D0847705

DAIRY INDUSTRY RESTRUCTURING

RESEARCH IN RURAL SOCIOLOGY AND DEVELOPMENT

Series Editor: Harry K. Schwarzweller

RESEARCH IN RURAL SOCIOLOGY AND DEVELOPMENT
VOLUME 8

DAIRY INDUSTRY RESTRUCTURING

EDITED BY

HARRY K. SCHWARZWELLER

Department of Sociology, Michigan State University, USA

ANDREW P. DAVIDSON

School of Sociology, University of New South Wales, Australia

2000

JAI
An Imprint of Elsevier Science

Amsterdam – New York – Oxford – Shannon – Singapore – Tokyo

ELSEVIER SCIENCE Inc.
655 Avenue of the Americas
New York, NY 10010, USA

First edition 2000

Library of Congress Cataloging in Publication Data
A catalog record from the Library of Congress has been applied for.

ISBN: 0-7623-0474-X
ISSN: 1057-1922 (Series)

♾ The paper used in this publication meets the requirements of ANSI/NISO Z39.48-1992 (Permanence of Paper).
Printed in The Netherlands.

CONTENTS

PREFACE

Each of the sixteen original contributions included in this eighth volume of *Research in Rural Sociology and Development* is concerned with an issue or problem relevant to the rapidly changing structure of the dairy industry in North America, Europe, and Oceania. Collectively, they reflect the leading edges of contemporary social science research and scholarship on this, one of the most heavily capitalized and most tightly regulated of all the food producing industries.

The first volume of *RS&D* (1984) focused on an exciting new wave of research and scholarship in the United States that, from the mid-1970s, was building toward a more comprehensive sociology of agriculture. At that time, questions about the changing character and organization of farms and farming were being vigorously debated and explored, in both the United States and Europe. Political economy perspectives and the pursuit of over-arching theoretical issues were emphasized. And, with great enthusiasm (and rightly so), commodity systems analysis was advocated as a useful methodological strategy to observe and take account of the very complex and often rather uneven interplay between production units, farm suppliers, marketing and processing systems, policy-makers, regulatory agencies, programs of research and extension, and (nowadays) the unrelenting forces of globalization.

Only recently, however, is the 'dairy problem' beginning to receive the concerted attention by rural social scientists that it obviously needs. Still sorely lacking is an intensive (grounded) debate on the reshaping processes, their differential impacts on affected families and communities, and the consequences of these structural shifts on the dairy industry's viability and integrity within the modern context. The impetus for a fuller, more socially sensitive discourse may be provided (as is the intent) by the papers presented here, for they specify some of the realities of what is happening and point to some of the critical issues that must enter into an extended discussion of how the dairy industry is being, and should be, restructured.

During the past decade, rural social science research on dairying in the U.S., long neglected, was revitalized by the U.S. Department of Agriculture when, in 1990, it approved a regional project (NE-177) that brought together a group of researchers, initially from nine states, to explore 'Organizational and Structural Changes in the Dairy Industry'. The project was subsequently revised in 1996 (11 states) so as to direct greater attention to 'Impacts of structural change in the dairy industry'. Some of the contributions in the present volume derive directly from NE-177 activities; support by the participating Agricultural Experiment Stations is acknowledged.

Andrew Davidson agreed to serve as co-editor. Earlier we had collaborated on a study of dairy farm changes in Michigan's Upper Peninsula and on a parallel study in the Lower Hunter Valley of New South Wales. Our association in the grueling editorial process for this volume was similarly pleasant and productive. His familiarity with the current concerns and styles of sociological inquiry in the European and Australian academic contexts, and with dairy industry problems on both sides of the world, were especially important.

Although great distances separated us, the editors, from each other and from the various contributors, e-mail technology facilitated communication. Even so, the editorial process for this particular volume of *RS&D* was exceedingly slow and strenuous. We worked very hard, and sometimes very long, with each of the contributors – aiming to assure a smooth flow of information and ideas from knowledgeable authors to intelligent readers. The patience and persistence of each of the contributors and their research teams is appreciated.

Personally, my interest in dairying was firmly established many years ago, through summer work on dairy farms in Vermont and upstate New York, and as an undergraduate in the College of Agriculture at Cornell University. Professor Stanley Warren was an especially influential teacher, for he made it clear that farming is a complex activity, that a farm should be viewed as an entity with many interrelated parts, and that success in farming depends on many factors, not the least of which is 'good luck' – the agricultural economy's vitality at a critical point in a farmer's career.

For many dairy farmers and their families in many parts of the contemporary world, the present times are especially difficult, as governments withdraw traditional price support mechanisms and protections in order to stimulate free-market efficiencies. This era of 'dairy industry restructuring' – the transition from one set of expectations to another, the explosion of new technologies, and the associated discontinuities – is a tangle of formidable challenges for those directly involved (dairy farmers and dairy industry leaders) and as well for rural social scientists whose research can make a difference in guiding the process and specifying its impacts.

Harry K. Schwarzweller
Series Editor

INTRODUCTION: RESEARCH AGENDAS AND FOCI OF CONCERN IN DAIRY INDUSTRY RESTRUCTURING

Harry K. Schwarzweller and Andrew P. Davidson

Dairy farmers and their families, in almost every industrialized country of the world, face an extremely uncertain future. The forces of change – locally, regionally, and globally – are formidable, persistent, and extremely complex. Many dairy farmers, in an effort to remain competitive, are being pressed to restructure their enterprises and to rearrange their lives. Some will make it, and some will not.

What shape will the dairy industry take in the years ahead? Will all small-scale family operations be phased out and will large-scale, industrially-organized dairies capture an even greater share of the market for fluid milk and milk products? Will current pricing and production control mechanisms, such as milk marketing orders, quotas, dairy boards, and other forms of governmental and quasi-governmental intervention, be modified to deal fairly with all stake-holders in the milk industry? Will a regional redistribution of dairy farms be affected by transnational institutions, such as GATT and the World Trade Organization? How will the coming generation of technologies influence the vitality and sustainability of the dairy industry, particularly in light of present production capacities and surpluses? What effect will major government and industry policies have on the future well-being of families that have dedicated their lives to dairying?

Research in Rural Sociology, Volume 8, pages 1–12.
2000 by Elsevier Science Inc.
ISBN: 0-7623-0474-X

The nature, causes, and significance of the changing structure of agriculture have been the subject of much debate. Some scholars argue that family sized operations, unlike their factory-style counterparts, are more flexible and more adaptable to local environmental and social circumstances; reliance on family reduces the need for 'profitability at all costs' and assures the availability of a reliable set of workers. Others argue that economies of scale are especially critical and enterprise expansion is a necessary condition for economic survival; consumers want cheap food and large farms can produce commodities at lower unit costs. A variety of related issues, such as the impacts of agricultural change on the quality of rural life and the vulnerability of large, corporate enterprises to industrial 'accidents', also enter into these disputations.

Little attention and relatively few research efforts by social scientists, however, have focused on the rapidly changing dairy industry. Indeed, there is a paucity of sociological literature that deals directly, or even indirectly, with dairying and dairy farm families. This is surprising, for dairying is one of the largest, most heavily capitalized, and most tightly controlled agricultural industries in the world. Further, it is an enterprise that does not lend itself to part-time farming practices; dairy farms, even the very smallest, are 'full-time operations' and, as such, represent in almost paradigmatic form the mutually dependent association between farm business and farm family.

****

Our concerns about current trends in the dairy industry (the 'dairy problem') have their origins in the intensive agricultural debate that was initiated by rural social scientists in the late 1970s. Many of the issues that were and still are being researched and discussed touch in one way or another on the historical and comparative restructuring of agriculture in contemporary capitalism. Rural social scientists turned to the writings of Marx, Kautsky, Lenin, and Chaynov, to construct an intellectually sound, theoretically grounded foundation for addressing these issues. At least three distinct yet related discourses can be identified within the contemporary literature: the decline of family-labor farms and the rise of large-scale, industrial-style corporate enterprises; uneven regional development and the consequent marginalization of certain rural populations and segments of the agricultural community; and the enormous changes occurring in the agri-food system (through mergers, vertical integration, and the state's role in overseeing the food industry.) Initially, the emphasis was on farm and farm family, but research soon shifted toward delineating commodity chains, and more recently to the complex and critical issues of food regimes and food security in the globalizing world economy (Buttel, 1996; McMichael, 1994).

This debate has not simply been about the mechanics or rhetoric of transformations within capitalism. At the forefront were and are contested images of what it is that constitutes 'the forces of change' and the directions those forces are driving society and its agricultural sector. Types of social relations and inter-institutional associations are considered important contingent conditions relative to the transformation process and its eventual impacts. Indeed, significant questions have emerged over how new socioeconomic patterns and political forms of power and authority will (re)shape agriculture and the agri-food system (Marsden, 2000).

Farming and husbandry practices, and their supportive norms, comprise some of the more puzzling ontological landscapes in the sociology of agriculture, especially the enigmatic divisions between social and nature, and between structure and agency (Lockie & Kitto, 2000). How the issues here are resolved will have great import in formulating a useful and valid approach to understanding the dynamics of agrarian change. Discourses on the restructuring of agriculture have been phrased from both within a modernist framework of grand narratives and total structures, and from within post-modernism, which argues for the primacy of location and diversity through an actor/agency approach. The earlier perspective, strongly influenced by Weber's theory of rationalisation, views the world as becoming increasingly efficient and calculable and with people using ever more sophisticated technology. Taken to its extreme form, which emphasizes the irrationality of rationality, farms are portrayed as factories in the field. The post-modernist perspective, on the other hand, is reflective of a new and discontinuous social form that directs attention to consumption and individual choice and how these in turn blunt the processes of globalization and reinforce socioeconomic and cultural diversity. In this view, agriculture is at once both global and local, but with an emphasis on diversification characterized by locally-based adaptive strategies (Arce & Long, 1999; Long & Long, 1992).

But, the agriculture debate is not as clearly formulated as it may at first appear. The rich tapestry of seemingly endless commodity chains criss-crossing the globe are not easily disentangled and interpreted. What the various perspectives seem to have in common is that agricultural industries in general, and virtually every agricultural producer and food consumer in particular, have been touched by what is known as 'globalization', the horizontal and vertical extension, integration, and control of agriculture by fewer and fewer multinational agri-food corporations. Still, the apparent indeterminacy of globalization suggests the need for different approaches and methodologies.

Despite certain misgivings, we believe that a broad comparative overview of a major agricultural industry, such as this volume presents, is relevant and useful because it encourages us, and our colleagues and students, to rise above the ideological fray that tends to locate problems neatly within paradigmatic niches. Though the sociology of agriculture literature is voluminous, scant attention has been accorded to structural shifts within the rapidly changing dairy industry, both in terms of description and theorisation. This is surprising given the prominence of milk products in the daily diets of people and the ubiquitousness of institutional structures that have shaped the expansion of the dairy industry in Western countries.

The dismantling of corporatism and the deregulation of agriculture is an underlying theme in the agricultural debate, particularly among European scholars. (For a comprehensive overview of corporatism in Western Europe, see Cox & O'Sullivan, 1988.) It is generally observed that longstanding arrangements between the state, producer groups and farmers are rapidly coming to an end in the name of 'economic rationalism'. In no other agricultural commodity is this more evident than in the dairy industry, where most Western countries had instituted some type of regulatory mechanisms in the 1930s to provide stability and order to an otherwise volatile market. Framed within this perspective, what can we expect with the demise of corporatism, given that it has long constituted an important cornerstone in the discourse on national dairy policies in the West? And, in the absence of some type of corporatism what types of institutional arrangements – if any – will emerge to fill their void, and how responsive will they be to the needs of local dairy farmers, particularly smaller-scale producers?

****

Current research literature relative to a restructuring of the dairy industry and the impacts of these great changes on farm families, rural communities, and the integrity of agricultural economies in America, Europe, and elsewhere in the world, is exceedingly sparse and diffuse. Indeed, the general problem of the dairy industry's transformation from a labor-intensive, highly regulated, strongly protected (corporatist) sector of agriculture, to a capital intensive system of production that is openly exposed to the unmerciful vacillations of the global market, is not being vigorously dealt with nor seriously debated in the regular channels of academic discourse, whether by rural social scientists, agricultural economists, or animal scientists/dairy management specialists. Concerns are being expressed, of course, especially in the popular press, industry newsletters, farm magazines, and the occasional book (as, for example, Grant, 1991). But the issues are extremely complex, the politics are very tangled, and the outcome of any posited solutions to the 'dairy problem' in America, the European Union, or any of the other industrial/developed regions of the world where the agricultural segment is no longer a vital part of the national economy, are, at best, tenuous. The knowledge base is weak, incomplete, and unreliable. Clearly, there is a need – an urgent need – for a concerted effort by the academic community and agricultural research institutes to explore, monitor, and instruct the process of dairy industry restructuring.

Our impressions derive, in part, from a systematic, though cursory search of some of the main journals that are most likely to report basic research and scholarly discussions relative to the organization and viability of the dairy industry. We browsed through the past five years (1995 to 1999) of *Rural Sociology, Sociologia Ruralis, American Journal of Agricultural Economics*, and the *Journal of Dairy Science*. Few relevant articles appeared: four in *Rural Sociology* and *Sociologia Ruralis* (Danks & Marsden, 1997; Davidson & Schwarzweller, 1995; Lyson, 1995; Schwarzweller & Davidson, 1997); seven in the *American Journal of Agricultural Economics* (Ahmad & Bravo-Ureta, 1995; Knutson et al., 1997; Kumbhakar & Heshmoti, 1995; McCorriston, 1996; Richards & Jeffrey, 1997; Schmitz et al., 1995; Sumner & Wolf, 1996), and eight in the *Journal of Dairy Science* (Bailey et al., 1997; Barney & Smith, 1998; Doering, 1995; Dryer, 1998; Losinger & Heinrichs, 1996; Marchant & Neff, 1995; Payne et al., 1999; Tauer, 1998.) Certainly, more research and focused debate should be allocated to this important, complex, and challenging issue.

****

Each of the sixteen chapters included in this volume is an original contribution on research relevant to the changing structure of the dairy industry in various regions of North America, Europe, and Australia. Although no attempt was made to classify them into issue-oriented subsections, an orderly progression is intended.

Many of the chapters report basic trends in the number and size of dairy operations and, without exception, they indicate a dramatic decline in number of dairies and a concomitant steady increase in average size of operation. The collective tone used by the various researchers in presenting their cold statistics is somber, almost fatalistic, sounding a death knell for the small, traditional dairy.

This transformation of the industry is made strikingly clear by Harper through a set of carefully chosen visual images and supportive arguments derived from a survey of dairy farmers in St. Lawrence County, New York. Profound differences are observed – huge, sharp contrasts – between the traditional, small dairy with its craft-based mode of production and the more modern, mega-dairy with its factory mode of production. As the large, industrial-style operation becomes dominant, is it irrational, asks Harper, for us to grieve the demise of the small dairy, "to lament the loss of a socially-harmonious and environmentally friendly system?"

In Ireland too, the dairy industry, which according to Tovey played a very important part in shaping Ireland's modern capitalist society, is changing rapidly, and small dairies, once an integral feature of the Irish countryside, are disappearing. Milk producers have become individualized entrepreneurs and are no longer influential agents of societal change. Among dairy farmers, says Tovey, "the family farm is losing its master-status as the definer of family identity and becoming one among a portfolio of family business activities." Thus, and not surprisingly, the recent history of Irish dairy farming is reflective of Ireland's economic transformation from an agrarian to an urban, industrial form.

In northern Germany, the pattern and associated problems of dairy industry restructuring are similar to what is observed elsewhere in Europe. The *Wesermarsch*, not far from Bremen, was once a premier dairy region, and the farm population constituted a very prosperous, socially dominant segment of the community. But, as Vonderach explains, dairy farmers have become marginalized, and are dependent now upon quotas and state subsidies to maintain their farms and to provide for their families; alternative job opportunities are limited. Inheriting the family farm is no longer a great privilege that assures a secure future and, consequently, there will be a continuing decline of the dairy industry here and the *Wesermarsch* will inevitably lose much of its distinctive rural pastoral character.

The situation is not much different in Australia. Dungog, a quiet farming community in the Lower Hunter Valley of New South Wales, was once dominated by a local milk processing plant that served a large number of dairy farms in the surrounding countryside. With the introduction of milk quotas in the 1960s, many dairies, particularly the smaller ones, were forced to close, and in recent years things have become even more difficult for the remainder. Through a unique, ten-year longitudinal study, Davidson has been monitoring the rapidly evolving situation, focusing especially on the dynamics of deregulation. Among Dungog dairy farmers, understandably, there is great pessimism about the future, for the political economy of Australia, like that of Europe's and America's, now favors an agriculture that is guided by market forces, not by dairy boards or government agencies.

Regional/state contexts vary, of course. In Wisconsin, for example, a state known as 'America's Dairyland', dairy herds average about 60 cows, while in California, where conditions favor mega, industrial-style operations, herds average over 500 cows. Thus, when speaking of "the demise of small dairies," regional/state contexts must be taken into account. But despite such great differences, the dairy industry is doing well in both states; California and Wisconsin together account for about a third of the U.S. total milk production.

Development of Wisconsin's dairy industry paralleled the urbanization of America's Midwest and its burgeoning markets for milk and cheese. Typically, the dairies were and still are diversified, producing their own fodder and feed concentrates, and relying mainly on family labor. But the pressures to expand are intensifying (and especially so since 1993, when Wisconsin relinquished its number one position in milk production to California). Exploring the dynamics of this restructuring process and the adjustments that some family-labor operations are making to survive, Jackson-Smith and Barham conclude that there are reasons for cautious optimism.

The situation is more positive in California, where the milk industry has been booming and where very large, very intensive dairy operations dominate. Because California does not participate in the federal milk marketing orders, many industry leaders believe that it has had an unfair advantage in the production and marketing of milk. Butler and Wolf systematically examine this assumption and determine that California's success does not derive from its unique dairy policies but rather from its advantages (climate, agro-ecology, wealth) and the enormous population growth of the western states.

Australia too manifests distinctive regional/state variations in basic trends and the organizational style of dairy farms. Berrevoets constructs a typology to characterize these differences. In Victoria, for instance, with over half of Australia's dairies, the emphasis is on land management, whereas in Tasmania the emphasis is on labor efficiency and in South Australia on cow management (herd average). Berrevoets's research concludes that the future viability of the Australian dairy industry will depend on a strategy of increasing milk production through improved pasture management, i.e. higher stocking rates and lower labor inputs.

Production efficiency is important and dairy farmers everywhere are being pressed to modernize and to adopt new, improved technologies. For those with small, marginal operations and limited capital, this is especially problematic, of course. Sometimes the pressures can be ignored, though returns to labor and land are reduced. But when changes in practices and equipment are mandated by government agencies in order to assure high quality milk and milk products, then new ways and major investments are inescapable.

In a marginal dairying community (San Jose de Gracia) in west-central Mexico (Michoacan), the imposition of quality standards is an exercise in power that, observes McDonald, has serious consequences for people's livelihoods and futures. But 'milk quality', he finds, has variable meanings depending on who is using the term and under what circumstances. The government's definition does not dovetail neatly with that of the processors' and farmers', and consequently, there is great potential for contradictions, misunderstandings, and conflict. It is not yet clear, says McDonald, whether San Jose's dairies will be 'invited' to struggle along on the technology treadmill, or if they will be forced, very soon and rather abruptly, to abandon dairying altogether.

Issues of milk quality are generating controversy also in Europe, stimulated by competition within the European Community and the public's increasing suspicions about food contamination and 'unnatural' production practices. Over-viewing the Dutch dairy industry, Frouws and Ploeg note that the various stakeholders – dairy cooperatives, government agencies, farmer's organizations, retailers, producer groups, dairy farmers – all of whom are concerned about milk quality, perceive of it in different ways. But some stakeholders are more powerful than others, and the policies they advocate will profoundly affect the future of the Dutch dairy industry.

From an individual dairy operator's point of view, the 'dairy problem' comes down to survival of the family/household and profitability of the farm enterprise. Regional circumstances, shifting governmental policies, vacillating or depressed prices, and the forces of globalization have much to do with the dairy sector's vitality. But why is it that, within the same general context, some dairy operations are more successful than others?

To explore this question, McIntosh and Luedke surveyed dairy farmers in a selected set of Texas counties. Three competing explanations are addressed by their research: herd size; the farm's location within Texas; and the personal rewards and enterprise goals that motivate and guide a farmer's activities. They conclude that both agency and structure affect dairy farm performance and production efficiency. Success in dairying depends on many factors, not the least of which are the farm operator's skills, aspirations, and values.

Concerned especially with the expansionist strategies of contemporary dairy farmers, Schwarzweller studied a mid-Michigan county where dairying is strong (farms average120 cows and production per cow is the highest in Michigan.) For most dairy farms, he observes, an increase in herd size and its requisite structural modifications bring into play economies of size that enable a dairy to produce milk more efficiently, increasing its profitability. But, for many small dairies expansion may not be a wise choice in light of family/ household goals and alternative opportunities. Further, the pattern for achieving an efficient dairy operation is open to innovation; smallness does not necessarily condemn a dairy to irreconcilable inefficiency.

Many things can interfere with the successful management of a dairy operation. In Kentucky, for instance, tobacco is a major cash crop and the tobacco quota is an important asset of most farming operations; 65% of the commercial dairy farms grow some tobacco. But, as Garkovich, Crist and Dyk show, though raising tobacco tends to detract from the use of good dairy farming practices, there are valid reasons, such as family traditions and the economic security that comes from a diversified operation, that reinforce the dairy/tobacco system. One wonders: if the tobacco quota program is terminated by the U.S. Congress, as it well might be, will this affect a strengthening of Kentucky's dairy industry and/or will it contribute to an increase in rural poverty?

Most of the current research on factors contributing to dairy industry restructuring looks to economic explanations, presupposing that the industry is being shaped almost entirely by market forces. But an emerging line of inquiry, such as that by Lyson, Guptill and Gillespie, gives primacy to non-economic, community-based factors as engines of change. Their innovative study, exploring the organizational, institutional, and interpersonal linkages of dairy farmers in upstate New York, finds that dairy farm performance and farm viability are directly related to a farm operator's level of civic (community) engagement. "Involvement in community affairs," they believe, "is one key element in a viable system of dairy farming."

Producer cooperatives, throughout the history of dairying, have been a major instrument for the marketing and processing of milk. But they now too, like the small dairies they once served so well, are struggling to survive. Even the larger cooperatives, such as the Michigan Milk Producers Association, are being overshadowed by huge, multi-national conglomerates that set the tone and virtually control the market. What can the small, independent dairy producer cooperatives do to remain functional and reasonably competitive?

Nilsson and Barnheim, working intensively with a small dairy cooperative in Sweden, have developed a new organizational model that is designed to change the system of incentives for its members. The idea is to bring the short-term aspirations of members into line with their long term interests via the introduction of a type of shares which members can buy voluntarily and which can be freely traded. The plan goes into effect in January, 2001 and, if successful, will provide a useful model for producer cooperatives elsewhere.

Governments have played a big part in subsidizing and regulating the milk industry, and as they back away from this protective role and/or rearrange the goals of these programs, which is the case in many parts of the world, the survival problems of small dairies are exasperated. Although European countries, pressured by increased competition from within the European Community, have been heavily engaged in making such adjustments (fine-tuning the milk quota system, for example), similar policy changes are being introduced or seriously advocated elsewhere.

Norway, which has made extraordinary efforts over the years to assist small dairy operations (the average dairy farm has 13 cows), set up a milk quota-based regulatory system in 1983. It was modified in 1991, as a 'buy out scheme', and again in 1996, as a 'buy and sell' scheme. Focusing especially on questions of distributive and procedural justice, Jervell and Borgen overview some of the problems and strengths of the relatively unique Norwegian system, which differs markedly from the Canadian and U.K. systems. Whether its present form will be retained depends in large measure on competition from within the European context and the political aggressiveness of Norway's agricultural community. For now, small dairies in Norway are being gently nudged to adjust to the realities and threats of global markets.

The United Kingdom too has been reorganizing its milk marketing system, encouraging a greater rationalization of the milk supply sector, both at the farm level and among dairy groups and processors. The state (England and Wales) is no longer directly involved in the day-to-day management and regulation of the industry (as it had been, since the early 1930s, through Milk Marketing Boards). Banks overviews these changes and the U.K.'s shift away from a close corporatist relationship between state and dairy farmer. He observes that "many farmers have entered the new millennium with a serious headache" and that many small scale dairies will be forced to close-out in the near future.

****

This volume, then, calls attention to the 'dairy problem', a complex issue that is intellectually challenging, for it relates directly to the agricultural debate of the past two decades, and of enormous practical import, for it concerns the socioeconomic well-being and life chances of a large segment of the agricultural community in most Western societies. The articles included here represent the cutting edge of current social science research on dairy industry restructuring and, as such, provide a strong base for further inquiry and focused debate. Collectively, they call into question the widely-held, one-dimensional view that tends to explain the industry's difficulties as an inevitable outcome of globalization, beyond state and individual farmer control, and therefore a necessary, albeit undesirable consequence of modernization. Rural social scientists, outreach specialists, and agricultural leaders can indeed make a difference in (re)shaping the dairy industry in ways that will be fair and socially responsible.

****

REFERENCES

Ahmad, M., & Bravo-Ureta, B. E. (1995). An Econometric Decomposition of Dairy Output Growth. *American Journal of Agricultural Economics, 77*, 914–921.

Arce, A., & Long, N. (Eds) (1999). *Anthropology, Development, and Modernities: Exploring Discourses, Counter-tendencies, and Violence*. London: Routledge.

Bailey, K., Harden, D., Garrett, J., Hoehne, J., Randle, R., Ricketts, R., Stevens, B., & Sulovicti, J. (1997). An Economic Simulation Study of Large-scale Dairy Units in the Midwest. *Journal of Dairy Science, 80*, 205–214.

Banks, J., & Marsden, T. (1997). Reregulating the U.K. Dairy Industry: the Changing Nature of Competitive Space. *Sociologia Ruralis, 37*, 382–404.

Barney, J. P., & Smith, T. R. (1998). How Local Dairy Communities Can Compete in the Global Marketplace. *Journal of Dairy Science, 81*, 1762–1768.

Buttel, F. (1996). Theoretical Issues in Global Agri-Food Restructuring. In: D. Burch, R. E. Rickson & G. Lawrence (Eds), *Globalization and Agri-Food Restructuring*. Aldershot: Avebury.

Cox, A., & O'Sullivan, N. (1988). *The Corporate State*. Aldershot: Edward Elgar.

Davidson, A., & Schwarzweller, H. (1995). Marginality and Uneven Development. *Sociologia Ruralis, 35*, 40–66.

Doering, O. (1995). Public Perceptions and Policy Imperatives: Animal Agriculture and the Environment. *Journal of Dairy Science, 78*, 469–475.

Dryer, J. (1998). U.S. Dairy Products for a Global Marketplace. *Journal of Dairy Science, 81*, 1749–1752.

Grant, W. (1991). *The Dairy Industry: An International Comparison*. Aldershot: Dartmouth.

Knutson, R. D., Romain, R., Anderson, D. P., & Richardson, J. W. (1997). Farm Level Consequences of Canadian and U.S. Dairy Policies. *American Journal of Agricultural Economics, 79*, 1563–1572.

Kumbhakar, S. C., & Heshmati, A. (1995). Efficiency Measurement in Swedish Dairy Farms: An Application of Rotating Panel Data, 1976–88. *American Journal of Agricultural Economics*, 77, 660–674.

Lockie, S., & Kitto, S. (2000). Beyond the Farm Gate: Production-Consumption Networks and Agri-Food Research. *Sociologia Ruralis*, 40, 3–19.

Long, N., & Long, A. (Eds) (1992). *Battlefields of Knowledge: the Interlocking of Theory and Practice in Social Research and Development*. London: Routledge.

Losinger, W. C., & Heinrichs, A. J. (1996). Dairy Operation Management and Herd Milk Production. *Journal of Dairy Science*, 79, 506–514.

Lyson, T. (1995). Producing More Milk On Fewer Farms: Neoclassical and Neostructural Explanations of Changes in Dairy Farming. *Rural Sociology*, 60, 493–504.

Marchant, M. A., & Neff, S. A. (1995). Interaction of U.S. and European Community Dairy Policies Through the International Market. *Journal of Dairy Science*, 78, 1191–1198.

Marsden, T. (2000). Food Matters and the Matter of Food. *Sociologia Ruralis*, 40, 20–29.

McCorriston, S. (1996). Import Quota Licenses and Market Power. *American Journal of Agricultural Economics*, 78, 367–372.

McMichael, P. (Ed.) (1994). *The Global Restructuring of Agri-Food Systems*. Ithaca, N.Y.: Cornell University Press.

Payne, M., Bruhn, C. M., Reed, B., Scearce, A., & O'Donnell, J. O. (1999). On Farm Quality Assurance Programs: A Survey of Producer and Industry Leader Opinions. *Journal of Dairy Science*, 82, 2224–2230.

Richards, T. J., & Jeffrey, S. R. (1997). The Effect of Supply Management on Herd Size in Alberta Dairies. *American Journal of Agricultural Economics*, 79, 555–565.

Schmitz, A., Bogess, W. G., & Tefertiller, K. (1995). Regulations: Evidence from the Florida Dairy Industry. *American Journal of Agricultural Economics*, 77, 1229–1251.

Schwarzweller, H., & Davidson, A. (1997). Perspectives On Regional and Enterprise Marginality: Dairying in Michigan's North Country. *Rural Sociology*, 62, 157–179.

Sumner, D. A., & Wolf, C. A. (1996). Quotas Without Supply Control: Effects of Dairy Quota Policy in California. *American Journal of Agricultural Economics*, 78, 354–366.

Tauer, L. W. (1998). Cost of Production of Stanchion Versus Parlor Milking in New York. *Journal of Dairy Science*, 81, 567–569.

REQUIEM FOR THE SMALL DAIRY: AGRICULTURAL CHANGE IN NORTHERN NEW YORK

Douglas Harper

INTRODUCTION

The following is a case study of agricultural change in a dairy farm neighborhood in St. Lawrence County, New York, which is located on the Canadian border, midway across the northern boundary of New York State.

St. Lawrence County, a leading dairy region of New York, is similar to other small dairy regions in New England (Maine, New Hampshire, Vermont and New York), the Mid-Atlantic states (New Jersey, Pennsylvania and adjoining states), and the Northern Midwest (Michigan, Wisconsin and Minnesota). There are variations in the climate and cultures of these areas, but dairy farming from one end of this region to the other is remarkably similar. These dairy farms, however, differ fundamentally from those that have developed in recent decades in southern and western United States.[1]

I am interested in the fate of the 50–125 cow farm, family-owned, largely dependent on local resources, and using what I will call a craft mode of production, in the context of emerging dairy farms milking up to a thousand or more cows, less dependent on local resources, and organized in what I refer to as a factory mode of production. This research extends research questions explored by many rural sociologists and other scholars.[2]

Research in Rural Sociology, Volume 8, pages 13–45.
Copyright © 2000 by Elsevier Science Inc.
All rights of reproduction in any form reserved.
ISBN: 0-7623-0474-X

METHODS

Data on early dairy farms were gleamed from agricultural censuses, two self-published memoirs by northern farm wives,[3] and several studies of northern dairy farming.[4] The transition to machine power during the WWII era is documented in the Standard Oil of New Jersey (SONJ) study of American culture (see Plattner, 1983). I used images from this archive to encourage elderly farmers to remember and interpret these transitions.

In 1989 I completed a 486 item survey of 48 St. Lawrence County dairy farms, 46 of which produced usable data. On these visits I observed, photographed and talked informally with most farmers for several hours. In 1999 I determined the subsequent fate of these farms through interviews with key informants. These various data all contribute to a general question as to the viability of the small dairy farm. The resolution of this question will have profound implications for the economies and cultures and environments of rural societies.

I summarized the evolution of northern dairy farms in Table 1. I suggest that change in dairy farming is primarily stimulated by new tools, machines and farm practices. Factors that influence the availability of labor, such as wars or attitudes toward gender roles, affect how and when available technologies are adopted. What is remarkable is that 'farm systems' comprised of tools, machines and a configuration of workers, animals, land and crops, shift rather abruptly from one stage to another, and then remain relatively constant for decades, until a technological revolution or social reconfiguration leads to another step in the evolution of farming. We are now in an era in which a fourth stage in this evolution appears to be underway. This new era may be the 'end of history' for the small farm.

FRONTIER SETTLEMENT TO EARLY MECHANIZATION

The first dairy farms in the United States, dating to the mid-18th century, were established by immigrants from several parts of the British Isles, Holland, and other European countries (Cohen, 1992). The animals and farming practices brought by these immigrants evolved, and in some sense de-volved, as dairy farming moved with pioneers into the Mid-Atlantic states. The pioneer farmers of the 1830s grew hay, grains, corn, vegetables, and fruit, and bred and raised horses, oxen, cattle, pigs and fowl, mostly feeding the farm family and the farm animals. Eric Sloan's illustrated and annotated diary (1965) of an 'early

Table 1. Structural Evolution on American Dairy Farms

	Farms of the New England frontier settlement (1700–1840)	Early mechanization (1850's-WWII)	Advanced mechanization (1950-present)
crops and feed	hay, grains (corn, oats), garden vegetables, fruit; farm is self-sufficient for animals and family.	hay, grains (corn, oats), some feed suppliments purchased for cattle. Self-sufficiency diminishes.	corn (silage) and hay. Some feed and all feed suppliments purchased. Self-provisioning rare.
animals	cows, horses, oxen, pigs, sheep, fowl	cows, horses, sheep fowl	cows
products sold or consumed	milk, cheese, butter, vegetables, honey, meat, fruit, juice, wool.	milk, cheese, butter, vegetables, meat.	milk
harvesting hay	loose hay cut with sythe, neighbors help.	loose hay cut with reaper; family accomplishes task.	mechanically baled or chopped for silo. Family or hired help.
harvesting small grains (oats, somctimes whcat)	cutting, stooking and moving by hand; threshcd by hand or horse.	cut with reaper; stooked by hand; moved to barn and threshed by neighbors.	combine replaces all labor; then small grains abandoned as crop.
harvesting corn (grain corn to silage)	as grain: picked and shucked by hand; sorted as whole ears or as grain; ground by miller.	as silage: cut and bundled by reaper; moved and chopped for silo by neighbors.	as silage: cut and chopped in the field with mechanical chopper.
housing and milking cows	rudimentary barns; cows milked in barnyard.	stanchion barn; bucket system for milking evolves to pipeline.	freestall barn; milking parlor.
manure storage and use	not gathered or used.	raked from barn into mechanical spreader; spread daily.	liquid manure stored in pit; spread infrequently.
motive power	horses and oxen	horses and tractors; 50 h.p. limit.	tractors and self-propelled choppers; up to 200 h.p.
labor	family; neighbors help with hay.	family; neighbors harvest grain, corn and share other tasks.	family and hired labor; little informal cooperation.
gender roles in work	relative gender equality; some tasks assigned to women.	less gender equality; women still assigned tasks.	women mostly leave productive work; assume tasks such as bookkeeping.
farm size	80–120 acres	80–120 acres	80–1,000 acres
herd size	15 to 20 cows	15–30 cows	50–1,000 cows

American boy' shows how even a fifteen year old farm boy in 1805 was skilled at blacksmithing, carpentry, and animal and crop work.

The family worked alone except for the hay harvest, which several farmers accomplished together. Each would contribute a worker or two and the informally organized crew harvested the hay on one farm after another, the first form of what farmers called 'changing works'. The collective work was a festive time, as each farm prepared meals for workers who moved from farm to farm.

McMurry (1995) tells us that the pioneer farmers did not use progressive farming practices. They did not rotate crops and thus drained their land of its nutrients; few used animal manure or other fertilizer to restore soil vitality. Cattle were outside most of the winter and foraged during the summer on natural grasses in declining fields. Overall, farm productivity was low, and it took a great deal of human labor to create a subsistence level of survival.

The Erie Canal in central New York (built between 1817–1825) and the first roads and railroads in northern New York connected New York farmers to national and international markets. Immigrants from the British Isles brought cheese-making skills to their new farms. In central New York the first dairy farmers were Welsh immigrants; in St. Lawrence County the most established farm families descended from immigrants from Scotland who settled in 1815.

By the 1840s there evolved, in these regions, a highly diversified form of agriculture that balanced animals, crops, products and family labor in a near-ideal mosaic. At the core of this was the 115 acre farm (the average farm size in New York for nearly a hundred years!) housing between 15 and 25 milk cows. The farms used two to five horses and perhaps a pair of oxen for power, and relied on eight to ten sheep for wool and food, and hogs for pork and a system to recycle the whey produced in cheese making.The pig manure was an important nutrient for field restoration. The farmers grew small grains (wheat, buckwheat, rye, oats, barley), corn, potatoes, peas, and root crops such as rutabaga, which was used for supplemental cow feed. Their orchards grew apples, pears, cherries, plums, grapes and other fruits. Farmers raised poultry for eggs and meat, and bees which pollinated plants and made honey. Large gardens provided for home consumption.

The typical farm of this era met the subsistence needs of the family as farmers purchased only a few products, such as tea, salt and spices, and also had sufficient resources and labor to produce a product for both home consumption and export, which was cheese.

The cheese-producing farm of the mid-1800s was an ideal balance of resources, animals, crops and labor in which "all activities circulated nutrients and energy endlessly" (McMurry, 1995, 40). The farm produced a rich variety of food for the family, from home grown beef, pigs, and sheep; poultry and eggs; home-grown wheat for flour, vegetables from gardens; fruits from orchards, honey from local bees, oats to feed the horse or oxen which powered the farm. The sheep provided wool for winter clothing; regular census reports included several yards of wool spun from most farm's sheep.

But most importantly, the 19th century family cheese farms were estimated to produce as many or even more calories than they expended, leaving out the contribution of human labor. It is estimated that the modern farm, by contrast, requires between 16 calories of energy to produce a calorie of energy of grain; and 70 calories to produce a calorie from meat. The cheese-making farm of the mid—19th century supported a family with nutritious and chemically-free food, produced a sizable cash crop, and did so without a net caloric loss. Family and neighbors worked together, and animals powered the small machines which were used in planting and harvesting crops. The farms prospered economically and socially.

At the beginning of this era, farmers primarily used tools to plant and harvest the food fed to cows and other animals; by the end of the second stage these tools were almost entirely replaced with machines. For example, on pioneer farms, farmers cut hay and grain with scythes, as farmers have for several centuries. Family members raked and turned the hay until it was dry; then gathered it, placed on horse-drawn wagons, and pitched by hand into barns. The first hay mower, pulled by two horses, was introduced during the Civil War, coincidentally helping relieve the labor shortage caused by the absence of men drafted into the war effort.

The mechanical mower revolutionized the hay harvest. A skillful worker with a scythe could cut two to three acres of hay a day (Weitzman, 1991, 60); a farmer with a mower did twenty (Canine, 1995, 47). All subsequent handling of the hay (raking for drying, picking it up in the field, moving it to the barn and storing it in a loft), however, was still done by hand, sometimes using simple, horse-powered elevators. This method of harvesting hay remained roughly the same until the post WWII era; the third stage of agricultural technology as presented in Table 1.

During the pioneer era farmers also cut (reaped) grain by hand, using scythes, to which long fingers had been added to guide the cut stalks into windrows. Workers then gathered and tied the grain into bundles and stacked them to dry. A worker with a fingered-scythe (called a 'cradler'), with four or five bundlers, could cut and bundle no more than three acres a day (Canine, 21).

Mechanical reapers, used to harvest grain fed to cows, horses and other animals, were invented in the early 19th century and in use by the 1840s. The first versions of these machines, which McCormick sold in the 1840s for $100, used two workers to cut ten acres of grain a day. The grain then had to be gathered by hand, bound into sheathes, and stacked to dry. The efficiency of the mechanical reapers improved during the 19th century, during furious competition among hundreds of inventors and companies, but the single overriding breakthrough was the development, during the 1880s, of a mechanical reaper-binder. This horse-drawn machine cut the grain, gathered it into bundles, and tied bundles together with twine. Workers then only had to walk through the fields to place the sheathes of grain in teepee-shaped stacks to dry. This machine, like the mower described above, was in use with little change until the third technological stage, and it is still used by groups such as the Amish who do not use gasoline powered machines. Again, we note a technological plateau of eighty or more years!

The grain, which was cut and dried in the field, had to be moved to a work area near a barn, and the grain had to be removed from the stalks. Removing the grain from the stalks is called 'threshing', and in the pioneer farms of the early 19th century used hand methods that had been used for centuries.

Mechanical threshers, developed at the end of the 18th century, made it possible for dairy farmers to grow more grain and thus to increase the quality of their herd's feed, leading to increased production. The first threshers were powered by turning cranks; next by horses on a treadmill. Steam power replaced horsepower, and, in the end of the 19th century, gasoline engines became the predominant mode of power. By the early decades of the nineteenth century, most grain was mechanically threshed, but threshing machines were incredibly expensive. In 1822 a horse-powered thresher cost $500, beyond the reach of nearly all farmers. More complex modes of power made the machine correspondingly more expensive. It was the cost of the thresher, in part, that led farmers to consolidate their efforts; to share labor and a thresher and to thus collectively harvest their grain.

The stationary thresher, like the mower and reaper-binder, changed little in basic design for nearly a hundred years, until contemporary technological developments.

Thus, crop harvesting, an integral part of a self-sufficient farm system, moved from hand-powered tools to machines, some of which were quite elementary and comparatively inexpensive (such as the horse-drawn hay binder); and others which were complex and expensive, such as the thresher. This second level of technology preceded the tractor and even gasoline power. It was powered by animals such as horses and oxen, by people, by steam and by other forms of mechanical power.

Milking and housing cows also found a form during the mid-19th century which was subject to little change for a hundred years.

On the pioneer farms of the mid-Atlantic region, cows spent much of the year outside. A milkmaid milked them in the barnyard. As the number of cows increased per farm, agricultural thinkers encouraged better cow housing to improve the conditions of the herd. Consequently, barns were designed to hold cows for the cold months of the year; the two-story structures typically included a mow in which loose hay for winter feeding was stored, and troughs in which manure was collected and removed from the barn. The first stanchion barns were designed in the 1830s (McMurry, 1995, 31). In these barns, cows were confined either by a chain, or by inserting their heads into parallel bars. While this sounds punishing, cows are easily habituated to such an arrangement. In addition, in the stanchion barn, it is safer and more convenient to milk cows. The stanchion barn requires a specific amount of space per individual animal and interior construction to hold and feed cows, and to gather their manure. Working conditions aside, fewer animals can be fitted into a stanchion barn than can be packed into the freestall barns that have become a defining feature of the modern factory farm.

Once again, an important technological form which came about in the middle of the nineteenth century, remained in place for over a hundred years. It limited the size of a herd which could fit into a barn most farmers could afford, but it also led to a pattern of animal/human interaction which nurtured the cow and created animal-smart farmers.

A key feature of the first two eras was the communal harvest. The farmers of the transitional era (the middle column of Table 1) grew ten to thirty acres of corn and grain in addition to hay used for pasture and meadow. They reaped and 'stooked' the grain with their own equipment and family labor, but shared threshers with neighbors. Farmers in the North East called this informal labor exchange 'changing works', and it was a key feature of the first eras of agricultural development.

The following photographs document aspects of the changing works threshing operation characteristic of farming in what I have referred to as the transitional era, represented on the middle column of Table 1.

The division of labor on these operations was informal. Two or three workers picked up the stooked grain in the field and stacked it on wagons (Fig. 1 shows a farmer transporting the grain to the barn); several others forked the bundles off the wagon and fed them into the thresher (Fig. 2 shows the thresher in operation at the barn; Figs 3 and 4 detail the work at the thresher itself). Another worker carried the bags of grain from the thresher to grain storage bins inside the barn, shown in Fig. 5. A typical field of ten acres could be threshed

Photo series: Changing works on the Threshing Crew 1945[6]

Fig. 1.
Transporting
stooked oats
to the
thresher.

Fig. 2. A
changing
works
crew
threshing.

Fig. 3. The owner of the thresher monitored the machine but did not work on the crew.

Fig. 4. Members of the changing works crew feed sheaths of oats into the thresher.

Fig. 5. One member of the crew fills bags with the threshed oats and carries them into the grain bin in the barn.

in one to three days. Thus a crew of ten to fourteen workers would spend at least two weeks threshing the grain of the neighborhood with a single machine owned by a prosperous farmer or a professional thresher.

Farmers finished the grain harvest by late August. They paused to show their animals and produce at the State Fair. In September they harvested corn. The same crew then went through the neighborhood filling silos, which is shown in Figs 5 through 8. Each farmer cut and bound his own corn, but the changing works crew picked the bundles of corn from the fields, stacked it on wagons, and unloaded it at silos where a chopper-blower crushed the stalks and ears and shot it into the silo. A worker, usually too old to work in the field directed the corn filtering into the silo to keep it filling evenly. This is shown in Fig. 8.

The labor exchange was formalized to the extent that farmers organized themselves to work together on the entirety of their farms for as many days as the harvests took, and they drew on their own resources for tools such as wagons and horses, and supplied food for the crews. The system balanced machines, labor and time. There had to be enough farmers to supply an adequate crew; there had to be enough machines to support the farmers of a region, and the farmers who changed works had to all be able to get their work done before the crops were ruined. At the core of the system was necessity. A farmer commented:

> Everybody needed help and that was the only way they could get it! That was the way things were done. There was not very close accounting in terms of a half of a day here and half of a day there . . .

While the shared labor was driven by economic need, it also answered a social thirst for connection to one's neighbors, as reflected in the following statement by an elderly farmer:

> It was a rich time! When I drove the back road to Gouverneur with my friend Homer Martin – we went past these Amish places and we both said Oh! "Look at those fields, all stooked up with grain!" But of course it was a lot of hard tedious work . . . but it wasn't any harder than a lot of things you do, because there was a big group to do it. The neighbors depended on each other for everything in those years. . .

Eating together enhanced the social dimension of the system. A farmer commented:

> The dinner was the highlight of the day. You changed works and didn't think nothing of that – but the highlight of the day was the dinner, the pies! Because you got a dinner like you would get at Thanksgiving or Christmas. The women back in them days was all home cooking. They really knew how to cook more than a woman does today because they did it all the time.

The changing works tradition provided a social dimension to what was usually solitary work. It reinforced farmers' identities and it brought neighbors into meaningful relationships. It stressed egalitarianism. One farmer commented that one of the members of his changing works crew had a smaller farm, and that he needed only half the time of the rest of the crew to harvest his oats. But he worked with the crew, contributing more labor to their farms than they did to his. He did it, the farmer said, "because he liked being with his neighbors."

As a mid-argument summary, I'd like to highlight two aspects of this historical overview. First, the technological evolution in two or three generations was from tools to ever more complex machines. This led to less human input per productive output, but greater capital investment. This evolution took a huge leap forward when the motive power shifted from human and animal to internal combustion engines.

Secondly, the technological changes described above influence how people work together. Some technological change led women out of agricultural

Photo series: Filling silos and feeding crews 1945

Fig. 6. A changing works crew gathers bundles of corn for transport to the chopper. A young boy drives the tractor.

Fig. 7. Usually two members of the crew unloaded the corn and fed it into the chopper/blower. Here a farmer from the crew works alone.

Fig. 8. Typically an older worker worked inside the silo, directing the chopped corn to fill the silo evenly.

Fig. 9. A changing works crew eats dinner.

production (as did the advent of factory cheese production) and other technologies altered how people worked among themselves. The horse drawn mower eliminated communal hay harvests. The combine replaced the thresher in the late 1950s on the small dairies, and the mobile corn chopper, adopted by most farmers during the 1950s, replaced the communal harvest of corn. Eventual development of machines and increasing labor efficiency further isolated the farmer from his and her neighbors.

STAGE THREE – MECHANIZATION

I now turn to the analysis of dairy farming in the past fifty years; that is, during the era described in the third column of Table 1. I refer during this discussion to data included on Table 2, which summarizes St. Lawrence County farming, and Table 3, which summarizes recent change in New York dairy farming.

Table 2. Number of Farms and Land in Production, St. Lawrence County, New York, 1910–1995[7]

	1910	1925	1940	1955	1959	1964	1969	1975	1990	1995
# farms	8224	7583	6236	4380	3426	2895	2190	1792	1367	575
average farm size (acres)	100	115	117	NA	210	230	248	259	290	NA
land in production (acres)	1,061,516	1,012,449	991,642	NA	NA	664,649	543,494	NA	493,073	396,721
cows/farm	12	12	14	14	19	22	32	35	46	54

Sources: U.S. Census of Agriculture (1925, 1945, 1954, 1959, 1969, 1992); Agricultural Census of St. Lawrence County, 1992; Huff (1996), New York State Agricultural Statistics, 1996.

Table 3. Number of Dairy Farms in New York State, 1987–97, by Herd Size[8]

Number of Farms

		1987	1992	1997	% change, 1987-1997
	1–9	1623	1068	777	–52%
	10–19	495	413	318	–36%
	20–49	4728	3340	2351	–50%
Herd	50–99	5178	4073	3506	–32%
Size	100–199	1492	1389	1210	–19%
	200–499	295	360	461	+56%
	500–999	29	47	88	+203%
	1000+	NA	06	21	+250%
	total	13840	10696	8723	–37%

Source: New York Agricultural Statistics 1987–1997.

Virtually all farmers mechanized during and immediately after the war years, which means they adopted tractors, corn choppers and mechanical milkers. Formal labor exchange disappeared during this time as farmers switched from threshers to combines (which required less labor) and then stopped growing grain altogether. Farms increased in size, became dependent on chemical fertilizers, herbicides and pesticides, and farmers became debtors. Many went out of business as neighbors absorbed each other. As the scale of farming increased, land went out of production, and milk production per cow more than doubled, from around 7,000 pounds per year in 1945 to 14,000 pounds at present. These patterns are summarized in Tables 2 and 3.

In Table 2, which presents data on St. Lawrence County, we see the remarkable loss in number of farms. More than eight thousand farms in 1910 have become less than 10% of that total. The declining number of farms is a function of two factors. One is declining land in agriculture. The land in agricultural production in 1995 is 30% of the land which was in production in 1910. In this region there has been little population growth or development, and much of this land, cleared by pioneer farmers in the 19th century, has returned to brush and forest. The second factor which informs the simple decline in the number of farms is the increase in farm size. But we see that farms have only tripled in size, from roughly 100 acres to around 300 acres at present. The average number of milk cows has grown slowly and steadily over the century, but only by a factor of about five.

Table 3 shows state-wide data on the change in dairy farms by size between 1987 and 1997. We note, in ten years, the rapid decline of farms with herds of up to 100 cows, and the corresponding growth of farms with an excess of two hundred, to now more than one thousand cows.

These data, as compelling as they are, need further elaboration. There have been several paths into and through the third era of industrialization. When I surveyed a neighborhood of 48 farms I found at least two versions of modern dairy farming, for which I have provided the label of 'craft' and 'factory'.

Like all labels, these are problematical. More accurate terms might be 'less' and 'more' mechanized. Calling some farmers 'craft oriented', points to features such as barn and milking systems, which have remained unchanged for one hundred or more years. Other aspects of the craft farms have evolved with those I have referred to as 'factory farms'. The label of factory farm does associate the most advanced dairy farms with features of agriculture which are organized on an ever increasing scale, and in the most formally rational manner. Still, the dairy cow is the same on both types of farms and the differences between farm types does not alter that defining fact.

I determined the types of dairy farms through a process of what Glaser and Strauss (1967) called 'grounded theory'. Prior to the survey, I completed about eight hours of tape-recorded interviews with two families of near retirement-aged farmers. When I visited the 48 neighborhood farms to complete the survey, I usually spent 4–6 hours informally talking, and often helping them with chores such as cleaning calf stalls while they milked the herd. I followed the survey with photo-elicitation interviews with several farmers in which my understanding of the farm situation became clearer. I came to see 'types' as constellations of factors including farm technology, divisions of labor, and the normal opinions and attitudes expressed in informal talk. There are some farms which are difficult to place into any of these categories (for example, one quite small farm, milking only 54 cows, is organized as a factory farm, with a small freestall and milking parlor), yet in general these categories seem to describe the current dairy system remarkably well.

In 1999 I updated these farm histories to determine which of these farms had gone out of business, which had expanded, which had changed their basic operating mode, and which had remained as they had been ten years before. The rate of change in dairy farms has been extraordinary, and by looking at these trends we may be able to anticipate future directions for the Northeast family dairy. The following discussion draws upon my survey and 1999 follow-up.

Table 4. Farm Characteristics, St. Lawrence County Survey, 1990

	Craft farms (n = 34)	Factory farms (n = 12)
number of cows	14–106	55–268
mean # of cows (milking)	46	108
annual calf mortality	3.7%	6%
3 x day milking	6%	38%
tillable land in production	205 acres	412 acres
corn	54 acres	146 acres
pasture/cow	0.82	0.46
liquid manure storage	11%	54%
full-time hired labor	0.37 (1 per 125 cows)	1.7 (1 per 63 cows)
total equipment horsepower	210	454

Source: St. Lawrence County survey

THE SOCIAL STRUCTURES OF DAIRY FARMS

On what I am calling the craft farm, the farmers make milk something like a craftsman makes a piece of furniture: an individual performs all tasks in the production system, and thus his or her knowledge of the overall system is comprehensive. The farmer uses more rudimentary tools and machines, and the worker controls and directs the machines rather than vice versa.

On the factory farm, workers make milk in a rationalized process which employs an advanced division of labor and mass-production technology. This produces work which resembles factory work, more directed by, and controlled by machines. I do note that these differences among craft and factory farmers are less dramatic than between a crafts worker and factory worker making a product. Still I argue that the metaphor explains a great deal of the tension in the current system.

The clearest difference between craft and factory farms lies in the type of barn and milking system. Farmers use the stanchion barn on the craft farm: cows stand in two long rows; their heads secured to keep them in place (see Fig. 11). The farmer moves from cow to cow, attaching a portable milking machine which pumps the milk to a tank in an adjoining room. The farmers feed the cows before they are milked, and the farmer modifies each cow's feed depending on her age, size, and breeding history. The craft farmer mixes each cow's feed on the spot the way a cook prepares a soup: a bit of several grains, vitamin supplements, even ingredients such as molasses to suit the needs and tastes of individual animals. While both craft and factory farmers buy some of

Fig. 10. Craft farm. The original barns remain in use. Outbuildings used in more diversified farming, such as pig sties, have been removed. In the foreground is a swimming hole, which is used as a skating rink in the winter (Figs 10 to 18 by the author).

their feed, the craft farmers are less likely to purchase high energy supplements, and less likely to ration balance their cow's feed. The result is less milk production per cow (less efficiency), and less stress on the animal herself.

A farmer who fits the craft farm profile explained:

Farmer: I think whether it's in a bigger operation or smaller one, the closer you push her to her maximum potential the more likely she is to have problems. It's going to put more stresses on her.

Interviewer: How do you push a cow harder?

Farmer: The better the quality of the feed you give her the more she's going to want to eat. And the more she eats the more she's going to produce. See, the maximum amount of milk you can make is when all the nutrients are in the proper amounts. So the limitations to any cow's milk production might be any one of these nutrients. When we play the game of balancing the rations, we're trying to bring 'em all up to the proper levels. And so, the closer you get these levels to the optimum amount, the more you're . . . you'd say 'pushing' the cow.

Interviewer: Like an engine that is built for high compression?

Farmer: Right. And the fuel mixture. And the air mixture proper. Then you're going to reach your maximum potential. Over the years we've been so far below potential of the cows that you could increase certain nutrients and others could still be lagging and the production would still increase. I think this is where you get your 'burnout', where you use the cows up. You increase a certain nutrient which pushes her hard, that way encouraging her to make production, but there may be some minor nutrient that is lacking. It can create foot problems with some kinds of things, or breeding problems with other things. It creates imbalances. And because a cow is working hard – in other words, her stomach is digesting all the time rather than 75% of the time. Anything that disrupts her is going to have a greater affect on her body and her functions than previously. You know, if the cow isn't working that hard she can get a disruption and maybe withstand it and not even know it.

Interviewer: Since 1940 there's been a doubling in the rate of production . . . in some cases a tripling. So, is it right to say that if you were able to balance the ration so that it dealt with a cow's physiological needs exactly, then it would probably be a good thing?

Farmer: No doubt it would be a good thing.

Interviewer: But the fact that it's not balanced exactly . . .

Farmer: I would say that's the biggest factor. It's like anything, if you get everything perfectly balanced and get this cow producing at 95% efficiency or something, most likely she won't last as long as one who is working at a slower rate. It's like if you take an engine and run it full speed, you know the whole time you have it it's not going to last as long as if you're moderate with it. There's no time for recuperation and so forth.

Fig. 11. Cows in a stanchion barn.

While the craft farmer may not feed their animals to produce the greatest milk production; they keep their animals up three times longer than do the their more industrially rationalized neighbors (three years as compared to up to nine years for the craft farmers).

The rationalized processes of what I have called the factory farm is characterized by the freestall barn and milking parlor. The freestall barn is simpler than the traditional stanchion barn with hay mow, essentially a one-story metal shed with a concrete floor. In some freestall barns there are slightly raised bunkers covered by a foot of sand, where cows may lay down, and feeding troughs down the center of the room. Otherwise cows mill about depositing manure on the concrete floor. Once a day a farmer drives a small tractor through the barn, pushing out the largely liquid manure with a snow plow blade. The cows move out of the way. The barn is never clean; it is rather slightly less filled with manure after the tractor has done its job.

At milking time the cows walk single file into an attached room called the milking parlor, where they stand in gated quarters waiting to be milked. Small parlors are 'double sixes', meaning two rows of six cows are milked at a single time. There are now parlors in which twice that number of cows can be milked. Milking is simple: one or more workers attach milking machines to the animals. When the milk is depleted, the machines generally detach on their own and swing out of the way. After the cows are milked, the gates swing open and they proceed out of the parlor and back to the freestall. Others amble to assume their places.

In the stanchion barn the worker moves from animal to animal; in the milking parlor system, the worker remains in one place while the work flows past. It is the introduction of the assembly-line process to what was a form of production which resembled the pre-assembly-line factory.

Milking in the parlor is not skilled work. The worker sprays the cows teats with water or disinfectant, attaches milk machines and removes them (or they remove themselves automatically) when the cow is milked. To the worker the cow are 'teats and feet', as pictured in Fig. 13.

The milking parlor de-skills milking. In the stanchion barn, the placement of animals and the pace of work encourages the farmer to evaluate how well the cow is eating and breathing; the condition of her manure and her general sensitivity to being milked. Farmers who milk in stanchion barns describe their engaged interest in individual cows, each named, located in the same place in the barn, and with a breeding history and personality. Workers in a milking parlor are not interested in nor knowledgeable about the animals they service.

Fig. 12. Inside a freestall, factory farm.

They are working an assembly line, which occasionally splatters them with manure.

The freestall barn allows the farmer to increase the herd size since the cows do not fit into specific places in a single building. Table 4 shows that the herds of the factory farms in my study average more than twice the size of the craft farms (108 cows vs. 46). The freestall also speeds up milking and allows the worker to milk the cows standing up, rather than sitting on a milking stool, pressed up against the cow. There is no doubt that it is easier to milk in a parlor, although the intimate connection to the cow is lost in the parlor.

The non-farmer visitor, or even a traditional farmer, finds the freestall an uninviting place. The order and neatness of the well-managed stanchion barn is replaced with a huge room filled with milling animals, always foul with manure (see Fig. 12). It is difficult to do veterinary work in the freestall barn since there are often no clean areas; the animals are not secure, and it is not simple to find a given animal. The room belongs to the cows, and it is unnerving to be among the huge, jostling creatures. While the stanchion barn is built to connect farmers to their animals, the opposite is true of the freestall barn.

More than half the factory farmers use liquid manure storage, as opposed to about 10% of the craft farmers. Here again we confront the price of efficiency.

The old system of cleaning 'solid' manure is more labor intensive but it has environmental plusses. The first step is to shovel bedding (straw or old hay) that is placed around the cow on a daily basis, and manure, into the trough behind stationary cows. This is a task that usually takes place after milking. Most farmers use gutter cleaners to move this mixture of manure and bedding out of the barn. These operate like a moveable walkway in the floor of the trough

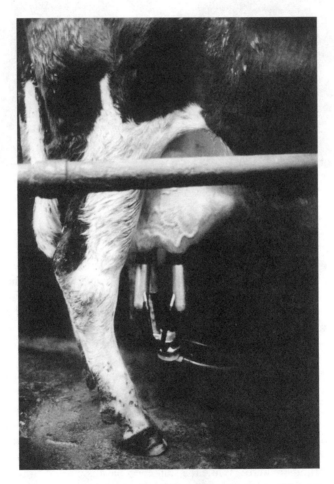

Fig. 13. The milker's perspective in the milking parlor. Because milking cows becomes assembly-line work, the milker is separated from other aspects of cow work, such as monitoring cow health as they are fed and milked.

behind the cows. It is peculiar indeed to see the slowly moving river of manure and bedding flow behind the cows when the gutter cleaner is switched on! The manure cleaner dumps directly into a manure spreader (Figs 15–18) which the farmer pulls into the field to distribute. This daily chore is time-consuming, and cold in the winter. But this system leaves the barn clean, and because the 'solid' manure contains plant material, it improves the substance of the soil as well as supplying nutrients.

The liquid manure system uses a lagoon adjacent to the barn (Fig. 14). Farmers spread the manure with large tank spreaders, on a limited number of days of the year. The new huge herds of up to 1,000 cows have created a surplus of manure and the manure pit has become an environmental hazard. Recently a failed pump caused a manure pit to empty back through a barn and to spill thousands of gallons of manure onto the adjoining land and road. A woodchuck dug a hole in the base of another farmer's pit and the river of manure fouled nearby land and roads. The quantity of manure has led to field run-off and the pollution of streams. The manure has threatened ground water, particularly where soil is sandy. Finally, when farmers spread liquid manure they create a

Fig. 14. Factory farm. The freestall is the large building in the center of the frame. Behind the freestall is the original barn, now used for calves and heifers. In front right is the liquid manure pit.

noxious odor which permeates the neighborhood. This stench is unprecedented in family dairy farming and ruins the pastoral idyll for farmers and others who share the country.

A farmer who lived his entire life in one of the most important farms in the neighborhood discussed the changing role of manure and the impact of the new manure systems:

Interviewer: Has the role of manure changed?

Farmer: It surely has! Manure was always considered a good fertilizer and years ago it was always piled in the winter neatly. It was taken out with the horses in a wooden box. You drove the sleigh through the barn, and shoveled it in from each side. Two men went to the field and shoveled it into a nice, neat, square pile, and the efficient, careful farmers were the ones who had the nicest looking manure piles. They were square and nice and didn't leach in all directions. Then, at the beginning of the season, in the early spring, the manure was spread quickly on the land, when the most good of it would be gotten, before it was cultivated or planted . . . or in the fall before they plowed the corn ground. Then we went through a stage where I can remember some of the farm magazines said that manure was so much work and now that we had commercial fertilizer it would be better if manure was just put in a lagoon someplace and forgotten about, because the commercial fertilizer grew so much faster crops and it was so much more efficient. Farms were getting larger and they said that all this time it was taking to spread manure was really wasted when you got right down to the dollars and cents of it. I read those things and I thought "what are we coming to next?" But then, when we got into the energy crunch and the price of fertilizer went from a few dollars a ton to $150 a ton or more, manure took on a much pleasanter face again, and the agricultural economists began to think up ways to treat the manure as it should be.

With the freestall barns, where there is no bedding, it would be impossible to shovel it and handle it by hand. So it has been necessary to think up these other ways of taking care of it [the liquid manure system]. They are also very expensive.

Interviewer: Do you have any opinions about the liquid manure systems – do you think it's a step ahead?

Farmer: Apparently it makes great crops but I certainly don't . . .

Wife of Farmer: Don't ask us!

Farmer: I wake up at night sometimes and would like to write to Cornell and tell them what I think of that. I just can't imagine living so close to such a stench! Some of our neighbors, when you go to visit them, if the winds are in the direction of the manure pit, or if they are spreading, which is probably thirty days out of the year – you just live in a horrendous stench. It's very maddening, especially to people who aren't in agriculture.

Wife of Farmer: We try to keep thinking – is it because we are not farming anymore that we mind the smell so much?

Farmer: I don't think so.. I like the smell of a lot of different manure's – fresh manure – But when you go into some of these barns now – it is just sickening.

As I write in 1999 the State has mandated that all farms using liquid manure systems have a plan in effect which will address the environmental and social

Fig. 15–18. Spreading manure and cleaning the spreader on a craft farm.

problems of the liquid manure system within five years. While some problems can be solved with different technology (for example, if the manure is injected into the ground, there will be less run-off) there are yet to appear solutions for most of the crises caused by the industrial production of manure.

The contrast between the craft and factory farms is also reflected in differences among the tillable land and crop sizes, although the increases are not uniform. For example, the pasture per cow on factory farms is half of that on the craft farm. In years since the survey many of the factory farms have eliminated pasture altogether. It is now typical that cows on factory farms spend their entire lives indoors, or sometimes venturing only to what are euphemistically called 'loafing pens', where they stand packed together with their herdmates in muck. Finally, the factory farms devote a larger percentage of their tillable ground to corn production, a high production crop which requires higher chemical inputs than hay or other crops.

FARM CULTURES

In the recent history of American agriculture, the culture of the craft farmer has been seen primarily as an impediment to modernization and progress.[6] The establishment of Cooperative Extension and Rural Sociology Departments has been predicated on the idea that farmers need to maximize their own human capital in the form of education, training, and the import of new ideas and techniques, in order to overcome their limited and 'pre-modern' cultures. Thus it is not surprising, that, compared to other industrialized countries, the U.S. has been remarkably unromantic about the need to preserve the family farm.[7] Nixon's Secretary of Agriculture George Butz's admonition to farmers to "Get big or get out" is but the most direct expression of this sentiment.

I observed two distinct cultures among the dairy farmers I surveyed in northern New York. The factory farmers epitomize the American ideal of rationality, efficiency and profit maximization, regarding expansion and modernization as the twin pillars of their professional identity. Many became farmers as adults and from outside the region, and farm to make a profit rather than participate in a lifestyle or extend a family tradition.

The factory farmers had all made sizeable investments during the past decade. Of the thirteen, several had built new freestall barns and milking parlors, an investment of a hundred thousand dollars or more. They had acquired adjoining farms and often installed field drainage systems to bring poorly drained fields into production. They moved more heavily into corn production (which yields the greatest tonnage per acre) despite its heavy reliance on chemicals and its heavy toll on the soil.

The differences between the two cultures were evident in their treatment of and attitude toward their cows. Factory farmers were more likely to milk three times a day and to consult professionals to balance the nutrients of their cowfeed. Fewer factory farmers pastured their animals at all, and several kept their animals inside year round. The factory farmers, on average, kept their milk cows for three annual milking cycles, while the craft farmers, on average, kept their animals for six. These differences point to the cultural differences between the two groups; they indicate the ways differing farmers defined the cow. For the factory farmer, turning cows over quickly allowed them to more quickly advance their genetic experiments, in other words, to selectively breed to improve milk production. Factory farmers were about twice as likely to purchase replacement heifers in addition to breeding their own replacements. Purchasing replacements typically is a way to bring proven genetic success into their herds. It is also an expensive way to improve the herd.

The factory farmers all knew their herd averages and were actively engaged in figuring ways to improve that measure of their success. In fact they knew the herd averages of other leading farmers in the neighborhood (or they asked me about them!) and measured themselves relative to others by that index. Several craft farmers did not even know their herd averages, or only placed it into a range.

The most striking difference, however, was in the regard for and connection to the animals themselves. The cows on the factory farm lived their short lives crowded in the freestall barn, standing in muck. The farmer of the factory farm is a manager of animals and machines, overseeing a complex configuration of disparate variables, but not intimately connected with any.

The craft farmers usually milk their cows themselves and know them well. I recall engaged arguments between fathers and sons over the breeding decisions which had produced a particular cow: perhaps she produced well and good teats and feet, but was the bad disposition worth it? Craft farmers often kept cows for as long as ten years, and they took care of these cows like members of an extended family. The craft farmers did much of their own veterinary work, both informally as they monitored their cows' health during the daily milking, and formally as they tested for pregnancy, assisted with difficult births, and did other rather extensive veterinary work. Since they kept their cows longer they represented a more important investment, and since they had smaller herds it was possible to have deeper knowledge of individual animals. As noted above, the layout of the barns facilitated the deeper animal/ human relationships experienced on the craft farm.

There were times when a well-managed barn of a craft farm reminded me of a monastery. The twice a day, seven days a week milking tied the farmer to an unvarying routine. For many people in contemporary life, such a routine would be unimaginable. But these farmers seemed to have gained from this life. They exhibited a depth of knowledge rare in today's world. They were confident in their knowledge and they did not question their identity. They were cut off from other people, but often well integrated as families.

It is fair to note that the group I have called craft farmers included individuals and families who did not live up to the ideals sketched above. There were farms with deteriorating barns and obsolete equipment; farmers who had not actively thought about different ways of doing things for decades or perhaps generations, whether or not they could afford them. These farmers were defensive about their vulnerability; most feared or even expected to go out of business before they retired. Of the thirty-three craft farms, five or six operations fit this description. They contrasted mightily with other farmers who shared their technology and general methods of farming. Several of these farmers were, indeed, out of business by 1999.

NEGOTIATING THE FUTURE

I complete this paper with reflections on the fate of the farmers ten years after I completed my survey, and suggestions about what this means for the future of small farm dairies in the U.S. I recall as a matter of context Table 2, which shows that by 1995, the last county-wide data available, the number of farms in St. Lawrence County had declined to slightly more than a fourth of the 1969 total, while the average size of farms had only slightly increased.

Of the thirty-four craft farms, nineteen (56%) remain in the business in 1999, ten years after my original survey (see Table 5). Fifteen of the thirty-five farms designated as craft farms in 1989 ceased their dairy operations during this period. Three of the fifteen families retired and did not pass the farm to a future generation. Four farmers sold their milking herds, but continued to crop their land and sometimes house heifers or calves in their barns.

Five of the fifteen craft farmers who left farming did so because of injury or death to one of the principal farmers of the operation. One farmer was killed and another seriously injured in separate farm accidents; two died as elderly individuals, and two others were injured in non-agricultural accidents sufficiently to force their retirement from dairy farming.

Six quit farming for various reasons: two farmers were newcomers who did not have the stamina or general acumen to remain in business; four others left farming apparently because of financial crises.

Table 5.   Change on 46 dairy farms, 1989–1999

	Remained in farming	# Farms	Closed dairy	# Farms
Craft farms (N = 34)	farms unchanged	11	ceased farming due to death/ injury of principal farmer	6
	same farm methods; generational transfer (or in process)	4	sold cows; continue auxillary agricultural work	4
	craft farm expanded to freestall/milking parlor	4	retired; land unused	3
			quit farming; land unused	2
Factory farms (N = 12)	farm unchanged	6	quit farming; land absorbed by neighboring farms	2
	significant expansion	4		
	Total	29 (63%)		17 (37%)

Source: St. Lawrence County survey update

The farmers who left dairying ranged from the smallest to some in the middle range. At the time of the 1989 survey those who were to go out of business averaged 41 cows and 215 acres of tillable land.

The land on six of the fifteen farms passed out of agricultural production when the farmers sold their herds; totaling approximately 1300 acres.[8] Most of these farms were on dead-end roads or in areas of the county which were heavily wooded, with small fields tucked into woods. In an era of the expansion of factory farms, most land which passed out of production did so because the farms were isolated and hard for another farmer to utilize. At least one of the farmers who has gone out of business in a prime agricultural area continues to live in the house; his barn has fallen in and his fields are unused and returning to weeds. Several adjoining farmers covet his land and disdain his disinterest in using his land or having it farmed by others.

Nineteen of thirty-five farms (54%) which were classified as craft farms in 1989 remain in business. Eleven of these operations are essentially as they were a decade ago. Four farms have not changed in size or organization, but they have transferred, or are in the process of transferring to the next generation. Four previously craft farms have built freestall barns, expanded their herds, and would, in 1999, be classified as factory farms.

What I rather tentatively called factory farms in 1989 (12 of 46, or 26% of the total) have become even more factory-like by 1999. In the neighborhood I surveyed (including the immediately surrounding region) there are now three 'mega dairies', each milking between 800 and 1,000 cows. One of these was, in 1989, the largest farm in my study, with 268 milking cows. This farm has tripled in size in ten years. The agri-business company Agway has plans for a 300 acre facility for raising calves and heifers on the site of a previously successful farm. The development of facility is temporarily on hold while the environmental impacts of the anticipated manure and other environmental effects are argued.

Four of the twelve factory farms have experienced significant growth, as 250–300 cow herds become common in the North Country. This has profoundly changed the character of farming in the North Country, and it has affected the surrounding community. As mentioned above, the factory farms have liquid manure pits which have been recognized as environmental hazards, around which energetic debate currently swirls. Beside their impact on the groundwater, streams and the land itself, the pits add a noxious element to the rural environment, symbolized in the now common stench and fouled roads caused by the routine work of spreading manure.

The expansion of the largest farms has also added large truck traffic (milk pickup for an 800 cow herd is itself a significant addition to the traffic flow) and equipment traffic. As the factory farmers buy the land previously belonging to their neighbors, their crop work becomes inordinately complicated. They must transport their tractors, plows, choppers and wagons sometimes miles from one part of their now extended farm to another. This adds to the caloric irrationality of the farms, as the fuel costs for heavy equipment are added to the caloric price of production. It also makes cropping inefficient and reduces the knowledge the farmer has of fields and lands. Finally, the increasing machinery on rural roads further alienates non-farm residents.

An important way to seek the meaning of these changes is to place oneself into the experience or perspectives of the farmers. Clearly many of those who left farming did so for common-sense reasons. These include those who retired or were injured, and, of course, those who died. In several cases the farmers sold their herds but continue growing crops and sometimes housing heifers or calves. They have become, in fact, contract workers for the factory farms in the area.

Some craft and factory farmers were flushed out of the system because they were less competent or motivated, or less lucky than their neighbors. For the most part their neighbors had been waiting for their seeming inevitable demise for years. The percentage of failures of this kind are not surprising given the general distribution of competence, motivation and luck. What is remarkable is that during these ten years no small farms began in place of those who left farming. Most of the land on the small farms which went under was purchased by larger farms. About a third of the land went out of agricultural production. These farms would be ripe for purchase by a new generation of small farmers. Interestingly enough, one of the only new small farms in the region (immediately adjacent to the area I studied) is run by a Vietnamese family who has earned the respect of their neighbors. By using a great deal of family labor, this farm is becoming a neighborhood showcase, supporting a family with a small herd and limited land holdings. And just ten miles in different directions from the neighborhood I studied are two Amish neighborhoods, who continue to show that a non-mechanized farm supported by informal collective work arrangements, can produce a viable agricultural system.

Yet these examples of viable small farms do not capture the imagination of most farmers. Many farmers see their fates, one way or another, tied to the factory farms and the new mega-dairies. There is spirited criticism of these trends by some farmers; resigned acceptance by others, and by some an enthusiastic endorsement that growth, even as represented by the mega-dairies, must be a good thing. At least some of the explanation for farmers' response has to do with the broader cultural embrace of entrepreneurial capitalism, the suspicion of government regulation, and our willingness, speaking as a nation, to replace craft with industrial capitalism.

I observe the seeming demise of the small farm and the growth of mega-dairies with concern. The old system was based on cooperation among neighbors. It used local resources almost exclusively. Farmers could grow most of what their cows required, and the manure produced on the farm was nearly sufficient to replenish the land used to grow the cowfeed. It would be unthinkable to consider it, as we do in the case of factory farms, as the manure as a potential or real source of pollution! Family farming was arduous work, but without the financial stress of the new system. The largest farmers in my study did not report working any fewer hours than did the smaller farmers. Their debt loads were often in the hundreds of thousands of dollars and while they had high cash flows, they were more vulnerable to fluctuations in the price of milk.[9] The biggest farms have absorbed not only the land of their neighboring farms, but have also turned previously independent farmers into workers or subcontractors. The vulnerability of the big farms is coupled with the dependence of so many rural families on a single economic unit. If the farm fails, it drags many others down with it.

The mega-dairies, and the generally increasing scale of dairy farming generally, threaten a rural culture. Not all cultures, of course, are worth saving. I am sure many of us lament the end of the craft era just as we enjoy the benefits of a mass-production world. But in farming it is different. Milk does not have to be made in a factory. In fact there is no benefit in doing it this way, and there are enormous costs. The big farmers were harried and driven by the demands of an incredibly complicated system, but I could not get away from many of the small farmers who had the time and energy to talk. I came away from these farm visits with respect for their ways of life. They were making something valuable and in the process treating animals and land well. In the meantime they were good neighbors. I thus end the paper with a question: Is it irrational to lament the loss of a socially harmonious and environmentally friendly system, and its replacement with a system based on factory work and environmental degradation?

ACKNOWLEDGMENTS

Many thanks to Karen Kline, who assisted in interviewing and data analysis; to Willie Louie, research assistant, and to Tom Lyson for inspiration and information. Thanks also to Rob Evans, patient chronicler of recent changes in the North Country. I also express my deep gratitude to North Country farmers who welcomed me to their farms and encouraged my interest in North Country agriculture.

NOTES

1. The data until the mid-1980s are summed by Gilbert & Akor (1988), and the implications of these two systems are explored by Geisler & Lyson (1991).

2. See, especially, Davidson & Schwarzweller (1995) and Lyson & Geisler (1992). The bibliography included in Davidson & Schwarzweller is comprehensive and cross-national in scope, and should be consulted for further research.

The ideas of Piore & Sabel (1984) on the possibilities of mixing forms and scales of production lie at the basis of much thinking on this subject.

3. Our previous neighbor, Emily Fisher, self-published a memoir (1985) of the immigration of the Fisher family and the subsequent five generations who managed the family farm. Doris R. Lee's *History of Pillar Point* (n.d.) draws on diaries and other information to detail the evolution of family farming in a community just south of the neighborhood I studied.

4. The best case studies dealing with New York agriculture are Cruise & Lyson (1991); Osterud's (1991) study of late 19th century dairy farming; Cohen's (1992) study of New England Pioneer farms; McMurry's (1995) study of cheese farms of the 19th century, and Elbert's (1985) study of gender roles in contemporary New York dairy farming. For case studies of dairy farming in other regions, see Davidson & Schwarzweller (1995) for the U.S.; Tovey (1982) for Ireland and van der Ploeg (1985) for northern Italy.

5. Figures 1 through 9 are reproduced with permission from the Standard Oil of New Jersey Collection, Ekstrom Library, University of Louisville, Louisville, KY. Figures 1 through 9 from Central and Northern New York, circa 1945.

6. This point is well developed in Buttel, Larson & Gillespie's masterful history (1990) of the sociology of agriculture.

7. The essays gathered by Comstock (1987) address the question of where there is a moral obligation to save the family farm. Geisler & Lyson (1991) describe environmental and social impacts of the shift from family to factory farms, a theme developed from Goldschmidt's classic (1940) study of social impact of agribusiness in a California farm region. Vogeler (1981) carried this argument into the 1980s.

8. This is difficult to determine exactly. Many farmers rent their land informally; not all farmers were available to question.

9. In the spring of 1999 the price of milk is slightly over $12/hundred. Just four months ago the price was over $17.

REFERENCES

Buttel, F. H., Larson, O. F., & Gillespie, G. W. Jr. (1990). *The Sociology of Agriculture*. New York: Greenwood Press.
Canine, C. (1995). *Dream Reaper*. Chicago: University of Chicago Press.
Cohen, D. S. (1992). *The Dutch-American Farm*. New York: New York University Press.
Comstock, G. (Ed.)(1987). *Is There a Moral Obligation to Save the Family Farm?* Ames, Iowa: Iowa University Press.

Cruise, J., & Lyson, T. A. (1991). Beyond the Farmgate: Factors Related to Agricultural Performance in Two Dairy Communities. *Rural Sociology, 56*(1), 41–55.

Davidson, A., & Schwarzweller, H. K. (1995). Marginality and Uneven Development: The Decline of Dairying in Michigan's North Country. *Sociologia Ruralis, XXXV*(1), 40–66.

Elbert, S. (1985). Amber Waves of Gain: Women's Work in New York Farm Families. In: C. Groneman, & M. B. Norton (Eds), *'To Toil the Livelong Day' America's Women at Work, 1780–1980* (pp. 250–268). Ithaca: Cornell University Press.

Fisher, E. 1985. *George Did It: A History of the Fisher Family.* self published.

Geisler, C., & T. Lyson. (1991). The Cumulative Impact of Dairy Industry Restructuring. *BioScience, 41*(8), 560–567.

Glaser, B., & Strauss, A. (1967). *On the Discovery of Grounded Theory.* Chicago: Aldine.

Gilbert, J., & Akor, R. 1988. Increasing Structural Divergence in U.S. Dairying: California and Wisconsin since 1950. *Rural Sociology, 53*(1), 56–72.

Goldschmidt, W. (1978). *As You Sow: Three Studies in the Social Consequences of Agribusiness.* New Jersey: Allanheld, Osmun and Co.

Huff, C. n.d. *New York State Dairy Statistics.* State of New York: Department of Agriculture and Markets. (pamphlet).

Lee, D. R. n.d. *A History of Pillar Point.* Self published.

Lyson, T. A., & Geisler, C. 1992. Toward a Second Agricultural Divide: The Restructuring of American Agriculture. *Sociologia Ruralis, XXXII*(2/3), 248–263.

McMurry S. (1995). *Transforming Rural Life: Dairying Families and Agricultural Change, 1820–1885.* Baltimore: Johns Hopkins University Press.

New York Agricultural Statistics 1996–1997 (1997). Albany: New York Agricultural Statistics Service.

Osterud, N. G. (1991). *Bonds of Community: The lives of Farm Women in Nineteenth-Century New York.* Ithaca: Cornell University Press.

Piore, M., & Sabel, C. F. (1984). *The Second Industrial Divide.* New York: Basic Books.

Plattner, S. W. (1983). *Roy Stryker. USA, 1943–1950. The Standard Oil (New Jersey) Photography Project.* Austin, Texas: University of Texas Press.

Sloan, E. (1965). *Diary of an Early American Boy.* New York: Ballantine Books.

Tovey, H. (1982). Milking the Farmer? Modernization and Marginalisation in Irish Dairy Farming. In: M. Kelly et. al. (Eds), *Power Conflict and Inequality* (pp. 68–89). Dublin: Turoe Press.

United States Census of Agriculture, 1925, 1945, 1954, 1959, 1969, 1987, 1992, 1997.

van der Ploeg, J. D. (1985). Patterns of Farming Logic, Structuration of Labour and Impact of Externalization: Changing Dairy Farming in Northern Italy. *Sociologia Ruralis, XXV*(1), 5–25.

Vogeler, I. (1981). *The Myth of the Family Farm: Agribusiness Dominance of U.S. Agriculture.* Boulder, CO: Westview Press.

Weitzman, D. (1991). *Thrashin' Time: Harvest Days in the Dakotas.* Boston: David R. Godine.

MILK AND MODERNITY: DAIRYING IN CONTEMPORARY IRELAND

Hilary Tovey

INTRODUCTION

During the 1970s much of the sociology of agriculture was preoccupied with debates about whether the family form of farming should be considered an obstacle to, or functional for, national socioeconomic development. This way of framing the agrarian question was challenged in the 1980s, when theorists like Long (1984), Friedman (1986), Long et al. (1987), insisted that family farmers be treated as acting subjects, who resist or collaborate with the state or agro-industrial corporations in the way they manage their farms. A similar action perspective is used here to look at Irish dairy farming, but I address farmer agency as a collective form which influences structurating processes in society, as well as on individual farms. How have dairy farmers contributed to the shaping of a modern capitalist society in Ireland? What specific features of Irish modernity can be traced back to their historical agency?

The historical significance of milk and milk products in Irish society is widely recognized. Cows, their ownership and their well-being were addressed in Brehon law tracts from as early as the eighth century. In early medieval Ireland, literary sources show that milk was an important element in the diet of adults as well as children. In the contemporary period, annual adult consumption peaked in 1984 at around 211 litres per capita (Doyle & Smith, 1989: 111) but is still more than treble the EC average, placing Ireland fourth among the world's milk-drinking countries behind Norway, Finland and Iceland (Lysaght, 1994a). Irish folklore is full of beliefs and rituals for the management of milk production and in particular, its protection against theft

Research in Rural Sociology, Volume 8, pages 47–73.
Copyright © 2000 by Elsevier Science Inc.
All rights of reproduction in any form reserved.
ISBN: 0-7623-0474-X

and interference by magic (Lysaght, 1994b). The cultural significance of milk has a clear material basis. Milk products, especially butter, were an important cash crop for generations of Irish farmers, whose sale generated money for land rent payments and for the purchase of necessities (tea, flour, tobacco) which households could not produce for themselves. As early as the mid-16th century, moreover, Irish butter was internationally traded. At that stage the trade was important enough to attract severe export duties from the British colonial rulers (Lysaght, 1994b: 209). By the 19th century it was being exported not only to Britain, but also to Europe, Africa, and the Americas.

However, there has been less recognition of the significance of milk producers, and the collective role they have played in the construction of modern Ireland. Irish dairy farmers have been involved in a range of attempts, over the past century, to act collectively on society and on the state, the most influential of these being the formation of the cooperative movement. Ireland's 'modernization' is usually dated from the industrialization strategies of the late 1950s, when the economy was opened up to investment by transnational capital after two decades of struggles for independent development or self-sufficiency. But the history of the cooperative movement suggests that Ireland's path to modernity began earlier than this, and was initially agrarian rather than industrial.

Today, while milk production is still in the vanguard of Irish economic success, milk producers are no longer important agents of societal change. From a particularly significant collective actor within an agrarian world, they have become individualized entrepreneurs, increasingly absorbed into the class structure of an urban capitalist society; in many respects the history of their transformation is also the history of the urbanization of Irish society. This chapter sets that transformation process in a wider societal context and addresses some of the conditions contributing to it. Starting with a brief account of the historical creation of a vision of agrarian modernity, through the cooperative movement, it goes on to contrast the contemporary situation of dairy farmers and of Irish agriculture more generally, and to outline the forces, political and economic, which have helped to shape the contemporary scene. One such force, perhaps the most significant, is the Irish food industry which itself, ironically, is the product of the earlier collective attempt by farmers to create an alternative, agrarian future.

MILK PRODUCERS IN RECENT IRISH HISTORY

Famines, evictions, and long-drawn-out struggles over fair rents and security of tenure left agrarian Ireland, by the end of the nineteenth century, demoralized and disorganized. From its commanding position in the international trade of 50 years earlier, Irish butter had lost virtually all its export markets, even the British market. Organizers of the cooperative movement in Ireland believed cooperation was the only way to revitalize Irish agriculture. Lack of rural organization left farmers vulnerable to exploitation by middlemen and dealers. Already by the 1880s the development of technology for mechanical butter-making was leading to a rapid spread of creameries, and most of these were privately owned. Often the major shareholders were butter buyers and merchant investors (Bolger, 1977: 65–6).

The Irish cooperative movement was a movement for the economic development of Irish agriculture and for the defense of Irish farmers against exploitation by industrial capitalists and merchants. But it became much more than this, providing institutional structures, opportunities for collective action, and discourses for interpreting and critiquing social arrangements which empowered farmers to participate in the subsequent development of Irish society as a whole. Cooperation was promoted not just as a form of business organization, but as a new way of organizing social relations along more egalitarian lines. The cooperative movement thus became also a movement for national development, for scientific and technological progress, even for the recreation of Irish civil society. The failure of demands for political independence at the end of the last century opened up a space in which other forms of independent development and autonomy could be pursued – linguistic and cultural, literary, organizational and administrative, and economic. The cooperative movement was one among a number of movements (the Gaelic League, the Sinn Fein movement of Arthur Griffiths) which used the political vacuum as an opportunity to develop a society capable of taking control of its own future, whether formally under British colonial rule or not. Agricultural cooperation provided conditions for mobilization, and a sense of organizational confidence, which later proved crucial to the success of the War of Independence (Rumpf & Hepburn, 1977). It articulated a discourse of economic nationalism which persisted as a feature of Irish society at least up to the 1960s. (Many of the private creameries in Ireland relied on capital investment from British wholesale grocery chains, so that the farmers' struggle against exploitative industrial capital merged into a struggle to maintain control over an Irish food industry in the hands of Irish people). But perhaps its most important contribution to the national independence movement was its vision of agrarian modernity, underpinned by a desire to demonstrate that the Irish were a rational, intelligent, innovative and disciplined people who deserved and who could make good use of self-government. Thus, the push by the cooperatives to reform Irish butter production standards, for example, was not only for economic reasons, to recapture the British market, but also for cultural ones, to demonstrate the modernity of the Irish nation (Digby 1949).

The growth of cooperation engaged Irish farmers in two further forms of collective action for societal change. One was a broad movement for rural development which has been described as fifty years or more ahead of its time (Bolger, 1977) in its commitment to self-help, empowerment and collective mobilization for marginal groups. Many of the cooperative movement's founding members understood what they were embarked on as nothing less than the creation of a new rural civilization – the re-valuing of rural society and its skills and culture in a world which was increasingly urban and industrial. Since Irish society at the time was still primarily rural and agrarian, recreating a rural civilization could also be understood as creating a distinctively Irish civilization. Secondly, the cooperative movement was also a movement for the technical improvement and modernization of Irish farming, and of Irish society more generally. The rural civilization to be created was to be a thoroughly modern one, owing nothing to tradition. Horace Plunkett, a founder of the cooperative movement, believed he had started 'an industrial revolution' (Bolger, 1977: 75) – one which, given Ireland's circumstances, would grow out of the industrialization of food rather than the importation of industries based on no indigenous linkages. The cooperative movement was not opposed to the industrialization of food production, but to industrialization through forms of social organization which left farmers powerless and dependent on those who controlled it. Movement leaders fought hard to ensure that the administrative and educational structures and knowledge to support a farmer-controlled food industry should be put in place. This emphasis on technical competence and economic efficiency in all areas of food production has probably been the movement's most enduring legacy, eclipsing more social objectives and aspirations. As we see later, it strongly influenced the sense of identity of Irish dairy farmers.

Once introduced, cooperativism developed rapidly in Ireland. The first cooperative society was set up in 1889; ten years later there were 374, with a membership of 36,683 (Bolger, 1977: 89), and by 1913, 985 (ibid: 103). More and more privately owned creameries also came into cooperative ownership, and by 1926, around 70% of all creameries in the Republic of Ireland were cooperatively owned (ibid: 215). Milk processing was the main focus of the early organisers' efforts, and it still remains by far the largest sector of Irish agricultural cooperative activity. But in the early period, and indeed until the 1970s (see below), milk production was not regarded as a specialized activity but rather as a line of production to which all or most farmers could aspire. The expansion of dairying, together with the cooperative organization of dairy processing, was thought of as a means of keeping smaller landholders in farming and equalizing access to rewards from farming, both seen as essential for maintaining a vigorous, economically and socially active population in the countryside. Over time, however, these impulses within the movement towards communalism, egalitarianism and resource dispersal began to run up against countervailing concerns about maximizing self-interest, efficiency and specialist interests.

DAIRY FARMING IN CONTEMPORARY IRELAND

The image of a modern agrarian social structure, forged in the early cooperative movement, remains part of the discourse of farming politics in the 1990s. That image was of a uniform, relatively egalitarian, producer society, a society based on independent, productive and efficient full-time family farms, where the land owned and worked by the farm family would be enough to absorb the labor of more than one generation and to provide family members with a moderate, stable level of comfort. It further assumed that inputs of family motivations and family skills can obviate the need for expanded control over land, giving rise to a form of highly technologically developed, intensive, high value-added farming which, in conjunction with a cooperatively organized food processing and agribusiness sector, would guarantee reproduction for farm households which have relatively small land-holdings (Chayanov, 1925; see also Roberts & Mutersbaugh, 1996). Of all Irish farms today it is dairy farms that come closest to being 'real farms' in terms of this Chayanovian vision. They are the most successful at combining family labor inputs with technical sophistication to produce a high quality product and generate comfortable incomes, on moderate sized farms. Closer consideration, however, reveals considerable variation. Externally, dairy farms are located in a broader rural context that is not uniform but highly differentiated, socially and spatially. Internally, there appear to be changes occurring in relations between household and enterprise, which portend profound transformations in the subjective meaning of family farming.

Dairy Farming and Irish Agricultural Restructuring

The Census of Agriculture defines specialization in an enterprise as when that enterprise accounts for at least two-thirds of the farm income. Using this definition, around one third of Irish farms today are specialized dairy enterprises, around 5% specialise in tillage, and the rest rely mainly on dry-stock systems – 44% on cattle and 18% mainly on sheep (Frawley & Commins,

Table 1. Farmland Size (Hectares), Comparing Dairy and Beef Farms, 1991

Size (hectares)	Dairy		Beef	
	%	cum. %	%	cum. %
0–<2	0.6	0.6	2.2	2.2
2–<5	2.3	2.9	10.9	13.1
5–<10	5.7	8.6	20.2	33.3
10–<20	22.5	31.1	34.8	68.1
20–<30	24.9	56.0	16.3	84.4
30–<50	27.7	83.7	10.6	95.0
50–<100	14.2	97.9	4.2	99.2
100 and above	2.1	100.0	0.8	100.0
Total %	100.0		100.0	
Total number of farms	41,552		71,786	
Average size (hectares)	32.9		18.7	

Source: derived from Census of Agriculture, 1991

1996: 5). Whereas in the past nearly all farms would have produced milk, if only for domestic consumption, today farms which produce milk are highly specialized in milk production, accounting for 93% of all dairy cows. Farms with only dry-stock production are thus in many cases the outcome of marginalization and exclusion processes rather than of positive decisions to specialize in this enterprise line. Commins and Keane argue, indeed, that the greatest contrast in contemporary Irish farming is "between systems which are based on, or incorporate, dairying and those systems based on cattle production" (1994: 93). In Tables 1 to 4 we compare dairy farming with dry cattle production, to illustrate the very divergent characteristics of these two farming types in Irish agriculture today.

The average size of a farm in Ireland is 26 hectares. Dairy farmers operate more land on average than all other farmers and considerably more than beef farmers. Yet they could hardly be described as large-scale, with 83% operating less than 50 hectares. However, measured by gross margins produced, dairy farming is more productive than the average in Irish farming (at 11.6 ESUs), and much more so than dry cattle farming (Table 2). Thus, despite the persistence of some very small dairy farms which return extremely poor incomes (Davis et al., 1997), it is hardly surprising that amongst farms rated by agricultural analysts as viable (farms which generate enough income to remunerate the family labor used at a level equivalent to the average agricultural wage, and also provide at least a 5% return on the non-land assets

Table 2. Economic Size Units,* Comparing Dairy and Beef Farms, 1991

	Dairy		Beef	
ESUs*	%	cum. %	%	cum. %
0–<1	0.8	0.8	19.2	19.2
1–<2	1.3	2.1	23.0	42.2
2–<4	2.8	4.9	27.4	69.6
4–<8	9.8	14.7	19.5	89.1
8–<16	25.2	39.9	8.3	97.4
16–<40	44.1	84.0	2.4	99.8
40 and above	16.0	100.0	0.2	100.0
Total %	100.0		100.0	
Total number of farms	41,552		71,786	
Average ESU	24.6		3.9	

Note: Economic Size Units (ESUs) are calculated using an EU–wide system for measuring standard gross margins per hectare (crops) or per head (livestock)
Source: derived from Census of Agriculture 1991

Table 3. Labor Input of Farmholder, and His/her Occupational Dependence on Farming, Comparing Dairy and Beef Farms, 1991

	Dairy		Beef	
Annual work units*	No.	%	No.	%
0–<0.25	436	1.1	5,680	7.9
0.25–<0.50	934	2.3	8,243	11.5
0.50–<0.75	1,106	2.7	9,637	13.4
0.75–<1.00	1,120	2.7	7,126	10.0
1.00	37,891	91.2	40,942	57.2
Total	41,487	100.0	71,628	100.0
Occupational dependence on farming				
Sole occupation	37,747	91.2	46,792	65.3
Main occupation	1,557	3.7	4,743	6.6
Secondary occupation	2,183	5.1	20,093	28.1
Total	41,487	100.0	71,628	100.0

*One Annual Work Unit is equivalent to the labour input of one full–time worker per year
Source: derived from Census of Agriculture, 1991

Table 4.   Percentage of Farmland Holdings in Different Economic Size Units,
1975, 1983, 1987, 1991

Farm Business size group (in ESUs)	1975	1983	1987	1991
Small (2 or less)	42.5	29.9	34.9	26.0
Medium (over 2 to 8)	43.6	40.3	34.1	34.3
Large (over 8)	13.9	29.8	31.0	39.7
Total percent	100.0	100.0	100.0	100.0

Source: Commins & Keane (1994: 43)

of the farm), dairy farms predominate. Nearly 70% of the 35,000 farms rated, on the basis of National Farm Surveys from 1991 to 1994, as 'large viable enterprises' were dairy farms (Frawley & Commins, 1996).

Dairy farmers tend to be younger than the average Irish farmer (61% are under 54 years, compared to 55% of all farmers and 49% of dry cattle farmers). More than 90% are categorized as full-time farmers, contributing a full man-year of labor input to their farm as well as having no other occupation (Table 3). They also make more use of family labour (52% of the total labor force in dairying in 1991 were spouses or other family members, compared to 36% in dry cattle farming; on average, dairy farms have 2.2 workers). Finally, recent National Farm Surveys show that dairy farming provides the best income per farm and per acre, with an average income in 1996 of £18,800 (c. US$24,400) on specialist dairy farms compared to just under £6,000 (c. US$7,800) in cattle farming, £7,800 (c. US$10,000) in sheep farming, and £15,600 (c. US$20,000) in tillage.

Contemporary 'specialist' dairy farmers, then, approach quite closely the ideal of family farming associated with agrarian modernity in the early years of the cooperative movement. But that ideal assumed a certain degree of social uniformity among farmers, whereas what has actually been emerging in Irish agriculture in recent decades is increasing heterogenity, on both class and regional dimensions (Commins & Keane, 1994; Commins, 1996). The diversity becoming visible in Irish agriculture is not taking the form of increased diversity in production systems. Over the past thirty years, in fact, Irish agriculture has become markedly more specialized in fewer products. Milk now accounts for one third of gross agricultural output compared to one fifth in 1960; cattle account for nearly 40%, compared to 29% in 1960; all other farm enterprises – pigs, poultry and eggs, cereals, fruit and vegetables –

declined significantly (Teagasc, 1995: 44). The differentiation is in how farm households are positioned in relation to agricultural production itself, the 'economic centrality' (Marsden et al., 1986) of the farm business to the farm household. Farm families are becoming increasingly diverse in terms of how much of household income comes from farming, how much of family labour time is devoted to it, how much, indeed, they define themselves as farmers or understand themselves to be seriously engaged in the occupation of farming.

Restructuring in Irish farming is not taking either of the 'classic' forms. There is little evidence of movement from family farming into more capitalist forms of management. In 1991, 'non-family farms' amounted to less than 700 in number. Similarly, there is no marked land concentration occurring, although smaller holding numbers are falling (Commins & Keane, 1994: 42); average farm size in 1991 was around 65 acres (26 hectares). The picture is complicated, however, by changes in the pattern of renting (Frawley & Commins, 1996: 3). In the 1960s, what land was rented (and it was generally limited and short-term) was rented by smaller farmers, whereas today it is mainly larger farmers, engaged in dairying, tillage or livestock enterprises, who rent in, often from smaller neighbors. Smaller landholders are withdrawing from farming as a livelihood, but without necessarily giving up ownership of their land. Irish agricultural restructuring is primarily a process of concentration of production, output and income on a steadily contracting group of farms. Commins & Keane (1994) estimate that 20% of Irish farms, currently holding about 40% of all agricultural land, account for some 60% of output. Table 4 shows the process of concentration of production in Irish farming over the past two decades.

The link between specialization and concentration is particularly clear in dairy farming. In 1975, dairy enterprises were found on 127,500 holdings (56% of all holdings), but by 1991 on only 49,100 (29%). Over the same period the average size of dairy herd increased from 12 to 27 cows (Frawley & Commins, 1996: 8). Furthermore, 62% of all dairy cows in Ireland are now found on farms with herds of at least 30 cows, compared to only 38% in the mid-1970s (Commins & Keane, 1994: 44). In fact 84% of dairy cows were found in 1991 on just 16% of the farms in the state – those with 16 or more ESUs (Frawley & Commins, 1996: 9). If these trends continue, it is estimated that milk producers will drop to around half their present number by the middle of the next decade (Fingleton, 1995). Similar trends are also evident in beef and sheep enterprises, in cereals, and most dramatically in pig farming; 35,800 farms kept pigs in 1973 but only 2,900 farms in 1991, and the average herd size had gone from 29 to 454 (ibid).

These processes of specialisation and concentration of production are also spatially patterned. During the 1980s, the small-farm counties of the northwest lost their national share of production for all farm enterprises. Even when they increased production (for example, of non-dairy cows), they did so more slowly than the large-farm counties of the southeast. Frawley and Commins point out that although cattle and sheep production are now the mainstay of farming in the west and north west, with tillage and dairying concentrated in the south and south-east, farms in the south and south-east still have larger cattle and sheep enterprises than in the west and north west (1996: 10). "Consequently, in the small farm counties, the intensity of resource use per farm – as measured by ESUs per hectare – is now little more than half of what it is in the large-farm counties..." (Commins, 1996: 104–5). Specialization in dairy farming is increasingly spatially concentrated: 57% of all specialized dairy farms are now in Munster, as is 52% of the 'national dairy herd' with a further 25% in Leinster. In the west and north west dairying is close to vanishing – from 18% of the total dairy herd in 1960, farmers there had 8% in 1991. Farming itself, we might say, is becoming concentrated in the south and southeast of Ireland, while the rest of the country becomes increasingly 'ruralised'.

As production becomes concentrated, farm incomes also become increasingly differentiated, spatially and socially. In 1996 large specialist dairy farms had an average income of £58,000, while small farms in dry cattle production had an average income of £1,800 (Teagasc, 1997). However, research on poverty suggests that income from farming has a diminishing relationship to the overall level of farm household income. "One of the remarkable features of Irish farming in recent years is the extent to which farm households have reduced their dependency on farming as a means of livelihood" (Frawley & Commins, 1996: 20). In 1994, only about 24% of farm households depended solely on their farms as a source of income; the smaller the farm enterprise and the more western or northwestern its location, the less likely it is to do so. In these cases, it is now the level of access by household members to non-farm income sources, and the type of income sources (welfare transfers versus employment, level and sector of employment) which determines the socio-economic status of the farm household, rather than the size of the holding or the scale or type of the farm business.

The result of such heterogeneity is that it is difficult even to establish with certainty how many 'farmers' or 'farm households' exist in Ireland today. The number of 'agricultural landholders' fell sharply from 263,219 in 1980 to 170,578 in 1991, but this was largely because census takers raised the land ownership threshold needed to qualify as a farmer (from one acre to one hectare). Debates take place about how many of the current 170,000 'statistical farms' are 'actual farms' or 'viable farms' – although 'viability', as Leeuwis (1989) points out, should not be confused with 'survivability'. The number of people "at work in agriculture, forestry and fishing," about 27% of the national labor force in 1970, is officially stated to have fallen steadily to around 143,000, or 12.5%, by 1993 (Teagasc, 1995: 62). Much, however, depends on what is counted as work. Commins (1996) shows, for example, that in 1991 a total of 312,729 people had "undertaken some farmwork" over the preceding twelve months (excluding casual, contract and relief workers), 96% of whom were family workers. The work of farm wives in particular is notoriously underestimated in calculating the Irish farm labor force (O'Hara, 1998). Thus some farm households or family members stop defining themselves as in farming, as their circumstances change, while others stop being officially regarded as such, whatever their own self-definition. In the drive to order and organize 'real' farmers, the project of modernity, as Bauman (1991) suggests, ends up by reproducing ambivalence and meaninglessness.

In sum, dairy farmers are the success story of contemporary Irish agriculture. In general they have been extremely successful – far more so than any other type of agricultural producer – in maintaining and developing a form of full-time family farming which, although moderate in scale, is nevertheless highly productive and highly profitable. But even as they have done so, the agrarian world in which such an ideal had purpose and value has fallen away around them. The conditions no longer exist which would encourage them to identify themselves as a collective agrarian actor in attempts to bring about societal change. What new meanings and ideas are emerging among them which may provide an alternative identity?

Dairy Farming: Subjective Transformations

If the structured social reality in which contemporary Irish dairy farmers live is quite different from that held out by earlier visions of agrarian modernity, there also appear to be some interesting changes occurring internally to the farm itself, in the relationships between enterprise and household, which suggest that the meaning of 'farming', and the meaning of "family farming', are undergoing some radical revision. Although enterprise and household on successful dairy farms appear, as we noted earlier, to be more tightly integrated than in other farm types, the direction of these changes – towards decreasing 'economic centrality' of the farm business – is in the end quite similar to those experienced by small landholders withdrawing from agricultural production.

We look first at how *dairying as a 'family' enterprise* is changing. Family farming is generally attributed two key characteristics – the farm labor system is organized to make the best possible use of a family labor force, with its necessarily different strengths and weaknesses from hired labor; and the production system on the farm is organised so as to best meet family members' needs. In contemporary Irish dairy farming, the close connection between labour system and the nature of the labor force has largely disappeared, but in some respects the second characteristic, the subordination of farm production to family needs, appears to have intensified. However, I argue below that this is happening in unexpected and ironic ways, leading over time to a situation in which the class reproduction or even upward mobility of the family is no longer closely dependent on the reproduction of the farm enterprise.

The gendered labor process which was once such a strong feature of Irish farming (women milked the cows, made the butter, and reared the calves; men walked the fields and took responsibility for growing crops and selling cattle) has vanished with farm specialisation. With it went a wealth of folklore which portrayed women as both guardians and 'thieves' of the milk 'profit' (the cream), "with supernatural knowledge, and the power to protect or promote, harm or hinder, by magic, the individual or collective dairying process" (Lysaght, 1994a: ix). The disempowerment of dairy women has been linked to mechanization: "The use of machines was regarded as a masculine pursuit, so for example, the task of milking – women's work, when done by hand – became redefined as a task appropriate for men" (Duggan, 1987: 57). Also important was the rise within middle class Irish society of ideals of domesticity and family privacy which, transferred to rural Ireland in the 1960s, deeply altered the role of farm women (Hannan & Katsiaouni, 1977), transforming them from co-producers into farmers' wives (Duggan, 1987). Many farm women of course, particularly on smaller farms, continued to supply labour to the farm but their work became increasingly invisible, and in an increasingly ancilliary role to the men; cleaning the milking parlour and utensils, keeping records, paying bills. On larger farms, particularly in more eastern regions, the most recent research suggests that farm wives now avoid farming, not in favor of domesticity but to pursue their own careers in the professions or in business (O'Hara, 1998). They are likely to see themselves not as part of a family farm, but merely as married to a farmer.

O'Hara (1997, 1998) demonstrates the continuing significance, nevertheless, of farm women when it comes to generational succession on the farm. Farm women strongly influence "the reproduction of family farming as a social form" through their control over the socialization of farm children, and particularly over their education (1997: 153). Particularly on smaller farms, women are educating their children out of farming; in such cases, the presence of a dairy enterprise on the farm often has more to do with establishing children in the world outside farming than with a commitment to reproducing family farming. O'Hara describes one family, for example, from a small farm in the west, who had educated three sons as engineers, and who were in dairying because it provided "a predictable and regular income to meet the cost of third-level education . . . The mother regarded dairying as a vital source of regular income when the children are being educated" (1997: 147). However, once that was achieved, they expected to cut down the work of their farm operation, perhaps by selling the dairy quota and switching into beef. O'Hara comments that "In this sense dairy farming is a means to an end, financing the education of children who will almost certainly not continue the enterprise on the smaller dairy farms when their parents retire" (idem).

On larger farms many women also aspire to place their children in careers outside farming but here, at least in regard to the expected heir, fathers are better able to contest their wives' aspirations "by virtue of their control over material resources which can provide a viable livelihood for a successor" (ibid: 152). Some research suggests that in this case farmers may choose to build up a dairy enterprise in an attempt to secure the farm succession:

> Quite a few of the dairy farmers said that they were staying in dairying because they thought that would make it more attractive to a son to take over from them, because it did guarantee a monthly salary and so was more like an urban job; but if no son showed any signs of wanting to take over, they would be quite glad to withdraw from dairying because they found it such a demanding job. . . . (Tovey 1995: 28).

However even on large, successful dairy farms and where succession is not an issue, we cannot assume that the farm enterprise is still central to the reproduction of the family. A number of interviews with what might be called 'vanguard farmers' in the *Irish Farmers Journal* during 1997–8 suggest that these farmers are starting to see dairying as a source of profits to be invested in whatever enterprise may best secure the continuing wealth of the family (possible investments mentioned included urban rental property and the Irish film industry). A good example is a liquid milk producer from the Leinster region, with 120 cows, quoted as saying:

> There is no doubt that farmers who are well set up in liquid milk are making money. Many have invested heavily in the farm, setting up good facilities . . . However the farmyard can be a bottomless pit for swallowing money and I will have to think very carefully about further development. Farmers have to learn how to become better investors outside the farm. With land prices so high, and expansion with quotas limited, it is an area where they can better develop their assets (31/1/98: 18).

The trend attracted approving editorial comment in the *Irish Farmers Journal* (22/11/97: 2): "Dairy farmers are showing a welcome capacity to run their farms in a business-like fashion . . . focusing on profit-generation from the

business, then assessing the best ways to invest that profit for the future . . .".
The business of family farming is becoming transformed into family business.

A second area where subjective transformations are evident is that of dairy
farming as an occupation. Compared to other farm systems, dairy farming has
long been seen as technologically demanding, requiring high skills and quality
standards on the part of the farmer. This idea is widespread within Irish farming
discourse; dairy farmers express it about themselves, farmers in other
commodity lines often refer to it in amused or exasperated ways indicating that
even if they do not endorse it they are well aware of the stereotype. Most Irish
farmers have had little technical education in farming but dairy farmers have
more than any other commodity group. They are twice as likely as the average
farmer to have done a Farm Certificate course or farm apprenticeship (8%) or
to have gone on shorter formal courses (12%) (Census of Agriculture 1991).
Dairy farmers are active in forming discussion groups around technical issues
in farm production, visiting each others' farms, attending open days at research
centers or 'monitor farms'. Within the farming media they are routinely
addressed as consumers of highly technical articles on breeding – not just for
high yields but also to increase specific milk constituents – on fertility
problems and achieving compact calving, on grassland and herd management,
and are encouraged to display their skills in these areas through entering
competitions and hosting farm walks.

Food industry intervention in the technical practices of milk production has
to be considered as one of the factors responsible for the falling numbers of
smaller producers in dairy farming (Tovey, 1982). Another is the lending
practices of the banks, which push farm families towards more technical
methods of production and formal levels of rationality. Irish banks too have
been very selective in giving credit to farmers. Their strategy is to pursue
'quality business' which they define as larger dairy farmers and more intensive
pig and mushroom producers, and to offer a "very competitive complete
financial package to larger-scale commercial farmers" in these categories
(Grant & MacNamara, 1996: 432). The preference of banks for lending money
to large dairy farmers emerges also in Smith & Healy (1996), and in Tovey
(1995) where it was explained on the grounds that they have a better, that is,
more regular, cash-flow situation. The more 'urban' financial arrangements that
accompany dairy farming make it easier for financial institutions to appreciate
and deal with dairy farmers. Given their conceptions of what constitutes
'quality farming', and their sponsorship, with the food industry, of competitions to generate particular styles of dairy farming, the banks too have
encouraged both structural concentration and the transfer of particular sorts of
technological practices and self-images into dairy farming.

State policy, since the 1960s, also strongly supported a technology-intensive or 'high-input high-output' (Leeuwis, 1989) approach to dairy farming which involved maximum use of purchased inputs to realise the maximum volume of outputs. Recently, however, that policy has given way to a search for 'more efficient' forms of milk production. The emphasis is on increasing profits by reducing costs, rather than by increasing output. This new policy direction can be, and indeed occasionally is, promoted by the state as a switch from 'productivist' to 'sustainability' goals in farming. More significantly, it is a response to the recognition that it is becoming extremely difficult to expand production under the current EU quota regime, and that in a globalized food market, the cost of their raw material is of critical concern to food processing companies. But what is most interesting about it is that it introduces farmers to a new way of thinking about farming, which presents this as less about technical production practices than about financial or business management. Contemporary dairy farming is not becoming less 'scientised', less dependent on bought-in technological packages, as a result of the new emphasis on efficiency; rather, this encourages the induction of the farmer into new and different sets of expert discourses, particularly around genetics and diet management, but also around economics. Technical skills and knowledge are still regarded as a central characteristic of the occupation of dairy farmer, but increasingly, milk producers are addressed also as people who run a business, that is, as entrepreneurs. The new orthodoxy, evident in the farming media and among farming experts in Teagasc (the state-supported institute for agricultural research and extension) and in the universities, is that dairy farmers are excellent at technical management of their farms but very poor at business skills. Teagasc itself is increasingly involved in organizing courses to develop financial and business skills in farmers. As one organizer of a recent course stated, "The emphasis in the past has always been on improving technical efficiency, but now financial management is even more important" (*Irish Farmers Journal*, 14/3/98: 41)

The growth of an entrepreneurial discourse to define dairy farming as an occupation is well illustrated in responses to the annual Dairy Farmer 2,000 Competition (a prestigious competition which is intended to highlight the requirements a dairy farm must meet if it is to survive and prosper into the year 2000 and beyond) which were extensively reported in the *Irish Farmers Journal* during 1997.The reports demonstrate the extent to which business rhetoric is now shaping conceptions of good dairy farming. The overall winner was portrayed as an enthusiast for a low input, high grass type of production, which gives him lowish yields (861 gallons per cow), but whose "financial performance and planning ability were high enough to make him Dairy Farmer

2000 for 1997 . . . [A good dairy farm business today] must be able to achieve high profits and grow in net worth, just as in any other business sector" (Editorial comment, *Irish Farmers Journal*, 22/11/97). And again, contestants

> should have been working to a well-defined plan to reach personal and business objectives. Unfortunately, there was very little awareness of the basic concepts of strategic business development. With the exception of a few farmers, many failed to identify or even calculate net worth or returns within their own business. In turn, this led to an inability to focus on, or even identify, long-term business objectives. Many farmers are so engrossed in the daily technical tasks that they fail, to their detriment, to focus on the broader picture of business development and wealth creation . . . (1996 overall winner and 1997 judge, *Irish Farmers Journal*, 22/11/97: 31).

The technicisation or scientisation of farming was a key element in the emergence of a professionalized conception of the modern Irish farmer. Professionalization, expressed in the formation of organizations like the Irish Farmers' Association, detached farmers from the rest of rural society (Tovey, 1997) and encouraged them to act on a sectoral basis only; but it did have the potential to unify and collectivize farmers, providing a role model of the vanguard farmer to which other farmers could aspire. The rise of a new business discourse, in turn, may be seen as part of a new process of class incorporation, in which successful milk producers are detached from other farmers and from an agrarian base, and encouraged to identify themselves with a class of 'small business entrepreneurs' emerging within Irish society as a whole. The transformation of developed and successful dairy farmers from vanguard farmer into part of the small business elite reduces their capacity to act as a role model for aspiring commercial farmers and suggests that they now have more in common with food industry and other business groups than with other farmers. The process indicates not only how subjective understandings inside farming are changing, but also a shift in the wider status system of Irish society in which the business person and entrepreneur has enjoyed remarkable upward mobility in recent years, while the status of farmer has heavily declined.

Dairy family farming has undergone a series of important economic, cultural and political transformations in recent decades. These include not only the marked fallout of smaller producers and the concentration of milk production on a declining number of large, specialized and highly productive farms, but also what seems like a gradual detachment of family and enterprise, as dairying becomes a strategy for generational class mobility out of farming, or merely one element in a wider range of family business interests. Looking at the declining centrality of agricultural production to farm household incomes in Britain, Marsden, Whatmore, Munton & Little (1986) say that this is not only a 'survival strategy' among small landholders for whom farming on its own can never generate an adequate income, but also an 'accumulation strategy' of large producers. However, this implies that it can be understood only as an expression of economic rationality. The Irish case shows that this 'declining centrality' is an expression of a wider process of transformation of the society and culture as a whole, in which farming and agriculture are losing ground to an increasingly urbanized world.

DAIRY FARMING AND THE POLITICS OF ECONOMIC DEVELOPMENT

A full understanding of this transformation to an urban modernity requires, finally, some account of the changing role of the state in managing the economic and social contexts in which Irish farming occurs. Through its pursuit of particular conceptions of 'economic development' over time, and of the contribution which agriculture can make to that, the state controls, endorses and legitimizes certain directions and types of change in farming. We touch only selectively on some of the more significant developments in state policy which have emerged in recent decades – the state's response to Irish accession to the EU in 1972; its fostering of the growth of an increasingly globalized Irish dairy food industry; and the changing practices of the dairy food industry in its relations with farmers. These have had particularly significant impacts in encouraging dairy farmers to turn away from seeing themselves as agents of an agrarian modernity, and move towards incorporation into the class of small entrepreneurs who are playing an increasingly significant role in Irish social and economic development.

State Policy for Agriculture After 1970: the Acceptance of Dualism

In the 1960s, state policy encouraged dairying as a form of production appropriate to smaller farms, and it was widely expected that once Ireland joined the (then) European Economic Community, the guaranteed prices for dairy products under the Common Agricultural Policy (CAP) would solve small farmers' income difficulties. Milk production expanded rapidly during the 1970s, but this coincided with a continuous decline in the numbers of smaller producers (Tovey, 1982). Through both its market supports and its aids for farm development, the CAP is now recognized to have had marked structural effects, encouraging the intensification and concentration of production and widening the gap between larger and smaller producers (Scott, 1995). National agricultural policy might have tried to correct these effects but it did not do so. During this period, state policy began to turn away from earlier ideals of a more egalitarian form of agrarian development towards acceptance of dualism and the legitimization of inequality:

> State policy in the 1960s seriously and imaginatively tried to address the peculiar structural and development problems of Irish agriculture. However, native state structural policy making seems to have virtually ceased since EEC entry, being concerned mainly with maximizing the total transfers from Brussels irrespective of their often quite perverse effects. The main 'successful' policies, from the point of view of the majority of farmers who are small-scale, have been those implemented by [other] government departments: mainly rural industrialization, and social welfare policies (Hannan & Breen, 1987: 60).

Agricultural policy discourse focused increasingly on levels of productivity in 'the agricultural sector' as a whole. Concern about the need to raise national levels of output became a justification for concentrating programs of aid for technological investment on the most 'progressive' farmers, who were also those with already the most resources. Intervention in the landholding structure to redistribute land more fairly between farmers was wound down, and the Land Commission abolished in 1980. The agricultural advisory agency ACOT (later absorbed into Teagasc) argued that what farmers needed was not material resources so much as education to modernise their production practices (Kelleher, 1983). The farmers themselves, through their representative organisations, largely supported the belief that technological modernisation is a better path to economic growth than structural change. As part of a corporatist bargaining structure vis-a-vis the state, the employers and the trades unions, the Irish Farmers Association was strategically committed to maintaining as large a population of farmers as possible (Smith & Healy, 1996), but it did increasingly accept the argument that many Irish farms would never become viable enterprises. Like the state, its response to this dilemma was emphatic promotion of capital-intensive, technically advanced farming.

The impact of these new political currents became critical when the European Union began attempting to control the surplus production encouraged by the CAP. When the milk quota system was introduced in 1984, member states had considerable scope to differ in the way they implemented the new regime (Cardwell, 1996). In Ireland, administration of the system was decentralized to the milk purchasers – effectively, the cooperatives. Quota was allocated to each cooperative on the basis of the number of its suppliers, and management of the quota to avoid or reduce superlevy is also carried out at the cooperative level. Until very recently this has been done through a system, specific to Ireland (Trotman, 1996: 266), known as 'fleximilk', where each cooperative assesses whether it is over or under quota in a given year. If it is under quota, none of its suppliers are liable for superlevy (regardless of the national situation). If over quota, the surplus milk from individual suppliers in the co-op who have not exceeded their quota is distributed among those who have. Only those who are still in excess after this are charged superlevy on their outstanding milk.

This form of implementation has some interesting effects. It transfers control over milk quotas, which legally belong to individual farmers, into the hands of the milk processors, and it enabled them to discriminate against smaller producers by using their unused quota to save larger producers from paying fines for overproduction. (Recognition of this has led to some changes in operation in 1998 – fleximilk is now known as 'disused quotas' and 70% of it must be allocated to producers with quotas of less than 35,000 gallons). Moreover, when the scheme was initially introduced the Irish state did not set up a national quota reserve which could have been used to allocate opportunities to produce milk more equally between farmers over time. It did introduce some limited measures to restructure production; quota was purchased for re-allocation to special cases of producers, and a small percentage of allocated quota (proportionate to the individual quota size) was siphoned off for new entrants and young farmers. But demand for such quota far exceeded the supply available (additional quota was received by 800 farmers, with 1.3% of all the herds in the country), and the re-allocation did not discriminate between older and younger farmers or between larger and smaller producers, leaving many smaller farmers unable to continue in dairying. In the first three years of operation (1984–1987), the impact of quota re-allocation in Ireland was minimal compared to other EU member states (Fingleton & Frawley, 1987: 105). Even farmers categorised under the Farm Modernisation Scheme as 'development farmers', that is, entitled to EU farm development funding, and whose development plans were officially approved by the Irish state, were never allocated the additional quota which it had been agreed that they needed to fulfil these plans. Some 1200 such farmers are still pursuing the issue through the courts today, 13 years later. The trend towards concentration of production, and decline in smaller herd-owners, which intensified during the decade, seems to have been facilitated rather than obstructed by the way the quota regime was implemented.

Allocation of quota represents, of course, a capital gain to dairy farmers, since it greatly increases the market value of their land if they decide to sell or lease it. Of the 38,588 milk quota holders identifed in the *Irish Farmers Journal* in 1998, 12% had a quota of over 50,000 gallons while nearly half (47%) had quota sizes of less than 20,000 gallons (14/3/98: 43). According to the same source (*IFJ*, 28/3/98: 6), there are currently about 9,000 'dormant' milk producers in the country, owning between them close to 100 m gallons of quota; most of this is privately leased. The state has been trying in recent years to encourage non-active quota holders to offer their quota to the state's Restructuring or Temporary Leasing Schemes (for social redistribution) instead of selling or leasing it themselves, by 'clawing back' up to 20% of any returns from private leasing. But the amount of milk available for temporary leasing has actually fallen in the past two years (from 70 to 60 million gallons), while private land-and-quota leases have increased (from 60 to 80 million gallons). Even with the clawback, the prices available on the open market seem enough to continue to tempt farmers to sell or lease privately. There are clear connections between this most recent form of commoditisation in dairy farming, and increasing inequalities among farmers, but state intervention to mitigate its impact remains quite ineffective.

Subordinating Farming to Food Industry Interests

State management of the quota system is linked to the increasingly dominant role that the interests of the food industry have come to play in Irish development policy. If the first major change in agricultural policy was the acceptance of a dualistic farming structure, the second is the subordination of the needs of agriculture to those of the food industry (Tovey, 1991). The desirability of that subordination was clearly articulated in an official report on *Ireland in the European Community* produced (1989) in anticipation of the creation of the single European market. This redefined farming (but without explicitly adverting to the fact) as the production of inputs for a food industry, and analyzed the well-known 'structural problems' in Irish agriculture as problems not for farmers but for the food processors. The seasonality, non-uniformity and insecurity of supply which the Irish food industry faces, it argued, can only be solved by getting farmers to enter into long-term supply contracts with processors, a development which the state should back by tying farmers' access to development aids to their becoming the sort of supplier the industry wants. Farmers who cannot achieve that should be helped to leave farming.

Re-orienting development policy to the needs of the food industry is widely justified on the grounds that it is a better bet than farming for generating employment. Since the 1970s it has provided a fairly stable 20–25% of manufacturing employment, whereas agricultural employment has fallen continuously: "The Irish economy may no longer be dominated by agriculture. But food [i.e. the food industry] employs 40,000 and remains one of the country's largest indigenous industries. Of the top 100 companies in Ireland 20 are food and drink manufacturers. Last year 640 companies exported almost £5 billion worth of product . . ." (*Irish Times*, 23/2/98: 17) The cooperative food industry (primarily dairy processors) in particular has experienced 'phenomenal growth', from a turnover of £20 million in 1970 to £6,000 million in 1995, and currently some 25,000 employees, nearly two-thirds of all food industry workers (Smith & Healy, 1996: 220). Probably far more significant than employment potential, in terms of influencing state policy, are the opportunities for accumulation generated in the food industry, which are not available in farming.

In the 1970s the Irish milk processing industry, operating in a context in which markets were guaranteed and export sales encouraged, consisted mainly of large-scale plants concentrating heavily on the primary processing of bulk commodities (milk separation, butter or powdered milk production). However, the leading cooperatives were beginning to look seriously at diversification in both their uses of their raw material, and their range of products generally. While bulk commodity production remains important today, there has been a strong shift towards consumer ready foods (cheese slices, spreads, dairy desserts, cream-based liqueurs) and food ingredients, which consistently generate higher profits than any other areas of cooperative activity (agri-trading has become a minimal activity in the biggest coops, and even liquid milk is now declining as a proportion of total sales). Compared to U.K. dairy companies (Banks & Marsden, 1977), Irish dairy processors today have flexible processing plants which are able to divert milk quickly into the best paying option, from liquid to casein to cheese. They are also diversifying into other, non-dairy based areas of production – lamb and beef processing (now generally also consumer-ready, branded packs rather than bulk slaughtering), fruit juices, soups and so on.

Two further features distinguish the industry today from earlier decades, increased integration, and increased internationalization. Different cooperatives are increasingly likely to have shares in each others' businesses or be involved in joint ventures of one kind or another, making the industry more integrated horizontally; vertical integration is also growing, where cooperatives which have not made it into the top rank of players but have not (yet) been absorbed through amalgamations, become transformed into virtual milk assembly plants for larger processors, either cooperatives or multinational companies or, increasingly, both. This is related to the internationalization and now, indeed, globalization of the industry in recent decades. Up to the 1980s, such internationalization as existed was the result of penetration into the Irish food industry by foreign capital, particularly British but also American. Since then the level of penetration of external capital has declined, and Irish companies are expanding overseas.

From Co-ops to PLCs

The emergence of Irish dairy companies as some of the first 'Irish TNCs' (trans-national corporations) has been accompanied by a crucial change in the nature of the cooperatives themselves. Irish dairy farmers are part of an industry characterized by near-monopolistic control of its raw material. In the 1960s and 1970s, that could be justified on the grounds that the cooperative organisation of the industry, by making farmers both suppliers to it and members of it, protected them against exploitation by external industrial capital. But the relationship between farmers and milk processors has changed a great deal since then, starting with the rationalization program of the 1960s which eroded the local identity of many of the societies, and later the expansion of the cooperatives into liquid milk supply. Members came to see themselves, and to act, simply as 'suppliers'. Equally, many societies increasingly treated their members as merely suppliers, while increasing numbers of 'members', i.e. shareholders, were not milk suppliers at all. By the late 1970s, the concept of cooperative membership seemed to have become little more than a smoke-screen, a discursive legitimation for the fact that the cooperatives monopolized outlets for the sale of milk by farmers, and accorded preferential treatment to larger and more technically advanced suppliers (Tovey, 1982). The convergence in ideology, activities, and attitudes to suppliers, with private food companies set the scene for the major cooperatives to float part of their holdings on the Irish stock exchange in the late 1980s.

'Privatization' was achieved by creating new companies in which the cooperative society had a specified level of shareholding while the rest of the shares were available for institutional or individual investment and in some cases, for limited distribution to employees. This could only be done by agreement of the cooperative membership and intense campaigns were launched to secure that, appealing to the economic self-interest of individual members and profiting from the split between 'member' and 'supplier' that had developed in many societies. The campaigns were uncontested by any significant voices on the Irish socio-agricultural scene, including the Irish Farmers Organisation and even ICOS (the central organisation for the cooperatives). The companies concerned have been strikingly successful, and co-op members' shareholdings have increased dramatically in value. At the 1986 floatation of the Kerry Group, for example, co-op members and employees were offered around 10 million shares at 35p each before trading; they started trading on the stock exchange at 52p each and are now worth some 780p (and extremely difficult to buy).

This success in itself has created the conditions for gradual further erosion of cooperative control. In July 1996, to take the example of Kerry again, to allow a new share floatation to raise money for expansion co-op members voted for a fundamental change in the Group's corporate structure which allowed the cooperative stake for the first time to fall below 51%. By early 1998 it had fallen to 37% (*Irish Farmers Journal*, 21/2/98: 14); 20% of the Kerry Group is owned by other local shareholders, and around 40% by institutional investors, of whom around 10% are from overseas. The floatation brought 6,000 shareholders in the company additional shares worth over £130 million, an average of £22,000 each: "The decision created at least 100 extra millionaires in north Kerry, local sources say" (*Irish Times Business Supplement*, 30/1/98: 5).

Analyzing the changing modes of regulation of milk production in Britain, Banks (this volume) argues that these have in fact promoted a new round of uneven development, which is both spatial and structural. From a different regulation history, spatial and social concentration of producers in the dairy industry is already well advanced in Ireland, suggesting that the formal organisation of regulation may be a less significant factor than cultural and ideological changes among state and food industry managers about the purpose of agricultural and food industry development. Given such changes, the increasing globalisation of the Irish industry, and the product diversification that seems bound up with this, may lead to a 'respatialisation of production' on a global and not just local scale. The historical development of the Irish food industry makes the process of 'substitutionism' identified by Goodman et al. (1987) – the development of a multinational food chain based on industrially- rather than agriculturally-produced inputs – unlikely here. Irish multinational food corporations remain solidly rooted in their control over an agricultural raw materials supply. But spatial substitutionism, as companies source supplies more widely and look for suppliers who can match not only cost requirements but also the preferences of consumers in diverse global locations for specific types of product, may come to be a significant problem. Can we expect the 'millionaire farmers' of North Kerry, with their modest herds and farms and their shareholdings in a dynamic multinational corporation, to move gradually from being milk producers into rentiers living on income from capital? What of those milk producers who have no such shareholdings?

We may note, finally, that these changes in the dairy food industry do not only affect farmers; they also significantly affect industry workers, members of the same rural communities and sometimes the same households as the farmers. Industry rationalisation has been accompanied by the shedding of workers, often by casualisation such as the transformation of milk delivery roundsmen from employees into self-employed contractors. Work opportunities become more concentrated in specific areas of the country. The Avonmore-Waterford merger, for example, brought an end to the Waterford Foods milk processing plant in the small town of Dungarvan in 1997, with the loss of 130 permanent manufacturing jobs ("Closure of town's oldest industry stuns community," *Irish Times*, 26/11/97). The 75 million gallons of milk which farmers produce in the hinterland of the town are to be transferred to another processing plant 60–80 miles away, but the workers are unlikely to find comparable jobs in their own area again. Overall, the AWG merger is expected to mean the end of around 750 jobs in the food industry in Ireland during 1998, and 550 in the U.K.

CONCLUSION: DAIRY FARMING IN AN URBAN WORLD

The recent history of Irish dairy farming is also the history of Irish society and its transformation from an agrarian to an urban industrial form. For most surviving dairy farmers this has been a history of success, but it also relates the defeat of a specifically agrarian project for an Irish modernity.

There is evidence to suggest that since the 1980s, farmers themselves increasingly perceive farming as drudgery without social reward (Shutes 1991; Tovey 1997). Among some successful dairy farmers, the family farm is losing its master-status as the definer of family identity and becoming one among a portfolio of family business activities. The extreme and counter-intuitive case of this is where milk producers who were also shareholders in their local cooperative may find themselves able to live from the returns to shareholding generated by a dynamic capitalist food industry, using their farmland as a resource for family recreation or consumption rather than for milk production.

Urbanization, in Irish terms, has also brought a reordering of social and political priorities to emphasise urban needs and values. One dimension of that is a transformation in the meaning of rural resources, from resources for production to resources for consumption. Rural society is being reshaped from a producer society into a location for tourism, environmental conservation, wildlife and leisure appreciation. Those landholders who remain in agriculture, such as successful dairy farmers, find their operations constrained and regulated in new ways by concerns about food safety and quality, or about the effects of their activities on water quality or on wildlife (for example their campaign to eradicate badgers who are seen as the carriers of brucellosis infections in cattle). "Discourses about food quality and value. . . geared more closely to perceived consumer norms and preferences" are increasingly influential in structuring dairy farming in Britain (Banks & Marsden, 1997: 394) and are also beginning to make an impact on Irish agriculture. But in comparison to other intensive agricultural producers (poultry and pork in particular) and to the other main product line, beef, Irish dairy farming generally enjoys high levels of consumer trust and satisfaction.

The impact on successful dairy farmers of new consumerist orientations to the rural is much less direct than their impact on other farmers. Landholders in the midlands, west and northwest have had much more direct experience of it. Thirty years ago, these were seen by the state as candidates to develop new dairying enterprises, to solve their income problems and boost national milk output levels. Today they are encouraged to diversify out of farming; they are constituted in both national and EU policy as surplus to food production needs and more appropriately engaged in the production of 'environmental goods'. Yet the two fates are interlinked: the spatial and class concentration of milk production, and the emergence of a global food industry based on that, is part of the same process whereby increasing amounts of other farm land are released for non-productive purposes and increasing numbers of other landholders coaxed or coerced out of seeing themselves as farmers.

Rural Ireland is being transformed from 'rural society' (based on the reproduction of family farming) into 'rural space' (available for conservation, urban leisure consumption and for regulated entrepreneurs) In Britain this process has been described as a process of 'moralisation' of the countryside (Lowe et al., 1997). In Ireland it might better be described as 'de-moralisation', the collapse of a collective culture and identity which once promised to be transformative, not just for farmers, but for Irish society as a whole.

REFERENCES

Banks, J., & Marsden, T. (1997). Reregulating the UK dairy industry: the changing nature of competitive space. *Sociologia Ruralis, 37*(3), 382–404.

Bauman, Z. (1991). *Modernity and Ambivalence.* Oxford: Polity.

Bolger, P. (1977). *The Irish Co-Operative Movement – its History and Development.* Dublin: Institute of Public Administration.

Cardwell, M. (1996). *Milk Quota – European Community and United Kingdom Law.* Oxford: Clarendon Press.

Chayanov, A. V. (1925). *The Theory of Peasant Economy.* Translated by D. Thorber, R. E. F. Smith, B. Kentlay. Madison: U. of Wisconsin Press.

Commins, P. (1996). Agricultural production and the future of small scale farming. In: C.Curtin, T. Haase & H. Tovey (Eds), *Poverty in Rural Ireland – a Political Economy Perspective* (pp. 87–125). Dublin: Oak Tree Press/Combat Poverty Agency.

Commins, P., & Keane, M. J. (1994). *Developing the Rural Economy – Problems, Programmes and Prospects.* National Economic and Social Council Report no. 97. Dublin: NESC.

Davis, J., Mack, N., & Kirke, A. (1997). New perspectives on farm household incomes'. *Journal of Rural Studies, 13*(1), 57–64.

Digby, M. (1949). *Horace Plunkett – an Anglo-American Irishman*. Oxford: Blackwell.

Doyle, P., & Smith, L. P. F. (1989). *Milk to Market (A History of The Dublin Milk Supply)*. Dublin: Leinster Milk Producers' Association.

Duggan, C. (1987). Farming women or farmers' wives? Women in the farming press. In: C. Curtin, P. Jackson & B. O'Connor (Eds), *Gender in Irish Society* (pp. 54-69). Galway: Galway University Press.

Fingleton, W. A. (1995). Structural changes in dairying in Ireland and in the EU, actual and projected. Paper presented to *Conference on the Dairy and Beef Industries*, Teagasc, Dublin.

Fingleton, W. A., & Frawley, J. (1987). Dairy farming in a milk quota context. In: *The Re-Structuring of the Agricultural and Rural Economy* (pp. 100-135). Rural Economy Research Centre 14th Annual Conference. Dublin: The Agricultural Institute.

Frawley, J. P., & Commins, P. (1996). *The Changing Structure of Irish Farming – Trends and Prospects*. Rural Economy Research Series no. 1. Dublin: Teagasc.

Friedmann, H. (1986). Family enterprise in agriculture – structural limits and political possibilities. In: G. Cox, P. Lowe & M. Winter (Eds), *Agriculture – People and Policies* (pp. 41–60). London: Allen and Unwin.

Goodman, D., Sorj, B., & Wilkinson, J. (1987). *From Farming to Biotechnology (a Theory of Agro-Industrial Development)*. Oxford: Blackwell.

Grant, W., MacNamara, A. (1996). The relationship between bankers and farmers – an analysis of Britain and Ireland. *Journal of Rural Studies, 12*(4), 427–437.

Hannan, D. F., & Breen, R. (1987). Family farming in Ireland. In: B. Galeski & E. Wilkening (Eds), *Family Farming in Europe and America* (pp. 39–69). Boulder Colorado/London: Westview Press.

Hannan, D. F., & Katsiaouni, L. (1977). *Traditional Families: from Culturally Prescribed to Negotiated Roles in Farm Families*. ESRI Paper no. 87. Dublin: Economic and Social Research Institute.

Kelleher, C. (1983). Implications of different theoretical approaches for policy and interventions, Parts I and II, *Irish Journal of Agricultural Economics and Rural Sociology, 9*, 133–160.

Leeuwis, C. (1989). *Marginalisation Misunderstood – Different Patterns of Farm Development in the West of Ireland*. Wageningen: Wageningen Agricultural University.

Long, N. (1984). Introduction. In: N. Long (Ed.), *Family and Work in Rural Societies* (pp. 1–29). London: Tavistock.

Long, N., van der Ploeg, J. D., Curtin, C., & Box, L. (1986). *The Commoditisation Debate*. Wageningen: Agricultural University.

Lowe, P., Clark, J., Seymour, S., & Ward, N. (1997). *Moralising the Environment – Countryside Change, Farming and Pollution*. London: UCL Press.

Lysaght, P. (1994a). Introduction. In: P. Lysaght (Ed.), *Milk and Milk Products from Medieval to Modern Times* (Proceedings of the Ninth International Conference on Ethnological Food Research) (pp. vii-ix). Edinburgh: Canongate Press.

Lysaght, P. (1994b). Women, milk and magic at the Boundary Festival of May. In: P. Lysaght (Ed.), *Milk and Milk Products from Medieval to Modern Times* (pp. 209–229). Edinburgh: Canongate Press.

Marsden, T., Whatmore, S., Munton, R., & Little, J. (1986). The restructuring process and economic centrality in capitalist agriculture. *Journal of Rural Studies, 2*(4), 271–280.

National Economic and Social Council. 1989. *Ireland in the European Community – Performance, Prospects and Strategy.* Report No. 88. Dublin: NESC.

O'Hara, P. (1997). Interfering women – farm mothers and the reproduction of family farming. *Economic and Social Review, 28*(2), 135–156.

O'Hara, P. (1998). *Partners in Production.* Oxford: Berghaan Books.

Roberts, R., & Mutersbaugh, T. (1996). On rereading Chayanov: understanding agrarian transitions in the industrialised world, *Environment and Planning A, 28*(6), 951–956.

Rumpf, E., & Hepburn, A. C. (1977). *Nationalism and Socialism in Twentieth-Century Ireland.* Liverpool: Liverpool University Press.

Scott, J. (1995). *Development Dilemmas in the European Community (Rethinking Regional Development Policy).* Buckingham/Philadelphia: Open University Press.

Shutes, M. (1991). Kerry farmers and the European Community: capital transitions in a rural Irish parish. *Irish Journal of Sociology, 1*, 1–17.

Smith, L. P. F., & Healy, S. (1996). *Farm Organisations in Ireland (A Century of Progress).* Dublin: Four Courts Press.

Teagasc. (1995). *Compendium of Irish Economic and Agricultural Statistics.* Dublin: Teagasc (Department of Rural Economy).

Teagasc. (1997). *National Farm Survey 1996.* Dublin: Teagasc.

Tovey, H. (1982). Milking the farmer? Modernisation and marginalisation in Irish dairy farming. In: M Kelly, L. O'Dowd & J. Wickham (Eds), *Power, Conflict and Inequality* (pp. 68–89). Dublin: Turoe Press.

Tovey, H. (1991). 'Of cabbages and kings': restructuring in the Irish food industry. *Economic and Social Review, 22*(4), 333–350.

Tovey, H. (1995). Farming, development and the environment in Co. Meath, Report on the Irish stage of the Research Project *Land Culture and Crisis: From Productionist Success to Fiscal and Environmental Impasse on European Farms 1940–1990,* funded by EU DG XII under the SEER Programme (unpublished)

Tovey, H. (1997). 'We can all use calculators now': productionism, sustainability and the professional formation of farming in Co. Meath, Ireland. In: H. de Haan, B. Kasimis & M. Redclift (Eds), *Sustainable Rural Development* (pp. 129–158). Aldershot, U.K.: Ashgate Press.

Trotman, C. (1996). *The Development of Milk Quotas in the UK.* London: Sweet and Maxwell Ltd.

DAIRY FARMING IN THE WESERMARSCH REGION OF GERMANY: A LONG HISTORY, DIFFICULT RESTRUCTURING, UNCERTAIN FUTURE

Gerd Vonderach

INTRODUCTION

My aim here – by focusing on what has been happening to dairy farming in the Wesermarsch Region – is to overview some of the very profound changes that have been and are taking place in the dairy industry of northern Germany and, insofar as possible, to specify some of the social and economic forces that drive this restructuring. In much of Germany, and throughout Europe, the future appears very uncertain for dairying. Many dairies – particularly the smaller operations – will soon be closed and those that manage to survive through the next decade will be markedly different. At this point, it is difficult to predict what the eventual outcome will be of this extremely complex, and sometimes unkind, restructuring process.

Once a premier dairy farming region of Germany, the Wesermarsch, in Lower Saxony, stretches along the western reaches of the Weser River to where it flows into the North Sea. To the south is the city of Bremen and to the north, Bremerhaven.

Research in Rural Sociology, Volume 8, pages 75–93.
ISBN: 0-7623-0474-X

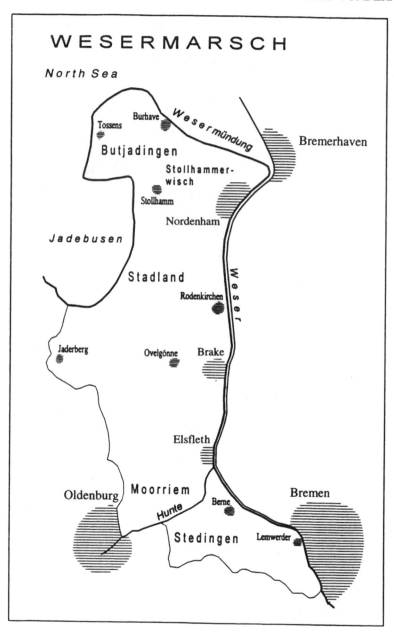

Fig. 1.

Landkreis Wesermarsch (an administrative entity, like a county) was formerly a part of the Duchy of Oldenburg. Its population today is about 94,500. There are several small dock-landing and industrial communities, including the *Kreissitz* (county seat) town of Brake, but otherwise the area is dominated by farms. Only a very small proportion of the work force (6.7%), however, is employed directly in agriculture (and fishing.)

The Wesermarsch landscape is flat and wide, with forestless marshes that are criss-crossed by drainage ditches. About 25% of the land is bog soil, 75% marshy soil. Only the sea marsh soil can be used for crop farming; the bog-land and brackish river marshes can only be used for grassland. About 97% of the farm land is in grass and most of the farms specialize in dairy and beef production. Dairying provides the biggest source of agricultural income, but this was not always the case.

HISTORICAL PERSPECTIVES

Wesermarsch farmers, from early on, had to struggle with the sea, in particular with storm tides and periodic breaches of the dykes, as well as with the problems and costs of draining lower-lying lands. Yet despite these difficulties, the marsh farmers were generally more prosperous than farmers in other areas. Indeed, in the late 1800s their crop yields (small grains, hay) and income were the highest in the Duchy of Oldenburg (Riedel, 1972: 27), for the flood-plain soils were very fertile. Conditions were less favourable, of course, in the heavier bog areas.

From the mid-1800s, pastoral agriculture and cattle raising began to be emphasized, made more feasible and profitable by the use of vaccinations to control cattle diseases, the introduction of Friesian cattle, improved land drainage systems, and most importantly, by favourable beef prices (Harjehusen, 1934: 3). The demand for beef in northern Europe accelerated, parallelling the rapid increase of urban populations. In those days cattle were driven to Bremen, Berlin, and the Ruhr area, and many were exported to England from Weser ports. But, by the early 1900s, beef farming in the Wesermarsch region had given way to dairying, and primarily the production of butter. This development was part of the agrarian modernisation that accompanied German industrialisation (Mueter, 1996: 177).

The construction of railways and the improvement of local roads were preconditions for the cost-effective transport of dairy products, especially butter, into the burgeoning urban and industrial markets. Also significant was the long term expansion of the national economy, from the 1890s to the First

World War. A steady rise in the real wages of industrial workers and miners led to a stronger demand for animal products (Muetter, 1996: 181).

Dairy stock too were improved qualitatively through selective breeding, organized through the efforts of local associations (Cornelius, 1908). Further, in the late 1800s, ten very large dairy cooperatives were established in the region; the Rodenkirchen cooperative was the biggest in Germany and probably in Europe before 1914 (Muetter, 1996: 191, 198). Even before the First World War, some dairy cooperatives were joined together into larger, central co-operatives, as for instance the *Verkaufs-genossenschaft Nordwest-deutscher Molkereien in Oldenburg* (Sales Co-operative of North-west German Dairies in Oldenburg.) As early as 1904, attempts were made to systematically control milk quality and its fat content. In 1908 a number of local cooperatives formed the *Garantie-Vereinigung Oldenburger Molkerei-genossenshaften* (Guarantee Organisation of Dairy Co-operatives in Oldenburg) to improve and standardize the quality of butter, and to market Wesermarsch butter under a common brand name. This cooperative effort in Wesermarsch gave impetus to the standardisation of butter quality throughout Germany.

As a result of these promotional and marketing activities, the Wesermarsch dairy industry attained a leading position in Germany prior to World War One. But milk prices fell after the war and the industry languished (Schreiber, 1928; Winkler, 1929). In 1932 there were 6,846 farms with cows in the region, but most were very small farms, averaging about 5.3 cows (Harjehusen, 1934: 13, 25). The average production of 3,283 litres per cow per year, though weak by today's standards, was considerably better than the German average of 2,374 litres (Harjehusen, 1934: 13, 25). Wesermarsch dairy farmers in the early 1930s, marketed their milk through 13 cooperatives and two private companies (Harjehusen, 1934: 51, 53). Most dairy farms in that era were diversified, growing grain, turnips, forage, and having a mixed livestock operation.

During the 60s and 70s,Wesermarsch farmers began to specialize in grassland and livestock agriculture and to purchase the necessary feed concentrates (grain, turnips). Because of the extreme parcelling of farmlands (inefficient arrangement of fields), water run-off problems, drainage difficulties, and poor soil conditions in some areas, the Wesermarsch and Moorriem regions participated in a federally financed program of farmland consolidation (*Flurbereiningungsverfahren*). It took several years to be implemented and, nationally, was one of the largest and most expensive agricultural projects ever undertaken by the German government (Mayhew, 1970: 4; Riedel, 1972: 25).

Livestock farming in the Wesermarsch region, until recent times, focused on both beef and milk production (Hinrichs, 1988: 145). Dairy farmers raised and fattened their own dairy steers and, consequently, dual purpose breeds were prominent. But when milk production became more profitable, the breeding emphasis shifted away from beef (Timmermann & Vonderach, 1993: 24). Beef prices during the 1990s were relatively low. Rearing beef stock and fattening them on grass requires considerably more land than for dairying and, nowadays, appeals mainly to farms that have a low milk quota and an excess of land.

For most of the century, until the 1960s, the number of dairy cows on Wesermarsch farms fluctuated between 30 and 35 thousand (except for a sharp drop immediately after World War Two.) Since the early 1960s, the numbers of dairy cows climbed steadily, reaching its contemporary peak of 55,000 in 1984, the year milk quotas were initiated (Timmermann & Vonderach, 1993). The reasons for this expansion were, basically, the good prices for milk and the introduction of labour-saving technologies, such as milking machines, modern milking parlours, straw-yard housing, and improved feeding and manure-handling equipment (Herrmann, 1996). However, dairy farming is still relatively labour intensive and it would be exceedingly difficult to operate a dairy as a part-time enterprise.

INTRODUCTION OF MILK QUOTAS (1984)

Milk surpluses occurred within the European Union (EU) countries in the early 1980s as a result of EU agricultural policies. Indeed, in 1983 milk production relative to home consumption (internal demand) was 122% in the EU and 131% in Germany (BMELF, 1985). Costs for the long-term storage of butter and skimmed milk powder as well as for their subsidized sale, a policy which encouraged dairy processors to accept more milk from producers, became politically unjustifiable.

Thus, as an emergency measure to constrain milk production, EU member states established a *Milch-Garantiemengen-Regelung* (Milk Quantity Guarantee Regulation) in 1984. This regulation mandated a reduction in milk production for West Germany of 6.7% less in 1984/85 and 7.7% less in 1985/86 than the 25.2 million metric tons that had been delivered to the milk processors in 1983 (BMELF, 1985). In face of these EU restrictions, the German federal government instituted a milk quota system of 'reference quantities' which prescribed for each farm an upper limit of milk production that could be sold and delivered to milk processors.

Cuts from the 1983 production basis, however, were graduated by dairy size and far more severe for larger dairies (12.5%) than for smaller dairies (2%). In addition to this differential, compensations were also given for economic hardships attributable to the imposition of quotas and, later on, several

Milchrente (milk pension) actions were taken in order to ease the adjustment process for individual farmers. Quotas were waived for some farmers because of hardship claims. Further, many of the larger dairies continued to expand despite quota restrictions on the assumption that the demand for milk would soon again increase. This led to a national surplus of reference quantities which, despite a series of additional quota cuts, could only be reduced from 1990 onwards through the continuation and special extension of the 'milk pension' actions (basically, an 'early retirement' system for dairy farmers). In 1993, milk quotas once more were cut by 4.74%.

In the Wesermarsch region, 44% of the dairy farms were recognized as cases of financial hardship, usually when they were able to prove financial investments in housing and milking installations exceeding 25,000 DM. This resulted in a remarkably unique situation, in contrast with other regions. Shortly after the introduction of milk quotas in 1984, even more cows were being milked in the Wesermarsch than had been previous to the imposition of quotas. Only later did cow numbers begin to decline.

At first the implementation of milk quotas triggered much anger among Wesermarsch farmers; it was a dominant issue at farmers' meetings and generated envy and resentment among neighbours. Opposition groups appealed to the *Kreislandvolkverband* (Wesermarsch Farmer's Association). Eventually, things calmed down somewhat as administrative authorities accepted numerous claims of hardship.

As it turned out, the larger farms could more easily demonstrate 'hardship' because their total financial investments were greater. Younger farmers who had just gotten started were especially disadvantaged by the quotas because it effectively blocked them from expanding their operations up to a level that could assure them a decent income; their only alternative was to purchase additional quota from dairies that had closed-out. Surprisingly, in this region only a few farmers applied for a 'milk pension' because those who intended to close-out or reduce their dairies quickly discovered that it was more profitable to rent-out their land and the attached quota.

Initially, additional milk quota could be obtained only by purchasing or leasing dairy land. Thus, land rental prices were driven up. The milk quota – an 'immaterial economic good' (Doll, 1989) – acquired an independent value that is determined by market demand. But by 1990/91 the regulations for transferring milk quotas were loosened. Transfer taxes were abolished and upper limits removed. It also became possible to lease milk quota (reference quantities) temporarily, on a yearly basis, within the given catchment area and independent of farm size. In 1993 the rules were further liberalized so that additional milk quota (reference quantities) could be obtained by purchasing or leasing land beyond the catchment area, within the administrative district. Initially during this early period, milk quota prices increased significantly. But in 1994/95, quota prices dropped greatly as milk deliveries became more balanced and, more importantly, because the nation-wide quota capacity had decreased (LWK Weser-Ems, 1996: 62). The current milk quota system is limited to the year 2006 and it is unclear if it will be retained or reshaped in the future.

CONTEMPORARY TRENDS: FEWER BUT LARGER DAIRIES

Dairy farming in the Wesermarsch evolved through a continuous process of structural change over the past four decades, influenced but not significantly altered by the imposition of milk quotas. Dairy farm numbers declined, but the average size of farm, in land holdings and number of cows, increased. Because of unfavourable milk prices and costs of production, smaller farms, particularly since 1984, were unable to survive. Subsidy measures and market regulations instituted by national and European agricultural policies at best only eased and cushioned the social consequences of these trends, but did not contain them.

Though not unlike what was happening to agricultural economies in highly developed industrialized nations elsewhere, the restructuring process seems to have been especially marked in the Wesermarsch region. The number of dairy farms had already dropped by 11% during the early post-war years, mainly

Table 1. Percent of all farms, by farm size (hectares), Wesermarsch region of Germany, 1949–1996.

Farm size (hectares)	1949	1960	1971	1982	1996
1–10	62.7	54.4	39.3	28.8	25.0
10–30	28.0	35.2	36.3	29.0	16.8
30–50	8.0	8.7	20.4	27.9	19.3
50–100	1.3	1.7	3.9	14.2	34.4
100+	–	–	0.1	0.1	4.5
total %	100.0	100.0	100.0	100.0	100.0
no. of farms	(5,927)	(5,271)	(3,475)	(2,258)	(1,490)
farm size average	11.4	12.8	20.6	27.1	41.5

Sources: Landwirtschaftskammer Weser-Ems 1938–1962, 1982; Statistiches Jahrbuch Niedersachsen 1973; Niedersachsen Landesamt fuer Statistic 1996.

Table 2. Percent of all farmed land, by farm size (hectares), Wesermarsch region of Germany, 1963–1996.

Farm size (hectares)	1949	1960	1971	1982	1996
1–10	21.9	17.3	9.0	4.7	2.4
10–30	43.7	49.0	37.4	21.1	8.0
30–50	26.8	25.5	49.6	40.9	18.9
50–100	7.0	8.1	12.3	32.7	57.4
100+	0.6	0.6	0.7	0.6	13.3
total %	100.0	100.0	100.0	100.0	100.0
no. of farms	(67,543)	(67,573)	(66,303)	(61,213)	(67,800)

Sources: See Table one

from closings of the numerous smaller dairies, those with less than 10 hectares; the number of farms with 10 hectares or more increased. This trend of 'expanding or retiring' continued and as a consequence, the number of farms declined by more than a third during each of the periods, 1960–71, 1971–82, and 1982–96; but the size of dairies became almost four times larger. During the 60s the decline was affected by the closing of farms with less than 30 hectares, but in the 70s, 80s, and 90s, the closings extended to dairies with 30

Table 3. Percent of all dairy farms, by herd size, Wesermarsch region of Germany, 1963–1996.

Herd size (no. of cows)	1963	1975	1982	1993	1996
1–19	96.9	58.2	37.1	18.8	12.4
20–29	2.8	24.5	15.8	15.0	11.0
30–39	0.2	11.7	16.8	16.1	14.2
40–49	0.1	3.3	13.6	16.3	12.7
50+	–	2.3	16.7	33.8	49.7
total %	100.0	100.0	100.0	100.0	100.0
no. of farms	(4,557)	(2,380)	(1,751)	(1,088)	(924)
av. herd size	7.7	17.4	30.2	40.4	50.3

Sources: Niedrsachsen Landesverwaltungsamt fuer Statisk 1963; LandwirtschaftslkammerWeser-Ems 1984/85; Niedersachsen Landesamt fuer Statisk 1993; Niedersachsen Landesamt fuer Statisk 1996.

Table 4. Percent of all dairy cows, by herd size, Wesermarsch region of Germany, 1963–1996.

Herd size (no. of cows)	1963	1975	1982	1993	1996
1–19	89.5	27.8	10.9	4.5	2.6
20–29	8.6	33.8	12.8	9.1	5.5
30–39	0.9	22.1	18.9	13.7	9.7
40–49	0.4	8.0	19.7	17.8	11.2
50+	0.6	8.3	37.7	54.9	70.0
total %	100.0	100.0	100.0	100.0	100.0
no. of farms	(35,042)	(41,375)	(52,837)	(43,958)	(46,510)

Sources: See Table 3

to 50 hectares. Since the 60s, only dairy farms with more than 50 hectares increased in number; in 1960 the few dairies with 50 hectares or more managed only 8.7% of the farmed land; by 1996, dairies of that size managed 70.6% of the farmed land.

Thus, agriculture (dairying), which once had been the dominant industry (apart from the commercial and harbour enterprises along the Weser River), became less important to the regional economy. In 1980, about 11.4% of the labour force was still employed in agriculture (including fishing and forestry); by 1995, it was only 6.7%. Nevertheless, agriculture's share of the Wesermarsch cross-national product (*Bruttowertschoepfung*) in 1995 was 6.6%, much higher than agriculture's national share of 1.1% (NLS, 1998: 168, 173); indirectly, this indicates the relatively high performance of Wesermarsh's dairy industry.

One must also take into account that farming in this region is very different from farming in other parts of (west) Germany. A much larger proportion of the farms, because they are mostly dairy operations, are run as full-time businesses. In 1991, 61% of the farms were full-time operations, compared with 42% nationally (BMELF, 1998). The proportion of rented farmland in the region, in 1991, was 62%, compared with 48% nationally. It is a common practice to pass along leasehold rights to an heir before the farm is actually bequeathed to that heir. It is not surprising then that the proportion of leasehold land in Wesermarsch increased during the first years of the milk quota because transferring a quota depended on leasing or purchasing the land to which it was assigned.

CURRENT SITUATION

Of the 1,490 farms in Kreis (county) Wesermarsch in 1996, 61.8% (924 farms) were dairy operations plus another 20.5% raised replacement heifers, breeding stock, dairy steers, etc. (NLS, 1997a, b). The latter are mostly part-time or retiree operations, often run by former dairy farmers who are pensioned or who have leased out their milk quota. Thus, the number of dairy farms now is only about 20% of the number in 1963. It is quite likely, according to some knowledgeable dairy farmers in the area whom we recently interviewed, that about half of the dairies now operating, particularly those with less than 100 milk cows, will close out in the not too distant future. In 1996, already more than a third of the remaining dairies were milking more than 60 cows, as compared with only 3.8% nationally (BMLEF, 1997: 12). Herd averages too are stronger in the Wesermarsch region, averaging almost 6,000 kg in 1994 (LWK Weser-Ems, 1996: 56) as compared with the German average of 5,264 kg (Stat. Bundesamt, 1997: 183).

The number of dairy cattle now (1996) is 48,500, not very much lower than the 55,000 in 1984 and, considering the great decrease in number of dairy farms, quite clearly a process of 'concentration' has occurred. There has also been an intensification of dairy production relative to the land used for dairying which, in turn, has led to manure management problems that are affecting some environmental damage, such as pollution of ground water and the consequent destruction of regional vegetation and bird habitat.

Milk and cheese factories too are fewer in number and much larger than they once were. In 1988 the two large dairy cooperatives of Oldenburg and East Frisia united to form the *Molkereizentrale Oldenburg-Ostfriesland* (Central Dairy Oldenburg/East Frisia), commonly referred to as MZO. Eventually, most of the remaining dairy companies joined the MZO, which is now one of the biggest milk processing cooperatives in Germany. There is some competition, but most dairy farmers now deliver their milk to them. Although the MZO is a cooperative, it is very large and individual farmers have very little say about management and marketing decisions.

RESTRUCTURING PROCESSES AND PROBLEMS

In 1991–93 we systematically interviewed, very intensively, a small, representative sample of Wesermarsch dairy farmers (Timmermann & Vonderach, 1993; Vonderach, 1993). We aimed to explore how they and their families were responding to the rapid changes occurring in the dairy industry, the managerial adjustments they were making to accommodate to the milk quota regulations and, in particular, to determine how they were dealing with the very serious and complex problem of generational transition. Our initial observations were followed up five years later, in 1998, by telephone interviews with this set of farmers.

Generational Transitions

It has been a long-established custom in this part of Germany for the family farm to be passed on to the youngest son. Initially the farm is leased out to the designated son soon after he is married, and only later is it bequeathed to him. This pattern provided families with unambiguous instructions for action, relieved the difficulties of decision making, and helped to hold together the farm and its property over several generations. Before the introduction of the old age pension this pattern also ensured financial security for the heir and his retired parents. Current legal regulations (1976 version) in effect support the established custom but also allow for other kinds of arrangements (Bundesgesetzblatt, 1978, 89). Although the farmers and their families that we surveyed are very much aware of the traditional pattern of bequeathing, the custom is currently realised in only a few cases (Timmermann & Vonderach, 1993: 144–165). There is now a remarkable diversity of solutions to the problem of inter-generational transition; special ways (often unique) to resolve the issue of farm inheritance are devised by each family in light of the family's particular circumstances, their children's career aspirations, their daughter-in-laws' wishes, and the general condition of the agricultural economy. In earlier times, children were keen to take over the family farm, but parents nowadays – if they wish to see the farm retained in the family – must cultivate a positive attitude by one or the other of their children relative to becoming a dairy farmer and assuming responsibility for the farm.

Several factors, we have observed, need to come together for a farm to remain within the family: (1) strong motivation by a potential successor to be a farmer; (2) necessary personal capabilities and training by the successor to manage a modern dairy operation; (3) availability of reasonably efficient farming equipment (i.e. operating capital); (4) relatively large milk quota; (5) sufficient land; and (6) good, reliable cooperation from parents and other family members. If these conditions are not satisfied, generational transition is not likely to occur, or the heir will give up after a few years. Then, the farm as a whole (with residence), or the land with attached milk quota (but without residence), is leased to a neighbouring farmer who wishes to expand, or to a newcomer who wants to start-up in dairying.

Today it can no longer be taken for granted that a designated successor, even when the farm is large and economically successful, actually wants to become a dairy farmer. If a son or, on rare occasions, a daughter seeks to take over the family farm it is generally because they appreciate this way of life, they enjoy farming, and they have a 'passion for agriculture'. Often, the successor begins his/her farming career early by getting an advanced degree in agriculture (*Landwirtschaftsmeister*), and sometimes even with a specialization in agricultural economics.

Nowadays too, it is rare for a dairy farmer's daughter to aspire to become a dairy farmer's wife. Rather, most farmers' daughters tend to develop other career interests, many going on to university. Consequently, it is not easy for a male heir who is designated to take over the family farm to find a marriage partner who is willing to join him in the struggles of managing a dairy farm.

Changing Family Dynamics

In our study of Wesermarsch dairy farms we noted a clear historical change from the traditional family labour enterprise that fully involved all members of a family (Tschajanow, 1987), to a more business-like organization that is managed as a father/son or husband/wife partnership or as a one-man operation (often with temporary and casual hired help). There are, of course, transitional family/farm situations, with characteristics of both the traditional and contemporary models (Timmermann & Vonderach, 1993: 165–179; Vonderach, 1993).

The parents of today's farmers used to work their farms in the traditional way as 'whole family' enterprises, though they already had begun to specialize and mechanize. For them, farming was a total way of life, with undifferentiated work and family roles, and they were assured that one of their children would eventually take-over and that the farm would remain in the family. It was expected that the farmer's wife and children would participate in the work and, as long as they could, so too would the elderly parents. There was never any question that the male (husband/father) was the patriarchal head of the household and the authoritative leader of the farm business. In those days, farm work was physically hard, especially because of the heavy marsh soils in this region, the difficulties of cultivating bog lands, and the frequent drainage problems. Larger and middle-size farms often employed some additional labour – unmarried workers and milkmaids who lived with the family on the farm. But the many small farms had to rely completely on family labour. In the 50s and 60s, as farms became more mechanized and more specialized in milk production, the work became easier and the need for hired labourers was reduced.

Dairy farm couples who are now middle-aged had to make some major adjustments in their life styles and work routines during the 80s when things began to change very rapidly. A number of such couples whom we interviewed in 1992 and who seemed to have strong, viable dairy operations, had, by 1996, closed out their dairies. In other cases, transition of their farm to the next generation appeared very unlikely, for their children had already completed the requisite training for some other occupation. Among these families, it was no longer taken for granted that their children would help with the farm work and to be involved with the family business. The husbands and wives in these situations are the main workforce and often the only workers. This is possible because equipment and management procedures have been modernized and made more efficient. Consequently, the sharing of work responsibilities and the reliance upon each other has made such husband/wife partnerships much stronger than in earlier times, where work roles were traditionally set and never questioned. Nevertheless, in our follow-up five years later some of these seemingly solid husband/wife partnerships had opted to lease out their farm and its milk quota to a neighbour.

The traditional pattern changed as young farmers, in the 1980s, took over their parents' dairy farms or established their own. In this new, modern mode, retired parents are inclined to leave the farm when their son marries; they no longer feel obligated to continue helping out with the farm work. Wives no longer assume that being married to a farmer means that they must conform to the traditional role of 'farmer's wife' Most of the wives of young farmers have been trained for non-farm jobs or professions and some continue to hold those jobs or expect to return to non-farm work after their children are grown. In cases where the young farmer and his wife manage the farm together, as a partnership, the wife more often than not wants to be recognized as an equal, not simply as a helper; dual management rights are sometimes legally established, by contract.

It is much more likely that a dairy will survive if husband and wife are both strongly involved in its operation than if the wife is pursuing some other, non-farm career. However, a dairy farm must be relatively large to support two full-time operators plus the necessary hired labourers and milkers, and to expand a dairy operation is not easy, given the milk quota restrictions.

Programmatic Assistance and Ecological Considerations

Wesermarsch dairy farmers who are managing relatively small dairies, but who want to run their farms as full-time operations, must find ways to expand the size of their herd and increase their total milk production if they wish to provide their family with a decent living and a secure future. Cattle farming is not a viable alternative to dairying nowadays because the prices for beef and cattle are very low; and Wesermarsch soil and climatic conditions do not favour the production of other, more lucrative agricultural commodities.

After the introduction of milk quotas, milk prices increased until 1988, but then dropped by almost one fifth by 1995 (LWK Weser-Ems, 1996: 57), bottoming out in 1996 (in the Weser-Ems region). During those years of falling prices there was, of course, a considerable drop in the incomes of farmers, leading many to consider ways to expand or alternatives to dairying. Those who closed out their farming operations made it possible for their neighbours to acquire more land and milk quota.

National agricultural policy has sought to support this consolidation process via financial assistance and various facilitating regulations and programs. On one hand, the expansion via consolidation of dairy farms was heavily subsidized, especially in the case of younger farmers. In addition to milk price premiums and easier credit, assistance included a relaxation in the assignment of milk quotas. On the other hand, early retirement was made more financially attractive.

Some years ago national policy also began to support farmers who wanted to change from dairying to less intensive farming alternatives. Here aspects of political economy are combined with environmental concerns. Apart from fostering ecological ways of farming there are measures to support an increase in green spaces and, more recently, special contractual projects to establish local nature conservancies.

The participation of Wesermarsch farmers in the ecologically oriented EU extension programs from 1989 to 1992 was higher than in other comparable coastal areas. This EU program was continued in 1993 to encourage an introduction or continuation of more extensive forms of farming. Participating farmers agreed, for a period of five years, to adopt grassland farming, including especially to reduce their stock of cattle and the use of fertilisers and pesticides. One hundred Wesermarsch farmers in 1996 were involved in the ecological and 82 in the grassland farming programs. This represented 12% of all Wesermarsh farmers and 13% of the farm land. The participating farmers received between 250 DM and 360 DM per hectare per year. A few of the farmers in the ecological farming program also started making cheese, as an income supplement; they are doing very well and are now employing additional workers and providing apprenticeship training.

A special supportive measure is the program for conservation of grasslands in Lower Saxony (*Feuchtgrünlandschutzprogramm*) which was ratified in 1995 and is financed jointly by the EU and the state of Lower Saxony. Implementation of this program began in 1995 in the northern part of Wesermarsch (Garden & Wilke, 1995) and soon after a second project was started in the southern area. Participation is voluntary and involved 88 farmers, with areas up to 31 hectares in size. Premiums range from 300 to 800 DM per hectare per year. Large parts of Wesermarsch were classified as important breeding grounds for various bird populations, and about one third of the agricultural land meets the criteria for nature preserve. For many of the farmers in this region, given the low prices for milk and beef, it is often economically attractive to accept certain farming regulations on some parts of their land. At the same time the voluntary participation of farmers in the program increases their readiness to make positive contributions to the general aim of a stronger protection of the natural environment.

CONCLUDING NOTE

Dairy farmers in the Wesermarsch region of Germany, in terms of their current situation and the available alternatives, are basically not very different from their counterparts in other parts of Germany and western Europe. For in other regions as well, dairy farmers are constrained by, and must deal with similar agri-economic circumstances and agri-political regulations, and they too are being increasingly influenced by powerful social and cultural forces. Nevertheless, some distinctions specific to the Wesermarsch region began to appear long ago as farmers adapted their enterprises and farming practices to local environmental conditions. This process of agricultural specialization accelerated during the past thirty years and a farming system evolved that focused on dairy and beef production and that provided Wesermarsch farmers and their families with a respectable income. Even before other regions, dairy farming in Wesermarsch became market oriented, and Wesermarsch early on became one of the leading dairy regions in Germany. Indeed, at the end of the last century, Wesermarsch dairy farmers constituted a very prosperous, socially dominant segment of the community, and enjoyed the perquisites and political advantages of being the largest taxpayer group in the Grand Duchy of Oldenburg.

Today, however, despite increased production efficiencies, dairy farmers in the Wesermarsch region are becoming a marginal sector of the larger community, with incomes considerably below average. They are dependent now upon quotas and state subsidies to maintain their dairy operations and to provide for their families; and, there are no feasible agricultural alternatives to dairying.

That is why inheriting the family farm, which in earlier times was regarded as a great privilege and distinguished a young man from his less fortunate siblings, is not an attractive prospect anymore for most farmers' children. We observe a paradoxical contradiction. On one hand, there is no longer a self-evident likelihood that the family farm will remain viable as a full-time operation into the next generation, and likewise, for similar reasons, there has been a considerable loss of status for a young person to be designated heir to the family farm. On the other hand, there is much pressure on the young farmer and potential heir to the family farm to acquire the necessary skills to manage a modern farming enterprise and to think in business-like ways. The latter is especially demanding given that most young apprentice farmers are associated with and involved in a family partnership that is headed by their father; such arrangements require, from both parties, a great deal of patience and cooperation.

Those young people who nevertheless assume the risk of taking over a farming operation, are no longer primarily guided by traditional motives, such as their duty to perpetuate the family farm, to hold fast to the family's lands, and to maintain the family heritage. Nor are they guided by a calculated desire to attain a respected and materially secure and prosperous future for themselves and their own children. Rather, there are certain (non-economic) cultural values and goals – a complex blend of modern or post-modern, and old fashioned – that make the way of life of a farmer seem attractive despite all its difficulties and uncertainties. Farming, according to this perception, offers independence and a family-friendly work and life style.

It is questionable, however, if such non-economic motives to rationalize the survival of family labour dairies can be sustained into the future. This is especially unlikely when weighed against the dairy industry's shaky prospects and the dependence of dairy farmers – particularly those with smaller-size operations – on state subsidies and regulations. With a continuing decline of the dairy industry here and the closing out of many more dairy farms, the Wesermarsch community and similar dairy farming regions, will lose their distinctive characteristics without at the same time gaining some alternative possibilities for regional development and the creation of non-farm jobs opportunities.

ACKNOWLEDGMENTS

I wish to thank Ina Dojen for help with the intitial draft, and Eileen Beyer for further translation assistance. The labourious and competent help of Professor Harry Schwarzweller in revising and condensing this article, and producing a final translation, is appreciated. I also thank Wiard Janssen, leader of the Wesermarsch district agricultural office (Lanwirtschaftsamt Wesermarsch) for his support of the survey and field work, and I especially want to thank the Wesermarsch dairy farm families for their cooperative spirit in granting us multiple intensive interviews. Hajo Timmermann and Steffen Hilber were involved in the empirical studies which are reported in this article. Thomas Garden, environmental consultant for Wesermarsch, cooperated with me in the investigation of farmers who had agreed to participate in the nature protection projects.

REFERENCES

BMELF (Bundesmin. Ernährung, Landwirtschaft and Forsten) (1985). *Agrarbericht der Bundesregierung 1985* [Agricultural Report of the Federal Republic 1985.] Bonn.

BMELF (1997). *Agrarbericht der Bundesregierung 1997.* Bonn.

BMELF (1998). *Agrarbericht der Bundesregierung 1998.* Bonn.

Bundesgesetzblat. [Federal Law Gazette.] 1978. No. 89.

Cornelius, P. (1908). *Das Oldenburger Wesermarschrind.* [The Wesermarsch Cow of Oldenburg.] Hannover.

Doll, H. (1989). *Milchquotenregelung und Struktur der Milcherzeugung.* [Milk Quota Regulations and Structure of Milk Production.] Münster-Hiltrup.

Garden, Th., & Wilke, J. (1995). Die Umsetzung des Feuchtgrünlandschutzprogrammes im Landkreis Wesermarsch. [The conversion into action wet green-land protection programs in Wesermarsch county.] In: *NAA-Berichte* 2/95.

Harjehusen, F. (1934). *Die Milchwirtschaft Oldenburgs unter Berücksichtigung der Neuordnung 1933/34.* [The Milk Industry of Oldenburg with respect to the new rules 1933/34.] Dissertation, University of Köln.

Herrmann, K. (1996). Vom Röhrchen zum Roboter. Die Geschichte der Melkmaschine. [From piping to robotics: history of the milk machine.] In: H. Ottenjann & K.-H. Ziesow (Eds), *Die Milch. Geschichte und Zukunft eines Lebensmittels.* Cloppenburg.

Hinrichs, E., Krämer, R., & Reinders, Ch. (1988). *Die Wirtschaft des Landes Oldenburg in vorindustrieller Zeit.* [The Economy of the Province of Oldenburg in Pre-industrial Times.] Oldenburg.

LWK (Landwirtschaftskammer) Weser-Ems (1996). *Landwirtschaftlicher Fachbeitrag zum Regionalen Raumordnungsprogramm für den Landkreis Wesermarsch.* [Agricultural Business Contributions to the Wesermarsch Regional Program of Spatial Ordering.] Brake.

LWK Weser-Ems. Ausgaben 1938–1962 (1982). *Die Landwirtschaftlichen Verhaeltnisse im Gebiet der LWK Weser-Ems.* [The Agricultural Conditions in the Region of LWK Weser-Ems.] Brake.

LWK Weser-Ems/Aussenstelle Brake, 1984/85. *Die Entwicklung der Landwirtschaft im Landkreis Wesermarsch.* [The Development of Agriculture in Wesermarsch County.] Brake.

Mayhew, A. (1970). *Zur strukturellen Reform der Landwirtschaft in der Bundesrepublik Deutschland, erläutert an der Flurbereinigung in der Gemeinde Moorriem/Weser marsch.* [The Structural Reform of Agriculture in the Federal Republic of Germany is an Explanation for the Re-parcelling of village fields in the Mooriem Community of Wesermarsch.] Münster.

Mütter, B. (1996). Der Aufbau einer modernen Milch- und Molkereiwirtschaft im Herzog tum Oldenburg 1871–1914/1932. [The building of a modern milk and dairy industry in the Duchy of Oldenburg.] In: H. Ottenjann, & K.-H. Ziessow (Eds), *Die Milch. Geschichte und Zukunft eines Lebensmittels.* Cloppenburg.

Niediedersachsen Landesverwaltungsamt – Statistik (1964). *Schweine-, Milchkuh-, und Huehnerbestaende im Verheltnis zur landwirtschaftlichen Nutzflaeche, 1963.* [Pigs, Milk cows, and Poultry Numbers in Relation to Agricuturally Productive Land, 1963.]

NLS (Niederesachsen Landesamt fur Statisk) (1994). *Agrarberichterstattung 1993.* [Agricultural Reporting.] Heft n.4.

NLS (Niedersächsen Landesamt für Statistik) (1997a). *Viehbestand am 3.12.1996.* [Livestock on 3 December 1996.] Hannover.

NLS (1997b). *Größenstruktur der land- und forstwirtschaftlichen Betriebe 1996.* [Size Structure of Agricultural and Forestry Businesses 1996.] Hannover.

NLS (Edit.) (1998). *Kreiszahlen. Ausgewählte Regionaldaten für Deutschland. Ausgabe 1997.* [County Counts. Selected Regional Data for Germany.] 1997. Hannover.

Riedel, K. V. (Edit.) (1972). *Moorriem. Landes-, volks- und sachkundliche Darstellung der Entwicklung in einer Großgemeinde.* [Moorriem. Land, People, and Relevant Information Representing the Development of a Large Commnity.] Oldenburg.

Schreiber, W. (1928). *Die Marschweidewirtschaft Butjadingens (Oldenburger Wesermarsch) und ihre Betriebsprobleme.* [The Butjadingens Marsh Grazing Economy and its Business Problems in the Oldenburg area of Wesermarsch.] Dissertation, Landwirtsch. Hochschule Bonn-Poppelsdorf.

Statistisches Bundesamt (Edit.) (1997a). *Statistisches Jahrbuch für die Bundesrepublik Deutschland.* [Statistical Yearbook for the Federal Republic of Germany.] Stuttgart.

Statistisches Bundesamt (1997b). *Ausgewählte Zahlen für die Agrarwirtschaft 1996/97.* [Selected Agricultural Statistics 1996/97.] (Fachserie 3. Reihe 1). Stuttgart.

Statistisches Bundesamt (1997c). *Milcherzeugung und -verwendung 1996.* [Milk Production and Utilization 1996.] (Fachserie 3. Reihe 4.2.2). Stuttgart.

Timmermann, H., & Vonderach, G. (1993). *Milchbauern in der Wesermarsch. Eine empirisch-soziologische Untersuchung.* [Dairy Farmers in the Wesermarsch. An Empirical-sociological Study.] Bamberg.

Tschajanow, A. (1987). *Die Lehre von die baeuerlichen Wirtschaft.* (first German edition: Berlin 1923). [Theory of Peasant Economy.] New Edition Frankfurt/M., New York [Alexander Chaianov. 1991. *The Theory of Peasant Cooperatives.* Columbus: Ohio State University Press.]

Vonderach, G. (1993). Bäuerliche Familienwirtschaft im Wandel. [Rural Economy in Change.] In: *Land, Agarwirtschaft und Gesellschaft, 10*(3).

Winkler, K. (1929). *Die landwirtschaftlichen Betriebsverhältnisse in Moorriem.* [The Agricultural Business Conditions in Moorriem.] Dissertation, Univ. Leipzig.

DAIRY RESTRUCTURING AND DEREGULATION IN AUSTRALIA: A CASE STUDY OF DUNGOG, NEW SOUTH WALES

Andrew P. Davidson

INTRODUCTION

The Australian dairy industry has been undergoing a dramatic transformation over the past three decades. Much of academic interest has focused on the rapid decline in the number of smaller dairies and an attendant rise in average farm size (Schwarzweller, 1988; Davidson, 1995), the structural reorganization of dairies (Lembit et al., 1991, ADIC, 1999a), and the concentration and consolidation of regional dairy cooperatives (Pritchard, 1996, 1998; Fisher, 1999).[1]

These changes are especially relevant in terms of the current debate over the effects of the deregulation of the dairy industry through the government's efforts to dismantle the corporatist or regulatory arrangements that underpinned the industry for so long. Although it is important to note the wider forces of agri-food globalization and international competition that are reshaping the dairy industry, changes in dairy practices are particularly expressive at the local level where adjustments must be operationalized and acted out. After all, dairy farming is not simply about milk or the judicious combination of production factors in the most 'efficient'[2] manner; it ultimately concerns the economic

Research in Rural Sociology, Volume 8, pages 95–113.

well-being of farm families and the future sustainability of many rural communities.

Since 1975, the number of 'registered' dairy farms in Australia has declined a staggering 57%, while cow numbers (in milk and dry) declined nearly 35% (ADC 1995; 1998; Safe Food Production, 2000). Average herd size, however, has risen from about 93 to 153 (and is currently estimated to be 161) (Safe Food Production, 2000). Interestingly, unlike other industrialised countries, the number of cows is again increasing, about 11% since 1995. Average annual yield per cow has also risen some 47% since 1990, an indication of better breeding and improved feed regimes (mostly improved pasturage). Commenting on these trends, many industry experts conclude that smaller farms will find it increasingly difficult to remain viable in a highly competitive international milk market (Pritchard, 1998, 1996; ADIC, 1999b; 1998; Kaine et al., 1994; Bardsley & Hughs, 1985). This opinion is particularly disturbing since about 25% of all dairies have less than 90 cows (ADC, 1998). It is estimated that in order to survive in a deregulated market, dairy farms will need to be milking between 400 and 500 cows, producing between 750,000 to 1.5 million litres of milk per year (Pearson, 1999). In fact, according to a report prepared on dairy deregulation for the Australian Senate, average herd size "is considerably below the level at which economies of scale are exhausted [which] is believed to approach a herd size of 2,000" (Moran, 1999: 4).

Quantifiable trends in the dairy industry, as in other agricultural sectors, are invariably associated with changes occurring in the agricultural and food supply system. Initially the forces driving the restructuring of the Australian dairy industry were technological innovations in milk production, transport, and storage in the early 1970s, which in turn were largely in response to changes in the demand for Australian dairy products (Lembit et al., 1991; Müller, 1978). There was, however, a second major stimulus for change; the entry of the United Kingdom, then Australia's largest market, into the European Community in 1973 which forced the Australian dairy industry to become more internationally competitive and to develop new trade export links (Moran, 1999). In an effort to bolster exports, the Kerin Plan in 1986 was introduced which directly linked domestic prices to international market returns thus enabling the dairy industry to respond more effectively to world market prices.[3] Additional pressures during the 1990s have come from the government's push towards the complete deregulation of the milk industry, both at the national and state levels. The resultant reordering of dairy farms, as indexed by share of milk market, appears to have come largely at the expense of the small and medium-sized operations.

This chapter focuses on industry adjustments made by dairy farms and explores the dynamics of deregulation on dairies in the community of Dungog, located in the Hunter Valley region of New South Wales. Specifically, I examine changes in dairying based on three surveys over a ten-year period (1990 to 1999), but especially change from 1995 to 1999. Furthermore, this chapter will pay particular attention to the reorganisation and survival chances of the remaining dairies, as well as provide a brief overview of those dairies that closed down their operations during this time period. I will also attempt to address the present debate in Australia as to whether or not smaller-scale family farms are inimical to an unregulated milk industry, and one that is increasingly oriented to producing milk for an export market.

DAIRY INDUSTRY RESTRUCTURING

Dairying is a major Australian rural industry, "comprising approximately 1% of gross domestic product and 13% of total processed food and beverage output" (Pritchard, 1998: 3). Australia's climate and pasture-based grazing system give it a comparative advantage and relatively low cost milk production (along with New Zealand).[4] Based on farm gate production values, it ranks third behind the wheat and beef industries. The gross value of dairy production in 1997/1998 was about AU$ 3 billion (ADC, 2000). Dairying is also one of the leading rural industries in terms of the proportion of downstream employment and processing it generates. At an ex-factory level, industry output was valued at around $7 billion in 1997/98, earning in excess of AU$ 2 billion in exports (ADIC, 1999a). More importantly, today more than half of Australia's annual milk is exported, and more than 60% of its manufactured dairy products, mostly to Asia. (Japan consumes 21% of Australia's food export sales and 37% of exports to Asia). Australia is currently the third leading dairy exporter with 12% of the global trade, compared with the European Union's 38% and New Zealand's 31% (ADC, 1999). According to the ADIC (1999b), however, "While the domestic industry has grown successfully . . . future growth lies in the expansion of export markets and the major exporters believe this requires the removal of price regulations."

Most export-oriented milk production occurs in the southern (colder) states of Victoria and Tasmania, with the remaining dairy regions (located in New South Wales, Queensland, South Australia and Western Australia) oriented towards satisfying local demand. Victoria is the major milk producing State with 43% of Australia's dairies and accounts for 63% of total milk production. In 1998/99, Victoria exported 83% of its total milk production (only 7% goes to fluid milk), earning 80% of the industry's export revenues. Dairying, however, is no less important in NSW. With 13% of the market, NSW is second only to Victoria in terms of milk production and number of dairy farms. Dairying is the fifth largest rural industry in NSW, with production at the farm gate estimated at about AU$ 462 million in 1999 (Safe Food Production, 2000). Unlike Victoria, NSW milk production is oriented towards producing milk year round to supply the fluid milk market (44% of its total milk production) (ABC, 1999b). Consequently, seasonal patterns are less pronounced than in either Victoria or Tasmania and require NSW dairy farmers to provide cows with supplemental feeding grains and concentrates when pasture growth is poor, which adds to their cost of production.

Trends in New South Wales' dairy industry have, in many ways, parallelled those occurring nationally and regionally – fewer dairy producers and larger herds. Since 1975, the number of 'registered' dairies has declined 63.4% and the number of cows 42.7%, although cow numbers have increased 19% since 1995 (ADC 1995; Safe Food Production, 2000). Average herd size has risen from 84 to 146, slightly less than the national average. Dairy farms in the other States are also getting larger; the current mean size dairy in Victoria is 164 cows, 124 in Queensland, 151 in South Australia, 166 in Western Australia and 192 in Tasmania (Safe Food Production, 2000). The smaller mean herd sizes in NSW and Queensland are probably due to the fact that these states lagged behind the others in the deregulation of their milk industries, most notably in their dairy quota systems which provide higher returns for liquid milk. Since 1994, the number of dairy farms has decreased 8.8% in NSW and 17.7% in Queensland, compared to the other states that lost 7.9% collectively.

Total milk production in Australia is steadily increasing. Much of this increase is due to increased productivity per cow, about 4,744 litres per year in Australia, but about 5,014 litres per year in NSW (ADIC, 1999b). Overall, then, the domestic and international demand for Australia's milk and milk products is steadily increasing, a demand which Australian dairy farmers are meeting. Unfortunately for the Australian dairy farmer, the wholesale price of milk remains comparatively low. Compared with the U.K. and U.S., the wholesale price in Australia is 40 and 29% lower, respectively (ADC, 1995); and, when factory prices paid to farmers for milk are adjusted for inflation, prices have remained relatively flat from 1982 to 1998 (ADIC, 1999b). It appears, then, that many Australian dairy farmers are caught in a cost/price squeeze; costs of inputs are rising more quickly than the price of milk at the farm gate.

The study of the restructuring of the dairy industry, as in agriculture in general, thus can provide important insights into the development processes. Figure 1 suggests that the differential pressures exerted by the wider political

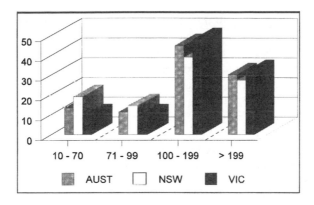

Fig. 1. Percent of Dairy Farms by Herd Size.
Source: Compiled from data from ABS, 1994.

economy can and do generate different developmental trajectories; in this instance, variations in dairy-farm scale within Australia and between NSW and Victoria. It also suggests that although economic forces and policies are pushing dairy farmers to expand, smaller and medium-scale operations persist (see, for example, Davidson 1997; Davidson & Schwarzweller, 1994; Schwarzweller & Davidson, 1997). Nevertheless, some dairy enterprises are better positioned to take advantage of changes within the wider political economy; in the present case, with changes associated with dairy industry deregulation. Still, it is not a foregone conclusion that the smaller family farm is inimical to a deregulated environment. The outlook, however, is rather bleak for many dairy farmers with industry experts anticipating a large shakeout, especially those "unable to survive on reduced real returns" and those who either do "not have the financial ability or inclination to achieve further efficiencies or to create economies of scale" (ADIC, 1999a: 2; Pearson, 1999; Koutsoukis, 1999; Mitchell, 1999). Thus, while it is important to document the presumed trend towards fewer but larger dairy farms, it is equally important to gain a clearer understanding of what is happening at the dairy farm level – to the farmers themselves.

DAIRY INDUSTRY DEREGULATION

Dairy regulation in Australia has its origins in dairy industry's attempts to stabilise milk production in the 1930s recession, parallelling in many ways the American experience of this time (Grant, 1991). Under the Australian constitution, the regulation of fluid milk falls under State jurisdiction, while the support scheme regulating manufactured milk is a federal prerogative (Domestic Market Support Scheme). Through complex market access arrangements and pooling systems, a two-tiered pricing mechanism was established for fluid and manufacturing milk (Pritchard, 1998: 3). Typically, dairy farmers receive higher prices for fluid milk than for manufactured. In New South Wales, for example, the average farm gate price for manufactured milk in 1999 was 24.6 cents but 47 cents for fluid milk.

The establishment of corporatist arrangements (a special relation between the state and interest organizations or sectors of the economy) facilitated a production system organised through regional cooperatives.[5] This administrative system remained largely unchanged until the Kerin Plan in 1986 which, as noted, was intended to bring cross-subsidy payments for exports more in line with international prices (usually manufactured milk), thus making Australian dairy imports more competitive (Pritchard, 1996). During the 1990s, deregulation efforts shifted to the state level – the fluid milk market, focussing primarily on price setting and zoning regulation (restrictions on interstate sales, especially of excess manufactured milk). Since 1990, milk prices have been deregulated beyond the farm gate such that market forces determine processor, vendor and retail margins, and retail price. Currently, farm gate prices and milk sourcing are in the final stages of being completely deregulated, leaving the milk industry completely exposed to market determinants.

From the beginning, the debate on the deregulation of the dairy industry has been driven by an ideology of 'economic rationalism'. N. Evans (1994: 47) goes so far as to claim that Australia and New Zealand have been labouring for the past century under 'socialism', and now are "cutting back government and freeing their economies." In this sense, policymakers hold firm to the idea that market forces generate the most efficient economic performance by creating appropriate investment strategies for both farmers and manufacturers alike, but regardless of the social consequences which are assumed to be externalities. In one study of 121 family-operated dairies in the Bega Valley and Eurobadalla Shires (NSW), it was estimated a five cent reduction per litre for their milk would make eight dairy farms unviable, a 10 cent reduction would make 70 farms unviable and a 15 cent reduction would place all at risk (Pearson, 1999).

Certainly too, dairy companies and manufacturing plants have been a significant driving force behind deregulation. During the 1980s and into the 1990s, a wave of consolidations and mergers occurred as companies sought to achieve economies of scale in order to compete domestically against each other and from imported products, and in the international market (particularly competition from New Zealand) (ADIC, 1999a). Three companies now process 90% of Australia's fresh milk output (Dairy Farmers with 35%; National Foods with 32%, and Pauls with 23%) (Fisher, 1999), and two cooperatives – Murray-Goulbunn and Bonlac – accounting for 70% of dairy exports (Pritchard, 1998). This worries many dairy farmers. In the words of one dairy farmer:

> Deregulation is meant to help the consumer. But it has been proved that supermarkets are the only winners out of deregulation. The producers are severely penalized by receiving less. Basically, the supermarkets are the big players screwing hell out of the primary producers (Blair, 1998: 55).

Not all dairy farmers view deregulation in this manner. Victorian dairy farmers with the bulk of dairy production view deregulation as a means to open up the markets of other states and give increased access to the powdered-milk export market (Mitchell, 1999).

Deregulation has also been ideologically charged with oblique references to consumer welfare: "Milk producers, through the monopoly arrangements they have persuaded governments to underwrite, are engaging in price gouging of the Australian fresh milk consumer" (Moran, 1999: 7). It is interesting to note, however, that farmers will receive monetary compensation to be funded by an 11 cents per litre levy on all fluid milk products; i.e. funded by the consumer rather than the industry (ADIC, 1999b). Furthermore, retail fluid milk prices have yet to fall although prices paid to dairy farmers has already.

STUDY SITE AND SURVEYS

The Shire of Dungog was selected as the research site because the pressures to modify and restructure the dairy industry are quite evident in the Dungog context and because I had access to data from an earlier study. In 1990, Harry Schwarzweller surveyed all dairy farms in Dungog Shire. Information was obtained from 69 dairy enterprises (one was missed) and on the 82 households that were associated with those dairies through various kinds of partnership arrangements. The original data set provided information on dairy management practices, scale of operation, labour utilisation, expansion aspirations, and related business matters. In August of 1995, I re-surveyed those same dairies (including the missed one) and gathered information on the remaining dairies, including the 76 households associated with those dairies. In 1999, I again re-surveyed those dairies, along with the 63 dairy farm households. Of particular interest was the future plans of those still dairying; how they saw themselves in a changing industry. As in 1995, information was also collected on the dairies that had closed out their operations.

Dungog, located about 80 kilometres west of Newcastle, is a small rural hamlet situated in the Williams River valley. To the north of Dungog, a range of mountains called the Barrington Tops (Mt. Barrington is 1,585 metres) provides a picturesque backdrop to the rich dairy country. The rugged topography of the area generally precludes broad acre agriculture. Early on, logging (especially cedar) along with several tanneries were the primary industries of Dungog's rural economy, although some farmers grew tobacco (Schwarzweller, 1988). Dairying and beef grazing now comprise the main agricultural enterprises. Unlike other areas of NSW, there are no sheep operations.

Does the Dungog area represent dairy farms in NSW? Consideration of published NSW Dairy Corporation (1998) statistics suggests that Dungog dairy farms are smaller than those in the Southern Region (particularly the Riverina) with a herd average of 157 and the Inland Local Areas averaging 143 cows, both of which rely heavily on irrigation for pasture production (Safe Food Production, 1999). On the other hand, in scale and character the Dungog dairies are not dissimilar to dairies in many other areas of NSW, particularly where small family owned dairies predominate and there is a growing competition for alternative uses of land (residential development, recreation, and hobby farming). The mean dairy herd in the Central Region (of which the Hunter Valley is a part) is 119 and 89 in the North Coast Region. Using data from 1995, the last time the New South Wales Dairy Corporation (1995) made more detailed dairy industry statistics available, the mean dairy herd average in the Hunter Valley was 110, 86 in the Mid North Coast and 154 in the Tablelands. I am satisfied that Dungog dairies, with a current mean herd size of 115 cows, is not unusual. Nevertheless, the pressures restructuring the dairy industry are quite evident in the Dungog context, located on the growing edge of the Newcastle/Sydney metropolitan sprawl.

CHANGES IN SCALE OF OPERATION

Central to the debate that only larger-scale dairy farms will prosper in a deregulated dairy environment is that smaller-scale dairy farms, those characterised as family operations, are decreasing in numbers and share of aggregate profits. It is important here to substantiate the assumed trend towards larger more industrialized-type dairy operations, with less dependence upon family labour and greater labour efficiencies. It is also important to draw out the dynamics of the mechanisms that contribute to the restructuring of dairying and to anticipate their impact in human terms. A number of interrelated structural factors are especially important to this debate: herd size and land holdings, family labour inputs and off-farm employment, and perception of the future of their dairy. Together these factors help explain present patterns of structural change and provide an answer to what the possible future of dairying will look like in NSW.

Herd size and land holdings

Herd size and land holdings provide an important insight into the outcomes of the restructuring process in dairying. With the impending reduction of prices paid to farmers for fluid milk and their attendant loss of income, dairy farmers will find that they must increase their herd sizes. Failing this, their ability to survive and prosper is doubtful. From 1990 to 1999, 28.6% of Dungog's dairies closed out their operations, a relatively constant rate of about 3% a year. Dungog dairies currently range in size from 52 to 270 cows. The mean herd size now is 115, 20 more than in 1990 but only one more than 1995 (median herd size is 110). Dairy farmers, of course, keep other stock; heifers, calves, bulls, and, increasingly, beef cattle. Given the hilly topography of the Dungog area, alternatives to dairying are limited; beef cattle are thus a particularly important strategy to diversify farm incomes. Currently, 44% of dairy farmers keep beef cattle; 26% keep 30 or more. The 50 remaining dairies were grouped into three categories; smaller, 70 or fewer cows; medium, 71 to 99 cows; and large, 100 or more cows. These categories are employed solely as analytical tools.

Table 1 indicates that smaller dairies are being pressured to get bigger or close out, although from 1990 to 1995, more dairies expanded their operations rather than contracted, as was the case in 1999; and, of course, realistic expansion will require adding more than four or five cows. But there seem to be few alternatives. The Senate inquiry into the impact of dairy deregulation in

Table 1. Number of Dairy Farms by Herd Size in 1989, 1995 And 1999 and Percent Change from 1990 to 1999.

Herd Size	1990	1995	1999	% change
smaller (< 70)	21	6	6	−71.4
medium (71–99)	25	24	17	−32.0
larger (≥ 100)	24	29	27	+ 11.1
Total (N =)	70	59	50	28.6

Table 2. Mean Herd Size by Herd Size in 1990, 1995, and 1999.

Herd Size	1990	1995	1999
Smaller (≤ 70)	60	63	58
Medium (71–99)	80	82	87
Larger (≥ 100)	130	143	146
Total (N =)	70	59	50

NSW and Victoria heard evidence that "selling dairy farms is now almost impossible due to industry uncertainty . . . there are very few buyers willing to invest" (ABC, 1999b). Consequently, when dairy farms close out in Dungog, increasingly the property is broken up and used for other purposes. Dairy expansion thus appeared somewhat more optimistic in the past than now (Table 2).

Smaller Size Dairies
- The future of smaller dairies is certainly less optimistic now than it was in 1995, and despite all dairies having to install effluent systems by the end of the year. Although four smaller dairies closed down their operations from 1990–1995, another 12 expanded their herd size an average of 23 cows; only five remained about the same size. In the 1999 survey, three smaller dairies closed out their operations, two reduced their herds an average of five cows and another remained about the same.

Medium-Sized Dairies
- Medium sized dairies exhibited a different trend in the 1995 survey than did their smaller scale counterparts. Although five closed out their operations, nine increased their herd size by an average of 39 cows; 11 remained about the same size and one scaled back its operation in anticipation of closing out (which it did in 1999). By 1999, medium-sized dairies appeared to be having a more difficult time; four closed out and another three downsized their operations an average of 17 cows. On the other had, five increased their herd size an average of 16 cows and the rest remained about the same size.

Larger Size Dairies
- Larger dairies, unlike the other two size categories, are better positioned to meet the challenges presented by the restructuring trends. Nevertheless, they

too are not overly optimistic. Of the larger dairies in the 1995 survey, four closed out, eight decreased their herd size an average of 17 cows, two remained the same, and 11 increased their herds by an average of 44 cows. By 1999, two more closed out, five downsized their operations an average of 36 cows, and the remainder are about the same size as in 1995.

In general, herd size is a strong correlate of gross sales because these dairies, like most other dairy farms in Australia, are not very diversified. The percent of milk sales of gross agricultural sales is about 93%, up from 91% in 1990 (nationally it is 88%). This of course means that dairies and dairy farm households are extremely vulnerable to the vacillations in the milk market and especially now with the deregulation of farm gate prices and the end of the quota system. According to one dairy farmer, "those relying on the quota for more than 75% of their farm income will be hard pressed when deregulation finally comes."

Dungog dairies average about 512 total acres operated with about 381 acres specifically for the dairy, slightly more than in 1995. Herd size and acres operated are closely associated ($r = 0.68$), these figures are only marginally higher than in 1990 and 1995. Furthermore, median herd size and acreage did not increase appreciably despite larger herd sizes on average. Aside from the general uncertainty over the future of dairying in this region, an additional factor includes the high cost of land due to Dungog's proximity to Newcastle and Sydney. Rather than buy additional land, farmers tend to lease land, but this too is increasingly in short supply. A number of dairy farmers complained about the rapid increases in the cost of land in the last 10 years. Some dairy farmers did, however, purchase lands from dairies that closed out.

The smaller dairies average 381 acres, the middle-sized farms 456 acres, and the larger farms 698 acres of dairy land operated. The mean averages are lower among smaller and medium sized dairies than in 1995, an indication that these farmers are unsure about their future and are anticipating possible closures. It is also noteworthy that recent dairy expansions operate larger holdings, while those dairies in a holding pattern have about the same or less. Lastly, larger dairies in 1999 tended to own more land but lease less, while this trend was reversed for medium dairies.

Labour inputs and off-farm employment

Dairying is a labour intensive enterprise that requires long hours, especially on dairies supplying fluid milk. It is estimated that one adult can effectively manage and milk 81 cows (Bardsley & Hughs, 1985). Farm labour inputs thus is a particularly important consideration in specifying any change in farm scale, for the number of labourers and the source and quality of that labour is directly relevant to the critical issue of survivability. Not surprisingly, total labour inputs are significantly correlated with herd size (r = 0.74), more so than in 1995 (r = 0.61). Larger farms too, tend to employ more labour; as herd size increases, dairies invariably find that family labour is insufficient to meet the needs of the growing operation. Of course, larger dairies are also better positioned to make use of labour saving technologies through increased economies of scale. On the other hand, family-based organisation of the workforce by smaller and medium size farms allows greater flexibility through 'self-exploitation' which enables farm families to compete with fully capitalist enterprises (Friedmann, 1986).

An indicator of 'adult work year equivalents' was devised (Schwarzweller, 1992) and used to differentiate the labour inputs by family and hired workers. The base, an index number of 1.0, represents the amount of labour assumed to be equivalent to that contributed by an adult actively involved 'full time' in the farming operation. A pattern of at least 40 hours per week throughout the year is taken to be full time. The farm related work of women is regarded as equal to that of men, but the farm related work of children is discounted by a factor of 20% for each year under 16 years of age. It should be noted that many dairy farmers work much more than 40 hours per week.

Overall, total labour inputs on the 50 dairy farms range from about 1.00 to 5.75. The median is 2.07, nearly the same as in 1990 and 1995. The mean is about 1.75 for smaller dairies, 2.14 for the middle dairies, and 1.99 for the larger operations. The important thing to note is that although smaller operations use more labour now, the mean herd size is now five cows fewer, indicating a greater degree of 'self-exploitation'. Middle-sized dairies also utilise slightly more labour, but then average herd size has risen by seven. Larger dairies, to the contrary, have become increasingly labour efficient over the past decade.

Hired labour currently accounts for about 20% of the total labour inputs (up from 13% in 1995); about 5% on small dairies, 11% on medium-sized dairies, and 26% on larger dairies. Smaller dairies employed slightly more hired labourers than in 1995, while larger dairies employed 11% more. Medium-sized dairies employ 2% less than in 1995, a further indication of their financial stress. Many dairies, of course, simply do not have the necessary economies of scale or the financial capability to hire additional labour on a regular basis. About 41% of all part-time and full-time hired workers are close kin of the operator (10% more than in 1995). Thus, one can generalise that these dairy operations depend for the most part on family labour, more so than in 1995 and 1990.

Equally important to diversifying farm income is off-farm employment as an effective household/farm survival strategy (Munton & Marsden, 1991). Overall, principal males and, especially, females work off the farm more now than in previous years. Both medium and larger size dairies have a slightly smaller portion of both principal males and females working off the farm than in 1995, but the smaller dairies have significantly more. In part, the lower rate of off-farm employment is a reflection of the lack of jobs in the area, due in part to the closure or privatization of many government services in rural Australia, as well as the closing down of many businesses in country towns. In some respects, the extra burdens of maintaining a viable dairy operation fall disproportionately on principal females who not only increasingly work off-farm, but also invest more hours in dairy work than in 1990.

EXPANSION OR CLOSURE

The attitudes and behavior of dairy farmers in Dungog in terms of modernization and herd expansion generally parallels the realities and structural constraints posed by the wider political economy. Most dairy farmers believe that dairying in many parts of NSW will be undermined by milk shipments from neighboring Victoria and New Zealand, making it increasing difficult for dairies to survive, particularly smaller dairies. Many dairies are already quite stretched. The significant expansion of a dairy operation – beyond adding a few cows to the herd – requires a considerable outlay of capital. In making such investments, farmers in an uncertain economic climate tend to be cautious. This is understandable, especially in the wake of the recent drought which had greater adverse impacts on medium dairies. More than twice as many medium size dairies than smaller and larger dairies reported greater debt burdens, increased feed costs, decreased milk production, and a reduction in income as a consequence of the drought. On top of this, all dairies in 1995 were given one year to install effluent management systems by the NSW Department of Agriculture; and now complete deregulation at the farm gate. On the other hand, not expanding their dairy enterprises may only be prolonging the inevitable closure.

In line with feelings of uncertainty, only a few of Dungog dairy farmers reported making some significant improvements between 1995 and 1999. Not surprisingly, only one smaller dairy made minor improvements to their dairies. Medium-sized dairies also evinced a reluctance to commit to the future; only three made some improvements to their dairies. Clearly, these farmers are loath to commit their limited resources to an expansion of the family enterprise at a time when the future of this industry is quite uncertain. Larger dairies, on the other hand, made more improvements to their operations, purchasing more equipment and modernizing milking facilities. In all probability, larger-scale dairies are intending to strengthen their position within the milk industry and are making the investments necessary to ensure their survival.

When asked about their future plans in the 1999, dairy farmers in Dungog remain pessimistic about the future of dairying in the region. In making investments, farmers in economically uncertain times tend to be financially conservative. Although 42% of the dairy farmers indicated that they will expand their herds in the future, 84% replied that they would not be increasing their land holdings. Furthermore, 62% said they would be making no or only basic improvements to their dairies. Only one smaller dairy farmer indicated that he would be making improvements and increasing his herd size. Medium-sized dairy operators were less cautious; 41% intend to make some or substantial improvements, as well as increase the size of their herds. Larger-sized dairy farmers were only slightly more optimistic with 44% intending to make some or substantial improvements but only 41% planning on increasing their herd size. In all probability, larger-scale dairies that are planning to undertake investments intend to strengthen their position within the milk industry. Overall, however, most dairy farmers in Dungog are in a holding pattern.

More revealing of the current dairy climate in Dungog is in managerial arrangements. A number of the dairies are operated as partnerships that involve two separate households in themanagement processes – 13 dairies, three less than in 1995. In part, multiple household operations can provide additional family labour and free up other household members to engage in off-farm employment; an additional household can also mean a smaller portion of the milk check. Furthermore, sons on five dairies shifted to a salary in lieu of a portion of the milk check; the generational transfer now in question. Overall, 50% of Dungog's dairy farmers were unsure if they would remain in operation in another 10 years, while 28% were certain that they would not. None of the smaller-scale dairies were positive, and only about 12% of the medium-scale dairies and about 33% of the larger-scale dairies were.

CLOSED DAIRY CHARACTERISTICS

An important question remains: How different were the closed out dairies from the dairies that are still operational? This can provide a better understanding of the dairy restructuring process, including the human impacts of dairy closures.

Table 3. Organizational Characteristics of Dairy Farms by Size of Operation:
Closed–1995, Closed–1995, and Open–1999

Characteristics	Small	Medium	Large
open–1999			
Herd size (mean)	60	87	156
Family labor (% farms)	95	91	75
Land ownership (mean)	381 acres	456 acres	698 acres
Diversification (% farms)	91	90	94
Operator age (mean)	52 years	50 years	49 years
Will close (anticipated) (% farms)	83	29	15
closed–1999			
Herd size (mean)	63	84	133
Family labor (% farms)	96	85	99
Land ownership (mean)	370 acres	409 acres	466 acres
Diversification (% farms)	100	91	95
Operator age (mean)	59 years	45 years	50 years
Will close (% farms)	100	75	50
closed–1995			
Herd size (mean)	60.0	82.0	126.5
Family labor (% farms)	81	100	100
Land ownership (mean)	376 acres	482 acres	503 acres
Diversification (% farms)	85	88	88
Operator age (mean)	57 years	38 years	49 years
Will close (% farms)	33	75	0

Table 3 summarises the assessment of various organisational characteristics of
the operational dairies in 1999, and the dairies that closed out by 1995 and
1999. It is possible to draw distinctions between the dairies that closed down
and those that remained operational. Nevertheless, what the data suggest is that,
possibly aside from the age of the operator, there are no appreciable differences
that can serve as structural predictors of dairy farm viability. Moreover, many
of those who closed out their dairy operations went into beef cattle. Given the
present beef market conditions, however, they appear to have gone from one
troubled industry to another. Unfortunately, aside from beef cattle, poultry and
deer farming, the landscape does not easily permit other agricultural activities
(Dungog Shire Council, 1994). Furthermore, many dairy farmers do not have
skills which easily permit a shift into non-agricultural occupations (see also,
Bell & Nalson, 1974).

CONCLUSION

The Australian dairy industry has been undergoing significant restructuring over the past 30 years. Trends in New South Wales are not unlike those that characterise Australia; a persistent decline in the number of dairy farms, an increase in the scale of surviving dairies and a steady increase in cow productivity. The effects of the present restructuring, however, have not been uniformly experienced. Many dairies continue to perform well, particularly with the strengthening of domestic demand for milk and the expansion of foreign markets. Yet many dairies, caught in the attendant price squeeze of recent years, have been forced to close down their operations, while many currently active dairies, particularly the smaller ones, are on the verge of closure.

Larger dairy farms in Dungog enjoy a relatively strong economic and social base for further expansion. The future of smaller dairies, on the other hand, is rather doubtful. The economic base for the expansion of the remaining smaller dairies is questionable. There are few alternatives and it is only a matter of time before they will close down their operations. Medium-scale dairies are at a crossroad; they will need to increase herd size in order to become competitive in an unregulated dairy environment; failing this, many will be forced to close out. In the end, the prognosis for Dungog's remaining dairies is rather bleak. Some dairies will survive into the future, many in all probability will not.

It is doubtful that there will be a return to corporatist arrangements which marked the past; but neither do we favor the rise of an economic environment where only the largest firms can exist. Current changes are generally expressed in terms of the neo-liberal rhetoric of freeing the market and taking government "off the backs of people." Any disadvantage arising from these seemingly necessary changes are referred to as externalities and transaction costs, to be borne by the public at large and benefited from by private individuals. Politicians are staying the course of 'economic rationalism', even though social indicators suggest the erosion of rural social cohesion. Now, rural Australia is in crisis. Not only is there a concentration in business enterprises, but closures of vital rural services such as banks, telecommunications, and hospitals worsen the situation in declining rural communities. Thus, when dairy farms close out, they are just a small part of a larger trend.

ACKNOWLDEGEMENTS

I gratefully acknowledge and thank Harry Schwarzweller for his original 1990 survey data, as well as Helen Earlam (1995) and Anne MacDonald (1995 and

1999) for their competent efforts in interviewing. Certainly too I recognize and appreciate the patience of the Dungog dairy farm families who provided information about their dairy activities in 1995 and 1999.

NOTES

1. Over the past decade there has been a paucity of agricultural research in the social sciences (with the exception of economics). For the past five years, research has been commissioned by Australia's primary industries by competitive tendering "on cost and scientific merit." A recent example of the types of research that are funded is the Dairy Research and Development Corporation's project on "the development of persistent legumes in tropical dairy pastures" (Radcliffe & Clarke, 1996: 1). While this is certainly worthy of industry funding, projects need to meet narrow guidelines that emphasize increasing productivity and efficiency, as well as expanding export markets. Little – if any – concern is accorded to the social aspects of farming. And with respect to the Australian Research Council (a primary source of research funds for academics), rural research is deemed to fall under the purview of the primary industries and thus ARC does not as a rule fund rural/agricultural research.

2. Within neo-classical economics, efficiency is configured as a mathematical construction to measure farm management decisions and frequently fails to take into account macro-level pressures – such as system-externalities – that also shape decisions.

3. According to the Australian Dairy Industry Council (1999b: 2), "From 1986 to 1982, export support was wound down from 44.2% above world parity prices to 22%. By 2000, the scheme [deregulation] will have reduced support to 10%."

4. According to the Australian Dairy Corporation, production costs are two-thirds of those in the European Union and three quarters of those in the U.S.; production costs are slightly lower in New Zealand (Moran, 1999).

5. Cooperatives have become quite powerful over the years, accounting for 75% of all milk output with the two largest (Murray Goulburn Cooperative and Bonlac Foods) controlling about 45% of all milk intake and around 50% of all milk used for manufacturing (Fisher, 1999).

REFERENCES

Australian Broadcasting Corporation National Rural News (1999a). Dairy Deregulation May Affect Property Market. *Country Hour.* 22/07/1999.

Australian Broadcasting Corporation National Rural News (1999b). The Pros and Cons of Dairy Deregulation. *The World Today.* 28/09/1999.

Australian Dairy Industry Council (1999a). The Australian Dairy Industry – Facts About Deregulation and the Restructure Package. *The on-line journal of the Australian Dairy Industry Council.* www.dairy.com.au/adic.

Australian Dairy Industry Council (1999b). Deregulation Discussions Continue Nationally *The on-line journal of the Australian Dairy Industry Council.* www.dairy.com.au/adic.

Australian Dairy Corporation. (2000). Push for Freer World Dairy Trade. Press Statement, 03/02/2000. www.dairy.com.au/news.

Australian Dairy Corporation (1999). *Influences on Farmgate Manufacturing Milk Prices*. Press Statement, 10/11/1999. www.dairy.com.au/news.

Australia Dairy Corporation (1998). *Australian Dairy Industry: In Focus 98*. Prepared by the Planning and Information Division. www.dairycorp.com.au/adc/ADC-PDF.

Australian Dairy Corporation (1997). Dairy Industry Profile. *Http://www.adc.aust.com/adc/adcpage.htm at June 4 1997*.

Australian Dairy Corporation (1995). *Dairy Compendium*. Melbourne: The Corporation.

Australian Bureau of Agricultural and Resource Economics (1991). *Dairy Industry Policy and Free Trade with New Zealand*. Canberra: Australian Government Publishing.

Australian Bureau of Statistics (1994). *Livestock and Livestock Products Australia*. Catalogue No. 7221.0. Canberra: Australian Government Publishing.

Bardsley, B. And T. Hughs. 1985. Measurements of Success in Dairy Farming. In: 1985 Dairy Production Conference Proceedings. *The Challenge: Efficient Dairy Production*.

Bell, J., & Nalson, J. (1974). *Occupational and Residential Mobility of Ex-Dairy Farmers on the North Coast of New South Wales: A Study of Alternative Occupations*. Armidale: Department of Sociology, University of New England.

Blair, T. (1998). Down on the Farm: Battered by Economic Change, the Bush – long the Pivot of Australia's Self-Image – Is Losing its National Influence. *TmeInternational, 150*(4), 54–55.

Davidson, A. (1997). Restructuring the Dairy Industry in New South Wales. *Rural Society, 7*(2), 17–28.

Davidson, A., & Schwarzweller, H. (1995). Marginality and Uneven Development: The Decline of Dairying in Michigan's North Country. *Sociologia Ruralis, 35*(1), 40–66.

Dungog Shire Council (1994). *Community Profile of Dungog Local Government Area*. Dungog: Dungog Shire Council.

Evans, N. Up From Down Under: After a Century of Socialism, Australia and New Zealand are Cutting Back Government and Freeing Their Economies. *National Review, 46*(16), 47–51.

Fisher, L. (1999). Land of Milk and Money. *The Bulletin*. 25/05/1999: 72.

Friedmann, H. (1986). Family Enterprises in Agriculture: Structural Limits and Political Possibilities. In: G. Cox, P. Lowe & M. Winter (Eds), *Agriculture: People and Politics*. London: Allen and Unwin.

Gebremedhin, T., & Cristy, R. (1996). Structural Changes in U.S. Agriculture: Implications for Small Farms. *Journal of Agricultural and Applied Economics, 28*(1), 57–66.

Grant, W. (1991). *The Dairy Industry: An International Comparison*. Brookfield, VT: Dartmouth.

Hinson, R. (1996). Structural Implications for Small Farms: Discussion. *Journal of Agricultural and Applied Economics, 28*(1), 67–72.

Kaine, G., Tozer, P., & Lees, J. (1994). *Context and Classification: Predicting Supply Response in the Dairy Industry*. Armidale: Rural Development Centre, University of New England.

Koutsoukis, J. (1999). Dairy Deregulation Causes Angst Down on the Farm. *The Age*. 28/08/1999. Www.the agecom.au/daily.

Lembit, J., Topp, V., Beare, S., & Sheales, T. (1991). *Dairy Industry Policy and Free Trade with New Zealand*. Canberra: Government Printing Office.

Madden, R. (1994). *Livestock and Livestock Products Australia*. Canberra: Australian Bureau of Statistics.

Mitchell, B. (1999). World of Milk Facing a Shake. *The Age*. March 6.

Moran, A. (1999). *Deregulation of the Australian Dairy Industry: Submission to the Senate's Rural and Regional Affairs and Transport Committee: Inquiry into Deregulation of the Australian Dairy Industry*. Melbourne: Institute of Public Affairs.

Munton, R., & Marsden, T. (1991). Dualism or Diversity in Family Farming?. *Geoforum*, *22*(1), 105–117.

Müller, P. (1978). *Dairy Farming on the North Coast of New South Wales: Social Change, Occupational Mobility and Future Development*. Occasional Publication No.1, Department of Sociology. Armidale: University of New England.

NSW Dairy Corporation (1998). *Dairy Industry Statistics Handbook*, Broadway, NSW: NSW Dairy Corporation.

NSW Dairy Corporation (1995). *Dairy Industry Statistics Handbook*. Broadway, NSW: NSW Dairy Corporation.

NSW Dairy Corporation (1985). *Dairy Industry Statistics Handbook*. Broadway, NSW: NSW Dairy Corporation.

NSW Government (1997). *Review of the NSW Dairy Industry Act 1979*. Issues Paper. Sydney: NSW Government.

Pearson, T. (1999). Dairy Deregulation: Milking Profits. *The Guardian*. October 13.

Pritchard, W. (1998). The Emerging Contours of the Third Food Regime: Evidence from Australian Dairy and Wheat Sectors. *Economic Geography*, *74*(1), 64–75.

Pritchard, W. (1996). Shift in Food Regimes, Regulation, and Producer Cooperatives: Insights from the Australian and US Dairy Industries. *Environment and Planning A*, *28*, 857–875.

Radcliffe, J., & Clarke, A. (1996). Rural Research in Australia. *Science*, *273*(5275), 612–613.

Safe Food Production (1999). *Dairy Industry Statistic Handbook*. Safe Food Production NSW – Dairy Division. www.dairy.nsw.gov.au.

Schwarzweller, H. (1988). *Agricultural Structure and Change in the Lower Hunter Valley of New South Wales: A Sociological Survey of Farm Families and their Work*. Agricultural Experiment Station, Michigan State University, Research Report 490, East Lansing, Michigan, U.S.A.

Schwarzweller, H. (1991). *Dairy Farm Restructuring in Australia*. Unpublished Manuscript.

Schwarzweller, H. (1992). *Dairying in Michigan's Thumb: Restructuring for the Future*, Research Report 521, East Lansing, MI: Michigan State University Agricultural Experiment Station.

Schwarzweller, H., & Davidson, A. (1997). Perspectives on Regional and Enterprise Marginality: Dairying in Michigan's North Country. *Rural Sociology*, *62*(2), 157–179.

Suter, K. (1999). Australia: Wealth and Despair. *Contemporary Review*, *274*(1598), 137–143.

DYNAMICS OF DAIRY INDUSTRY RESTRUCTURING IN WISCONSIN

Douglas Jackson-Smith and Bradford Barham

INTRODUCTION

Medium-sized, diversified, family-labor farms[1] have long defined the structure of dairy farming in 'America's Dairyland'. The red barns, silos, farmhouses, and fields of hay, grain, and pasture associated with these operations have given rise to the state's distinctive pastoral landscapes. As family businesses these farms have been successful enough to provide their operators with 'middle-class' standards of living. Nationally, in the 20th century, Wisconsin's dairy sector produced more milk and especially more cheese than any other state in the U.S. Among Wisconsin residents, much cultural pride stems from the state's preeminence in dairying – car license plates bear the motto 'America's Dairyland', while sports fans are particularly infamous for donning foam 'cheeseheads' to identify themselves as from Wisconsin.

Over the last 50 years the dairy farm sector Wisconsin has witnessed considerable changes in the size of their milking herds, use of production technologies and management practices, and mix of livestock and cropping enterprises. Despite these changes, most dairy farm operations have typically remained at a scale such that they are still operated and managed predominantly by farm household members. Indeed, until quite recently, Wisconsin only had a handful of large dairy farms that rely heavily on hired labor. At the same time, it has typically had fewer 'very small' dairy farms typical of some other midwestern or southern states. The distinctive character

Research in Rural Sociology, Volume 8, pages 115–139.
Copyright © 2000 by Elsevier Science Inc.
All rights of reproduction in any form reserved.
ISBN: 0-7623-0474-X

of Wisconsin dairy farming has been attributed to the state's unique political, cultural, and socioeconomic history (Gilbert & Akor, 1986).

In recent years, a belief has emerged in Wisconsin and throughout the Upper Midwest that the leading role of medium-sized, family-labor dairy operations is ending, and that these operations are being converted rapidly into large herd, industrial-style dairy farms that will look more like the dairy operations that are typical in California, Arizona, New Mexico, Idaho and other western states (Boehlje, 1997; see also Lyson & Geisler, 1992). As evidence for this trend, observers point to the highly publicized recent construction or expansion of very large dairy farms in the state; the growing number of 200-plus cow herds with modern milking parlors and freestalls; reports that medium-sized dairy farms are financially stressed; and increased rates of net farm losses, especially among farms that milk smaller herds. The view that medium-sized dairy farms are particularly vulnerable and being replaced by larger commercial dairy farms (on the one hand) and growing numbers of small, part-time farms without dairy cows (on the other) is consistent with the overall trend toward a bipolar or dualistic farm structure in U.S. agriculture as a whole (Buttel & LaRamee, 1991).

Many in the farming community and general public have viewed these dairy sector trends in a negative light (Buttel & Jackson-Smith, 1997). Their concerns tend to be directed to the implications for farm families, the vitality of rural towns and communities, rural land use patterns and landscapes, the quality of the state's rural environment, and even the state's economy (Strange, 1988). At the same time, many dairy industry leaders and professionals working with the dairy sector have tended to evaluate the apparent rise of larger scale farms in more positive terms, i.e. as evidence that Wisconsin's dairy sector is taking steps to remain competitive given the advent of new technologies and changing market conditions (Jones, 1999; Palmer et al., 2000). Often overlooked is another large group of industry participants and professionals who see this same structural change as inevitable, even as they worry about its effects on their own enterprises or activities or about the social and environmental consequences.

Given the importance of dairy products to U.S. regional and national farm economies, surprisingly little empirical research has been undertaken on the recent trends and dynamics of structural change in the American dairy farm sector, other than observing that a rapid transformation is occurring. We draw on data from a wide variety of sources[2] to explore recent patterns of structural change in Wisconsin dairy farming and compare them to long-term trends in Wisconsin and the U.S. We also examine the underlying patterns of expansion, entry, and exit which are shaping the evolution of dairy farm structure in the state. What are the forces that underlie recent structural changes? By clarifying the dynamics of what is occurring perhaps we can better anticipate future changes in this critical industry.

THE U.S. AND WISCONSIN DAIRY SECTORS

Aggregate Performance

Over the last several decades, the U.S. dairy industry has experienced the loss of several hundred thousand dairy farms and a decline in total dairy cow numbers. However, productivity growth (per milk cow) was sufficient to increase total milk output (Perez, 1994). Table 1 reports annual estimates of the performance and size structure of the United States and Wisconsin dairy sectors between 1993 and 1998. Herd numbers in the U.S. have fallen by over 25% in this 5-year period, while cow numbers are down 4%, and productivity increased by 9%. Overall milk output increased by 4.5%, but saw significant

Table 1. Changes in the Size and Production of the U.S. and Wisconsin Dairy Sectors, 1993–1998.

| | 1998 total | | Changes, 1993–1998 | | | |
| | | | Net Change | | Percent Change | |
	USA	Wisconsin	USA	Wisconsin	USA	Wisconsin
Farms by Herd Size						
Under 30 cows	35,690	4,300	–22,940	–2,000	–39.1	–31.7
30–49 cows	25,155	7,300	–9,655	–2,990	–27.7	–29.1
50–99 cows	34,277	8,900	–7,833	–1,900	–18.6	–17.6
100–199 cows	13,748	1,950	–882	–340	–6.0	–14.8
200 + cows	7,560	550	+590	+230	8.5	71.9
Total farms	116,430	23,000	–40,720	–7,000	–25.9	–23.3
Milk Cows (no, 1,000s)	9,158	1,369	–423	–174	–4.4	–11.3
Herd Average (lbs. milk per cow per year)	17,192	16,685	+1,470	+1,880	9.3	12.7
Total Milk Production (millions of pounds)	157,441	22,842	+6,805	–2	4.5	0.0

Source: Milk Cows and Production: Final Estimates, 1994–1997, USDA/NASS Statistical Bulletin #952, 1999; also published figures for 1998 from http://usda.mannlib.cornell.edu/reports/nassr/dairy/pmp-bb/.

volatility. In Wisconsin, where the largest number of U.S. dairy operations are located, herds were lost at a slightly lower rate than the national average, but dairy cow numbers dropped almost three times as fast, by over 11% in 5 years. Because productivity per cow increased more rapidly in Wisconsin than in the U.S. as a whole, the state's milk output remained virtually unchanged over this period.

Any discussion of the aggregate performance of the dairy farm sector in recent years must make mention of the tight profit margins and increasingly volatile milk prices that have come to characterize the life of a dairy farmer. Indeed, farmers in Wisconsin and the U.S. received average annual real milk prices[3] in the late 1990s that were roughly 20% lower than in 1960, and about 40% lower than the peak price paid for milk in 1979. More recently, price swings have become extremely dramatic, with a 25-year high and low nominal milk price both recorded during 1999. Overall, low real prices (combined with higher real input costs) have reduced profit margins in dairying and generated pressure to milk more cows in order to maintain levels of income sufficient to support a family. More volatile prices cause monthly income to fluctuate widely, which can adversely affect the survival of cash-poor beginning farmers and others with high relative fixed costs and little income from off-farm sources.

Changes in the structure and performance of the aggregate dairy sector are also related to broader regional shifts in the geographic location of dairy farming in the United States (Jesse, 1995). Table 2 summarizes the relative importance (in herd numbers, cow numbers, and milk output) of the major dairying regions of the United States. It is apparent that the Western and Southern 'industrial' dairy states (listed in the table) have rapidly increased their share of U.S. milk production since 1950, and now produce over a third of U.S. milk with less than 10% of the dairy farms. Herds in these states are typically 4 to 5 times larger than average herds in other regions and tend to have noticeably higher levels of productivity per cow. The rise of this industrial dairy region has come while dairies in the Corn Belt and Mid-South regions saw significant declines in herd numbers and milk output.

It is worth noting that while the Northern Tier states in the traditional dairy belt have lost market share since their peak in 1980, in 1997 they still had over half of U.S. dairy farms and produced almost 40% of the nation's milk. As we will argue below, the dynamics of dairy farm structural change in Wisconsin – while not particularly indicative of trends in the industrial dairy states – is representative of how dairy farming is changing in the rest of the important U.S. dairy farm regions, and can provide critical insights into the pace and direction of future changes in the U.S. sector overall.

Table 2. U.S. Dairy Sector Characteristics and Changes by Region.

| | % of U.S. Total | | | | | 1997 Avg. | |
| | Total Milk Production | | | Dairy Farms | Milk Cows | Herd Size | Herd Avg. |
Region	1950	1980	1997	1997	1997	(cows)	(lbs/cow)
Northern Tier States[1]							
(Traditional Dairy Belt)	38.4	45.6	39.6	50.1	40.6	61	16,448
Wisconsin	*12.7*	*17.4*	*14.3*	*20.2*	*15.1*	*56*	*16,057*
Western/Southern States[2]							
(Industrial Dairy Belt)	12.6	21.0	35.0	9.5	31.1	246	19,008
California	*5.1*	*10.6*	*17.7*	*2.3*	*15.0*	*497*	*20,197*
Corn Belt States[3]	21.0	12.5	9.5	16.8	10.2	46	15,694
Mid-South States[4]	5.8	5.0	3.4	6.1	4.2	51	13,684
ALL OTHER STATES	22.2	15.9	12.5	11.9	14.5	59	15,161
U.S. TOTAL	100.0	100.0	100.0	100.0	100.0	85	16,451

Source: Milk Cows and Production: Final Estimates, 1994–1997, USDA/NASS Statistical Bulletin #952, 1999.
Notes: [1] Wisconsin, New York, Pennsylvania, Minnesota, Michigan, Vermont. [2] California, Texas, Washington, Idaho, New Mexico, Florida, Arizona, Oregon. [3] Ohio, Iowa, Missouri, Illinois, and Indiana. [4] Kentucky, Virginia, and Tennessee.

Changing Size Structure

The overall shift towards larger dairies in the U.S. and industrial dairy states, is viewed by some as evidence that the traditional family-scale dairy farm is an anachronism. While the total number of U.S. dairy operations fell by almost 41,000 between 1993 and 1998, the rate of net decline was significantly higher among smaller dairy operations (Table 1). Farms with less than 30 dairy cows lost almost 40% of their numbers – or almost 23,000 farms – over the last 5 years, while net losses of farms with 30–49 and 50–99 cows were somewhat slower. The largest farms (those with over 200 cows) actually increased in number.

In Wisconsin, the rates of net decline were generally under the national average for farms with less than 100 milk cows, but higher than average among those with between 100–199 cows. Almost 5,000 of the net decline of 7,000 dairy farms in Wisconsin occurred among dairies with under 50 cows. At the other end of the spectrum, Wisconsin saw its number of farms with over 200 cows nearly double. Of course, Wisconsin's rapid rate of increase in this category is partly a reflection of the relatively low numbers of firms it had in this size class in 1993 (relative to the overall size of its dairy sector), and the fact that many 100–199 cow operations increased their herd sizes across the 200-cow threshold during this period.

The effect of these different rates of decline has been to produce an increasingly concentrated dairy farm sector in the U.S. and Wisconsin. As noted in Table 3, U.S. dairy herds with under 50 cows still dominate (in terms of a share of operations), but they declined from 59.5% of all dairy farms in 1993 to 52.3% in 1998. While numerous, their share of U.S. milk output declined to less than 10% of the total. Since their numbers decreased less than the overall average, the mid-sized U.S. dairy herds (with between 50–99 milk cows) actually increased as a share of all operations (from 26.8 to 29.4%), but their share of total milk production fell slightly. Meanwhile, the largest dairy

Table 3. Size Structure of Wisconsin and United States Dairy Farm Sector, 1998.

	United States	Wisconsin
	(percent)	
Dairy Farms by Herd Size Class		
Under 30 cows	30.7	18.7
30–49 cows	21.6	31.7
50–99 cows	29.4	38.7
100–199 cows	11.8	8.5
200–499 cows	4.4	2.1
500 cows or more	2.1	0.3
Total	*100.0*	*100.0*
Milk Produced by Herd Size Class		
Under 30 cows	2.1	3.1
30–49 cows	7.1	21.0
50–99 cows	24.0	41.0
100–199 cows	20.0	21.0
200–499 cows	16.8	10.0
500 cows or more	30.0	3.9
Total	*100.0*	*100.0*

Source: Milk Cows and Production Reports:
http://usda.mannlib.cornell.edu/reports/nassr/dairy/pmp-bb/
Note: See Table 1 for total farms and total production figures.

farms in the U.S. (those with over 100 cows), increased as a percentage of all operations, and their share of milk output rose considerably. The role of the roughly 2,500 very large U.S. dairies (with over 500 cows) is particularly noteworthy, since they accounted for just over 2% of the farms but produced 30% of all milk in 1998. When you include farms with between 200–499 cows, the largest 7,500 dairies now produce almost half of all the milk in the United States.

When compared to the U.S. totals (Table 3), Wisconsin has proportionately fewer very small (under 30 cow) and very large (over 200 cow) dairy operations. Currently, farms milking between 30 and 99 cows represent roughly 70% of all Wisconsin dairy operations. What is surprising to many observers is that this same group currently owns almost two-thirds of all the milk cows and produces 62% of the milk in the state. Relatively large farms (those with over 200 cows) represented just 2% of the herds in 1998, but – due to their larger scale – produced 14% of the state's milk. Very large, industrial-scale operations are even less common. For example, out of the more than 21,000 Wisconsin dairy farms in 1999, fewer than fifty were large enough to require manure storage permits from the state's Department of Natural Resources (permits are required on farms with more than 1,000 'animal units', which corresponds to roughly 700 milk cows).

Clearly, despite rapid changes in dairy farm structure in the 1990s, the medium-sized family-labor dairy farm using traditional production technologies remains the backbone of the Wisconsin dairy sector (as well as in most of dairy states outside of the industrial dairy regions in the west and south). Why this is the case is addressed later in this chapter. First, we turn to a more detailed consideration of the dynamics of structural change; the patterns of dairy herd expansion, entry, and exit

DYNAMICS OF STRUCTURAL CHANGE

Aggregate changes in the dairy sector reflect the combined impact of three very distinct processes. First, they mirror any changes in the way *existing* dairy farms are organized and operated, particularly efforts to expand the size of dairy herds. Second, they are influenced over time by the characteristics of new dairies started or taken over by the next generation of *entering farmers*. If, for example, new dairies tend to be larger than average, then adding them to the sector will produce an increase in the average farm size overall. Finally, the aggregate changes in farm structure are also influenced by the decisions of individual farm operators to *exit* dairy farming. For example, if farms that are ceasing to milk cows tend to have smaller herds, then their exit from the sector will *ceteris paribus* create an increase in the average size of the remaining farms.

Dynamics of Dairy Herd Expansion

Perhaps the most important type of structural change made by dairy farm operators is the decision to expand the size of their herd.[4] Though expansion is often discussed as a relatively contemporary phenomenon, Fig. 1 shows that dairy herds have been steadily growing larger in Wisconsin and the U.S. since 1950. In fact, the typical Wisconsin dairy herd has quadrupled in size over the last forty years – from fifteen cows in 1950 to almost sixty cows today. Average-sized U.S. dairy herds have increased from less than 10 cows to almost 80 cows per farm over the same period. When annualized rates of growth are considered, the average Wisconsin and U.S. herd size has been increasing by roughly 3 and 5% a year, respectively, in almost every period since the 1950s. Somewhat surprisingly (given the heightened attention to dairy herd expansion activity in the state and nation in recent years), by historical standards the 1990s have seen relatively slow annual rates of growth in the average size of U.S. and Wisconsin dairy herds, though Wisconsin's rate slowed more than the nation's as a whole.

In order to express the incidence of different types of herd expansion in Wisconsin, we surveyed over 1,000 Wisconsin dairy farm operators in 1997 and asked them how many cows were in their milking herd last year (in 1996), five years ago (in 1996), and how many they expected to be milking in 2001.[5] Our findings (Table 4) suggest that herd expansions were relatively common in the early 1990s, with almost 44% of Wisconsin dairy herds increasing their cow numbers by 5% or more. Looking forward, only a third of the dairy farms expected to stay at the same herd size for the next 5 years. Interestingly, almost a quarter of Wisconsin dairy farm operators were planning to exit or milk fewer cows by the year 2001. While rate of herd growth is the most common measure of expansion, we also observe (Table 4) how many cows were added to a herd. Relatively few Wisconsin dairy farmers added significant numbers of cows to their herds in the early 1990s (only 3% added 50 or more cows, and less than 20% added more than 10 cows). This suggests that many of the relatively rapid herd expansions (in percentage terms) actually involved growth from relatively small herd sizes to more medium-sized operations (rather than growth from a medium-sized to a much larger sized operation).

To further examine expansion trends from 1991–1996 we created a transition matrix (Table 5). Several interesting patterns are observed. First, the overall size distribution of this group of Wisconsin dairy farms changed relatively

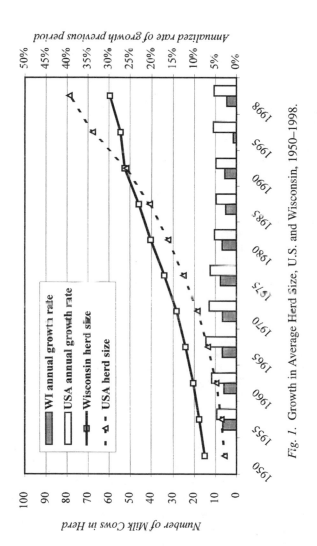

Fig. 1. Growth in Average Herd Size, U.S. and Wisconsin, 1950–1998.

Table 4. Past and future herd expansion activity, 1997 Wisconsin Dairy Poll respondents.

	Expansion Activity	
Type of Change in Herd Size	Actual[1] 1991 to 1996	Planned[2] 1997 to 2001
	(percent of respondents)	
Rate of herd size growth		
New Dairy (entered since 1991)	6.7	n.a.
Downsized (more than 5%)	12.8	5.5
Stable (+/–5%)	36.9	33.9
Slow Growth (5–25%)	25.6	16.5
Rapid Growth (25% or more)	18.0	22.4
Plans to Exit by 2001	*n.a.*	21.7
Total percent	*100.0*	*100.0*
(n)	*851*	*820*
Change in cow numbers		
New Dairy (entered since 1991)	6.7	n.a.
Downsized (by more than 10 cows)	3.4	1.7
Stable (+/–10 cows)	71.3	52.7
Slow Growth (+ 10–49 cows)	15.8	17.5
Rapid Growth (+ 50 or more cows)	2.7	6.4
Plans to Exit by 2001	*n.a.*	21.7
Total percent	*99.9*	100.0
(n)	*851*	*820*

Notes: [1] Respondents were asked how many cows they were milking in 1991. New entrants were prompted to write '0' for their 1991 herd size. [2] Respondents were asked how many cows they expected to be milking by 2001. People expecting to exit were prompted to write '0' for their expected 2001 herd size.

slowly in the first half of the 1990s.[6] More than two-thirds of all dairy farms were still in the same size 'category' in 1996 as in 1991 (denoted by the cells on the diagonal), and most of those that expanded increased by just 1 herd size category. Only 2.3% of all dairy operations increased by two or more herd size categories (most of whom were relatively small farms that expanded to between 100–199 cows in 1996.) There is some weak evidence that farms reaching the 200 cow threshold begin to enter a more aggressive pattern of further expansion. Survey respondents reported very similar types of expansion plans when asked how many cows they thought they would be milking by the year 2001.

Table 5. Estimated Number of Wisconsin Dairies in Each Herd Size Class in 1996, By Herd Size in 1991.

| | | Size of Dairy Herd in 1996 | | | | | | | |
		1 to 24 cows	25 to 49 cows	50 to 74 cows	75 to 99 cows	100 to 199 cows	200 to 499 cows	500 or more cows	1991 total
Size of Dairy Herd in 1991	Entered since 1991	264	821	498	59	29	0	0	1,671
	1 to 24 cows	1,173	528	59	0	0	0	0	1,759
	25 to 49 cows	381	7,534	2,052	88	0	0	0	10,055
	50 to 74 cows	0	616	5,306	938	410	29	0	7,299
	75 to 99 cows	0	0	176	1,466	674	0	0	2,316
	100 to 199 cows	29	0	29	147	1,143	264	0	1,612
	200 to 499 cows	0	0	0	0	0	264	29	293
	500 or more cows	0	0	0	0	0	0	29	29
	1996 total	1,847	9,498	8,120	2,697	2,251	557	59	25,034
	Percent of 1996 herds	7.4	37.9	32.4	10.8	9.0	2.2	0.2	100.0

While incremental expansions on medium-sized dairy farms are numerically the most common in Wisconsin, it is also worth noting how they contribute to dairy cow numbers (and milk output) levels in the state. We divided respondents into three major herd size categories: those with small (under 50 cows), medium (between 50–199 cows), and large herds (over 200 cows). An analysis of farms that increased their cow numbers between 1991 and 1996 suggests that incremental expansion on modest-scaled farms actually brought in two-thirds of the total number of new cows that were added to the Wisconsin dairy sector during this period. Just over half of the cows brought in via herd expansions were on farms that were entering or expanding into the medium-sized category (25% of the total) or were associated with expanding medium-sized farms that ended up with less than 200 cows by 1996 (29%). Another 17.4% of the cows brought in through expansion were introduced on smaller dairy farms that milked less than 50 cows in 1996. Growth among the larger operations was responsible for adding the remaining 33% of cows.

Dynamics of Entry

Net declines in dairy farm numbers (discussed above) are often misconstrued to be the number of dairy farms that have 'exited' or quit over a given period of time. But the net change is a balance or residual sum of subtracting exiters and adding back new or 'entering' farms. We know from various sources of information that there has been a dramatic reduction in the total number of new dairy entrants in Wisconsin and the U.S. over the last 15 years, and that this has accelerated the rate of net farm loss in the sector as a whole. Meanwhile, the increase in average dairy herd size, rising rates of adoption of new dairy technologies and management practices, and the belief that economies of scale are essential have led many industry observers to assume that any successful new dairy entrant in the 1990s would have to start with modern facilities and large herds. Presumably, fewer prospective dairy farmers have the management ability and/or sufficient capital to farm in this modern, large-scale way, and thus some may have been discouraged from pursuing a dairy farm career. Also, America's relatively robust non-farm economy has provided the already declining number of farm children with strong non-farm employment opportunities during the last decade.

There has been relatively little study of the characteristics of recent dairy farm entrants in Wisconsin or elsewhere in the United States (Jackson-Smith, 1994; Buttel et al., 1999). In a 1996 study of dairy farm entrants in Wisconsin, we defined an entrant as *someone who owns some or all of the dairy herd on the farm and began making major management decisions on this operation in the previous three years.*[7] Among the 321 respondents who met this definition, most entrants were found to have started new dairies, while a significant minority were junior operators on a parent's or some other farmer's operation. Land ownership per se was not a criteria for being considered a new dairy farmer, and almost 40% of our dairy entrant sample actually rented in all of their farmland (Buttel et al., 1999).

The characteristics of Wisconsin's recent dairy farm entrants and their operations are presented in Table 6 (and are compared to a statewide sample of all dairy farms taken the following spring). The results do not provide evidence that a rapid transformation of Wisconsin's dairy farm sector is underway. Indeed, if anything, entrants continue to begin in the old-fashioned way, with operations that are somewhat smaller than the state average and with technologies that are standard on most medium-sized farms. Despite the fact that most grew up on dairy farms, surprisingly few have taken over their parents family farm, and most rely heavily on off-farm employment to make ends meet. While many entrants express the intention to expand their operations, most appear likely to do it gradually.

Compared to other Wisconsin dairy farmers, recent entrants tend to pursue production strategies that minimize fixed investments in land and equipment and use fewer of the 'production-maximizing' technologies. Many have

Table 6. Characteristics of Entrants to Dairy Farming in Wisconsin, 1993–1996, Based on 1996 Wisconsin Survey of New Dairy Farm Entrants.

Characteristic	Dairy Farm Entrants (1996)	All Dairy Farms[1] (1997)
Number of respondents	321	1,019
Average age principal operator (years)	34.3	46.9
Average size milking herd (includes dry cows)	43.9	65.9
Farms by herd size (%)		
0 to 24 cows	25.9	7.7
25 to 49 cows	39.4	36.8
50 to 74 cows	27.2	31.5
75 to 99 cows	4.7	11.0
100 or more cows	2.8	12.9
Total	100.0	99.9
Tenure and labor force (%)		
Operator owns some farmland	60.4	95.1
Operator rents some farmland	57.6	69.1
Employs regular, nonfamily workers	18.4	36.8
Management practices (%)		
Production records kept on individual cows	54.4	66.9
rBST use	5.4	11.8
TMR machinery	16.2	23.0
Parlor milking facility	4.4	9.4
Rotational grazing[2]	29.6	14.8
Family Background (%)		
Operator or spouse farm reared	88.2	99.1
Inherited or purchased farm from relative	18.4	61.0
Off farm work (%)		
Operator works off-farm	33.8	15.4
Spouse works off-farm	40.1	35.4
Either or both works off-farm	55.5	41.0
Source of most household income (%)		
All from farming	34.4	54.1
Most from farming	17.8	38.3
Most from off-farm	47.9	7.6
Total	100.1	100.0

Notes: [1] = Random sample of all Wisconsin dairy operations conducted by PATS in spring, 1997.
[2] = Relied on pastures to feed milking cows and moved cows as least once/week to fresh pastures.

followed a 'herd-first' acquisition strategy, renting land and building their herd to a scale that fits their goals and their capital and labor resources prior to buying land and major equipment. Almost a third of recent entrants used management intensive rotational grazing, a management practice that requires relatively little investment in facilities or equipment, but rewards specialized management skills and cost-minimizing strategies.

The fact that entrants are, on average, in their mid-30s also suggests that the medium-sized and low fixed investment character of their operations reflect what is or has become possible for most entrants, which is to start modestly and go forward from there. This inference is also supported by the responses of entrants when asked to identify the main obstacles they encountered when entering dairy. The most frequent response, reported by 56% as a serious obstacle, was maintaining an adequate cash flow; 32% said it was acquiring equity. About 20% reported that "evaluating the risks and returns involved in dairying" and "getting loans once I had some equity" were key obstacles. Thus, among a long list of potential obstacles, financial constraints are considered the most serious by new entrants. By contrast, relatively few entrants (under 10%) regarded arrangements with parents, herd management skills, or setting up the business organization as serious obstacles to entry.

Overall, recent entrants do not appear to be a source of rapid structural change in Wisconsin. Small- and medium-sized operations predominate among new dairy operations, and careful study has unearthed relatively few 'new' dairy farms in the state that started out at a relatively large scale (i.e. greater than 200 milk cows). This is not to suggest that new entrants will remain small forever. Rather their experiences and strategies demonstrate how dairy farming in Wisconsin continues to be dominated by family initiatives, built off of low initial levels of equity and lots of hard work, where some farm families may eventually grow their operations into larger ones.

Dynamics of Exit

Patterns of exit from Wisconsin's dairy sector provide additional insights into the forces of farm structural change in the 1990s. Studies of Wisconsin dairy farms over time (Cross, 1994; Jackson-Smith, 1995; Jackson-Smith et al., 1999) suggest that gross exit rates often exceed 7 to 10% per year, and there are usually considerably more farms closing their doors than new operations entering across the state (hence the longstanding decline in farm numbers noted above). Many of those who quit dairying remain in agriculture, however, often raising beef cattle, dairy heifers, or crops. Others either look for work outside of the farm sector, or begin their retirement.

It is widely assumed that farmers who have decided to quit dairy farming are largely doing so because they are no longer able to compete economically. Similarly, higher rates of farm loss among smaller dairy operations are also taken as evidence to support the importance of economies of scale favoring farms at the larger end of the size spectrum. Yet, while closing a dairy farm may often be an emotionally painful and difficult process for farm families, many farm families quit not so much because they cannot survive economically, but rather because age, health, or the lack of a successor make it difficult for them to make the financial and labor investments necessary to keep the operation. Also, as Bentley & Saupe (1990) show, some farmers quit when better opportunities arise outside of dairy farming. Since a farm's structural characteristics may be associated with the farmer's age (older farmers who are nearing retirement tend to operate smaller herds with less debt and lower levels of investment in new facilities), it is possible to confuse the effects of normal lifecourse events (like retirement or better opportunities) with an underlying process of structural transformation based on the economic competitiveness of the farms (Jackson-Smith, 1995).

In order to characterize the farms that had closed out their dairy operations recently, we tracked the fate of roughly 300 dairy farmers between 1995 and 1997. We found that smaller dairies were indeed much more likely to exit than larger dairies (Table 7). Operations with under 40 cows in 1995 contributed more than half of the total exits over the two-year study period. At the same time, exit rates were much lower among farms with more than 100 cows. The strong association between herd size and exit rates underscores a point raised earlier that exits can be a primary basis for dynamic changes in the size structure of the dairy sector. However, inferring that scale of operation is the main determinant of exit can be potentially problematic. As Table 7 shows, there are many other characteristics of farms, farm operators, and farm households that might be influencing exit outcomes.

The most important factors associated with the closing out of dairies is the age of operator (Table 7). Relatively young operators were also somewhat more likely to exit, perhaps because they have higher levels of debt, less experience, fewer fixed investments, and more non-farm job opportunities than well established dairy farmers. Farm operators entering their mid-career phase (40–55 years old) were the least likely to exit. Meanwhile, those in the later stages of their careers (over 55) were by far the most likely to exit, underscoring the importance of normal lifecourse events (retirement, health problems, and transition of a farm to a new generation) in determining the fate of a farm operation.

Table 7. Rate of Exit from Dairy Farming, 1995–1997, by Various Farm and Household Characteristics, Wisconsin Longitudinal Dairy Farm Study.

	% of all farms in longitudinal panel sample	% exiting between 1995–1997
ALL HERDS	100.0	16.1
Herd Size (1995)		
Under 20 cows	5.4	25.0
20–39 cows	32.0	21.2
40–59 cows	34.7	14.0
60–79 cows	13.2	14.7
80–99 cows	7.8	12.5
100 or more cows	7.0	2.8
All Farms	100.0	16.1
Operator Age (1995)		
Under 35	13.9	11.3
35–39	13.1	14.9
40–44	20.9	15.0
45–49	12.3	12.7
50–54	11.9	8.2
55–59	11.4	19.0
60–64	9.6	32.7
65 +	6.8	25.7
All Farms	100.0	16.1
Debt-to-Asset Ratio		
No farm debt	20.5	21.0
Debts <= 10% assets	11.5	11.9
Debts = 11–39% assets	26.5	12.5
Debts = 40–59% assets	25.3	13.8
Debts = 60% assets or more	16.2	22.9
All Farms	100.0	16.1
Household Income Total		
Less than $10,000	16.5	18.1
$10,000-$19,999	25.2	15.7
$20,000-$34,999	27.0	11.8
$35,000-$49,999	16.1	14.8
$50,000-$74,999	7.9	17.5
$75,000 or more	7.3	29.7
All Farms	100.0	16.1
Household Labor Force Status		
No off-farm employment	59.9	14.9
Operator has off-farm job	6.3	18.2
Spouse has off-farm job	28.2	15.8
Both work off-farm	5.6	33.3
All Farms	100.0	16.1

Note: Based on panel of 294 dairy farms responding to surveys in both 1995 and 1997.

We also found interesting non-linear associations between exit rates and indicators of debt leverage, household income and participation in off-farm work. While it is not too surprising that those who are highly leveraged are more likely to fail, the increased rate of exit among those with no debt likely reflects the typically debt-free status of late-career farmers preparing to retire. Participation of operators or their spouses in off-farm work seems to increase the chances that a farm operation will quit dairying. Where households have very low income and no off-farm job, it is likely that the lack of sufficient farm income (and the absence of outside sources of income that can pay for living expenses) make farms particularly vulnerable. Alternatively, while a farm household member's off-farm employment may provide income and benefits that can enhance the farm's viability, it also links the household to opportunities in the community and can facilitate the process of closing down the dairy operation.

Overall, our exit data strongly suggest that much of the decline in smaller-size farms (more than 40%) can be viewed as part of a lifecycle process that involves retiring farmers who may have wound down their operations over time. Another group of small and mid-sized exiting dairies represent younger farmers who face significant challenges in their first few years of operation. What is not clear from these results is the degree to which these farmers were 'pushed' out by lack of competitiveness or 'pulled' out by alternative opportunities, especially during this past decade when labor markets in Wisconsin were very tight (i.e. rising wages, low unemployment). Smaller-scale operators may have found it easier to exit, both because they had not sunk as much investment into their farms and because they may have already had a solid footing in off-farm labor markets. Put differently, operators of smaller farms may be more likely to exit (and those with larger herds may be less likely to exit) for reasons other than economic competitiveness.

Balancing Entry and Exit Trends

Since entrants do not seem to represent a 'new breed' of dairy farmers in Wisconsin, and because most continuing farmers engage in relatively modest types of expansion, it is worth asking why the size structure of the dairy sector is changing so rapidly. A key lies in how the balance of entry and exit trends over time can produce notable impacts on the overall structural characteristics of the aggregate dairy farm sector. Specifically, several studies in Wisconsin suggest that dairy farm entry rates are at historic lows while exit rates persist at relatively high levels. We used Census of Agriculture data to estimate the annual number of new dairy farmers who entered the sector, the number of dairy operations that closed, and the resulting net change in dairy farm numbers over the last 20 years (see Gale, 1994 for details on the methodology employed).

Figure 2 notes that the annual number of dairy farm exits in Wisconsin has held relatively steady – at between 1,800 and 2,000 a year – throughout the 1980s and 1990s. However, the number of new dairy operations fell dramatically from nearly 1,400 annually in the early 1980s to less than 350 annually between 1992 and 1997. The associated rapid increase in net dairy farm losses in the mid-1980s and 1990s is primarily the result of significantly fewer young people entering dairy, and not – contrary to most popular accounts – a product of more farm closings. (Of course, since the base of dairy farms is declining, the actual exit *rate* increases throughout the period).

Given that both exiters and entrants tend to operate smaller than average dairy farms, and that exiters now vastly outnumber new entrants, sheer demographic momentum – and not so much dramatic expansion activity among surviving farms – has produced much of the apparent growth in average herd size that we noted earlier. Put differently, a considerable proportion of structural change at the aggregate population level (in Wisconsin and in the United States) is the direct result of a growing imbalance between entry and exit rates, combined with the typical characteristics of the entrants and exiters.

COMPETITIVENESS OF MEDIUM-SIZED DAIRY FARMS

While medium-sized dairies remain important to the Wisconsin dairy sector, their position is definitely slipping relative to larger dairy operations. For most industry observers, higher rates of exit among small and medium-sized dairies are usually attributed to a lack of economic competitiveness, linked to an inability to capitalize on economies of size. In this section, we examine some of the theoretical and empirical evidence for how economic competitiveness is related to the patterns of structural change noted above.

There are a number of reasons why larger herd size may increase the economic performance of a dairy farm. First, volume premiums paid to large milk producers and volume discounts for large purchases of certain inputs are a likely source of size economies. So are the potential labor savings associated with the efficiencies of milking herds in parlors rather than in stanchions (Jones, 1999). In addition, larger operations may also be able to exploit modern milking facilities more efficiently by spreading the fixed costs of purchasing equipment or obtaining management information over a larger number of cows.

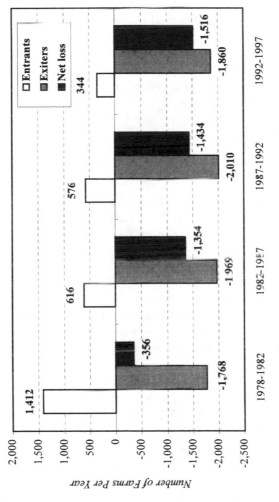

Fig. 2. Estimated Number of Wisconsin Dairy Farm Entrants and Exiters, and Net Change in Dairy Farm Numbers per Year, 1978–1997.

Specialization in labor tasks on larger farms can also produce potential unit cost savings, though labor specialization strategies can occur on medium-sized operations as well.[8]

Many observers forget that larger size operations may also face serious diseconomies, especially in a management-sensitive activity like milking cows. For example, herd health, breeding, and nutritional management are critical to productivity and economic outcomes on dairy farms. Palmer et al. (2000) found evidence that Wisconsin dairy farms that had recently undergone major increases in herd size had reduced productivity per cow and were more likely to have higher cull rates or extended open periods where cows are not producing milk. In addition to increased management demands on operators of large farms, these operations are also more likely to rely on hired labor whose effort and capacities may not be comparable to an owner-operator for both incentive and experience reasons.

Recent empirical studies of Wisconsin dairy farms support the contention that size economies are either not present or if present are relatively small in Wisconsin's dairy sector. In a study of over 900 Wisconsin dairy farms, Frank & Vanderlin (1999) found that average total allocated costs per hundredweight of milk were actually about 10% lower on the 51 to 75 and 76–100 cow herds than on operations of over 250 cow herds. Similar results were found five years earlier by Trachter & Splett (1994) and in recent case studies of 38 Farm Credit Services loan recipients in the Upper Midwest (Krutza, 1999). Recent data from Pennsylvania are consistent with these findings (Hoards Dairyman, 2000). Certainly, evidence from the actual farmer experiences suggest that the size economies in dairying are much less than suggested by engineering studies of new facilities that tend to assume away associated labor and management problems (Kriegl, 1998).

Perhaps just as importantly however, Jones (1999) shows that gains in herd productivity may be more important than increasing herd size in improving the competitiveness of dairy farms in Wisconsin. In other words, differences in management ability and sophistication among farms with similar herd sizes tend to be much more dramatic than cost-differences across dairy farms of different scales. Kriegl (2000) has also shown how low-cost strategies involving the use of management intensive grazing can provide comparable net financial returns to operators in Wisconsin.

Ultimately, the individual decisions that shape aggregate patterns of structural change – whether to exit dairying, expand the herd, or stay put – are usually made by households, not business managers or absentee investors (Gasson & Errington, 1993). As such, they are likely to rest on more than just the unit costs of milk production or the rate of return on assets and labor generated by their dairy operation. Does one of the family members have a good off-farm job that helps to achieve income goals and other benefits? How important are intangible benefits; autonomy, working outside and with animals, of a farm career? Does the family value the quality of life offered by rural living and having their children or grandchildren grow up on a farm? Do they anticipate passing the farm on to a child or another family member or friend? Conversely, do they see no future for the farm in their family? Or, are they tired of being tied to the farm and the relentless daily milking of cows?

Additionally, the fate of particular farm operations (of all sizes) will also be shaped by the market and institutional policy contexts in which they live and work. When comparing farm viability across regions, it is critical to take note of the federally mandated milk pricing system that pays producers in the Upper Midwest significantly lower prices than they would likely get in a more competitive free market pricing system (Cox et al., 1997). Regional labor markets also exert a strong influence over the viability of dairy farm operations, since tight overall labor markets and the absence of large pools of immigrant labor in the Upper Midwest make it expensive and often impossible to find adequate non-family laborers to work on larger dairy farms. Similarly, local and state environmental and land use policies can influence the competitiveness and viability of dairy farms differently based on where you live and the size of your dairy herd. Declining farm numbers in some places may fall below the critical mass required to support a good infrastructure of input suppliers, veterinarians, and processors that more densely populated dairy regions have. Finally, farmers living in states that invest in dairy-related university research, and that have county extension staff with expertise in dairy farming, may face different prospects than those who try to survive without the support of their public land grant institutions.

When considered next to these sorts of questions, the issue of survival of medium-sized family farms is more complex than one of looking at a single measure of economic competitiveness. In other words, there is no simple economic statistic, such as unit cost of production, that reveals the ideal farm size of the future or predicts patterns of structural change. Similarly, the relative rates of farm survival across regions (or across herds of different sizes in a single reason) are not easily interpreted as de facto evidence of superior economic competitiveness. While it is likely that on average Wisconsin dairy will continue to grow bigger (with the increased presence of some significantly larger farms), the evidence suggests there is plenty of room for medium-sized family operations to continue playing a major role.

DISCUSSION AND CONCLUSIONS

Our detailed exploration of the underlying dynamics of structural change among Wisconsin dairy farms leads us to conclude that the industry changed gradually in the 1990s and that the future of dairying in Wisconsin and many similar 'dairy belt' states will be one that is shaped by a number of factors. These include: (a) the continued presence of a large segment of medium-sized family-labor dairies, many of which will be expanding gradually and experimenting with new technologies and management practices that boost labor efficiency, milk output, household quality of life, and business profitability; (b) an increased number of relatively large dairy farms milking more than 200 cows in parlor/freestall facilities with significant hired nonfamily labor forces; and (c) significant growth in the number of dairy farms that seek to minimize unit costs by reducing labor and capital investments through the use of intensive grazing of improved pastures, purchased feeds, and low-cost milking and housing facilities (like New Zealand-style swing parlors, flat barn parlors, and greenhouses). In addition, Wisconsin is likely to continue to see its share of national milk production (and dairy farms) decline relative to the more 'industrial' dairy regions, but the state (and the other traditional dairy belt states) will remain a major force in the production of milk well into the future.

Our findings in Wisconsin suggest that the relatively simplistic view of structural change as an economically straightforward process of modernization and adjustment to new technical economies of scale is not very accurate. This may well challenge scholars who study structural change to revisit their assumptions about how and why farm structure changes in other regions. Though Wisconsin's situation may be rather unique, until careful empirical work is done in other states and regions, we will not know for certain whether the patterns we observed are or are not typical of the processes elsewhere in the country. The fact that Wisconsin's overall patterns of structural change are similar to national trends, and that research on the underlying microdynamics of change are similar to those observed in other places where detailed empirical data are available (e.g. in Canada, see Ehrensaft et al., 1984) provide ample reason to believe that similar results will be borne out elsewhere, particularly in other parts of the traditional dairy belt.

ACKNOWLEDGEMENTS

This research was supported in part by grants from the University of Wisconsin Agricultural and Natural Resources Consortium as well as the USDA Regional

Hatch Project NE177. The authors would like to acknowledge the contributions of several of our colleagues who assisted in the preparation of this paper. Marcia Ostrom and Fred Buttel helped design and implement the many studies that are summarized here and reviewed earlier drafts of this paper. Spencer Wood, Monica Nevius, Lucy Chen, Lisa Stefanik, Glenn Wavrunek, Roberta Anderson, Lisa Bargender and Eric Finnin all assisted in the collection and analysis of the survey data. We also greatly appreciate the patience and constructive criticism of the co-editors of this volume. Any errors and omissions are the full responsibility of the authors.

NOTES

1. These terms are used with specific definitions in mind. 'Medium-sized' refers to farms that can be operated with predominantly farm family labor. Because of technological changes, the scale of dairy operation that might be called 'medium-sized' has changed throughout the 20th century, though the concept remains relevant. 'Diversified' dairy farms are those which raise a significant portion of their livestock feed on farm. 'Family farms' are those where the ownership, labor, and management functions are all performed primarily or entirely by members of the farm operator's family. Overall, medium-sized family dairy farms are markedly different than the large herd, industrial-style dairy farms that are more typical of dairy states in the west and southwest. Industrial-style dairies refer to farms that use modern milking parlors and freestall confinement housing, often purchase the majority of their herd feed requirements, and rely principally on a hired non-family labor force. They also differ from, 'small' dairy farms that are not big enough to productively employ available household labor, and usually rely mainly on off-farm income to survive.

2. Most of the data used in this paper are drawn from ongoing research on dairy farm restructuring by staff of the Program on Agricultural Technology Studies at the University of Wisconsin-Madison.

3. Real milk prices were computed by dividing nominal all-milk prices by the published values for the U.S. Consumer Price Index.

4. We do not discuss herd contraction in much depth here, though many such adjustments are made. Usually, down-sizing is a step toward an eventual exit from the sector. However, some herd reductions are made in order to utilize labor and capital more efficiently, or to accommodate family quality of life or lifestyle concerns. We observed that expansions are more common than contractions among continuing operators.

5. The 1997 Wisconsin Dairy Farm Poll was sent to a random sample of Wisconsin dairy farm operations (obtained from dairy producer list maintained by the state Department of Agriculture, Trade, and Consumer Protection). Of the 2,098 surveys initially mailed out, 116 producers reported having quit dairying, and 1019 useable surveys were returned (producing a response rate of 51.2%). The characteristics of the responding dairies were compared to state estimates of the underlying size distribution of herds, and we determined that the sample was quite representative of the overall population though we had a very slight oversampling of larger dairy farms, and undersampling of the very smallest dairy farms.

6. It is important to recognize that the 1991 data do not include any of the operations that exited or quit dairy farming before 1997. Hence, the actual 1991 size distribution would likely include more small- and mid-sized dairies.

7. Using our specific definition of an entrant, we compared state lists of dairy farms from the spring of 1994 and the fall of 1995 to identify all new dairy farms that had begun operation over this period. Mail surveys were sent to all farms where new names appeared on the 1995 list that were not present in 1994. As reported in Buttel et al. (1999), we had about a 45% response rate, and received 320 completed and useable surveys from recent entrants who fit our definition.

8. Examples include management-intensive rotational grazing, whereby the producer can concentrate on managing pasture and herd performance, especially if grain is purchased rather than cultivated (Jackson-Smith et al., 1996). Similarly, some operators are going to a strategy of buying all of their feed and just concentrating on milking cows.

REFERENCES

Agriview (1999). Direction, not size, is key to dairy success. September 30, Pg. B–3.

Boehlje, M. (1997). *Industrialization of agriculture: Implications for the dairy industry.* Paper presented at the Mid-Atlantic Dairy Management Conference, Hershey, PA., February 28–March 1.

Bentley, S., & Saupe, W. (1990). *Exits From Farming in Southwestern Wisconsin, 1982–1986.* Agricultural Economics Report No. 631. Washington, DC: Economic Research Service, U.S. Department of Agriculture.

Buttel, F. H., & LaRamee, P. (1991). The 'Disappearing Middle': A Sociological Perspective. In: W. H. Friedland, L. Busch, F. H. Buttel & A. P. Rudy (Eds), *Towards a New Political Economy of Agriculture* (pp. 151–169). Boulder, CO: Westview Press.

Buttel, F. H., & Jackson-Smith, D. (1997). *Livestock Expansion in Wisconsin: Farmers' Views on the Benefits and Costs of Large-Scale Livestock Production.* PATS Research Paper No. 2. Madison: Program on Agricultural Technology Studies, University of Wisconsin.

Buttel, F. H., Jackson-Smith, D. B., Barham, B., Mullarkey, D., & Chen, L. (1999). *Entry into Wisconsin Dairying: Patterns, Processes, and Policy Implications.* PATS Research Report No. 4. Madison: Program on Agricultural Technology Studies, University of Wisconsin.

Cox, T. L., Chavas, J.-P., & Jesse, E. V. (1997). *Regional Impacts of Reducing Dairy Price Supports and Removing Milk Marketing Orders in the U.S. Dairy Sector.* Department Staff Paper No. 377. Madison: Department of Agricultural and Applied Economics, University of Wisconsin.

Cross, J. A. (1994). *Entry-Exit Behavior of Wisconsin Dairy Farmers.* ATFFI Research Paper No. 6. Madison: Agricultural Technology and Family Farm Institute, University of Wisconsin.

Ehrensaft, P., LaRamee, P., Bollman, R. D., & Buttel., F. H. (1984). The microdynamics of farm structural change in North America: The Canadian Experience and Canada-USA comparisons. *American Journal of Agricultural Economics, 66* (December), 823–828.

Frank, G., & Vanderlin, J. (1999). *Milk Production Costs in 1998 on Selected Wisconsin Dairy Farms.* Staff Paper. Madison: Center for Dairy Profitability, University of Wisconsin.

Gale, F. H. (1994). *The New Generation of American Farmers: Farm entry and exit prospects for the 1990s.* Agricultural Economic Report No. 695. Washington, DC: Economic Research Service, U.S. Department of Agriculture.

Gasson, R., & Errington, A. (1993). *The Farm Family Business*. Wallingford, UK: Centre for Agriculture and Biosciences International.

Gilbert, J., & Akor, R. (1986). Increasing structural divergence in U.S. dairying: California and Wisconsin since 1950. *Rural Sociology, 53* (Spring), 56–72.

Hoards Dairyman (2000). *News in Brief*. January 25, pg. 43.

Jackson-Smith, D. B. (1994). *Getting in While the Going's Tough: Entry into the Wisconsin Farm Sector*. ATFFI Technical Report No. 1. Madison: Agricultural Technology and Family Farm Institute, University of Wisconsin.

Jackson-Smith, D. B. (1995). *Understanding the Microdynamics of Farm Structural Change: Entry, Exit, and Adaptations among Wisconsin Family Farmers*. Unpublished dissertation. Madison: University of Wisconsin.

Jackson-Smith, D. B., Barham, B., Nevius, M., & Klemme, R. (1996). *Grazing in Dairyland: The Use and Performance of Management Intensive Rotational Grazing among Wisconsin Dairy Farms*. ATFFI Technical Report No. 5. Madison: Agricultural Technology and Family Farm Institute, University of Wisconsin.

Jackson-Smith, D. B., Chen, L., Nevius, M., & Anderson, R. (1999). *Results of Wisconsin Longitudinal Dairy Farm Study*. Unpublished manuscript. Madison: Program on Agricultural Technology Studies, University of Wisconsin.

Jesse, E. V. (1995). *Factors affecting the competitive environment of the Upper Midwest*. In: Proceedings: Four-State Dairy Expansion Conference. Rochester, MN and Stevens Point, WI, November 7–8.

Jones, B. L. (1999). *Growth in Dairy Farms: The Consequences of Taking Big Steps or Small Ones When Expanding*. Staff Paper. Madison: Center for Dairy Profitability, University of Wisconsin.

Kriegl, T. (1998). *To Expand or Not Expand – Which Strategy Pays?* Staff Paper. Madison: Center for Dairy Profitability, University of Wisconsin.

Kriegl, T. (2000). *Wisconsin Grazing Dairy Profitability Analysis: Preliminary Fourth Year Summary*. Paper presented at Wisconsin Grazing Conference, Wausau, Wisconsin. Madison: University of Wisconsin, Center for Dairy Profitability.

Krutza, M. (1999). *Knowing Business Factors is Key to Modernization*. FCS Report. Wausau: Farm Credit Services of North Central Wisconsin.

Lyson, T. A., & Geisler, C. C. (1992). Toward a second agricultural divide: the restructuring of American agriculture. *Sociologia Ruralis, 32*, 248–263.

Palmer, R., Bewley, J., Jackson-Smith, D., & Hemken, D. (2000). *Dairy farm modernization in Wisconsin*. Paper submitted for annual meetings of American Dairy Science Association.

Perez, A. M. (1994). *Changing Structure of U.S. Dairy Farms*. AER No. 690. Washington, DC: Economic Research Service, U.S. Department of Agriculture.

Strange, M. (1988). *Family Farming*. Lincoln: University of Nebraska Press.

Trechter, D., & Splett, N. (1994). *Factors Associated with Superior Performance Among Dairy Farms*. Agribusiness Research Working Paper. River Falls, WI:Rural Development Institute, University of Wisconsin.

CALIFORNIA DAIRY PRODUCTION: UNIQUE POLICIES AND NATURAL ADVANTAGES

L. J. (Bees) Butler and Christopher A. Wolf

INTRODUCTION

In 1970, California dairy farms produced 8% of the milk in the United States. This represented just over one-half the milk production of Wisconsin dairy farms and ranked California fourth among all U.S. states. But, by 1993, California had passed Wisconsin and is today the largest milk producer with almost 20% of the U.S. total. An increase of this magnitude – 18 billion pounds greater in 1998 than 1970 – begs for an explanation. We believe that this enormous production spurt, and the accompanying development of a large-scale, intensive dairy industry in California, can be attributed to a unique combination of many factors, chief among which are the burgeoning population, rapid rise of incomes, and favorable climate and agro-environmental conditions.

Nevertheless, despite a general recognition of natural advantages for dairying, and the accelerating demand for milk, the unusual vigor of its dairy industry has focused considerable attention on the unique dairy policies in California. California is the only major milk producing state outside the U.S. Federal Milk Marketing Order system. Instead of participating in the federal orders, California administers its own milk pricing and pooling rules. And, the California state order includes a quota that many dairy industry leaders in other

Research in Rural Sociology, Volume 8, pages 141–161.
2000 by Elsevier Science Inc.
ISBN: 0-7623-0474-X

states believe is responsible for increasing – artificially and unfairly – the milk prices to California producers.

Thus, our primary aim in this chapter is to explain how several of these controversial California dairy policies came into being, why they were formulated, how they work, and their effect on milk production. To what extent have these polices favored the rapid expansion of the California dairy industry? We then overview some of the advantages that California enjoys relative to other states – geographical, socio-demographic, economic, and historical. Can the California rise to the forefront of U.S. milk production be attributed to such advantages?

Misconceptions About California Dairy Policies

Misconceptions about the impact of marketing policy differences have provoked harsh words about the California dairy industry in national policy debates. Low milk prices often lead dairy industry leaders in other states to point at California as the over-production culprit (Dairy Profit Weekly, 1999). This notion of an unfair California dairy advantage has also been evident in national policy discussions. At a Congressional hearing in 1987, legislators from the Northeast and Upper Midwest were 'shocked and dismayed' that California would continue its growth in milk production despite an attempt to decrease U.S. milk production by 12 billion pounds through the Dairy Herd Buyout Program (U.S. Congress, 1987). In 1988, a series of Congressional hearings addressed the issue of regionalism in the U.S. dairy industry. A presumed unfair advantage for California was discussed. As one witness put it,

> ... there remains a sizeable number of dairymen who view the real and perceived advantages of West Coast dairymen as unfair and discriminatory. To many Upper Midwest producers, California issues are being used as excuses preventing necessary change to become competitive in today's dairy world ... Irrespective of the reasons, management of the California state order system is viewed as inequitable (Professor Larry Hamm, Michigan State University in U.S. Congress, 1988).

Another prominent expert witness testified,

> ... California has been pointed to as the guilty party for problems with the price support program ... California's quota plan has been charged with distorting price signals and encouraging expansion. Those who make such accusations don't understand how the plan works ... California's economic formula has been criticized for cushioning market shocks. Perhaps rather than finger pointing, it should be recognized that the pricing formula is probably more in keeping with the goals of the price support system ... than is the current [FMMO] system (Professor Harold Harris, Clemson University in U.S. Congress, 1988).

During debates on the 1990 Farm Bill, some congressional legislators looked for ways to force California into the federal milk marketing orders. The general perception was that California had an unfair advantage in milk production and the marketing of dairy products, and, as a result, the 1990 Farm Bill contained a clause known as Section 102. Using this clause, Congress attempted to force California to reduce butter, powder, and cheese 'make allowances' that processors receive to partially cover the costs of processing surplus milk into storable products. Make allowances are processing margins built into minimum prices. This was a divisive strategy because California 'make allowances' are directly connected to prices that the producer receives. As the make allowance declines, producer milk prices in California increase. Congressional legislators no doubt thought that California producers would support such a policy because it would mean that they received higher prices for their milk. However, Section 102 was not implemented and died quietly in 1995 when it was clear that there was no basis for the congressional action. Ironically, the proposals for the reformed Federal milk marketing orders are so similar to the California milk marketing order that one can barely notice any differences. Even today, the dairy industry and the California Department of Food and Agriculture are staving off lawsuits brought by out-of-state processors challenging, among other things, the unique California fluid milk standards.

California and U.S. Milk Production Trends

To understand the basis for all the fuss about the burgeoning dairy industry in California in recent decades, consider some U.S. and California trends. From 1950 to 1998, in response to increases in both population and income, U.S. milk production increased by 35%. This was accompanied by a 58% decrease in the number of milk cows and a 223% increase in milk per cow (Table 1). Over the same period, California milk production increased by 361%, milk cow numbers increased by 82%, and milk per cow increased 152%.

Milk is produced and processed in every state, but more than half of the U.S. total, since 1980, comes from five states: California, Wisconsin, New York, Pennsylvania, and Minnesota (Table 2). Some comparisons of California and Wisconsin are useful because they are the top two milk producing states with similar U.S. market share but exhibit very different dairy farm industry structures. The common perception is that Wisconsin farms tend to be relatively small and vertically integrated while California farms are usually much larger and specialized.

Consolidation of milk production onto fewer, larger farms is occurring in every U.S. state and region and has resulted in an 89% decline in the number

Table 1.   Dairy Industry Changes, U.S. and California, 1950–1998

Year	Milk Cows (1,000 head)		Milk Per Cow (pounds)		Total Milk Production (million pounds)	
	U.S.	California	U.S.	California	U.S.	California
1950	21,944	777	5,314	7,710	116,602	5,991
1960	17,515	824	7,029	9,800	123,109	8,075
1970	12,000	755	9,751	12,384	117,007	9,350
1980	10,799	896	11,891	15,153	128,406	13,577
1985	10,981	1,041	13,024	16,102	143,012	16,672
1990	10,127	1,135	14,642	18,461	148,313	20,953
1995	9,458	1,254	16,433	20,211	155,425	25,344
1998	9,143	1,420	17,192	19,442	157,441	27,607
% change 1950–98	−58	+45	+223	+152	+35	+361

Source: U.S. figures from U.S. Department of Agriculture, National Agricultural Statistics
Service, 1951–1999. California figures from California Department of Food and Agriculture
California Dairy Information Bulletin and *California Dairy Industry Statistics,* 1951–1999.

of U.S. milk cow operations from 1965 to 1997 (Table 3). The number of dairy
farms decreased by 72% in Wisconsin and by 75% in California over that
period. More significant, the net loss of dairy farms in Wisconsin was over
seven times the number in California; huge numbers of small dairies in
Wisconsin were lost.

Table 2.   Percent of Total U.S. Milk Production, Top 5 States

	1950	1960	1970	1980	1990	1995	1998
State	(percent of U.S. milk production)						
Wisconsin	12.7	14.4	15.8	17.4	16.5	14.8	14.5
New York	7.6	8.3	8.8	8.5	7.5	7.5	7.5
Minnesota	6.9	8.3	8.2	7.4	6.8	6.1	5.9
California	5.1	6.5	8.1	10.6	14.1	16.3	17.5
Pennsylvania	4.8	5.6	6.1	6.6	6.7	6.8	6.9
Total 5 States	37.1	43.1	47.0	50.5	51.6	51.5	52.3

Source: U.S. Department of Agriculture, National Agricultural Statistics Service, 1951–1999.

Table 3. Number of Dairy Farms,* Top 5 Milk Producing States

State	1965	1970	1980	1985	1990	1995	1998	% change (1965–1998)
				(thousands)				
Wisconsin	86.0	64.0	45.0	41.0	33.0	28.0	23.0	–73
New York	39.0	28.0	19.0	16.5	13.0	10.0	8.7	–78
Minnesota	72.0	46.0	27.0	23.0	15.5	12.0	9.7	–87
California	11.3	7.2	5.6	5.2	4.5	3.3	2.7	–76
Pennsylvania	42.0	30.0	22.0	21.0	15.5	11.8	10.9	–74
U.S. Total	1,108	648	334	272	194	140	116	–89

Source: U.S. Department of Agriculture, National Agricultural Statistics Service, 1951–1999.
*The dairy farms are actually 'operations with milk cows' as defined by NASS.

Average herd size has been increasing the United States, and so too in California and Wisconsin, since 1959 (Table 4). In 1997, Wisconsin herds averaged 59 cows, whereas California herds averaged 530 cows (U.S. Department of Agriculture, 1997). The difference in average herd size between California and the U.S., or Wisconsin, has been increasing in both absolute and relative terms.

Table 4. Average Herd Size: U.S., California, and Wisconsin

Year	U.S.	California	Wisconsin
1959	9	39	20
1964	13	63	24
1969	20	98	28
1974	26	134	33
1978	33	173	37
1982	39	204	42
1987	50	295	47
1992	61	400	50
1997	78	530	59
% change 1959–97	767	1259	195

Source. U.S. Department of Agriculture, *Census of Agriculture*, 1959–1997.

CALIFORNIA POLICIES

The first impression one gets of the California milk marketing system is that it is so different from the Federal order system that regulates most of the market grade milk in the U.S. (Boynton, 1992).

A set of state administered dairy policies forms a context for the California dairy industry and, because it is unique, is the basis for much attention. We focus on four policy instruments that seem to have stirred the most controversy: the state's unique marketing order, make allowances, fluid standards, and water subsidies.

California Milk Marketing Order

Federal dairy policy has historically consisted of three instruments: (1) The dairy price support program, which commits the federal government to purchase selected storable dairy products at minimum purchase prices; (2) The milk marketing order system, which regulates fluid quality, grade A, milk and affects regional milk prices paid by users and how these prices are translated into farm level prices; and, (3) Trade policy which includes import barriers and export subsidies, that insulate the U.S. domestic market from foreign competition, and increases demand for certain manufactured dairy products.

While California is able to participate in the dairy price support program and is protected by national import barriers, it does not participate in the federal milk marketing orders. Because of a quirk in timing with the implementation of federal milk marketing orders in the 1930s, and a federal restraining order forbidding California from joining the federal orders, California operates a state milk marketing order outside the federal marketing order system. It consists of classified pricing (minimum prices for milk by end-use) and, since 1969, order-wide pool pricing (revenue pooling).

The unique California milk marketing order and stabilization plans have allowed the industry the luxury of experimenting without having to coordinate its plans with neighboring states.

Given the scrutiny that California policies have received over the years, it is indeed ironic that the new federal milk marketing order reforms, effective January 2000, are quite close to the current California milk marketing order. Both the new multiple component pricing (MCP) scheme and the associated make allowances are very much in alignment with the California order.

Two potentially significant differences exist between California and federal milk marketing orders: the pricing system and the pooling system. California's state marketing order prices milk based on five end-use classes, rather than the four classes under reformed federal orders. California prices are set by milk component by the California Department of Food and Agriculture (CDFA) using formulae. Pricing concerns are reviewed through a hearing system which allows the CDFA to respond quickly to changes and challenges. In fact, one major reason that California has resisted entering the federal order system may be the responsiveness of its pricing system relative to federal orders, which require major legislation and politicking to change. Federal order reforms include moving all federal order pricing to multiple component pricing using formulae similar to California.

Another reason California may be hesitant to enter the federal system is the quota that governs milk revenue pooling. The quota was an integral part of the implementation of order-wide pool pricing in 1969. From its inception, in 1935, until 1969, the California state marketing order operated with classified pricing but without market-wide pooling. In the 1969 move to market-wide pooling, the quota was created to reflect historical class 1, or fluid, contracts. To facilitate passage of market wide pooling, the quota was used to maintain higher revenue for those producers who historically marketed in the higher-valued fluid market. The quota was allocated based on historical production but is freely traded among licensed California milk producers. This is not a marketing or production quota. Rather, it is a method of allocating pooled revenues to producers who historically marketed their milk in the higher-valued fluid market. The existence of the quota has production implications, as the farmers in California receive the non-quota price as their marginal price, while producers in federal orders have identical average and marginal prices (Sumner & Wolf, 1996).

The major effect of quota is to redistribute revenues from classified pricing. Individual producers in California receive a weighted average price of the quota and non quota pool prices with the weights determined by individual ownership of milk quota relative to milk production. The result is that the marginal incentives to produce milk are actually lower than they would be without the quota under a federal-style blend price. Sumner & Wolf (1996) estimated that 1991 California milk production would have been about 7% more without the quota because it changes the marginal incentive to produce milk (not because it restricts supply).

The net effect of the California dairy policy on milk production relative to the federal order system is not clear. The quota results in less milk production than would occur under a federal-style blend price. The responsive pricing system means that California producers see market incentives more quickly than their federal counterparts resulting in a more efficient and productive allocation of resources. One obvious place that the effects of California policy can manifest themselves is in the milk price. California milk producers have consistently received lower milk prices than the vast majority of producers under federal orders yet milk production has increased rather than fallen off. This evidence alone is enough to lead us to examine other factors that might explain California milk production.

California 'Make Allowance'

A make allowance is a portion of the minimum price that processors are allowed in order to cover their manufacturing costs. Originally defined for use in the dairy Price Support Program, the support price is not set such that plants were required to pass on a given price to farmers. Rather, the price is set so that plants could achieve returns sufficient to pay their farmer patrons the minimum price. Essentially, the make allowance is added to the desired farm-level milk price to arrive at the price paid to dairy product manufacturers.

Before the January 2000 reforms, Federal milk marketing orders did not explicitly use a make allowance, but rather priced milk from a base derived from surveys of competitive markets (at one time the Minnesota-Wisconsin price series and, until January 2000, the Basic Formula Price). The Price Support Program make allowance played a role in federal minimum prices to the extent that the support price provided a floor for the surveyed dairy products that in turn provided the basis for all federal classified prices.

The classified pricing system in California uses make allowances to derive component prices from product prices. In California, the make allowance is transferred from producers to processors by subtracting it from the established base price for raw milk used for butter/powder and cheese. The make allowance, or manufacturing cost allowance, can be thought of as a fee paid by producers to processors in order to help defray the costs of processing surplus raw milk into storable products, namely, butter, powder and cheese.

In contrast, in federal orders, processors did not receive a make allowance (unless they sold commodities to the government). Instead, they covered the costs of processing raw milk into butter/powder and cheese by levying an upcharge or over-order premium on higher classes of milk, or through cooperative retains paid directly by producers. If California were to do this, it would increase the retail price of milk.

Historically, the California make allowance used in the determination of Class 4 prices has been set to allow the higher cost manufacturing plants, often referred to as 'balancing' plants, to earn an adequate return. The rationale has been that due to the geographical isolation of California, the state cannot afford to have inadequate manufacturing capacity, which would require milk to move large distances east, at great expense, for manufacturing or to be dumped. Thus, the state has attempted to encourage adequate manufacturing capacity by regularly updating the make allowance to keep it current with plant costs, which are audited by the California Department of Food and Agriculture.

At the same time, the California make allowances are a major balancing mechanism. Since Class 4 prices are inversely, but directly, related to the make allowance, both producers and processors economic well-being are affected by its magnitude. If the make allowance is set too low, processors go out of business, and the states' manufacturing capacity is decreased. Meanwhile, producer prices would increase, thus increasing the potential for surplus milk production. If the make allowance is set too high, processor over-capacity and a decreased milk supply (because producers would get a lower price) would make the manufacturing sector inefficient.

The 1990 Farm Bill contained a section (102) explicitly aimed at changing the California make allowance. It was reasoned that the California make allowance resulted in a higher profit margin for cheese and butter/powder plants located there. While the make allowance is seemingly generous, California historically experienced relatively higher costs to manufacture butter, milk powder and cheese, and also has lower yields of product (per hundredweight of milk), particularly for cheese. Mandating lower make allowances in California would increase producer prices which would encourage surplus milk production, decrease state manufacturing capacity, and, under the Price Support Program, the surplus milk production translates to increased sales of butter, powder and cheese to the government at taxpayer expense (Butler, 1990).

The California make allowances are a different way of allowing manufacturing plants to cover their costs of converting raw milk into storable products. In federal orders these costs are covered in a less transparent way, by passing some of the costs on to consumers and some back to producers. The newly reformed federal orders, with the move to multiple component pricing, also have make allowances of much the same magnitude as California. Given the uproar in recent years over the California make allowance, this is indeed an ironic turn of events.

California Fluid Milk Standards

California has long had standards for fat and solids content in fluid dairy products that differ from the rest of the country (Table 5). California standards require fluid milk to be fortified by replacing removed fat with solids-not-fat (SNF), either a powdered or condensed milk, such that total solids are at least

Table 5. Minimum Standards for Fluid Milk Products, U.S. Federal and California

Product	Federal	California
Whole milk		
Milkfat	3.25%	3.5%
Solids-not-fat	8.25%	8.70%
Protein	8 g	8 g
Calcium	290 mg	310 mg
Sodium	120 mg	130 mg
Calories	140 Kcal	150 Kcal
Lowfat milk		
Milkfat	0.5–2%	2%
Solids-not-fat	8.25%	10%
Protein	8 g	10 g
Calcium	290 mg	350 mg
Sodium	120 mg	150 mg
Calories	120 Kcal	140 Kcal
Extra-light milk		
Milkfat	0.5–2%	1%
Solids-not-fat	8.25%	11%
Protein	8 g	10 g
Calcium	290 mg	320 mg
Sodium	120 mg	160 mg
Calories	100 Kcal	120 Kcal
Non-fat Milk		
Milkfat	<0.5%	<0.25%
Solids-not-fat	>8.25%	>9%
Protein	8 g	8 g
Calcium	290 mg	320 mg
Sodium	120 mg	130 mg
Calories	90 Kcal	80 Kcal

Source: National All-Jersey Inc. (1992).

12%. As a result, California fluid milks are more consistent than those of other states where fat is removed without replacement by an equivalent amount of solids. Taste tests have shown that consumers often prefer the richer, more consistent fluid milk resulting from California standards.

California milk standards emerged from a compromise between producers and processors in the early 1960s. At that time, processors wanted statutory authority to market a lowfat milk product (prior to 1962 only two fluid milk products were defined – whole milk and skim milk). But since producers were paid on the basis of the fat content of their milk, they were afraid of what reduced fat products would do to Class 1 sales of milk fat. If the extracted milkfat was not sold at Class 1 prices, it would be sold at the lower priced Class 4a (butter) or 4b (cheese) price. The resulting agreement mandated that producers would be paid for both fat and solids-not-fat content (known as multiple component pricing, or MCP) and that the 12% standard (10% SNF, 2% milk fat, or later 11% SNF and 1% milk fat) would become the standard for California milk.

However, among the many provisions of the Nutrition Labeling and Education Act (NLEA) of 1990 is a requirement that standards of identity be uniform in all states. This, in effect, preempted California milk standards, no longer allowing them to differ from those prescribed by the federal government. Many in the U.S. dairy industry believed that the higher (more nutritious) California standards should become the national standard. However, processors in other states opposed this change when it was proposed in the 1990 Farm Bill.

California applied for an exemption from the lower federal milk standards in 1991, arguing that federal minimum nutritive (protein and calcium) standards are significantly lower for every fluid milk product, and the federal fat standard for non-fat milk is double the California standard. While the FDA has never ruled on the California exemption, the 1996 Farm Bill (FAIR Act of 1996) specifically exempted California from the federal milk standards and allowed California to maintain its higher standards.

In November 1999, the *Los Angeles Times* argued that November California retail prices were $0.60 to $1.20 per gallon higher than the national average, and that this was due to California's more stringent milk standards. Since the fortification process involves the addition of extra solids to fluid milk, some fluid milks in California are more expensive than non-fortified milk in other states. We estimate from California fortification allowances that it costs on average about 16 to 20 cents per gallon to fortify milk to California standards. Some California consumer groups have argued that this added expense denies poor people the nutrition that milk affords them, and that out-of-state milk should be allowed to enter the state, or alternatively, that the state should change the standards. But the extra 16 to 20 cents per gallon for fortification should not add $0.60–$1.20 per gallon at retail level. Thus fortification is a relatively minor factor influencing California retail fluid milk prices.

Salathe & Price (1992) estimated that if California standards were adopted nationwide, it would raise farm-level milk prices 1 to 2% in the long run and the average retail price of milk would rise 9 to 13 cents a gallon.

A number of out-of-state fluid milk processors have attempted to sell fluid milk in California that meets the federal standards, but does not meet the higher California standards. They argue that the NLEA preempts California standards. Since the California standards are mandated by statute, the California Department of Food and Agriculture has had to order such milk to be withdrawn for sale in California. This, in turn, has prompted several court challenges to California's statutes and standards. The courts have generally ruled in California's favor, and California has been able to maintain its higher standards for milk. However, in August 1999, a San Diego Appeals Court decided that California law could not ban federal standard milk from entering the state. As of this writing (January 2000), State officials have asked the California Supreme Court to review the Appeals Court ruling.

This issue is a particularly tricky one for the California dairy industry. On one hand, California standards for milk provide consumers with a richer, more nutritious and more consistent milk than do the lower federal standards. The fat and SNF content of milk changes seasonally and by geographic location. If it is not fortified then its consistency changes week-to-week, month-to-month, potentially leading to a loss of consumer confidence in milk. On the other hand, disallowing the sale of the lower federal standard milk from other states can be construed as an unfair trade barrier. Some state legislators have argued that consumers should have a choice of which milk they want to purchase, and that the increased competition created by allowing the lower federal standard milk to be sold in California would help boost consumption and result in an increased intake of calcium. Numerous surveys carried out over the last few years have shown that milk prices vary between retail outlets (not just in California, but all over the nation) by as much as $2.50 per gallon. Lower-than-average priced milk is available in most cities and towns throughout the nation. What is clear is that most consumers do not take much notice of the price they pay for milk, as long as it is reasonable.

Abolishing the standards themselves would reduce prices by 16–20 cents per gallon. But the extra milk required to obtain the daily requirements of calcium and other nutrients would probably make the price reduction a wash. Although it is not illegal for California to continue to produce the richer milk that consumers prefer these issues clearly pose a dilemma for the industry. First, approximately 50 million pounds of solids-not-fat used for fortification (worth about $50 million), and a significant amount of butterfat (from the lower federal fat standards) would be displaced, which would flood dairy products markets. Most of this surplus butterfat would be purchased by the government through the current price support program. Thus, taxpayers would foot a large chunk of the bill. Second, California consumers would pay significantly more than this to obtain the nutrition equivalent to that offered in milk. Third, the effect of the displaced solids and fat would likely depress the price of milk for all U.S. dairy producers. Dual standards would likely create considerable confusion for consumers.

It would not be any great loss to processors if fortification of fluid milk were replaced by the lower Federal standards. This would reduce the cost of producing California fluid milk, resulting in California processors being more competitive with surrounding states. At the same time, a large volume of non-fat solids would be released onto the market, reducing the price of all milk in the U.S.; and the losers would be California consumers and all U.S. producers. Thus, California fluid milk standards, have historically benefitted not just California dairy producers but all U.S. dairy producers.

Water Subsidies in California

California is prone to drought because of the irregularity of winter rain and snow pack patterns and, therefore, the unreliability of supplies from the state's water storage and distribution system. Water demands of a rapidly increasing population threaten agriculture's historic claims, while complaints proliferate about subsidized water prices to agriculture.

Dairy per se is not a large water user. Shultz (1990) estimated that an average cow drinks about 25 gallons of water a day, but noted that milk is 90% water and that manure and urine are usually recycled as fertilizer. While an average dairy will use 50 gallons per cow per day to clean the cow and sanitize the milking equipment, this water is used over again to flush the barns and feeding areas, and eventually ends up on farmland. The daily water use per cow is less than the 100 to 150 gallons that an adult living in Fresno uses for drinking, showering, cooking, and watering the lawn.

The water shortage in California may affect dairy through irrigated alfalfa rather than direct water use. Dairy producers rely heavily on alfalfa grown in the state because of its high quality. Bringing alfalfa in from elsewhere (except for some from nearby western states) is costly. There is a notion that California producers have an economic advantage due to federal water subsidies. The fact is, water subsidies are limited to just three districts, and these districts provide only a limited amount of feedstuffs to California producers. There are no feed grains raised in those water districts, and less than 3% of the alfalfa is grown there. The elimination of water subsidies then, would not likely affect milk production significantly, if at all.

Besides alfalfa, California dairy producers have available large quantities of certain crop byproducts, which may be substituted when alfalfa prices are high.

Some of the by-products fed are from perennials that have first claim on agricultural water when it becomes scarce, e.g. almond hulls and citrus pulp. While they are not substitutes for the high quality alfalfa that California producers are accustomed to, these by-products give the dairy industry an important flexibility that may help some dairies survive when water is in short supply.

The net result is that, while water subsidies may help dairy production indirectly through alfalfa and by-product production, this is a small effect and water use is more likely a constraint, rather than an advantage, for California dairy production.

EXPLAINING THE ROBUST GROWTH OF THE CALIFORNIA DAIRY INDUSTRY

Do California dairy/water policies give the milk producers a substantial advantage over milk producers in other states? Our analyses of four key policy instruments – the milk marketing order, make allowance, fluid milk standards, and water subsidies – indicate that they do not. Indeed, the California policies actually serve to restrain production, often benefitting producers in other regions. The state milk marketing order results in less aggregate milk than would be produced under a federal-style milk marketing order; California make allowances result in a lower milk price for producers than the federal system which also suggests less milk production ceteris paribus; California fluid standards do provide higher milk prices, however, the solids removed from the milk market also benefit dairy farmers in other states; and water is a constraint rather than a benefit for California dairy farmers. The role of California policy to explain milk production growth has often been greatly exaggerated. Other factors, most of which are derived from the vast natural resources present in California, had a far greater effect on stimulating growth in milk production.

Many factors outside of policy contribute to milk production and industry structure that are, or historically have been, unique to California. While a detailed model explaining the evolution of the dairy industry is beyond the scope of this chapter, there are some obvious factors we can examine that move us towards an understanding of California milk production.

Climate

California agriculture operates in an almost ideal climate with an abundance of natural resources. One advantage of this climate is that dairy cattle can be housed with little or no shelter. Indeed, California dairy farmers domestically pioneered the now common technologies of the milking parlor and dry-lot housing and/or free-stall barns. Dry-lots or simple shade barns represent a cost advantage over the more elaborate, and thus expensive, housing often used in colder regions. However, recent advances in animal husbandry have led to the adoption of open barns with retractable curtains in colder climates, and this advance partially mitigates the cost advantage that warmer climates, such as California, have enjoyed. The low humidity, especially during peak production times is also advantageous, for it is primarily humidity rather than heat that stresses cows, resulting in decreased milk production. Simple sunshades and inexpensive water-misters are all that cows require during California summers.

Complementary Crops

The California climate also contributes to the production of high quality alfalfa, and agricultural commodities whose by products help to minimize the costs of milk production. The ability to grow high quality alfalfa in California results from the controlled nature of alfalfa production afforded by irrigation. While most other regions of the U.S. rely on rain to grow alfalfa, it generally does not rain in the Central and Imperial Valleys of California from May through October. However, a lack of winter precipitation in can create droughts which result in a limited amount of water available for alfalfa and other crops.

More than 250 crops are produced by almost 78,000 farms on 7.8 million acres of harvested cropland in California, including more than half the U.S. output of fruits, nuts, and vegetables (Carter & Goldman, 1997). The dairy industry realizes an indirect benefit from this plethora of crops, and their by-products, serving as a residual market for those that do not make the grade, or for some other reason are not sold in their primary market. These by-products include but are not limited to cottonseed, almond hulls, and citrus pulp which often represent cost-effective alternatives to conventional feeds. To obtain these feed products, dairy farmers in other states and regions must pay added transportation costs.

Geographic Isolation

California is geographically isolated relative to other historical U.S. population and milk production centers, and this limits the amount of milk that flows into, or out of, the state. The Rocky and Sierra Nevada Mountain Ranges are a major obstacle to moving raw milk either east or west; the vast expanse of sparsely settled land to the east of California adds considerably to the costs of transporting milk. Thus, California has always had to assure itself of sufficient in-state processing capacity. In fact, the ultimate limit to California milk production is determined by the amount of processing capacity in-state. With the remarkable population growth in California in recent years, both production and processing capacity have increased without direct competition from outside states. While technology and population growth in surrounding states have changed in recent years, the infrastructure and efficiency of the California dairy industry were already in place to meet these challenges.

Population Explosion

California has a large and diverse population that provides some unique marketing opportunities for milk and dairy products as well as a diverse pool of labor for the industry. That a significant percentage of U.S. milk production has moved west and south over the past several decades is not surprising, for milk is heavy and perishable, and its production has parallels with population growth.

More than one in ten Americans now reside in California, and for much of the 1970s and 1980s, its population grew at twice the rate of the U.S. This population explosion had two principal effects on the size and structure of the dairy industry. One, it provided an ever-increasing demand for dairy products and thus an impetus for aggregate industry growth. And two, the growth of urban areas resulted in a fiscal windfall to dairy farmers who, because fluid milk is highly perishable, traditionally were located close to cities. These population effects generated wealth, in the form of land equity, available for the latest production technologies and for increases in herd size. Farms in southern California (e.g. the Chino Valley) that supplied milk to Los Angeles, were able to sell land for high-priced urban uses and then relocate their dairies in the south Central Valley. These moves often resulted in significant increases in farm size and milk production because the wealth gained from land sales was reinvested to both take advantage of the latest production technology and avoid taxes. Related effects are discussed with respect to technology below.

Investment Timing and Technology Adoption

Where California started with respect to natural resources and when it started with respect to production technology are significant factors in explaining the size, structure, and efficiency of the California dairy industry today – especially relative to other states and regions. There is an economic concept termed 'asset fixity' that captures the essence of this advantage by explaining why investment and disinvestment by dairy farms may be discrete and asymmetric.

Though a rigorous dynamic explanation of dairy industry structural evolution is beyond the scope of this paper, it is worth noting that the dairy industry is relatively 'young' in California. Dairy production technology has not been stagnant in any recent time period and California dairy production increases corresponded with adoption of the current dominant production technology set. Regions with less temperate climates are rapidly adopting similar production technologies (i.e. parlors and free-stall barns) in recent years. However, adopting this technology during initial growth is different than changing technologies from an older set of production assets as it gives California the early adopter advantage on the 'technology treadmill'.

Asset fixity with adjustment costs may explain capital movement, or lack of movement, over time. Adjustment costs are the costs associated with changing the capital stock such as the facilities and equipment needed on a modern dairy farm. Asset fixity occurs when returns to current use are higher than the salvage value of an asset, but current returns are not sufficient to make expansion profitable (Johnson, 1956). This asset fixity may partially explain the continued preponderance of stanchion barn use in the Midwest and Northeast United States. The opportunity costs of using these older, smaller facilities are low, but the current use is still higher than the salvage value which is close to zero. The opportunity costs that may fix an asset in its current use range from opportunity costs between enterprises on a given farm to opportunity costs in other industries in a region.

When asset returns, salvage values, and acquisition prices differ across individuals or regions, as they have in California relative to other parts of the United States, growth rates and firm sizes differ. For example, new dairy farms are able to organize production according to current facilities and equipment acquisition prices and the expected path of prices, without regard to the past pattern of prices. Entering dairy farmers have the potential advantage of being more flexible in their choice of technology, scale of operation, and timing of entry. In contrast, the active dairy farmer has investment capital already sunk on the farm, and only the decisions on future investments or on currently reversible investments can be treated the way an entering farmer can treat the whole package. Because of sunk costs, and perhaps because of capital constraints and inertia as well, the tendency will be for active farmers to move slowly in changing technology than if previous investments could be easily reversed.

CALIFORNIA DAIRY INDUSTRY DYNAMICS

Each of these characteristics – climate, complementary crops, geographic isolation, population growth, and investment timing – is an advantage also found, to at least some extent, in other states and regions. However, none are combined as they are in California. The exploding population contributed to a large and steadily growing demand for dairy products. Metropolitan expansion also resulted in demand for land which led directly to increases in wealth for dairy farmers who chose to move their operations away from the urban areas as technologies became available to economically transport milk (at least within state boundaries). The climate, crops, wealth, and technological advances contributed to an ever-increasing supply of dairy products and the geographic isolation meant that the supply must come from California.

In the 1920s and 1930s, the major dairying area in California was in Los Angeles county, close to the largest California city. Transportation of milk from outside the region was expensive, so the milk production was necessarily close to the city. However, land in Los Angeles county even then was expensive, because there were a number of alternative agricultural commodities that could be produced on a few acres of land (mainly specialty crops such as vegetables, small fruits, and flowers). Most dairy farmers could only afford small plots of land and soon learned to specialize and support many cows on few acres of land by eliminating cropping operations, purchasing the majority of their feed, and managing cows in dry-lots rather than pastures. As the dry-lot technique on smaller-than-usual plots of land was adopted and refined, dairy producers also found ways of expanding their herds and capturing significant economies of size. Herd sizes began to grow from 100–150 cows to 300 or more.

In the 1940s the population of Los Angeles exploded. More and more of the land that previously was devoted to agriculture became real estate for housing. The enormous prices that dairy producers were able to garner as a result of the real estate boom in Los Angeles county allowed many to sell their small plots of land and move their dairy operations to nearby Orange county. Larger tracts of land were purchased, more modern technologies were adopted, and, using the same techniques that they used in Los Angeles county, dairy operations grew larger.

In the 1950s, the same thing happened in Orange county that had happened earlier in LA county. Population growth forced real estate prices to skyrocket, and many dairy producers once again garnered large prices for their land, and many relocated further away from the burgeoning city, but still in reasonable (transportation) proximity to Los Angeles. The areas around San Bernardino, Riverside, Ontario and Chino became the new dairying areas. Once again, dairy producers were able to afford larger tracts of land, and more modern technologies, which meant even larger dairy operations of 500–800 cows or more. At the same time, other dairy producers were attracted by the rapid growth that was occurring in California's central valley, and many relocated to the counties of Tulare, Kings, Fresno and Kern in the south of the central valley. During the 1960s and 1970s, many more dairy operations spread further north up the central valley to Merced, Madera, Stanislaus and San Joaquin counties. By this time the intensive, drylot feeding style of dairying was an established and recognized technique.

Often called 'California-style' dairying, it is precisely this historical movement of dairying that led to the tremendous growth in milk production, and explains the structure of the current dairy industry. More importantly, California dairy producers have learned some valuable lessons. First, they have learned to successfully expand and, when sufficiently lucrative, to relocate their operations. Second, they have learned to increase milk production efficiency by concentrating the herd in drylot feeding operations, purchasing rather than growing their own feed, and minimizing other costs of operation like land and housing facilities, thus capturing significant economies of size. Third, they have overcome asset fixity by specializing, simplifying, and being able to continually update technologies.

CONCLUSIONS

California dairy production increased enormously in recent decades. Because of this remarkable vigor the unique set of policies that affect milk production, processing, and marketing in California have become a source of controversy in national dairy policy debates. However, from our examination of the state marketing order, make allowances, fluid standards, and water subsidies we conclude that the effects of these policies on milk production have been greatly exaggerated. For the California industry as a whole, the quota does not affect total revenues. But, the quota does affect marginal revenues and tends to reduce total milk production, thereby benefitting other parts of the country. The California 'make allowance' plays an important role in the state's ability to maintain processing capacity which, in turn, keeps retail prices lower and acts as an additional balancing mechanism on the supply of and demand for milk. Fluid standards result in consistent, nutritious milk available to California consumers as well as the use of a substantial volume of solids that would otherwise depress farm-level milk prices. Water subsidies have a negligible, indirect effect on milk production and likely constrain production. None of these unique policies explain the huge expansion of California dairy production; other factors have likely had a far greater effect.

Favorable climate, geography, natural resources, population growth and technology have influenced the size and performance of the California dairy industry. A mild climate provided a cost advantage in facilities and contributed to the abundance of crops that provide alternative feeds. Geographic isolation meant that fluid milk requirements must be met from within. The population explosion provided both an ever-increasing market demand and urban pressure which increased land equity and encouraged herd size increases. The timing of these population and income growth factors coincided with induced innovation and technology adoption that encouraged the formation of large, productive dairy farms.

That California policies are often a lightning-rod in national policy debates is an example of the regionalism present in the U.S. dairy industry today. However, despite the level of government intervention in regional milk markets, milk marketing is a highly competitive activity. As long as California remains outside of the federal orders, and as long as there are regional differences in fluid differentials, commodity production, and other factors that differentiate one region from another, there will be regionalism in public policy debates. The California policies have had a role in demonstrating alternative methods that later have been widely adopted by Federal policy makers as in the case of the most recent Federal Milk Marketing Order Reform.

ACKNOWLEDGMENTS

The authors benefitted greatly from comments offered by Harry Schwarzweller and Andrew Davidson.

REFERENCES

Boynton, R. D. (1992). Milk Marketing in California. Sacramento, CA: Dairy Institute of California.

Butler, L. J. (1990). The California Make Allowance, Testimony submitted to the House Agriculture subcommittee on Livestock, Dairy and Poultry, Washington, D.C.: April 30.

Butler, L. J. (1992). *Maintaining the Competitive Edge*. Davis, CA: University of California, Agricultural Issues Center.

California Department of Food and Agriculture (1951–1999). *California Dairy Industry Statistics*, Sacramento, CA: Annual Issues.

California Department of Food and Agriculture (1951–1999). *California Dairy Information Bulletin*, Sacramento, CA: December issues.

Carter, H. O., & Goldman, G. (1997). The Measure of California Agriculture: Its Significance in the State Economy. Chapter 2 of *California Agriculture: Issues and Challenges*. Berkeley, CA: University of California Giannini Foundation.

Dairy Profit Weekly (1999). *X*(40), October 18, 1999.

Jesse, E. (1994). Section 102: The California Make Allowance Issue. University of Wisconsin, Department of Agricultural Economics Staff Paper No. 46. Madison, WI: April 1994.

Johnson, G. L. (1956). Supply Functions – Some Facts and Notions. In: E. O. Heady et al. (Eds), *Agricultural Adjustment Problems in a Growing Economy*. Ames, IA: Iowa State University Press.

Los Angeles Times (1999). Does fortifying milk add cost Los Angeles CA: November 24, 1999 page A9.

National All-Jersey Incorporated (1991).Equity Newsletter, *XVI*(4), August 1991.

Salathe, L., & Price, J. M. (1992). Implications of raising the nonfat solids standards for beverage milk. *Southern Journal of Agricultural Economics, 24* (December), 197–209.

Shultz, T. (1990). The Environmental Impact of a Cow. Annual Report, Tulare Dairy Herd Improvement Association.

Sumner, D. A., & Wolf, C. A. (1996). Quotas without Supply Control: Effects of Dairy Quota Policy in California. *American Journal of Agricultural Economics, 78* (May), 354–366.

U.S. Congress (1988). Review of Regionalism as an Issue in the U.S. Dairy Industry, Vol. II: Background Papers, April 1988, for the Subcommittee on Livestock, Dairy and Poultry of the Committee on Agriculture, U.S. House of Representatives, 100th Congress, 2nd Session, Washington, D.C.: June 1988.

U.S. Congress (1987). Review of the Dairy Termination Program and other ongoing Dairy Program Initiatives Mandated in the Food Security Act of 1985, Hearing before the Subcommittee on Livestock, Dairy and Poultry, Committee on Agriculture, House of Representatives, 100th Congress, 1st Session, Washington, D.C.. March 4, 1987.

U.S. Department of Agriculture (1959–1997). *Census of Agriculture*. Washington, D.C.

U.S. Department of Agriculture, Economic Research Service (1985). Dairy: Background for 1985 Farm Legislation. Agricultural Information Bulletin No. 474. Washington, D.C.: April 1985.

U.S. Department of Agriculture, National Agricultural Statistics Service (1951–1999). *Milk Cows and Production*. Washington, D.C.. Annual Issues.

Wisconsin Department of Agriculture Trade and Consumer Protection (1951–1999). *Wisconsin Dairy Facts*. Madison, WI.

DAIRY FARMING IN AUSTRALIA: A DECADE OF CHANGE 1983/84–1994/95

Erik Berrevoets

INTRODUCTION

Powerful economic and political forces are reshaping Australia's dairy industry, not only nationally but also differentially between regions. But while the effects of dairy restructuring are well known at the national level, little is known about what is happening at the state/regional level. This is unfortunate. Research in Europe and the United States has pointed out the importance of understanding the differential impacts associated with dairy restructuring (Gilbert & Akor, 1989; Lyson & Geisler, 1992, DuPuis, 1993; Davidson & Schwarzweller, 1995; Van der Ploeg & Long, 1994; Van der Ploeg & Van Dijk, 1995). But to date, there has been very little concern in Australia about regional differentiation, about the impacts of change forces and national policies on dairying in the various states, and about the uneven development of Australia's dairy industry (with the possible exception of Davidson, 1997.)

This paper specifically explores changes in the structure of dairy farms by state in Australia between 1983/84 and 1994/95. It also explores the implications of these changes on the economic returns to dairy farmers and resource use, in order to better understand the differential affects of dairy restructuring in Australia.

Research in Rural Sociology, Volume 8, pages 163–180.
ISBN: 0-7623-0474-X

EXPLANATIONS OF DIFFERENCES IN MILK PRODUCTION

Australia's dairy industry developed along the southeastern coastal fringes of the Australian continent because of the favorable environmental conditions and the concentration of population in these areas (Ashton, 1949–1956; Davidson, 1981; Edwards & Drane, 1961; Sillcock, 1976). Since the Second World War, the industry has become increasingly concentrated in Victoria. Now, more than half of Australia's dairy farms are located in this state. New South Wales and Queensland combined have a quarter of the number of dairy farms. The remainder are distributed over South Australia, Tasmania and Western Australia. The number of dairy farms in Australia's two territories (the Australian Capital Territory and the Northern Territory) is too small to be included in the major national statistical data collection (BAE, 1985 and ABARE, 1997). Although the states differed in the rate of decline between 1983/84 and 1994/95, their relative ranking was not affected. On average, three quarters of Australia's milk production was used for manufacturing purposes.

Early in the development of Australia's dairy industry two distinct milk markets were created, each with its own marketing arrangements. Victoria, South Australia and Tasmania geared their milk production predominantly towards the manufacture of cheese and butter for export purposes. Dairy farms in New South Wales, Queensland and Western Australia oriented their production towards the supply of fresh milk for the domestic market (Ashton, 1949–1956; Davidson, 1981; Edwards & Drane, 1961; Sillcock, 1976; ABARE, 1997).

A range of policy measures regulated both market segments and cushioned price fluctuations and provided dairy farmers with income stability. Beginning in the 1970s this situation changed. The Australian government introduced a range of measures that dismantled government support and exposed the dairy industry to global market forces. These initially affected the manufacturing component of the industry, but with the introduction of the Kerin Plan in 1986, the prices of the fresh milk market were linked to those of the international market (Griffith, 1989).

The different market segments in Australia had different production requirements and received different returns per litre of milk (see DuPuis, 1993 for the U.S.). The production of fresh milk requires year round production. This means more extensive animal husbandry practices and a higher labor input. Dairy farms producing milk for use as fresh milk enter into quota arrangements with dairy factories that provide a higher price per litre in return for a guaranteed supply of milk. The manufacturing market segment accepts a seasonal supply of milk. This means that during the winter period when pasture is less nutritious, cows are dried off to avoid the cost of supplementary feeding (Ashton, 1950; Davidson, 1981). But the situation is changing and dairy farms that produce milk for manufacturing purposes also aim for milk production throughout the year (Dairy Research and Development Corporation, 1993).

In addition to changes in the structure of milk production associated with milk market segmentation, a review of the literature suggests a number of alternative explanations. Davidson & Schwarzweller (1995; and Schwarzweller & Davidson, 1997) argue that the differences in farming structures can be regarded as the geographical expression of the extent to which regions are able to participate effectively in the global economy; that is, some regions become marginalized as they become increasingly remote from economic centres. This research argues that the concentration of milk production in certain regions was associated with differentials in scale and productivity (see also Lyson & Geisler, 1992). Farms in marginal regions were found to be dominated by small-scale dairy farms with low levels of production, efficiency and economic returns, and regions at the 'economic core' of the development by large scale, highly productive and efficient dairy farms with high economic returns.

Hofstee (1985), who originally developed the farming styles perspective, argued that the cultural characteristics of regions are also reflected in farming practices. His concept was modified by van der Ploeg in the 1990s who argued that as a result of the modernization of agricultural production with its focus on increases in scale and the adoption of technology, farming styles structure farming practices through the extent to which farmers have incorporated technology and are dependent on the market for inputs (van der Ploeg, 1994; van der Ploeg & Saccomandi, 1995).

Additional research on the existence of regional differences in agricultural production in the U.S. suggests some further explanations. One of these is the historical development of agriculture in particular regions (Gilbert & Akor, 1988). In relation to the dairy industry in Australia, the state government of Victoria had a stronger focus on the establishment of dairy farming as an export industry than the state government of New South Wales. This might explain current regional differences in the production of milk in Victoria for manufacturing purposes and in New South Wales for the fresh milk market.

The historical development of the dairy industry in each state has also played a role in the scale of production. The size of farms in states where dairy farming was established relatively early (Victoria and New South Wales) appears smaller than farms established in areas where the dairy industry was established at a later date (Western Australia). The reasons why dairy farms in Western Australia have the largest farm area is because they were established in areas that were environmentally less suited for dairying as a result of lower levels of rainfall which, in line with the pasture based nature of dairying in Australia, required larger farm areas. Furthermore, these farms were often not set up purely as dairy farms but as mixed enterprises (Ashton, 1949–56).

Other factors that help explain differences in the structure of dairy farms are the importance of agriculture in the economy of each state in Australia and the level of government support to the rural sector. States like Victoria and New South Wales have a more developed manufacturing sector than states like Queensland and Tasmania (Australian Bureau of Statistics, 1986). Dairy farms as a proportion of the total number of farms also varies substantially between states. In 1983/84 dairy farms made up about one tenth of all farms, varying from less than 4% in Western Australia to almost 25% in Victoria and Tasmania (see Table 1). The importance of agriculture in a state economy and the importance of dairy farming for each state can affect the political influence of dairy farmers on government policies that determine government levels of expenditure on outreach services (extension) and support to the industry.

Differences also exist in climatic conditions between different states. Southern Victoria and Northern Tasmania have a cool temperate climate with high rainfall. Northern New South Wales and coastal Queensland are sub-tropical dairy regions with a warm climate and high rainfall. Northern Victoria and inland New South Wales have relatively dry climates with a need for irrigation. Western Australia and South Australia are characterized by a Mediterranean climate with low summer rainfall and cool relatively wet winters.

Table 1. Number of dairy farms as proportion of total number of farms in Australia, 1983/84

	No. of dairy farms	Total no. of all farms	Dairies as % of all farms
New South Wales	3,232	52,704	6.1
Victoria	10,455	45,560	22.9
Queensland	2,778	33,948	8.2
Western Australia	1,309	19,289	6.8
South Australia	630	16,584	3.8
Tasmania	1,245	5,586	22.3
Total Australia	19,655	174,025	11.3

Source: ABS, Australia Yearbook, 1986.

METHODOLOGY

For the purpose at hand, differences in the structure of dairy farms in Australia by state are examined using data collected by the Australian Bureau of Agriculture and Resource Economics (ABARE) and its predecessor the Bureau of Agricultural Economics (BAE), and presented in their Farm Survey Reports. ABARE uses the Australian Standard Industrial Classifications (ASIC) as a basis for selecting a sample for farms for inclusion in its surveys. The ABARE selects a sample of farms stratified by geographic area and with an estimated value of agricultural operations that is equal to, or above $20,000. ABARE survey officers interview farm operators or farm managers. ABARE obtains further information from accountants, selling agents and marketing organizations (ABARE, 1997). The population and sample size for 1994/95 is presented in Table 2.

A number of terms need qualification. Productivity refers to the output per production factor, such as herd average (milk yield per cow), stocking rates (cows per hectare), and milk production per week worked. Efficiency refers to the financial returns per production factor such as returns per week worked. Hence, it is possible to have a high level of production but a low level of efficiency, as the returns per litre of milk impact on the level of efficiency, but not on the level of productivity. Net value of production refers to total financial returns minus the total variable costs. Gross margins refer to total returns of a production factor minus the variable costs (this calculation excludes fixed costs).

Some of the variables presented here are derived directly from the ABARE *Farm Survey Reports*. These include milk production per farm; farm area; herd size; number of weeks worked per year; milk yields per cow; financial returns

Table 2. Population and samples of dairy farms, by state, 1994/95

	Population	Sample
New South Wales	2086	75
Victoria	7824	87
Queensland	1852	40
Western Australia	505	57
South Australia	831	43
Tasmania	759	30
Total Australia	13857	332

Source: ABARE, 1997.

to dairy farmers; cost of production; dairy receipts (specialization in milk production). In addition, some variables are combined, such as stocking rates (number of dairy cows divided by farm area), price per litre (dairy receipts divided by the milk production per farm), net value of production or gross margin per farm (total returns minus variable costs), gross margin per week worked, gross margin per cow and gross margin per hectare (financial returns minus total cost, and divided by the number of dairy cow, or weeks worked, or farm area).

The variables used to assess level of market integration associated with the structure of milk production are specialization in milk production (dairy receipts as proportion of total returns), and the cost of production. This consists of financial data on materials (the cost of fodder, fertilizers, etc.), services, and interest repayments, but excludes the cost of family labor.

OVERVIEW OF DIFFERENCES IN MILK PRODUCTION BY STATE: TOWARDS A TYPOLOGY

Between 1983/84 and 1994/95, milk production per farm more than doubled in Tasmania but increased by less than three-quarters in Queensland. Similarly, changes in farm area increased by more than three-quarters in South Australia, but by less than 5% in Queensland. Herd size almost doubled in Tasmania but increased by less than one fifth in Queensland. Increases in herd averages varied from approximately two thirds in Queensland to a little over one-tenth in Tasmania. And stocking rates increased by almost three-quarters in Tasmania but decreased by more than a quarter in South Australia. The number of weeks worked increased by less than a tenth in Victoria but declined by about the same rate in South Australia (see Table 3).

An examination of the differences in milk production per farm by milk market segments shows that milk production per farm is not distributed evenly across each segment. Victoria enjoyed high milk production per farm, South Australia had an average milk production per farm, while Tasmania labored under small milk production per farm at a time when all three states dominated the production of manufactured milk. A similar observation can be made for states where the majority of milk is used as fresh milk (Table 4).

It appears that between 1983/84 and 1994/95 two basic strategies were being employed to increase milk production. Some states focused on increasing herd averages, whereas other states focused on increasing stocking rates. There is some indication that such strategies are associated with the use of milk for either fresh milk or manufacturing purposes (see Table 4). Dairy farms that serve the fresh milk market require high yielding cows such as Holstein-

Table 3. Changes (%) in the scale and productivity of milk production, by state, 1983/84–1994/95

	New South Wales	Victoria	Queensland	Western Australia	South Australia	Tasmania	Total Australia
No. of dairy farms	-34.2	-23.0	-31.6	-16.5	-33.2	-36.2	-27.4
Milk per farm	73.6	88.9	72.7	77.3	99.3	116.4	87.8
Farm area (Ha.)	28.2	6.6	4.5	50.0	80.8	11.8	16.5
Herd size	51.8	42.6	17.6	32.7	37.8	99.1	43.3
Labor (wks/yr)	-4.3	7.0	-5.3	-5.0	-6.3	0.9	1.6
Labor efficiency (ltr milk/work week)	81.3	76.6	82.5	86.7	122.7	114.6	84.8
Herd average	25.1	31.0	63.8	33.0	45.3	13.6	33.0
Stocking rate (cows/Ha.)	14.3	27.4	—	—	-26.0	71.4	20.0

Source: data adapted from BAE, 1986; ABARE, 1997.

Table 4. Scale of milk production and productivity of dairy farms, by state, 1994/95

	New South Wales	Victoria	Queensland	Western Australia	South Australia	Tasmania	Total Australia
Milk total per farm (ltr)	520,997	626,596	399,385	680,000	580,874	618,951	579,118
MFG grade (%)	44.4	90.2	48.8	56.2	72.0	100.0	78.1
Farm area (Ha.)	264	146	233	402	320	189	198
Herd size	208	210	147	260	175	235	202
Labor (wks/yr)	135	123	124	133	119	116	125
Labor efficiency (ltr/work week)	3,859	5,094	3,221	5,113	4,881	5,335	4,632
Herd average	4,269	4,148	4,337	4,787	5,402	4,000	4,256
Stocking rate	0.8	1.4	0.6	0.7	0.5	1.2	1.0

Source: data adapted from ABARE, 1997.

Friesians. Dairy farms that produce milk for manufacturing purposes require cows that give milk with a high butterfat and protein content such as Jerseys, (Australian Dairy Corporation, 1996). This would imply that herd averages are lower for states where the majority of milk is used for manufacturing purposes.

So too could it be expected that market segmentation would have a determining influence on stocking rates. The pasture based nature of milk production in Australia, in combination with substantial periods in which dairy cows are not producing milk (and require less nutrition) on dairy farms that serve the manufacturing milk market would be higher than stocking rates in states where the majority of milk is used as fresh milk. This is the case in Victoria and Tasmania however, stocking rates in South Australia are the lowest in Australia. However, this is not the case and suggests that herd averages and stocking rates are not solely determined by cow breeds or the production requirements of particular market segments.

The majority of milk in states producing predominantly for the fresh milk market realized increases in milk production primarily through raising herd averages. In states where the bulk of milk is for manufacturing purposes, higher milk production was achieved through increases in stoking rates. From this perspective, there are marked differences in the structure of milk production by state. These differences can be classified according to their main structural characteristics (see Table 5).

New South Wales Dairy Farms: Labor Intensive

In 1983/84 New South Wales dairy farms were characterized by high labor input but low labor efficiency. These farms had a relatively high level of market integration as reflected in a high cost structure. In relation to other characteristics, the structure of milk production is similar to the Australian average. On the basis of the high labor input and low labor productivity, milk production on dairy farms in New South Wales can be described as 'labor intensive'. Despite the changes in the structure of dairy farms in this state between 1983/84 and 1994/95, the description of 'labor intensive' is appropriate to describe dairy farms in New South Wales relative to other states.

Queensland Dairy Farms: Traditional

Milk production in Queensland is characterized by large land area with small herd size. Dairy farms in this state have an average to low herd average and low

Table 5. Overview of structural differences in milk production by state, 1983/84 1994/95

State	Production Orientation	Herd Size	Land Size	Labor Input	Labor Efficiency	Market Integration (Cost structure)	Stocking Rates	Herd Average	Output per farm	Net value of production
New South Wales: labor intensive	Fresh milk market	Average	Average	High	Low	High	Average	Average	Average in 1983/84 Low in 1994/95	Average
Victoria: land management	Manufacturing milk market	Large	Small	Low in 1983/84 Average in 1994/95	Average	Average in 1983/84 Low in 1994/95	High	low	High	Low in 1983/84 High in 1994/95
Queensland: traditional	Fresh milk market	Small	Large	Average	Low	Low	Low	Low in 1983/84 Average in 1994/95	Low	low
Western Australia: large scale	Fresh milk market	Large	Large	High	High	High	Average	High	High	high
South Australia: cow management	Manufacturing milk market	Average in 1983/84 Small in 1994/95	Average in 1983/84 large in 1994/95	Average in 1983/84 High in 1994/95	Average	Average	Average in 1983/84 Low in 1994/95	High	average	Average in 1983/84 High in 1994/95
Tasmania: small scale	Manufacturing milk market	Small in 1983/84 large in 1994/95	Small	Low	Average 1983/84 high in 1994/95	Low in 1983/84 Average in 1994/95	Average in 1984/85, high in 1994/95	Average in 1983/84 Low in 1994/95	Low in 1983/84 Average in 1994/95	Average

Source: data adapted from BAE, 1986; ABARE, 1997.

stocking rates. They also had a high labor input, but low labor productivity, although it is also characterized by a low level of market integration (cost of production). On the basis of these characteristics Queensland dairy farms can be described as 'traditional'. Between 1983/84 and 1994/95 dairy farms in Queensland increased milk production by increasing herd averages; however, other characteristics of milk production in this state remained similar relative to that of other states throughout the period 1983/84 and 1994/95.

Western Australian Dairy Farms: Large Scale

Western Australian dairy farms are characterized by a high output per farm, large land area and large dairy herd. They achieved high herd averages but had average stocking rates. Dairy farms in Western Australia also have high labor inputs, high labor efficiency and high level of market integration. This farming style can be described as 'large scale'. Between 1983/84 and 1994/95 the structure of milk production in Western Australia remained similar relative to that of other states and can still be described as 'large scale'.

Victorian Dairy Farms: Land Management

Dairy farms in Victoria were characterized by a high output per farm. Their structure of milk production was characterized by a large herd size but a small farm area. In terms of productivity Victorian dairy farms had a low herd average, but high stocking rates (productivity of pasture). They worked relatively few weeks per year, but had a high milk production per week worked. They have a relatively low cost structure. Milk production in Victoria was characterized by high stocking rates and their structure of milk production can be described as 'land management'. The changes that took place between 1983/84 and 1994/95 did not change the characteristics of milk production in Victoria.

South Australian Dairy Farms: Cow Management

In 1983/84 dairy farms in South Australia were characterized by medium range milk production per farm, had large land area but small herd sizes, and enjoyed the highest herd averages but with low stocking rates. They had low labor inputs and medium range labor efficiency. Furthermore, these dairies had an average level of market integration. Dairy farms in South Australia were characterized especially by their high herd averages and consequentially they can be described as focused on 'cow management.' Between 1983/84 and dairy farms in this underwent some marked changes. In 1994/95 the dairy industry in South Australia was still characterized by a small herd size and the highest herd averages, but farm area had increased to become the second largest in Australia. Between 1983/84 and 1994/95 the milk production in South Australia changed as a result of increases in farm area and herd averages rather than stocking rates. Milk production per week worked increased to become similar to the national average. During this period the structure of dairy farms in South Australia became similar to that of Western Australia.

Tasmanian Dairy Farms: Labor Productive

In 1983/84 milk production in Tasmania was characterized by large herd sizes and average farm area resulting in high stocking rates. They had low labor inputs and the highest labor efficiency. They had low herd averages, and an average level of market integration. Tasmanian dairy farms of this period can be described as 'labor productive'. Between 1983/84 and 1994/95 dairy farms in Tasmania also underwent some marked changes. They experienced the highest increase in milk production per farm and the largest increase in herd size in Australia. Dairy farms in this state had the largest increase in stocking rates but the lowest increase in herd averages. Stocking rates became the second highest, while herd averages became the lowest in Australia. The result of these changes in milk production per farm in the state changed from one of the lowest in Australia to above the national average. So too, the size of the dairy herd changed from one of the lowest to the second largest in Australia while farm area remained the second smallest in Australia. Milk production in Tasmania increased as a result of increases in herd size and stocking rates rather than increases in herd averages or farm area. The structure of milk production in Tasmania became similar to that of Victoria during the period 1983/84 and 1994/95. The relationship between differences in the structures of dairy farms and the implications of the two strategies for the economic returns to dairy farmers is explored below.

REGIONAL DIFFERENTIALS AND THE ECONOMIC RETURNS TO DAIRY FARMERS

An exploration of changes in the structure of milk production by state shows that during the period 1983/84 and 1994/95, returns increased more than twofold in Tasmania but by less than one and a third in South Australia. The cost of production increased almost threefold in Tasmania but by less than one and a half in Victoria. Victoria was the only state where the increase in the rate of returns was greater than the increase in the cost of milk production (see Table 6). One concludes that at least half of the dairy farms currently in operation will be forced to close out in the not too distant future. State differentials in the degree of vulnerability are all too evident.

Dairy farms in New South Wales received the highest price per litre of milk in Australia. However, they have a net value of production (NVP) which is below that of dairy farms in Victoria and Western Australia, which receive a lower return per litre. Dairy farms in New South Wales also have a gross margin per week worked that is below that of dairy farms in Western Australia and Victoria, which receive a lower price per litre of milk. Gross margins per cow in New South Wales are also below those of dairy farms in Western Australia and Queensland and gross margins per hectare are below those of dairy farmers in Victoria and Tasmania, all of who receive a lower return per litre of milk (see Table 7).

Dairy farmers in Victoria received the second lowest returns per litre but they are the only state in Australia where, between 1983/84 and 1994/95, the increase in rate of returns was greater than the increase in rate of the cost of production. Their NVP was higher than that of dairy farms in all states except Western Australia. Too, their gross margin per week worked is one of the highest in Australia, and is higher than that of dairy farmers in New South Wales, Queensland and South Australia who receive a higher price per litre of milk They also had the highest gross margin per hectare in Australia and their gross margins per cow were slightly above the national average. Similar observations can be made in relation the price per litre and net returns.

When differences in efficiency and returns are examined in relation to particular farming structures, there is some indication that farming structures that focus on increasing milk production by increasing stocking rates and number of cows (Victoria and Tasmania) are more efficient than farming structures that have increased milk production by increasing herd averages (Queensland and South Australia).

DISCUSSION AND CONCLUSION

This analysis of the dairy industry in Australia makes a number of observations. Based on an examination of data over the period 1983/84 and 1994/95, it suggests that two major dairy farming strategies appear to have developed in Australia. The first strategy focuses on increasing milk production by increasing herd averages while other focuses on increasing milk production by raising stocking rates. The literature on the development of the dairy industry in Australia does not provide any clear explanation for these differences.

Table 6. Changes (%) in economic returns of milk production, by state, 1983/84–1994/95

	New South Wales	Victoria	Queensland	Western Australia	South Australia	Tasmania	Total Australia
Gross returns	144.2	143.3	153.5	157.3	130.1	215.6	157.6
Cost of production	190.0	139.3	176.8	189.1	194.0	274.9	183.1
Price per litre	40.3	44.9	48.4	40.7	34.4	61.0	45.6

Source: data adapted from BAE, 1986; ABARE, 1997.

Table 7. Economic returns of milk production ($A), by state, 1994/95

	New South Wales	Victoria	Queensland	Western Australia	South Australia	Tasmania	Total Australia
Gross returns	233,002	192,723	78,376	302,289	197,354	186,866	200,819
Cost of production	176,244	126,400	36,699	223,227	153,526	141,174	151,242
Net value of production	56,758	66,323	41,677	79,062	43,828	45,692	49,577
Price/litre (cents)	36.9	24.2	36.8	30.4	28.9	23.5	28.4
Hired labor (% total costs)	6.2	3.6	1.8	3.9	2.8	4.1	3.6
Sharefarming (% total costs)	1.8	7.2	—	0.2	6.9	4.9	4.3
Gross margin per week worked	420.40	425.90	335.30	594.40	368.30	393.90	396.60
Gross margin per cow	272.90	249.50	282.30	304.10	250.5	194.40	245.40
Gross margin per hectare	215.00	358.80	178.44	196.7	137.0	241.80	250.40

Source: data adapted from ABARE, 1997.

An analysis of economic returns to dairy farmers reveals that the differences in the structure of dairy farms by state were associated with economic returns that cannot be derived from the price per litre. Instead they appear related to the structure of dairy farms. Dairy farms that are able to increase production by increasing stocking rates are in a better financial position than dairy farms that increase milk production by increasing herd averages. This is likely to be a result of the fact that the latter strategy allows for increases in milk production at a lower cost of production than strategies that increase milk production through increasing herd averages.

At the start of the new millennium the Australian dairy industry continues to be subject to government policies that advocate greater deregulation. And its future continues to be uncertain as the likelihood and effect of certain trends is unknown at present. My analysis suggests that rather than accept that there is only one pattern of development, an adequate understanding of the development of the Australian dairy industry involves an analysis of the extent to which differences in the structure of dairy farms mediate the processes that operate external to the farm unit.

ACKNOWLEDGMENTS

The author gratefully acknowledges the input and comments of Dr Andrew Davidson and Professor Harry Schwarzweller on earlier versions of the manuscript.

REFERENCES

Ashton, L. G. (Ed.) (1949). *Dairy farming in Australia – Victorian Edition*. Canberra: Department of Agriculture and Trade.

Ashton, L. G. (Ed.) (1950). *Dairy farming in Australia – New South Wales Edition*. Canberra: Department of Agriculture and Trade.

Ashton, L. G. (Ed.) (1951). *Dairy farming in Australia – Queensland Edition*. Canberra: Department of Agriculture and Trade.

Ashton, L. G. (Ed.) (1952). *Dairy farming in Australia – South Australian Edition*. Canberra: Department of Agriculture and Trade.

Ashton, L. G. (Ed.) (1955). *Dairy farming in Australia – Western Australian Edition*. Canberra: Department of Agriculture and Trade.

Ashton, L. G. (Ed.) (1956). *Dairy farming in Australia – Tasmanian Edition*. Canberra: Department of Agriculture and Trade.

Australian Bureau of Statistics (1984–85a). *Census of Manufacturing Establishments: Summary of Operations by Industry Class, New South Wales*. Cat No 8201.1.

Australian Bureau of Statistics (1984–85b). *Census of Manufacturing Establishments: Summary of Operations by Industry Class, Victoria*. Cat No 8201.2.

Australian Bureau of Statistics (1984–85c). *Census of Manufacturing Establishments: Summary of Operations by Industry Class*. Queensland. Cat No 8201.3.

Australian Bureau of Statistics (1984–85d). *Census of Manufacturing Establishments: Summary of Operations by Industry Class, Western Australia*. Cat No 8201.5.

Australian Bureau of Statistics (1984–85e). *Census of Manufacturing Establishments: Summary of Operations by Industry Class, South Australia*. Cat No 8201.4.

Australian Bureau of Statistics (1984 85f). *Census of Manufacturing Establishments: Summary of Operations by Industry Class, Tasmania*. Cat No 8201.6.

Australian Bureau of Statistics (1986). *Australia Yearbook, 1986*. Canberra: Australian Bureau of Statistics.

Australian Bureau of Agriculture and Resource Economics (1991). *Farm Surveys*. Canberra: Australian Bureau of Agriculture and Resource Economics.

Australian Bureau of Agriculture and Resource Economics (1997). *Farm Surveys*. Canberra: Australian Bureau of Agriculture and Resource Economics.

Australian Dairy Corporation (1995). *Australian Dairy Compendium*. Glen Iris: Australian Dairy Corporation.

Australian Dairy Corporation (1996). *The Australian Dairy Industry*. Glen Iris: Australian Dairy Corporation.

Australian Farm Journal (1994). *Property: Rural Land Around the Nation*, May, 108–122.

Australian Farm Journal (1995). *Kangaroo Island Cheese Enterprise Expands*, August, 44–45.

Australian Farm Journal (1996). *Premium Cheese Market Up for Grabs*, September, 26–27.

Australian Financial Review (1998). *SA Victory for Dairy Farmers*, 25 February, 1998.

Bock, L. (Ed.) (1995). *Natural Farming Australia*. Brisbane: Cynaco.

Bureau of Agricultural Economics (1986). *Farm Surveys*. Canberra: Bureau of Agricultural Economics.

Cottrell, R (1987). *The Sacred Cow, The Folly of Europe's Food Mountains*. London: Grafton Books.

Dairy Research and Development Corporation (1993). *Dairy Development in Western Victoria*. Glen Iris: Dairy Research and Development Corporation.

Dairy Research and Development Corporation (1995). *The New South Wales Dairy Industry: a Strategic Analysis of Research, Extension and Related Needs for Industry Development*. Glen Iris: Dairy Research and Development Corporation.

Dairy Research and Development Corporation (1995). *A Regional Plan for Dairy Industry Development in the Murray Basin*. Glen Iris: Dairy Research and Development Corporation.

Davidson, B (1981). *European Farming in Australia*. Amsterdam: Elsevier Scientific.

Davidson, A. P (1997). Restructuring of the Dairy Industry in New South Wales. *Rural Society*, 7(2), 17–28.

Davidson, A. P., & Schwarzweller, H. K. (1995). Marginality and Uneven Development: the Decline of Dairying in Michigan's North Country. *Sociologia Ruralis*, 35(1), 40–66.

DuPuis, E. M (1993). Sub-National State Institutions and the Organization of Agricultural Resource Use: The case of the Dairy Industry. *Rural Sociology*, 58(3), 440–460.

Drane, N. T., & Edwards, H. R. (Eds) (1961). *The Australian Dairy Industry an Economic Study*. Melbourne: F. W. Cheshire.

Gilbert, J., & Akor, A. (1988). Increasing Structural Diversity in U. S. Dairying: California and Wisconsin since 1950. *Rural Sociology*, 53(1), 56–72.

Griffith, G. R. (1989). *Policies and Trends in the Australian Dairy Products Market: 1964/65 to 1988/89*. Sydney: NSW Agriculture and Fisheries, Division of Rural and Resource Economics.

Gow, J. (1994). Farm Structural Adjustment – an Everyday Imperative. *Rural Society, 4*(2).

Hefford, R. K. (1985). *Farm Policy in Australia*. St Lucia: University of Queensland Press.

Industry Commission (1991). *Dairy Industry*. Canberra: Australian Government Publishing Service.

Kiley-Worthington, M. (1993). *Eco-Agriculture: Food First Farming*. London: Souvenir Press.

Lawrence, G. (1987). *Capitalism and the Countryside*. Sydney: Pluto Press.

Lyson, T. A., & Geisler, C. C. (1992). Towards a Second Agricultural Divide: The Restructuring of American Agriculture. *Sociologia Ruralis, 32*(2/3), 248–263.

Maso, B. (1987). *Rood and Zwart*. Wageningen: Mededelingen van de Werkgroup Sociologie Landbouw Hogeschool Wageningen.

O'Sullivan, D. (1992). *Dairying History of the Darling Downs*. Toowoomba: University of Southern Queensland Press.

Piore, M. J., & Sabel, C. F. (1984). *The Second Industrial Divide*. New York: Basic Books.

Pusey, M. (1991). *Economic Rationalism in Canberra*. Melbourne: Cambridge University Press.

Salamon, S. (1985). Ethnic Communities and the Structure of Agriculture. *Rural Sociology, 50*(3), 323–340.

Sillcock, K. (1972). *Three Lifetimes of Dairying in Victoria*. Melbourne, Victoria: Hawthorne.

Van der Meulen, H., & Ventura, F. (1994). Transformation and Consumption of High-Quality Meat: The Case of Chianina Meat in Umbria, Italy. In: J. D. van der Ploeg & A. Long (Eds), *Born from Within* (pp. 128–159). Assen: van Gorcum.

Van der Ploeg, J. D. (1995). From Structural Development to Structural Involution: the Impact of New Developments in Dutch Agriculture. In: J. D.van der Ploeg & G van Dijk (Eds), *Beyond Modernization: the Impact of Endogenous Rural Development* (pp. 109–146). Assen: van Gorcum.

Van der Ploeg, J. D., & Saccomandi, V. (1995). On the Impact of Endogenous Development in Agriculture. In: J. D. van der Ploeg & G van Dijk (Eds), *Beyond Modernization: the Impact of Endogenous Rural Development* (pp. 10–27). Assen: van Gorcum.

Ventura, F (1995). Styles of Beef Cattle Breeding and Resource Use Efficiency in Umbria. In: J. D. van der Ploeg & G van Dijk (Eds), *Beyond Modernization: the Impact of Endogenous Rural Development* (pp. 219–232). Assen: van Gorcum.

MILK QUALITY AND GLOBALIZATION: METAPHORS OF MODERNITY IN NORTHWESTERN MICHOACÁN, MEXICO

James H. McDonald

INTRODUCTION

The ability to define and impose a particular set of standards over others involves the exercise of power. As new quality standards are imposed on local producers and processors, the variability of the meaning of quality becomes an important problem. Given that the idea of milk quality varies according to an actor's position in the structure of the dairy industry, my aim is to take account of the rationale for those differing conceptualizations and their implications. Through a series of cases, I examine how farmers, processors, state officials, and consumers understand the meaning of quality and how the new demands for quality shape local practice and, in some instances, resistance. Specifically, each group has its own image and perception of 'milk quality', its own notions about the validity of diverse standards of quality and their relative importance, and its own sense of the economic cost-benefit involved in assuring 'quality' at their particular level in the system of production and processing.

The idea that milk quality can vary and that it is often important for milk to meet a certain standard is certainly not new to these different groups. Until recently, however, it was not a major issue among any of the key players in the dairy industry, and consumer demands for a safe and nutritious product

Research in Rural Sociology, Volume 8, pages 181–209.

received little attention. Foreign competition in the globalizing, market-oriented Mexican economy has changed that. With the opening of the Mexican economy under the North American Free Trade Agreement (NAFTA) in 1994, the Mexican state, in concert with large dairy processors, has begun to impose new and more rigorously maintained standards for the fresh fluid milk that is destined for commercial processing into cheese, yogurt, and the like. What is being imposed are milk quality standards that derive from Western dairy science (based on the percentage milkfat, non-fat solids, and the presence of bacteria and other contaminants).[1] By adopting what might be termed 'global-technical standards' similar to those of the U.S., their aim is to produce dairy products that rival the international competition.

As Zárate (1998: 141) aptly observes, however, the process of globalization is one in which, 'diverse habitats of meaning' found at the local level intersect with the ideas and practices of global origin, often though the mediation of more proximate institutions (e.g. government agencies and large commercial dairies) (see also McDonald, 1999a). 'Milk quality' has variable and contested definitions, and takes on different meanings depending on whom is deploying the term and under what circumstances. Understanding the emic frameworks of the key players in the dairy industry will aid in the formulation of development strategies by revealing the potential for contradictions, misunderstandings, and conflicts at the different levels of dairy production and processing. This approach has the added advantage of taking into account local-level knowledge and material conditions that are often overlooked in more macro-oriented research.

SETTING

The setting for this exploratory research is in Michoacán, a west-central Mexican state (Map 1). Fieldwork was conducted in the state's northwestern highlands in the community of San José de Gracia; some additional information was obtained in nearby Cotija. San José is located about an hour and a half south of Guadalajara in a region that is a bit like a green desert; it appears lush, but its mountainous terrain and thin soils are poorly suited for agriculture, and this is exacerbated by a lack of irrigation. Additionally, it is characterized by significant environmental degradation from overgrazing and deforestation. San José is a marginal dairying community insofar as it is dominated by small-scale farmers utilizing a peasant-like system of 'tradi-tional' production methods characteristic of the highlands and many other parts of Mexico – a labor intensive regime in which cows graze on open rangeland (with supplements of commercial feed) and are milked by hand once per day,

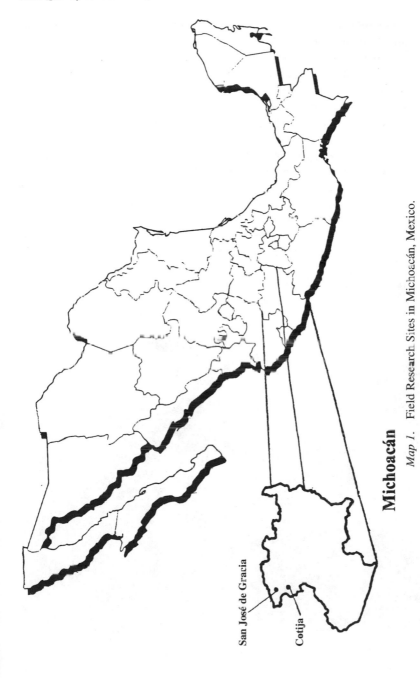

Michoacán

Map 1. Field Research Sites in Michoacán, Mexico.

San José de Gracia

Cotija

often in the field (see Fig. 1). Only one of the large farmers in my sample had a mechanical milking machine.

The 1996 membership list of the Local Dairymen's Association of San José, reflects the domination of independent, small-scale producers in the area: small farms with less than 20 head of cattle comprise 82.9% of all farms; 11.3% are small-medium farms with 20–49 head; 5.1% are medium-large farms with 50–100 head; and only 0.7% are large farms with over 100 head. The Dairy Association reports a total of 6113 milk cows (an average of 15 head per member).[2] Herds consist of cows that are a Holstein-Cebu mix, and cows in milk (on average seven months per year) produce only about seven liters and no more than 12 liters of milk per day. Farmers, however, claim these cows are well adapted to life on the range and are resistant to the numerous parasites and problems that would plague finer stock.

Dairying is supported by the production of maize supplemented by commercial feed during the dry season (November-May) and open rangeland grazing during the rainy season (July-October). Farmers typically do not have enough rangeland (about 1–2 hectares per animal) or seasonal agricultural land (5–10 hectares on average, producing only 3–4 tons of maize per hectare) to

Fig. 1. Farmer milking in the field.

support their herds, nor is there adequate water for irrigation (let alone for cattle to drink). Only two farms in my sample had any irrigation, and that was limited to small plots of groomed pasture. Consequently, no farmer is self-sufficient in forage crops (typically maize) or rangeland, and each has to supplement these with purchased feed (commercial grain mixtures) and forage (hay, alfalfa, and maize). This dependency on commercial feed is most acute during the dry season, especially toward its end when even the farms with the most agricultural land run out of stores of their own forage crops. While most farmers use limited amounts of commercial feed during the rainy season, they also complain that their rangeland is of poor quality and insufficient even during the best rainy season.

During the summer of 1996, farmers also complained bitterly about rising costs of production coupled with the declining price for their milk (US$0.23–0.25 per liter, a significant drop from the US$0.31 they were receiving during the dry season).[3] This theme is an old one and can be traced back to the beginning of year-round dairying in the 1960s. Historian Luis González notes that even during the relatively stable economy of the 1960s:

> Dairy men complain that prices of milk and milk products rise slowly in comparison with the rapidly increasing costs of feed and consumer products; but they realize that, even so, they are making more money than they used to, although it is still not enough to merit them living well and to increase their operations [L. González, 1974: 274].

The opening of the Mexican economy in the 1990s created a far harsher economic environment. As Rodríguez (1997: 7–8) notes, with few exceptions the 1990s witnessed sharply rising costs for dairy production, declining prices for raw, fresh milk (with a momentary exception during mid- to late-1995), expensive credit, and an overall reduction of subsidies.

Several cases underscore how the crisis impacted farmers in San José de Gracia. In the summer of 1997, one medium-scale farm, for example, with 42 cows in milk, yielding 550 liters per day, was netting only US$12.50 per week. A smaller counterpart with only 10 cows in milk, yielding 120 liters per day, was losing $381 pesos per week (US$47.63).[4] This complemented similar data obtained in July 1996 by a local veterinarian and several other dairymen. In their study, the smallest farm had three cows in milk and was losing US$6.00, a small-medium farm with 20 cows in milk was losing US$27.11, and a medium-large farm with 90 cows in milk was losing US$95.87 per week.[5] Farmers openly talked of their 'decapitalization' – selling cows to pay off their debts to local feed sellers and others.

Although farmers face serious financial problems and herds are being reduced, this is, nevertheless, still an important milkshed within the state of Michoacán. The municipality of Marcos Castellanos, in which San José is located, alone accounts for almost 10% of the state's annual milk production (259,539,000 liters are produced in the state and 25,086,700 liters in Marcos Castellanos) (INEGI, 1993). Indeed, approximately half of the state's production comes from the northwestern region including the highlands and an adjoining lowland area known as the Ciénega de Chapala. According to M. A. González (1997), 71% of the state's milk production is dedicated to fluid consumption and the other 29% to processing. He estimates that the per capita consumption of fresh milk is 54 liters per year, which is well below the FAO recommendation of 131 liters (M. A. González, 1997: 3). Not surprisingly, considerable quantities of pasteurized milk flow into the state from elsewhere in the central region – Jalisco, Guanajuato, and Aguascalientes.

The commercial processing of milk in Michoacán, however, has been expanding. Twenty years ago there was a single pasteurization plant in the state that was operated by LICONSA (the milk processing and distribution branch of CONASUPO, the National Company for Popular Subsistence) (see Fig. 2).

Now there are seven functioning plants and another three, which for various reasons, are not in operation (Ricardo Rodríguez, SAGAR-Morelia, personal communication, June 1997). Two new pasteurization plants in La Piedad and Pátzcuaro were funded by the state's Alianza para el Campo Program in

Fig. 2. Farmers delivering milk to the LICONSA plant in Jiquilpan, Michoacán.

1995–1996. Additionally, in the 1994–1995 cycle, FIRCO (the state's Trusteeship of Shared Risk) funded four milk refrigeration tank projects (milk collection centers) in Zacapú, Tlazazalca, Vista Hermosa, and Cotija. The Cotija project was completed in 1996 at a cost of US$22,728, of which US$6,494 was paid by local producers. The Cotija project is the only one that has yet to get up and running. The Cotija project sits idle because they cannot find a buyer in the region willing to pay them enough to make it cost effective to run and maintain their expensive new equipment. A separate milk refrigeration tank project is being financed by LICONSA, which has established 12 milk collection centers throughout the state.[6]

Northwestern Michoacán, consequently, represents a significant, but under-developed, milk producing region. Additionally, milk production in San José is complemented by perhaps as many as 60 or more local dairy processors that range from numerous small, family-run operations to three relatively large-scale processors.[7] It is estimated that the commercial processing of elaborated products, such as cheese, cream, and yogurt, is 188,400 liters per day in the municipalities of Marcos Castellanos, Michoacán and Valle de Juárez, Jalisco (M. A. González, 1997: 14, 17). Annual consumption by processors, however, is 68,620,000 liters.[8] This implies a local deficit in production of 43,533,300 liters (without accounting for production in neighboring Valle de Juárez, Jalisco). In other words, the area represents a fairly robust and elastic market for milk that is being made into processed dairy products. Overall, however, the local dairy economy in San José de Gracia is far from healthy and, in general, farming methods are rudimentary. It remains to be seen whether this region will be able to modernize and compete in the globalizing Mexican economy.

The northwestern highlands are surrounded by other important dairying regions in central Mexico. For example, the area contrasts with Mexico's top milk producing zone, the Altos de Jalisco (to the immediate northeast), not so much in terms of scale or organization of production, but in terms of the presence of large-scale commercialization of milk (Rodríguez & Chombo, 1998). It also contrasts with the large-scale, heavily capitalized farms associated with the Laguna Region near Torreón, Coahuila yet further to the north, which has the highest yields per cow in the country (ITESM, 1994). To the east, Guanajuato has a geographically advantageous location in the Mexican economy with direct access to Mexico City and major crossings along the Texas-Mexico border. While dairying in Guanajuato is a mixture of small and large-scale operations, there is a marked trend toward the concentration of dairying into larger-scale farms (with herds averaging 50 cows or more) (McDonald, 1994, 1996, 1997, 1999b). The Laguna area has seen heavy investment for the development of high-tech farms in tandem with industrial integration through the Leche Lala dairy (one of Mexico's largest dairy processors), as well as Alpura, Queen, and Bell. The Altos de Jalisco region, in contrast, has seen private corporations, such as Nestlé, buying from traditional small-scale farmers who receive little added investment in technology or organizational infrastructure, yet manage to produce large volumes of milk. Guanajuato represents a middle ground between the two.

The Michoacán community, then, is a more marginal case from a commercial perspective. Given the importance of dairying to the region, the collapse of this key industry would have dire consequences for the area. Therefore, the ability to produce a quality product that conforms to rising national and consumer standards is an emerging issue. And to comprehend the variable meanings of quality held by diverse government officials, dairy processors, dairymen, and consumers, along with the priorities they assign to the various standards being promulgated by the government is critical to producing safe and nutritious milk and creating sustainable regional development.

RESEARCH METHODS

Data for this article were collected during the summer of 1996 and 1997 via in-depth, semi-structured interviews with 47 farmers and the managers or owners of 11 dairy processing plants. A stratified sample was drawn from a listing of 410 dairy farmers in the community: 27 small farmers (1–20 cows); 15 medium (21–100 cows); and five large (over 100 cows). Another stratified sample of dairy processors was drawn from the approximately 60 businesses in the community and surrounding area. These processors included five small businesses (1000 to 1200 liters daily); five medium (5,000 to 10,000 liters daily); and one large (27,000 liters daily).

Supplemental macroeconomic data and policy information were also obtained from records and five interviews at the main SAGAR (Secretariat of Agriculture, Livestock, and Rural Development) office in the state capital of Morelia and a local district office Sahuayo, Michoacán, and one interview was conducted with an official with FIRA (The Bank of Mexico's Office of Instituted Trusteeships in Relation with Agriculture, also located in Morelia), and another with an official at the Morelia Dairymen's Association. Relevant information was also obtained from individuals associated with the local dairy industry, including officials of dairymen's associations, veterinarians, local politicians, and consumers.

THE VARIABLE MEANINGS OF QUALITY IN MICHOACÁN

From my vantage point in Michoacán, there were considerable differences between local conceptualizations of quality and the global-technical one being imposed on them. The quality concept, then, can be thought of as a point of articulation between the global and the local. How its definition and associated practices work out in Michoacán, of course, has tremendous implications for local well-being. Indeed, just to the north of San José in the Altos de Jalisco, new quality standards imposed by large processors, such as Nesté and Sello Rojo (Red Seal), is forcing farmers to reorganize and invest in costly new equipment. The end result is that many small farms have failed (Rodríguez & Chombo, 1998). And, as is known from work on the industrialization of agriculture in the U.S., this forces small-scale producers to go out of business because they cannot or will not meet new technical requirements or quality standards, and entire regional rural economies collapse with devastating results (Fitchen, 1991; Griffith & Kissam et al., 1995).

The imposition of quality standards, thus, becomes an exercise of power, and its exercise has serious consequences for people's livelihoods and futures. Consequently, a consideration is, "quality according to whom, and with what consequences?" With this in mind, I will now turn to a discussion of the government's position in conjunction with the consumer's position as a starting point for defining the health interests of the Mexican people. This will be followed by a discussion of dairy processors who implement these standards. Finally, farmer's understanding of milk quality will be examined in light of the imposition of new standards.

State Government Officials and Consumers

Government officials working at SAGAR in the state capital of Morelia advocate the adoption of global-technical standards for milk quality that would support greater competitiveness in domestic and international markets, as well as address public health concerns. They emphasize basic standards in bacteria levels, milkfat, proteins, and other solids, and the absence of antibiotics or milk from diseased animals. They also show an understanding, however, of local constraints and challenges faced by processors and farmers in areas like San José de Gracia where there is a tremendous variability throughout the entire chain of production. When focusing specifically on farmers, these officials feel that perhaps the biggest problem faced by them is their dependency on commercial feed for their cattle. Grazing in open pasture lands during the rainy season poses a problem because the wild grasses and weeds contain little protein. The commercial feeds they use during the dry season are often purchased in insufficient quantities to properly maintain their cows at optimal production levels.

A second major problem noted by these officials is the milking methods employed by dairymen. They attribute the continuation of milking-by-hand to an interaction of the local ideology and the local economy. On the one hand, farmers have traditionally milked-by-hand and, according to these officials, feel that it is a superior method (i.e. less likely to damage the cow and also most likely to thoroughly drain the udder of all its milk). They also note, however, that milking-by-hand quickly spreads diseases like mastitis,[9] and they acknowledge the high frequency of subclinical mastitis found in herds milked-by-hand, especially under the conditions found in areas like San José. On the other hand, they observe that the area is characterized by abundant and cheap labor, facilitating the dependence on manual labor rather than machinery. Furthermore, machinery would not be cost effective for many of the area's farmers anyway. Additionally, they realize that farmers are slowly decapitalizing and have little or no money to invest in costly new technology were it cost effective.

Consequently, these officials appreciate the economic realities that conditioned farmers' decisions, but offer few ideas about how to change the existing pattern of production. Without support from industry in the form of better infrastructure (more large dairy processing plants and local pasteurization plants for fresh fluid milk), there will remain little stimulus for developing farms into more efficient production units. They remark, for example, that existing plants in the area do not offer bonuses for producing quality milk nor is there any degree of vertical integration with large dairy processing plants.

Consumers are also becoming increasingly vocal in their demands for safe and nutritious milk. This is evident in Guadalajara where a number of dairies are spreading leaflets door-to-door advertising 'high quality milk' sold in pharmacies, specialty stores, or delivered directly to the consumer's doorstep. A flyer from Leche Tepatitlán, for example, claims that their fresh pasteurized milk is "made with the highest quality currently possible, carries a Sanitary Certification that is periodically verified by the Secretary of Health, and it is 100% natural . . . containing vitamins, carbohydrates, and an energy source found only in true milk . . . [and] no vegetable oil, extenders, synthetics, or preservatives." Most interesting and suggestive, however, is that their milk is being sold through the Guadalajara Pharmacy chain. Pharmacies in Mexico are associated with holistic rather than allopathic health. As such, they are not unlike health food stores in the U.S., such as General Nutrition Centers. It is not unreasonable to interpret this move as a response to consumer fears about impurity and lack of control, since pharmacies, as extensions of the laboratory, are seen as controlled and disease-free environments.

Throughout urban Mexico, middle-class consumers are increasingly buying expensive ultra-heat treated milk rather than pasteurized fresh milk. In northern Mexican markets, dairy products from the U.S. (fluid milk, ice cream, and yogurt) are flooding the market, carry competitive prices, and pose a serious challenge to domestic products (McDonald, 1996). All these are indicators of consumer preferences and demands for safe and nutritious milk. In San José, a few questioned local milk in terms of those qualities (one of the local veterinarians emphatically claims that he would never consume cheese produced during the rainy season because of poor sanitation), but the vast majority would simply shrug when questioned about milk quality. It must be all right because no one, they say, seems to get sick.

While many urban and some rural dwellers question the quality of what they consume, many have little choice but to buy raw milk sold on the street or uncooked white cheese produced by small processors as cost effective alternatives to their commercial counterparts. A series of recent milk scandals, however, have thrown the quality of those commercial products into question as well. Though able to evade formal prosecution, Raúl Salinas (brother of former President Carlos Salinas [1988–1994]) has been linked with the alleged importation in 1986–87 of radioactive powdered milk while he was Director of CONASUPO (Zamora, 1997). In 1996 Mexico began a campaign to test commercially pasteurized milk in high production and consumption areas of the country (González Pérez, 1996) and it was reported that 30% of Mexico's commercially pasteurized milk was substandard or adulterated (*Siglo 21*, 1996a). In Jalisco, the majority of its 400 large commercial dairies were found to be in violation of basic sanitary standards (del Castillo, 1995). In addition, pasteurized skimmed milk now has to have clearly marked packages stating that its nutritional characteristics are different from whole milk (*Siglo 21*, 1996b).

Back in San José, townspeople commonly joke about the cheese coming out of the area's commercial processing plants as tainted or made out of anything but dairy products ('plastic cheese' as they would say). One person noted, "You don't see anyone selling [dairy's name] cheese around here. We know better. No one would eat it." Many voice the opinion that they would prefer to eat non-commercial products because, whatever their problems, they are safer than their commercial counterparts. For many people, then, it seemed that quality and commercial production are anything but inherently synonymous.

While this evidence is anecdotal in nature, it certainly suggests that Mexicans are aware of milk quality problems. The key will be if and how this awareness becomes a force to shape the market and create a more accountable national system of dairy production and consistently safe and nutritious fresh milk, as well as processed products such as cheese, cream, and yogurt.

Dairy Processors

San José, as noted earlier, has many dairy processors (or creameries as they are called locally) ranging from extremely small, rudimentary operations to those that are very large and technologically sophisticated (see Figs 3 and 4). Not surprisingly, as we move downward in terms of scale of operation, processors' concept of quality begins to diverge rather sharply with the global-technical definition.

The one large creamery owner who took part in this study embraced the global-technical perspective in terms of milk quality. Indeed, one of his engineers who attended the interview told me the precise levels of protein, milkfat, and so on that needed to be met or exceeded for raw fresh milk to be accepted for processing at his plant. In fact, they did not feel that international quality standards could be met by many farmers nationally:

> Those of us that produce cheese would like milk with 3.6 [%] of fat and 3.6 [%] of protein. But we aren't in a position to demand this level of milk. What we want is milk that is well treated from the moment it is milked until we get it. We can't talk of higher quality, or in regard to the composition of milk, because we still don't have it . . . We don't have the cattle nor the system to feed them. A few ranches [in the country] are better organized. Their business is to sell milk and produce milk. Well obviously they can do it.

As far as he was concerned, if farmers cannot produce quality milk at a national level, local farmers:

> well . . . none of them [can produce with this level of quality]. Here you're a dairy farmer because you have three or four cows and you let them loose to graze, you milk them once-a-day, and the little bit of water they give them, the little bit they give them to eat – and this guy's a dairy farmer! This small-scale stuff isn't dairy farming, he isn't a producer of milk.

Indeed this processor does not buy any milk locally, but rather imports it from the Altos de Jalisco where he has a large milk collection center. His reasoning, however, has far less to do with quality factors than with volume:

> Unfortunately here in our area [in San José], we can't demand quality. Why? Because there is no quality. In the area of Los Altos [de Jalisco] they've begun, for example, to put in refrigeration tanks for the small dairy farmers, no? But unfortunately, a tank of 2,000 liters serves five or six dairy farmers. Automatically this milk doesn't have quality. The milk

Fig. 3. Workers at a medium-sized creamery in Cotija, Michoacán.

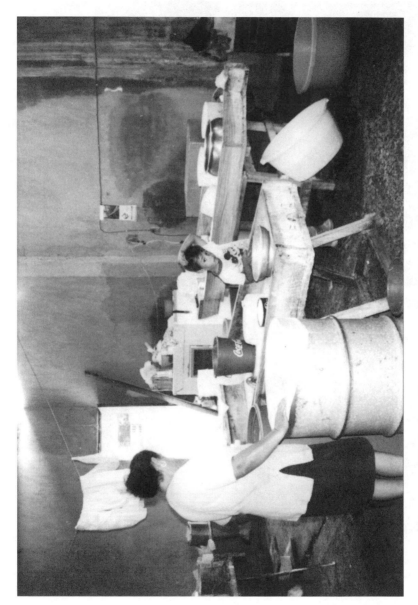

Fig. 4. A small creamery near San José de Gracia, Michoacán.

would have quality if it went directly from the milking machine into the [refrigeration tank], but if you have a tank, there are five dairy farmers within two to three kilometers, when they arrive [at the tank] with the milk the milk has already lost quality.

This case underscores a fundamental irony in San José. The plant most likely to help farmers organize and provide them with a stable market and an equitable price brings in milk from the Altos de Jalisco where milk costs slightly more per liter than in San José.[10] The owner only wants to work with farmers who are organized and can sell him milk in bulk:

There no milk in San José . . . we use 27,000 liters per day. We couldn't get that much milk here since there are so many competitors. But as far as I am concerned the quality is about the same even though farmers' milk is refrigerated once it arrives at the collection center in Los Altos. Some farms are further away than others, and acidity and bacteria multiply with distance. It all balances out.

Where he does have an edge in quality is through rigorous testing of milk: acidity, protein, milk fat, bacteria, antibiotics, and every 15 days they run a California test on each farmer's milk to test for mastitis.

When asked if he had tried to organize farmers in San José in order to avoid the shipping costs, as well as produce the level of quality he needs, he responded:

I don't believe anyone has asked them [to organize] for the simple reason that there are so many buyers. All the dairymen look to see who will pay them [more money] for their milk. Why? Because we are so many [commercial processors]. . .On the other hand, the 100 processors of cheese that are here, normally their process is very simple. So much so that they don't need refrigerated milk because they'd have to spend money to reheat it in order to pasteurize it. So why would they want refrigerated milk?

Medium-sized creameries do use raw milk purchased from local dairy farmers, as well as powdered milk, other dairy derivatives, and vegetable fats to make their various products. Most produce several different types of cream and cheese, and some also make yogurt. For example, one creamery, La Jolla (a pseudonym), produces three types of cream: *natural* (made with pure raw whole milk that sells wholesale for US$1.87 per kilo), *base* (made with 20% raw whole milk, powdered milk, and vegetable fat that sells wholesale for US$0.67 per kilo), and *vegetal* (made with 10% raw whole milk, vegetable fat, maize flour, and water that sells for US$0.27 per kilo). They also produce three types of cheese: *añejo* (made with pure raw whole milk that sells wholesale for US$2.67 per kilo), *cotija* (made with 60% raw whole milk, 40% powdered milk, and vegetable fat that sells wholesale for US$2.00 per kilo), *sierra* (made with about 50% raw whole milk and 50% powdered milk along with vegetable fat that sells wholesale for US$1.60 per kilo), and finally *doble crema* (while this has about the same percentage of whole milk and powdered milk as the previous type, its high water content results in a slightly lower wholesale price of US$1.33 per kilo). Additionally this creamery also produces yogurt.

Owners of medium-sized factories typically define milk quality in less specific terms than their larger counterpart. From the perspective of smaller processors, quality milk contains lots of nutrients, and specifically milkfat. When probed further, they are most interested in protein content. This became clear when one owner noted the problems he has during the rainy season. The price for milk drops not just because volume increases, but because the milk is 'thinner'. That is, it has a lower protein and milkfat content. He noted that this is because farmers allow their animals to graze and provide them with very little supplemental commercial feed or purchased forage. The problem is that the grasses and weeds found in the rangeland have little protein. As a consequence of this and increased competition in the market, he reduces the amount of fresh milk he works during the rainy season by 50%. Another owner does the opposite, processing less milk during the dry season (3,000 to 4,000 liters per day) than during the rainy season (7,000 liters). He too notes the seasonal variability – "well, the climate influences the amount [of cheese we get per liter]. In the rainy season [farmers] drop balanced concentrates altogether and during the dry season they never feed them enough." As a palliative for the problem of seasonal milk quality variability, these owners suggested that: (1) farmers need to purchase better quality commercial feed with higher protein. Many believe that farmers are more concerned with price than with the quality of the feed they purchase; (2) farmers need to produce their own high protein forage crops (this requires more intensive farming techniques anchored by irrigation through the construction of dams to capture the often abundant summer rains); and (3) that dairy practices also needed to change. The high bacteria levels found in local milk is a notable problem. One medium processor felt this is the most pressing problem that he faces: "Farmers are sometimes lazy and they don't get the milk here early. It's a real problem." He urged farmers to adopt sanitary techniques including the use of mechanical milking machines, but perhaps even more importantly, the education of the workers conducting the milking. Yet most medium owners are pragmatic, noting that farmers could not afford additional technology, such as milking machines or small milk refrigeration tanks.

A striking feature of medium-sized creameries is the limited capacity for testing milk and the other products they use in their cheese, cream, and yogurt. Those that have labs can only test for bacteria levels, protein and other solids, and the presence of water. Most contended they have had few problems with farmers watering down their milk. The owner of 'El Campesino' (a pseudonym, as are all names in this article) uses a simple empirical test:

Quantity [of cheese per unit of milk]. If we suspect that milk is being adulterated [with water], we compare how much cheese we get from it versus milk we know is good . . . Otherwise, all I can do is ask farmers for clean milk without antibiotics. They tell me it's clean. Who knows?

What bothers most of the medium-sized owners is their inability to test the milk for antibiotics and other medicines that farmers give their animals. They are certain that farmers continue to sell milk when their animals are receiving medical treatments. Not only is it unhealthy for humans to ingest these antibiotics, but their presence retards the effects of special bacteria cultures used in the production of high quality speciality cheeses, such as cheddar. Another related problem is the use of what they called 'neutralizers'. These are substances that farmers put into their milk to slow the growth of bacteria in the warm, raw milk. As El Campesino's owner noted, "Imagine if you break down or for some reason it takes you just one extra hour to get your milk to the factory. And, of course, antibiotics in the milk will also reduce the bacteria in the milk." Toward those ends, he felt that farmers would be better off if they adopted the practices he had heard about in the Altos de Jalisco and created their own small collection centers with a refrigeration tank. But he could not afford to help the farmers he works with financially to purchase such equipment. In fact, he thought that if he demanded refrigerated milk of his farmers, they would simply find another creamery that would buy their milk without making such a demand.

Another problem is the lack of capacity to test the additives that processors mix in with the milk in the process of making elaborated dairy products. These include such things as vegetable fat, tints, flavorings, and the like. The owner of another medium-sized business, 'El Tigre', complains, for example, that he received shipments of old or spoiled vegetable fat in the past, especially when he has had to purchase from other than his regular supplier. Overall, quality control for these products seems to be low. Yet El Campesino's owner claimed little problem with quality control. But at the market in Morelia, he had to take back cheese he had sold the previous week because it tasted bad according to his client, who could not (and would not) sell it (Armando Cortez, personal communication, 1996). While it is unclear how widespread these quality control problems are, this event made it clear that they do exist.

A major contradiction ran through the medium- and large-scale owner's discourse on quality. On the one hand, these owners valued milk with high protein and fat content, but at the same time they pay only for volume. "That is the custom here," one noted. At the same time, this processor also feels that the industry's role in stimulating change toward higher quality milk will be to pay a premium for milk that exceeds basic standards. But not he, and not now.

Small-scale dairy processors have a more general notion of milk quality. They typically make one or two types of cheese: *fresco* (a soft, high-water content white cheese) and *cotija* (a dense white cheese with lower water content). They often process 1,000 or 1,200 liters daily (resulting in 100 to 120 kilos of cheese) and sell on a weekly basis to regional markets in larger towns or small cities, such as Paracho or Uruapan. For one small processor, Camilo, the key to milk quality is 'good feed' for the cows, though he could not specify exactly what it was about feed that makes it either good or bad. Additionally, he felt that good cows were also important, and you get good cows by using fine bulls for insemination. Both dimensions result in cows that produce more milk. But when probed further he noted,

> Well, good milk is natural, clean, it doesn't have mamitis [sic] or it isn't the milk from a cow that's recently given birth; that the cattle are recently milked and that the milk is clean, and that it hasn't gotten hot in the sun, that it arrives early so that we can make good cheese.

Yet at the same time, Camilo says that he needs to use warm rather than refrigerated milk. His explanation is simple. Refrigerated milk separates. He does not have the equipment (nor wants to spend the additional money) to reheat and homogenize the milk. He also feels that farmers might find it tempting to skim off the cream if it is refrigerated.

Aside from milk that has sanitary problems, his biggest problems center around milk that arrives with high acidity[11] and that has been adulterated with water (". . . fat gives more cheese. The more fat [content] you have, the more you get out of it"). But no small processor has any way to test for these problems other than the basic empirical test of how much cheese is rendered from the milk.

In general, Camilo maintains that the quality of milk he buys is essentially all the same. The distinction he makes in quality is between milk from the area and milk produced in the mountains. In the latter case, it is colder and farmers' herds are primarily Cebu, which give less milk, but with a higher fat content. And while he values milk with a high fat content, low acidity, and so on, he does not pay anything extra for quality milk nor does he feel he can demand it of his clients who would simply sell their milk elsewhere.

In sum, then, dairy processors, regardless of size of operation, embrace a notion of 'quality'. As we move from large to smaller processors, the conceptualization of 'quality' becomes increasingly general in detail but maintains some basic similarities (i.e. relative to fat content, milk solids, acidity/bacteria, disease and other sanitation problems). At each successive level, processors lose control of the ability to demand quality of their dairy farmer clients. The large processor does not buy milk locally at all because he feels that they do not and will not organize and sell milk in large quantities. The medium-sized processor tests for some basic quality factors (e.g. water), but feels that he cannot demand other quality standards of his farmers. The small processor finds all milk that he buys to be of essentially the same quality (some may be more or less acidic, more or less sanitary, but it all balances out in the long run).

Dairy Farmers

Dairy farmers have their own understandings and relative importance of the quality standards. As a group, they tend to associate quality with increased milk production and lower costs of production, not with the definition offered by medium- and large-scale dairy processors or government officials. Farmers here, whether large or small, produce for economic gain that is shaped by the contingencies of the local market. Even two of the largest dairy farmers in the community do not process their own milk even though one owns a large dairy plant and the other a medium-sized creamery. In the former case, don Ramiro sells his milk to a local cheesemaker and prefers to truck in fresh fluid milk in bulk from nearby Altos de Jalisco. In the latter case, don Elio sells his fresh milk on the local market while at his plant he purchases powdered milk and vegetable fat which he turns into a low cost butter substitute. Interestingly, it is not that local dairymen will only change their practices when forced, most cannot change because of severe economic and infrastructural limitations. Additionally, there is no pressure to change from the local market, and there are no bonuses paid for 'quality' milk.

Another feature of dairying in the area is a lack of collective action to organize and to become better integrated into the market (McDonald, 1999b). There is no demand to do so, and farmers also have access to a stable if poorly paying market for warm fresh milk. Farmers tend to be pragmatic realists when it comes to the issue of modernizing their farms. Most use a cost/benefit calculation to plan farm development. Since quality is not demanded nor paid for by processors, such things as milking machines and milk refrigeration tanks would be an unnecessary expense. Furthermore, many farms have no electricity to run these machines, and are not inclined to install it since there is no viable market alternative as there is in the Altos de Jalisco (cf. Rodríguez, 1997). On the other hand, farmers would consider changing their system of production if it were cost effective. Since they are currently losing money and decapitalizing and the local market does not demand or support such changes, farm modernization is not a priority nor a possibility for most of the area's dairy farmers.

While these generalizations provide a broad frame of reference by which farmers in the region operate, it is useful to further separate farmer's conceptions of quality. Small producers form the largest bloc in the region. These farmers equate quality first and foremost with quantity, secondly with milkfat content which they link to cattle health, and thirdly with adulterating milk with water. They will also mention purity (typically linked to cattle health, lack of adulteration, and sanitation) and nutrition (typically linked to milkfat). Curiously, no farmers says that their product is 'safe', which is simply a fundamental, shared assumption (see Fig. 5).

They note, however, that none of the local creameries that buy their milk demand anything other than volume. Indeed many contend that creameries prefer to receive warm milk. As a consequence, they see the purchase of milk refrigeration tanks as an illogical and unnecessary expense. Milking machines are seen as time- and labor-saving devices that allow farmers to milk more cows in less time. Nevertheless, some argue that milking machines can damage cattle and hand-milking, therefore, is preferable. None of these farmers link either type of technology with quality,[12] but rather see them as ways of dealing with a high volume of production. Thus, given the small scale of their operations (and the fact that many ranches do not have electricity), these machines are seen as unnecessary luxuries, especially during bad economic times. Others argued that such expensive technology would have marginal utility, costing more to purchase, operate, and maintain than they would return in profit. Cotija's farmers, however, value milk refrigeration tanks (one of which had been installed in the Local Dairymen's Association in 1996) somewhat differently. For them this technology signifies a way to pool their milk and sell it in bulk for a better price.

The closest that small farmers come to the global-technical model of the state is when they observe that quality is inherent in the health and productivity of their cows (i.e. good quality cattle produce more and better quality milk as embodied in fat content). They also explicitly link volume and milkfat content with the type of feed consumed by their cows, and believe that commercial concentrates increase fat content. And, most claim that their cows eat very well (often resulting in the owner's self-exploitation – a frequently repeated joke is, "Fat cows, skinny peasants"). Farmers look to commercial feeds as the way to enhance the fat content and volume of milk produced per cow, rather than improving their rangeland or working their agricultural lands more intensively. This line of questioning would invariably lead to a discussion of the need for the government to subsidize cattle feed which had risen astronomically in price over the past year (around US$6.82-$7.68 per 40 kilo sack the previous year and US$9.87-$10.40 in the summer of 1996).

Fig. 5. A farmer making a *pajarete*—a combination of raw milk, chocolate, and often a shot of alcohol that is consumed in the morning by most farmers in the region.

Though all farmers claim that their cattle are sound and healthy, most feel their herd can still be improved by gaining access to fine bulls. However, farmers claim that the average productive period for their cows was seven or eight lactations. That is, farmers exploit their cattle well past their peak productive period. Nevertheless, most feel that their animals are hearty and well adapted to life on the open range and have few health problems. This assertion is certainly called into question in a study by M. A. González of San José which found levels of subclinical mastitis at 80% in a medium-sized ranch in the municipality.

Middle-level farmers have a more variable conception of milk quality, and they consider more factors. Some focus on the basics of volume, milkfat percentage, and the water noted above, but there are a number of other considerations. One farmer, for example, breaks the concept down into qualitative and quantitative dimensions. By 'qualitative' he means basic hygiene – "milk that is free of impurities." By 'quantitative' he means milkfat, protein and other solids, as well as higher volume (he also refers to this constellation of traits as 'efficiency'). He also adds that while local dairy processors do not pay for quality, there is a de facto quality control system at work in San José; processors know who produces good milk and bad milk. If you produce 'bad milk', you have a harder time finding a processor to buy your milk.

Another farmer notes that while his neighbors pretend to know about animal care and the health of their cattle, they really know little: "We are very backward in our knowledge about dairying. Everyone says that their cows are healthy. Well, they're lying." He talks about all the problems he has had with his cows, one of which came down with gangrenous mastitis: "Imagine, you wash your hands before milking and then you come into contact with that cow and then go on to milk all your others without washing your hands! How many of your cows are going to get sick?" His son also had reproductive problems with a number of his cows and lost a year's worth of reproductive potential. "You have to feed them even though they only give two or three liters per day." What is noteworthy here is that he was most likely selling this cow's milk even though she was on antibiotics. Additionally, rather than immediately selling such animals for beef, he keeps them at the risk of infecting other animals and at the expense of on-going treatments.

Local cows are not necessarily as well adapted to local conditions, one of the farmers said, but perhaps no animals would be highly productive under local constraints. He spoke of a test he conducted with a local cow (Holstein-Cebu mix) and a purchased high quality Canadian Holstein. Both were corralled and given the same water, feed, and other treatment. He observed: "[T]he Canadian cow didn't beat out the [Holstein-Cebu] in production. Bring in high quality American cows and they will produce the same as cattle we've already got. We will only get higher production with better methods." The cow's breeding makes little difference when they are not well fed.

On a more positive note, a farmer with dual purpose cattle[13] started experimenting during the 1996–97 cycle with high-yield grasses on a plot of land (12 hectares) with some river-fed irrigation (5 hectares). He grew both a summer and winter variety, and each yielded three cuttings. He observed that his cows responded positively in terms of increased conditioning and greater milk production (he claims an increase of 30 to 40%). It was so successful that he plans to expand the cultivation of these new varieties if he can find a way to afford more equipment to augment his existing river-based irrigation system. He is also experimenting with dry farming 25 hectares of winter oats (primarily on rented land) and between one and two hectares of yellow maize that he says will not yield a larger volume than the regional average of three or four tons per hectare, but is more nutritious. Further farm diversification includes raising small steers; he sells them young because he does not yet fully understand this complex and highly competitive market. But he is proud that the quality of his young steers brought him US$1.35 per kilo (at an average of 230 kilos) when the going rate was US$0.96 to US$1.03 per kilo in the summer of 1997. He is also experimenting with cut flowers that he sells to a middleman. This is a small-scale venture (a quarter hectare of irrigated land) which does not yet turn a profit. Finally, he owns a hog-raising operation. He is employing an important strategy of diversification that is especially adaptive in a volatile economy.

Large-scale farmers provide a more nuanced view of milk quality, relating it with technical efficiency, using available resources to their maximum productive ends. One farmer notes, for example, "As I understand 'producing better milk', is to be more efficient within your unit of production. Or rather, with the same resources you use them better and get higher production." This and other farmers transformed their maize crop into silage, using their resources as intensively as possible and staying as self-sufficient as possible in terms of forage crops.

> Quality milk is milk that comes with all of its milkfat. It has it all. While milk has to have milk fat . . . But to produce quality milk you have to give high quality feed, like alfalfa, to high quality cattle. Alfalfa is number one in the world. If there isn't alfalfa, the milk is of lower quality.

Large farmers (and some of their medium-scale colleagues) consistently emphasize the relationship between more intensive cultivation of their land, the production of nutritious crops, and their milk's fat content. But even the largest farmers had little non-irrigated, arable land to produce forage crops or groomed pasture land, and only two had limited amounts of irrigation (15 of 300 hectares and 30 of 80 hectares, respectively).

In most cases, technical efficiency also means increased hygienic methods of milking. As a large dairyman notes, "[W]here I want to enhance my milk is hygiene on the one hand that leads to public health and on the other . . . [w]e should also strive for producing milk with less fat and higher protein." Given the abundance of inexpensive wage labor, only one large farmer in the area uses a milking machine. Again, while most of these farmers are familiar with the connection between technology (milk refrigeration tanks and milking machines) and hygiene, few see any benefits of investing in such technology when they receive no economic incentive in the local market that only pays for quantity.

Although farmers in northwestern Michoacán differ in their conceptualiza-tion of quality, they felt that given the structural constraints within which they operate (e.g. relatively small herds of low-productivity cows, limited arable land, scrubby range land, lack of water, lack of electricity in many ranches), they produce a 'quality' product. These constraints bar them from other options in the modification of the local system of production or make those options unrealistic in terms of their net benefits. But the shift toward more intensive and diversified farming strategies is beginning to emerge as farmers attempt to find a way to survive in an increasingly hostile economy.

CONCLUSION

Unlike other Mexican milk producing areas, such as the nearby Altos de Jalisco, there is no well-established discourse about milk quality being shaped in Michoacán by the penetration of large commercial dairy processors or a demanding public. To make the hour and a half trip from northwestern Michoacán to Guadalajara is to move into a different world where industrial giants are introducing new standards for milk quality to small-scale farmers. As Rodríguez (1997) observes for the Altos de Jalisco, in Mexico's top milk producing region, the quality concept is used as a form of control over formerly disorganized small- and medium-scale farmers who are being told to "organize for quality" and purchase expensive milk refrigeration tanks, or lose their market. Yet at the same time these farmers receive few financial benefits from these changes. In the Altos de Jalisco, the new quality standards of the state are being deployed both as a set of practices and a rationalizing ideology intended to reshape farmers and their relationships, as well as the market in which they are embedded. As Murdoch & Ward (1997: 331–312) see it,

> Diverse actors, to greater or lesser degrees, become incorporated into networks through their (sometimes willing, sometimes enthusiastic) adoption of common rationalities and forms of calculation. . . . Liberalism is thus marked out by the degree to which power is exercised, not so much by direct repression, but by the more invisible strategies of normalization in which apparently free subjects come to calculate and monitor themselves in terms derived from dominant modes of governmentality.

Among farmers in the Altos de Jalisco, this process of taming the domestic economy is hardly being greeted with enthusiasm.

To the immediate south in San José de Gracia, in contrast, milk quality has yet to become a politicized concept. This was reflected in the comment by the small-scale processor discussed earlier who noted that, "here all the quality is the same." Far from being conservative traditionalists, however, farmers in the region are interested in more efficient production but recognized that pragmatically, they have neither the infrastructure (both in terms of natural and material resources) nor a market that would stimulate and support further development of their farms. Indeed, they complain about decapitalizing their equity, given current economic conditions. This, coupled with a lack of subsidies and limited access to credit or government programs, calls into question the viability of small- and medium-scale dairy farms, let alone any movement towards their modernization. In fact, most processors believe that their role in stimulating farm development is to offer premiums for quality milk production. But they also recognize they would have to demand new milk quality standards as a group, and with so many processors in the area, this would be very difficult. And few have the trained personnel, laboratories, or equipment to actually test their milk. The implications of structural constraints on farmers in this region is best summarized in the words of a medium-sized dairy processor:

> Farmers here shouldn't look for price. They need to find a way to lower their costs. They need to grow more of their own intensive forage crops. The price of milk isn't going to go up . . . As a businessman, logically, yes, yes to lower the price [of your products], well you drop the price of milk. The one who gets the boot, well, are [the dairy farmers]. They have to work more and more and more, in order to keep going . . . I'll always find a way to make my product.

Gazing across the town's rooftops from my room in the town's newest boarding house (built by the owner with dollars saved from working many years in California), what immediately strikes even the most casual observer is an emerging stratification reflected in house architecture. The town is alive with construction, but it is not the local dairymen who are, in their poverty, embracing a rising lifestyle. Rather, much of the mortar, brick, and labor is purchased through remittances as mostly younger members of the community head off to Chicago, Los Angeles, or Dallas. Those who remain at home speak of dairying as a fight – a war they are not winning.

In the Altos de Jalisco, a global-technical definition of quality is being used as a rationale to tame dairy farmers and reap profit. Ironically the large processor in San José who trucks in his milk from Los Altos does so not to get milk that more closely meets new quality standards, but for the convenience of buying in bulk. It is interesting that Rodríguez (1997: 2, 18) also uses the war metaphor to characterize the relationship between large dairy processors and dairy farmers in Los Altos – imposing on farmers new practices and cultural logics in the name of quality, but without reward for compliance. Many will find little additional profit, and many will likely go out of business, detritus from the politics of quality. According to this conventional wisdom, dairymen who go out of business must be 'bad' because they lack competitive efficiency. Taken a step further, their going out of business can be interpreted as a social good. Who, then, wins the war? Extending this neo-Darwinist logic, goodness is efficiency that translates into agribusiness profit. This might be well and good if dairymen shared in the benefits, but Rodríguez's (1997) work certainly suggests otherwise. In Los Altos, farmers are given little choice but to get with the program or get out. Within this discourse, farmer resistance can be easily delegitimized and attributed to antiquated conservatism or worse, inefficiency. In San José it is not clear whether farmers will be 'invited' onto the technology treadmill on which they either modernize or lose their market, or if they will go out of business altogether as a casualty of Mexico's rapidly changing rural economy.

ACKNOWLEDGMENTS

This research was supported in 1996 by funding from Mexico's Consejo Nacional de Ciencia y Tecnologa (CONACYT) for a project entitled, 'Mejoramiento de la Calidad de la Leche: Problemática y Alternativas para Jalisco y Michoacán' [Enhancing Milk Quality: Problems and Alternatives in Jalisco and Michoacán] and in 1997 by a University of Texas at San Antonio Joint Faculty-Graduate Student Grant. Additional support came from UTSA Division of Behavioral and Cultural Sciences Research and Travel Funds (1996 and 1997). I would like to thank Guadalupe Rodríguez Gómez, the project's PI, from the Centro de Investigaciones y Estudios Superiores en Antropologa Social de Occidente (CIESAS-Occidente), Patricia Chombo Morales from the Centro de Investigación y Asistencia en Tecnologa y Diseño del Estado de Jalisco (CIATEJ), and Armando Cortez from UTSA who worked diligently as my graduate research assistant during the 1996–97 field seasons. Additional thanks are due to the volume's editors, Harry Schwarzweller and Andrew Davidson, for their helpful comments and suggestions on earlier drafts of this article.

NOTES

1. Milk's composition ranges from 85.5–88.7% water, 2.4–5.5% milkfat, and 7.9–10.0% non-fat solids (protein, lactose, minerals, etc.). In the U.S., the Food and Drug Administration's standards regulating the interstate trade of fresh fluid milk require a minimum of 3.25% milkfat and 8.25% non-fat solids. Other quality problems stem from bacteria that should have a standard count of no more than 50,000 per milliliter of fluid milk and the presence of antibiotic residues (Outlaw, Knutson & Schwart, 1993). From a consumer and public health standpoint, the immediate and pressing problem is the presence of high levels of bacteria (e.g. coliform) and other contaminants.

2. Though officials at the Dairymen's Association were quick to point out that farmers often under-report the number of head they own, this figure is generally consistent with my experience in the area. M. A. González (1997: 19), however, estimates that there are as many as 800 dairymen in the area with perhaps as many as 30,000 cows.

3. This and all subsequent Mexican peso to U.S. dollar conversions are based on the following rates. In the summers of 1995, 1996, and 1997, the U.S. dollar was worth on average 5.9 pesos, 7.5 pesos, and 7.8 pesos, respectively.

4. These figures should be taken with a bit of caution since they are not representative of the entire annual cycle, but rather June is one of the hardest months for farmers. By then (1) they have run out of forage crops, (2) the rainy season has not yet refreshed their rangeland, and (3) the price of milk is beginning to drop to its low rainy season level. Nevertheless, these figures do underscore the delicate economic balancing act in which farmers are currently engaged, since these farmers have to make up losses incurred during these difficult periods.

5. The third example is a case of dual purpose cattle which produce less milk than regular dairy cattle, but which are also are sold as beef cattle. Consequently, this owner is making up for his losses through the sale of cattle for beef.

6. These are located in the municipalities of Vista Hermosa, Tarimbaro, Jiquilpan, Maravato, Villamar, Rio Lerma, and Uruapan for a total of 20 tanks of either 5,000 or 2,100 liter capacity.

7. M. A. González (1997: 16) lists the largest creameries in San José de Gracia: four are large (processing 20,000 or more liters per day), 5 are medium (processing 10,000–20,000 liters per day), and 17 are small (processing less than 10,000 liters per day and most are processing less than 2,000). While these are the most visible operations in San José, it is reasonable to expect many other small-scale operations working 1,000 liters or less in the municipality.

8. These figures are crude estimates, but still a useful point of departure for understanding the consumption patterns of the local market. Two cautionary notes are worth mentioning. First, the daily consumption figures vary between the dry and rainy season. For example, one medium processor, which M. A. González (1997) says processes 10,000 liters/day, only does so in the dry season. During the rainy season their

use of fluid milk drops to 5,000 liters/day. Second, this figure does not, for the most part, reflect the milk processed in small family-run creameries.

9. Mastitis is inflammation of the udder caused by infection. Subclinical mastitis results in lower milk production by as much as 20–25% (M. A. González, personal communication).

10. In June 1997, for example, the wholesale price was US$0.26 per liter in the Altos de Jalisco while the wholesale rate varied between US$0.23 and US$0.25 in San José.

11. It is important to note that Camilo is also a *rutero* who picks up milk from his clients who cannot transport their milk directly to his small factory. The time between milking and pick-up is enough to cause problems, especially during periods when the weather is warm.

12. So, for example, one farmer explicitly questions the purity of his milk, but does not link this to any alternative production methods using new forms of technology: "The hygienic quality of our milk, well . . . that's impossible for us. We milk by hand and you know that during the dry season there's a lot of dust. There's a lot of manure where we milk in the corral because we have no milking salon. So all this dust is around and it doesn't make any difference what you use to cover your receptacles for the milk. No matter what, it's full of dust. We don't have the salons where we could wash the udder and tits before milking. What do you do [under these circumstances]? Try to have someone keep everything clean? What a waste of time I tell you."

13. Dual purpose cattle are raised for both milk and beef, though their milk production is considerably lower than cows that are raised for milk production only.

REFERENCES

del Castillo, A. (1995). Empresas de lácteos violan la sanidad. [Dairy Plants Violate Sanitation Standards]. *Siglo 21* September 4.

Fitchen, J. M. (1991). *Endangered Spaces, Enduring Places: Change, Identity, and Survival in Rural America.* Boulder, CO: Westview Press.

González, L. (1974). *San José de Gracia: Mexican Village in Transition.* Austin: University of Texas Press.

González, M. A. (1997). *Proyecto para la construcción de una bodega de almacenamiento de granos y forrajes en la localidad de San Miguel, Municipio de Marcos Castellanos, Michoacán.* [Project for the Construction of a Grain and Forage Storage Facility in the Area of San Miguel, Municipality of Marcos Castellanos, Michoacán]. Proposal submitted to Alianza para el Campo (Fomento Lechero).

González Pérez, L. (1996). Analiza Profeco principales marcas de leche. [Profeco Analyzes the Major Brands of Milk]. *El Financiero* July 25, 27.

Griffith, D., & Kissam, E. with Camposeco, J., Garcia, A.,Pfeffer, M., Runsten, D., & Pizzini, M.V. (1995). *Working Poor: Farmworkers in the United States.* Philadelphia: Temple University Press.

ITESM [Instituto Tecnologico y de Estudios Superiores de Monterrey]. 1994. *Diagnóstico y plan estratégico para los productores lecheros de la Región Lagunera.* [Strategic Plan and Diagnostic Analysis for Milk Producers in the Lagunera Region]. Mexico: Centro de Planeación Agropecuaria and Centro de Estudios Estratégicos.

INEGI [Instituto Nacional de Estadstica, Geografia, e Informática]. 1993. *Annuario estadistico del estado de Michoacán*. [Annual Statistical Summary for the State of Michoacán]. Mexico: INEGI.

McDonald, J. H. (1994). NAFTA and Basic Food Production: Dependency and Marginalization on Both Sides of the U.S./Mexico Border. *Research in Economic Anthropology, 15*, 129–143.

McDonald, J. H. (1996). The Milk War: The Effects of NAFTA on Dairy Farmers in the United States and Mexico. In: K. Roberts & M. I. Wilson (Eds), *Policy Choices: Free Trade among NAFTA Nations* (pp. 75–105). East Lansing: Michigan State University Press.

McDonald, J. H. (1998). La calidad de leche en San José de Gracia-Cotija: Una mirada sociocultural y poltica a la globalización. [Milk Quality in San José de Gracia-Cotija: A Sociocultural and Political Examination of Globalization]. In: G. Rodríguez Gómez & P. Chombo Morales (Eds), *Los rejuegos de poder: Globalización y cadenas agroindustriales de la leche en Occidente* (pp. 275–295). Mexico: CIESAS.

McDonald, J. H. (1999a). The Neoliberal Project and Governmentality in Rural Mexico: Emergent Farmer Organization in the Michoacán Highlands. *Human Organization, 58*(3), 274–284.

McDonald, J. H. (1999b). Commercial Family Farmers and Collective Action: Dairy Farming Strategies in Mexico. In: W. M. Loker (Ed.), *Globalization and the Rural Poor in Latin America* (pp. 41–60). Boulder, CO: Lynne Rienner Publishers.

Murdoch, J., & Ward, N. (1997). Governmentality and Territoriality: The Statistical Manufacture of Britain's 'National Farm'. *Political Geography, 16*(4), 307–324.

Outlaw, J., Knutson, R., & Schwart, R. (1993). Minimum Solids-not-fat Standards for Fluid Milk. Working Paper, Department of Agricultural Economics, Texas A&M University.

Rodríguez Gómez (1997). Los tanques rancheros de ganaderos de leche en Los Altos de Jalisco: Organización por y para la globalización. [Dairy Farmer's Milk Refrigeration Tanks in the Altos de Jalisco: Organization for and by Globalization]. Paper presented at the Second International Seminar Concerning National Dairy Systems in North America, Mexico City

Rodríguez Gómez, & Chombo Morales, P. (Eds) (1998). *Los rejuegos de poder: Globalización y cadenas agroindustriales de la leche en Occidente*. [Power Games: Globalization and Milk Agroindustrial Chains in the West]. Mexico: CIESAS.

Siglo 21. (1996a). Diariamente se adultera 30% de la producción lechera. [30% of Daily Milk Production is Adulterated] June 4.

Siglo 21. (1996b). Las lecheras deberán decir de qué están hechos sus productos. [Dairies Ought to Say What Their Products Contain]. June 5.

Zamora, G. (1997). *Caso CONASUPO: La Leche Radioactiva*. [The Case of CONASUPO: Radioactive Milk]. Mexico: Editorial Planeta.

Zárate H., & Hernández, J.E. (1998). Ethnography, Culture Change, and Local Power. *Journal of Historical Sociology, 11*(1), 138–149.

ISSUES OF QUALITY IN DUTCH DAIRYING

Jaap Frouws and Jan Douwe Van der Ploeg

INTRODUCTION

Quality is an old and recurrent issue in the Dutch dairy industry. In the past, the concern with quality focused primarily on the minimal nutritional, hygienic and organoleptic properties of milk. This is no longer the case. Issues of milk quality now are more complex with multiple and frequently contradictory definitions, reflective of the diverse interests both within and outside the dairy industry. The idea that the notion of quality cannot be solely limited to the intrinsic properties of milk or cheese has become widely accepted by consumer organisations, state institutions and, increasingly, by farmer unions and the dairy industry as well. A wide range of issues relating to the sustainability of production, animal welfare, and nature and landscape preservation are increasingly being included in quality definitions. As the national Council for the Rural Areas (RLG, 1998) recently argued, the food production system should not only produce safe and good food, it "has to produce trust as well; i.e. trust that food is produced with the required care for the eco-system, animals, landscape and natural values." How these competing and contested definitions of milk quality are negotiated will probably be decisive in the re-emergence or demise of the Dutch dairy sector. A crucial question here is whether or not a more direct link will emerge between differentiation in primary production on one hand, and differentiation in dairy processing on the other.

Research in Rural Sociology, Volume 8, pages 211–228.
ISBN: 0-7623-0474-X

The importance of dairying to Dutch agriculture cannot be overstated. Dairying occupies about one third of the area available for farming and the Netherlands is one of the largest dairy exporters in the world. The Dutch dairy industry has a gross production value of over 10 billion Dutch Guilders (NLG) per annum ($4.8 billion), three-quarters of which is earned through exports. Apart from its economic significance, dairy farming is also considered to be an important social carrier. In this respect, it is seen as supporting the countryside, both by contributing to employment and by maintaining the open, green space, that is increasingly valued as an intrinsic part of the country's cultural capital. Nevertheless, there have been significant changes within the Dutch dairy industry. Between 1985 and 1995 there was an annual decrease of 4.3% in the number of dairy farms. This decline is expected to continue during the coming decade, with a further reduction of dairy holdings by another 50%. Dairy processing too has restructured and is now dominated by two very large cooperatives. These are adjusting their financial, control and ownership structures to enhance their competitive strength on the national and international market. As quality is a crucial asset in market competition, a massive quality project has been launched in order to have each and every part of the Dutch dairy sector certified by the year of 2000.

According to Nicolas & Valceschini (1993), changes in perceptions of quality have come about from growing international competition and trade liberalisation. The current contrasting notions of quality are supported by different actors, interests and public policies. These in turn are associated with differing production systems, control mechanisms, chain linkages, market strategies and consumption patterns. In effect, this has led to different and competing technological trajectories; industrial-style dairying and counter-initiatives instigated by primary producers and their organisations as they strive to create special quality circuits under their own control, and changing consumer preferences. Although the Dutch dairy sector has been successful in industrialising its dairy industry, there are questions over its sustainability. It is also questionable whether the quality associated with bulk production can withstand the competition emerging from the new, high quality-oriented circuits of production, transformation and marketing. In short, the competitive advantage (Porter, 1985) of the Dutch dairy system is under a double threat. On one hand, new international competitors, able to realise far lower costs, are emerging. On the other, there is a demand for increased quality differentiation that can only be realised by more localised and specialised producers.

To explore the relation between conceptions of milk quality and different production strategies, we begin by briefly noting definitions of quality and consumer demands. We then review the current social, political and economic context in which dairying takes place in the Netherlands. We go on to examine recent structural developments in primary production, processing and marketing. We then focus on the central theme of this chapter, namely the interplay of strategies and interests in the struggle over quality as these are played out by the farmers, farmer organisations, dairy cooperatives and processors, retailers, and government institutions. In conclusion we reflect on the crucial choices and dilemmas that dairy farmers and processors are facing and the possible outcomes of the current struggle for milk quality.

MULTIPLE DIMENSIONS OF QUALITY

Quality is a multifaceted concept that incorporates a wide range of interests stretching from farmer to consumer. Increasingly, the demands of consumers, retailers and the general public must be taken into account. The definition of milk quality has expanded from intrinsic product qualities to include methods of production. Now, both the qualities of the physical environment and landscape where dairies are located, as well as the welfare of the dairy cows, is part of this broader Dutch notion of milk quality.

Clearly, the consumer demands perceived by retailers greatly influences definitions of quality which, in turn, are passed on to the primary producers. Consumer demands, with respect to food products and production, nevertheless appear to be highly diverse (Meulenberg, 1996; Dam & Scholte, 1997). The *price oriented consumer*, for example, searches for low-priced food (including fast food) and pays little attention to health, animal welfare or the environment. The *quality consumer*, on the other hand, values aspects of health (fresh, rich in vitamins, low calorie, and safe), the environment, and animal welfare, and is prepared to pay for these. Lastly, for the *conscious consumer*, environmental friendliness, animal welfare, naturalness and healthiness are crucial; they are prepared to pay high prices for exclusive food products (Bokma et al., 1997).

Notwithstanding this diversity, quality criteria are generally being raised in all consumer categories. Consumers are becoming more critical of milk safety and animal well being because of a greater demand for fresh dairy products (with higher contamination risks), wider application of biotechnology, and greater awareness of health risks (due to animal diseases and use of antibiotics and growth stimulators).

The government's agricultural policies too reflect these changes in public concerns and societal standards and anticipate that they will intensify over the coming years. In this respect, the use of artificial means such as anti-microbe growth stimulators is to be gradually suppressed, while consumers will be guaranteed maximum freedom of choice via separately certified chains of production for gmo-free and/or organic food. Farmers surpassing the legal environmental, welfare and veterinary standards will be subsidised. Government policies thus still leave room for different degrees of quality. However, taking into account the increasing emphasis on safety, environment, health and animal welfare, the room for differential qualities is going to be minimised through increasingly formalised and integrated systems of chain monitoring and certification (Bokma et al., 1997). It is within this context, then, that we begin to understand recent changes in the Dutch dairy industry.

DAIRY RESTRUCTURING AND THE CONTEXT OF POLITICAL AND ECONOMIC CHANGE

Concomitant with a decrease in the number of dairies and an increase in herd size, processors have also gone through a series of mergers and milk processing is now dominated by two, very large co-operatives. These two co-operatives are leading the massive quality project that is heading for the certification of all Dutch dairies by the year of 2000. The Dutch dairy industry is now among the most regulated of the agricultural sectors. From the early days of the Common Agricultural Policy milk prices have been supported by an extensive system of import levies, export subsidies and intervention bureaus that have purchased and stocked surpluses of butter and milk powder.

By 1984, the increasing budgetary burden of price support policies led to the introduction of milk quotas. A national quota was assigned to each member state and subsequently divided among its respective dairy farmers. In the Netherlands, milk quotas became tradeable, subject to minor restrictions based on the relationship between land and quota. The costs of securing a milk quota – NLG 4.00 per kilogram ($1.93) – are considerable. Dutch quota prices are the highest in the European Union. Thus, if individual dairy farmers want to increase their milk production by 50,000 kilogram, for example, they will have to make a quota investment of NLG 200,000 ($96,000).

Since 1984, the milk quota has been reduced several times, leading to a severe, 15% reduction in national milk production. Attempting to secure a higher quota, at least 50% of Dutch dairy farmers have started administrative procedures to try and obtain a larger quota than the one initially assigned to them. Besides lodging appeals and trying to buy more quotas, farmers have also resorted to different types of strategies to counteract the effects of quota restrictions. These include raising the fat content of milk to get better prices, processing raw milk on the farm, leasing milk quotas and practising cow tourism by out-sourcing cows or milk either on paper or in reality (Elégoët & Frouws, 1991).

Although the current quota system can be expected to continue into the near future, prices and income policies for the European dairy sector as a whole are going to change considerably as a result of the renewal of the GATT agreement in 2001 and the entry of Central and Eastern European countries into the EU. Consequently, Dutch dairy farmers can expect a significant reduction in export subsidies and a considerable decline in raw milk prices; they will, however, be compensated for this decline by direct income payments. Government payments to farmers, in all probability, will be linked to farming in an environmentally friendly way, adding to an already impressive body of national environmental regulations developed since the 1970s. Regulations are currently in place covering the quantity, timing and methods of liquid manure application, manure storage, animal housing (measures aimed at reducing ammonia emission), as well as pesticide usage. Regulations to enforce dairy farm extensification are also being drafted that will set a maximum animal-land ratio. Furthermore, levies have been imposed on energy use and manure production, while potentially damaging practices such as sprinkler irrigation, drainage and soil levelling have been brought under strict license.

Dairy farmers are also being confronted by more stringent controls on animal health and welfare; healthy and happy cows are coming to be seen as crucial to dairy quality and image. To this end, the dairy farmers' association and the processing industry are currently setting up programs to prevent or eradicate cattle diseases. Moreover, a compulsory and extensive system of animal identification and registration is being imposed to make it possible to trace the source of any contagious outbreak of disease. Welfare requirements for animal housing, feeding and grazing systems complete the complex of regulatory prescriptions designed to maintain and restore the quality of Dutch dairy products.

STRUCTURAL FEATURES OF DUTCH DAIRYING

Primary Production

In 1980, there were 67,000 dairy farms in the Netherlands,[1] but by 1997 the number had fallen to about 36,000. This significant reduction was accompanied by a considerable increase in size of dairy operations, from an average of 35 cows per farm in 1980 to 44 in 1997. Most of the dairies that disappeared had less than 30 cows. Some 22,000 went out of business between 1980 and 1995, whereas the number of farms with more than 70 milk cows declined by only 800 during the same period. Quota size is also uneven within the dairy sector: 10% of the dairies have a milk quota of over half a million kilograms representing 27% of the national quota, while 43% do with a milk quota of less than 200,000 kilograms, representing 18% of the national quota.

Almost 90% of all farms with dairy cows can be classified as specialized dairy farms. There are about 1.6 million cows in the national dairy herd producing 11 million tons of raw milk each year, worth more than NLG 8 billion ($3.8 billion). In spite of an increase in operational size and an increase in specialization within the Dutch dairy industry, the last decade has seen a more extensive use of land due to the introduction of milk quotas. As the average milk production per cow continues to grow, the number of cows has been reduced considerably. This has resulted in decreases in the animal-land ratio, although quota reductions and productivity gains are frequently offset by purchasing or leasing additional quota. On average, the number of milk cows per hectare of land used for grazing or silage decreased from 1.76 per hectare in 1985 to 1.34 per hectare in 1995. However, this average conceals the considerable variations that exist between regions and individual holdings.

Today, the average Dutch dairy farm owns about 28 hectares, milks about 45 cows, and has a milk quota of about 300,000 kilograms. Despite being relatively small, the average farm is worth about NLG 3 million ($1.4) due to high land and quota prices. Expanding a dairy farm, therefore, requires considerable financial outlay and the take-over of such a farm without family support has become almost impossible. The annual turnover of milk quota transfers – both for farm succession and free quota trade – and lease contracts amounts to well over NLG 1.5 billion ($720 million). This has contributed to a significant cost increase in Dutch dairy farming (LTO 1997b).

Until the introduction of milk quotas, Dutch dairy farmers typically pursued a strategy of production-maximisation. Since 1984, however, there has been a gradual transformation towards a cost-minimising strategy, producing a fixed quantity of milk in the least expensive way. These seemingly uniform production strategies nevertheless hide a significant diversity of farm management trajectories. Empirical research has shown several paths – or styles of farming – each of which can provide a good income for the dairy farmer (Ploeg, 1995). The relationship between scale (number of dairy cows and hectares per unit of labour) and intensity of production (operationally defined as gross value of production per cow and/or hectare) appears to vary significantly. Farming styles not only reflect farmers' notions and values concerning the way farming ought to be organised, but the impact of the relations between the farm enterprise and the surrounding markets, techno-logical packages and policy incentives as well.[2]

Dairy Processing and Marketing

Dutch dairy companies process more than 95% of the raw milk produced in the Netherlands with dairy co-operatives accounting for about 80% of the total raw milk. In recent years, mergers have reduced the number of dairy companies from 43 to 12. The co-operative sector is now dominated by two very large companies, one collecting milk in the northern and eastern parts of the country,[3] and the other in the west and south. More than 50% of all raw milk is transformed into cheese, 20% into milk powder and condensed milk, and 15% is sold as fluid milk. Most of the remaining 15% is processed into desserts, ice-cream and butter. The total production value of the Dutch dairy industry is NLG 10 to 12 billion ($4.8 to 5.5 billion) with three-quarters of this derived from export earnings. Skimmed milk powder and cheese are the most important export products.

The Dutch dairy industry is generally considered to be an efficient bulk producer (McKinsey, 1997). When compared to Danish processors, for example, Dutch dairy processors add 18% less value to raw milk, primarily because Danish dairy processors produce more premium products. However, with 27% more value per hour worked, productivity in Dutch dairying is much higher than in Denmark. This higher productivity is the result of the extremely large-scale plants in which milk powder and cheese are made, the intrinsic productivity gains derived from the Dutch product mix and the more automated production processes used to manufacture bulk varieties. These efficient bulk producers are under increasing pressure, however. The deregulation of European price protection, the entry of low-cost countries into the European Union and improvements in long-distance logistics will probably lead to severe competition with countries such as Poland and New Zealand, especially in the bulk commodity markets where Dutch dairy processors currently earn most of their profits.

There are two basic strategic options open to Dutch milk processors seeking to counteract these impending threats. Either they become premium food producers or they evolve into global, low-cost, bulk food producers (McKinsey, 1997; see for a more general discussion Porter, 1985). The premium food strategy entails differentiating the range of products, creating strong, innovative brands and developing close relationships with retailers and supermarkets. To be able to realise the premium food option, milk processors have to ensure they have the size and ownership structure that will allow them to make sufficient investments in R&D, advertising and marketing. Pursuing the second option, on the other hand, means competing efficiently and developing global operations that give access to low-cost labour and farm products. This requires global sourcing by establishing strong farmer networks and distribution systems in low-cost countries and setting up processing plants in these countries. It also means forging close ties with local wholesalers and retailers. More than the premium food strategy, the success of the second strategy requires a strong capital base.

Dutch dairy co-operatives are in fact pursuing both strategies by simultaneously creating new brands and acquiring production capacity in countries such as Poland. They are revising both their financial and ownership structures in order to obtain operational funds and provide room for executive decision-making that is unfettered by membership consent. Options that are actively being pursued involve issuing tradeable supply rights to farmers or tradeable stock delinked to supply rights, either amongst farmers or within broader groups of investors, creating institutional barriers between the co-operative as an association of members and the co-operative as a company composed of business units.

Regardless of the strategy, the outcome of each bodes poorly for the farmer. The premium food strategy tends to lead to a more selective purchase of raw milk, as smaller quantities are needed to produce bulk products such as cheese and milk powder. This selectivity threatens farmers' supply rights and signifies the end of the co-operative obligation to purchase. Selective sourcing, in fact, brings the milk quota under the control of the dairy companies. So too with the international, low-cost strategy. Although it can generate significant growth opportunities abroad, it also tends to undermine the position of dairy farmers in the Netherlands. While the demand for processed food in emerging markets is expected to grow rapidly, it may lead to the substitution of global sourcing and manufacture for domestic raw milk supply and bulk production.

Shifting Powers

The above analysis shows that both of these strategic options undermine the appeal of the co-operative 'umbrella' as both the security of supply and the maximization of raw milk prices are scaled back. Dutch dairy co-operatives have long maintained a tradition of maximizing the milk prices paid to their members. This tradition was based on their profit-sharing mechanism and ownership structure, as well as the need to attract and retain members in order to ensure a stable volume of supply. Gains from efficiency and productivity were largely passed on to farmer members whose obligation to supply was equal to their right to supply. The co-operatives were obliged to purchase, process and sell whatever quantities of raw milk their members supplied.

The co-operatives' 80% share of the raw milk supply market gave them almost complete control over raw milk prices. The guaranteed purchase of surpluses financed by the European Community has helped support high price levels. This relative immunity to market pressures and demands has come to an end. The fierce struggle for outlet markets has turned the dairy industry upside down. It is now demand rather than supply driven and the demands of buyers have become increasingly powerful. Power is concentrated in that part of the dairy chain that is closest to final consumption. It is the large retailers who articulate consumer concerns and desires and who are steadily capturing a growing share of total food sales. Dairy processors are becoming more and more dependent on them for their domestic sales. The share in domestic food sales of the top-five Dutch retailers has grown from 33% in 1990 to 50% in 1995 (Koninklijke Nederlandse Zuivelbond FNZ, 1997). In addition, many retailers are moving towards private labels, even in the case of the important 'A brands', thus limiting food processors' opportunities for marketing their own products. One of the largest retailers in the Netherlands is already selling about a third of its food products under its domestic label. As a result, retailers increasingly determine the conditions under which food products are supplied to consumers.

Retailers are not insensitive to consumer demands given their growing purchasing power. They now find that they must take into account consumer preferences, most notably through the guarantee of milk quality. This relates not only to human health and safety but also, for example, to the effect of dairy farming on the environment, animal welfare, naturalness (aversion to the use of hormones or genetically modified organisms) and social justice. Incidents such as the outbreak of mad cow disease and the contamination of animal feed with carcinogenic aflatoxine have clearly demonstrated the relevance and potential impact of consumer concerns. These can only be met if total transparency and control are assured in all product-related activities conducted by suppliers, producers, processors, traders and transporters and if (potential) offenders can be smoothly spotted and eliminated. Protection against possible health risks as well as reliable and clear information that enables the consumer to make conscious choices have become crucial requirements and reflect the close relationship between quality and trust (Karpik, 1992).

REGULATION OF QUALITY

Quality control in dairy products has a long history in the Netherlands given the importance of dairy exports to the Dutch economy. Official control, based on agricultural quality legislation, is implemented by the Central Body of Dairy Quality Affairs (COKZ) which inspects dairy products at plant level and controls for such factors as fat, salt and water content. The National Food Inspection Department also examines dairy products and follows general European directives on hygiene. This department is mainly concerned with the safety and healthiness of food. Besides these official control mechanisms, there is a voluntary milk recording system organised by the National Society for Cattle Improvement (a private association), that covers about 80% of all Dutch dairy cows and takes on-farm milk samples every three weeks. Lastly, all dairy processors have their own system for controlling the quality of raw milk supply and dairy products. These enable them to pay farmers according to the quality of their production, as well as to trace sources of pollution and contamination.

The Dutch Dairy Quality Project

In spite of the impressive array of control mechanisms, the farmers' union leadership, co-operative leaders and dairy company leaders seek to extend and systematise quality controls to each and every part of the dairy commodity chain. It is anticipated that such an endeavour will enable the Netherlands to achieve a leading position on international markets by strengthening and maintaining consumer confidence. The Dutch Dairy Organization (NZO) represents all Dutch dairy companies whether they are private enterprises or co-operatives. Together with the Dairy Farmers' Association of the National Farmers' Union (LTO), it has launched a common project known as Chain Quality Milk (KKM). KKM is a system of certification that is meant to apply to all raw milk produced at farm level from 1 January 2000. Prior to that date, all dairy farms are visited by KKM-appointed inspectors and those who do not comply with KKM standards are given a chance to improve their performance. Since all industrial raw milk processors participate in the scheme, no dairy farmer can escape from KKM inspection. The only exceptions are those farmers who process and sell all their raw milk themselves.

A separate and more demanding certification system is being set up for the several hundred Dutch organic dairy farmers. This will be known as the Quality Guarantee for Biological Dairy Farming (KBM). Raw milk that is not certified will not be sold for human consumption and will only be able to command one third of the price of raw milk produced under KKM standards. These standards will be uniform and applied nation-wide. Initially, these standards will be set at relatively lenient levels such that all dairy farmers can meet them fairly easily except when there is a lack of hygiene.

The KKM system clearly reveals the heterogeneity and contingent character of the quality concept. This applies not only to the safety of purchased feed and veterinary products, but also involves such items as animal welfare and environmental pollution. However, in spite of their broad, encompassing character, the initial requirements for obtaining the KKM certificate remain close to current practices and prevailing government regulations. Simple rules for animal welfare, like prescriptions for grazing and outdoor exercise, are absent, for example. The environmental module is equally modest and simply refers to existing legislation. Additional requirements, let alone raising standards, are not being considered at this time.[4]

Societal Acceptance

As it is currently operationalised, a primary concern of the KKM quality project appears to be image building. The KKM does not encourage dairy farmers to undertake substantial quality improvements, rather its aim is to reassure customers, accommodate public criticism, and prevent the enactment of any further constraining environmental regulations. The KKM is largely motivated by a fear of the consequences of such discrediting affairs as BSE, the use of growth stimulating hormones, the carcinogenic contamination of milk, and the excessive nitrate pollution of ground water. The prime mover of the KKM's quality project thus is its preoccupation with the public image and social acceptability of dairy farming.

In their policy paper on the future of the Dutch dairy industry, the leaders of the LTO Dairy Farmers' Association stated that the sight of grazing cows is a generally appreciated feature of the Dutch landscape, arguing that it might possibly become a more important reason for the continuation of dairy farming than the sector's contribution to employment and the economy (LTO 1997a). They went so far as to claim EU support for dairying because the Netherlands, with its very high production costs, could be considered a less-favoured-area as far as dairy farming is concerned. This new legitimation for land-based dairy farming also serves to justify the relatively large area devoted to it in the Netherlands. Dutch agricultural areas are still protected by spatial planning regulations. If this protection is withdrawn because of increasing pressure from other quarters, such as the need to build houses, provide recreation areas, conserve nature, and establish infrastructure, land prices will rise beyond that which dairy farmers can afford. This makes the socio-political acceptance of dairy farming and the extensive land use it involves a matter of dairy farm survival.

CONFLICTING STRATEGIES AND INTERESTS

How do quality regulations relate to farmers' strategies, choices and responses, touching as they do on issues of professional autonomy, craftsmanship and self-consciousness? Both the premium food strategy and the international low-cost strategy make the position of dairy farmers less secure. The first turns supply guarantees into supply favours that are selectively distributed in accordance with externally determined, uniform quality requirements. The second will threaten supply rights by favouring low cost producers, penalising dairy farmers who do not employ cost-minimising strategies and those farmers working relatively remote holdings. In fact, the entire high-cost area of Dutch dairying will be disadvantaged because there is a growing tendency to look for replacement, low-cost suppliers elsewhere. Premium product quality realised through product differentiation is regarded primarily as an addition or adjustment to the process of industrial processing, packing and marketing (Ploeg & Ettema, 1990).

Overall, the premium food strategy has little interest in the specific quality efforts made by farmers so long as they comply with strict hygiene and security standards. There is no difference with the bulk processing strategy in this respect. The common chain quality project KKM thus involves both a disciplinary definition of quality and an essentially negative definition of quality. Most KKM modules are of a preventive or prohibitive nature. Thus, the raw milk that farmers supply should not be contaminated or endanger human health, and should not lead to environmental pollution.

But, while substandard milk is penalised, producing milk with special or extra qualities is neither encouraged nor remunerated, since relevant linkages to the quality or identity of the final products are not taken into account. It is hardly surprising then that such a top-down quality project provokes resistance among farmers. They are aware that marketing and image building of processed dairy products are the main concerns. Nevertheless, farmers' grievances concern their limited freedom and cooperative relationships becoming increasingly business-like. They also fear reduced milk prices and that retailers will be the ones to profit; hence, they are suspicious of supermarkets that might change from one supplier to another without warning and they resent sacrificing the interests of individual farmers to processor and retailer interests and uniformity. In other words, farmers object strongly to the increasing standardisation and dependence associated with what they consider to be retailer-led industrialisation in dairy farming.

Many of the agri-environmental regulations which represent the state's articulation of society's demands on the quality of dairy farming, also reflect a negative definition of quality, that is experienced by dairy farmers as constraining, rigid, unjust and frequently ineffective (Frouws et al., 1996). Ways of farming are prescribed to ensure that farmers do not harm nature, the landscape and the environment, and that they do not produce surpluses. This regulatory approach does not encourage farmers to work to achieve a better performance or higher standards. It is only concerned with imposing limits through licensing and standardised practices.

Farmers' Responses

In essence, issues of quality in Dutch dairying can be summarised by asking: "What difference do the capacities and initiatives of the individual dairy farmer make?" The external regulation of quality, analysed above, reveals a tendency towards de-qualification (denying the relevance of distinctive or specific capabilities) and the undermining of farmer autonomy.[5] This tendency is, of course, being contested and these counteractions are based on distinctions predicated on the specific or unique characteristics of primary production and marketing. Region-specific produce is an example. The production process is often characterised by the use of local fodders, unique techniques of preparation, special ingredients, and the use of organic practices and inputs. Specific marketing strategies involve direct delivery to consumers. Some farmers extend this service to producing prepared foods, and customer-made packages of fresh or frozen food (see for examples, Broekhuizen et al., 1997).

This distinction in production and marketing characteristics can also be categorised as a collective, usually region-bound, asset. A well-known example is traditional Parmesan cheese production. The use of a selected milk race, particular roughage ingredients, un-cooled raw milk delivered on schedule, and traditional processing, all contribute to its special taste and other product qualities (de Roest, 1990).

Some styles of farming are more suited to pursuing such strategies of distinction. For other styles, these strategies may make too many demands on the time, craftsmanship and customer relations. In the Netherlands, the production and marketing of local cheese varieties in the densely populated west is mainly done at relatively extensive dairy farms where there is a strong interest in artisan techniques and a sensitivity to the naturalness of products. It is an example that illustrates the relevance of farming styles (Ploeg & Roep,

1990; Broekhuizen et al., 1997). The distinguishing characteristic of specialised products can be institutionalised through certification and labelling. These institutions can serve then to appropriate and redistribute the monopoly rent found in publicly recognised exclusivity and limited supply (see, for examples, Perrier-Cornet, 1990; Menard, 1996).

Alternatives to constraining, agri-environmental regulations involve an emphasis on the distinct and distinguishing characteristics of local soils, water systems, scenic beauty and bio-diversity and warrant tailor-made environmental rules and practices. These alternatives are primarily developed by voluntary, region-based farmers' associations that tend to combine their proposals for environmental self-regulation with agreements involving contracts for nature and landscape preservation.

In terms of agri-ruralist discourse, dairy farmers' responses to the industry restructuring can be seen more generally as an essential element that contributes to the quality of the rural areas (Frouws, 1998). In the ideal countryside of agri-ruralist discourse, dairy farmers have renewed their social contract with society, practising multi-functional agriculture that meets society's demand for items that range from healthy food and pure drinking water, to attractive landscapes and country recreation. According to this discourse, the quality of the rural, regarded as a co-production of man and nature can be considered to be a precondition for the quality of society at large (Ploeg, 1997).

CONCLUSIONS

Many different strategies and interests in the dairy sector are legitimised by an appeal to quality. Definitions of quality are being disputed and negotiated more so today than in the past. For some, it is associated with specificity and distinction, and for others with uniform standards. Many dairy farmers see a further industrialisation in dairy farming as being equivalent to de-qualification and loss of autonomy. For them, industrialisation reduces farmers to mere suppliers of raw material and thus food quality is a matter of industrial control. This is linked to a one-dimensional quality strategy with an exclusive focus on commercial image building. However, other dairy farmers (Ploeg et al; 1992; Roep et al., 1991) regard industrialisation along the lines of further expansion, intensification, productivity increases, and large capital investments as the only viable way of achieving future competitiveness.

A similar divergence is found in research circles. A prognosis is made of straightforward industrialisation of the dairy farming sector by extrapolating dominant trends in technological development and economic liberalisation

(Eck et al., 1996). From this perspective, industrial dairying is only concerned with producing milk; most inputs, such as roughage and replacement calves, are produced by specialised firms. Similarly, disposed manure is industrially processed and mineral surpluses are exported. The average herd size of these industrialised dairies is about 1000 dairy cows, producing 13,000 kilograms of milk per annum through genetic modification and Bst. Cows are kept in stalls and are no longer pastured, and are milked with mechanical milkers. Somewhat less radical is the perspective advanced by the National Farmers' Union LTO, an organisation that also promotes the further enlargement of dairy holdings although it does not endorse its industrial character because it is assumed that this will harm the image of naturalness and rurality. From the perspective of the LTO, standardisation, large-scale production, and automation will be camouflaged by grazing cows in the green meadows around the dairy farm.

From a very different perspective, dairy farming can be seen as gradually turning towards ecological methods of production whether or not these are part of a multi-functional rural holding that combines raw milk production with farm-made dairy products, domestic sales, agri-tourism, the provision of social or educational services on the farm, nature conservation, and part-time jobs outside agriculture. Such developments can be seen as secondary to a dominant industrial trend or, as other researchers have suggested, an indication that the ecological modernization and ruralization of dairy farming is an inevitable alternative to the perceived insustainability of large-scale industrialised dairies that is meeting growing social resistance and increasing competition from low-cost countries.

For the time being, dairy co-operatives, government institutions and research stations, farmers' organizations, retailers, primary producer groups and individual dairy farmers all have a common preoccupation with quality. They do not define it in the same way, and the definition provided by some players is more powerful than that of others. This is one reason why strategies adopted by the large dairy companies is so important. Their current response is to communicate images to consumers that imply a pattern of qualitative upgrading. This is associated with an artisanal approach that is in line with the conservation of landscapes, natural values and rural interests. Developments in the dairy industry, however, continue to follow the pattern of further cost-reductions. Furthermore, there is an evident tension between images and real practices. This is being bridged through the imposition of ever-tighter regulatory systems designed to underpin the notion of quality and to avoid new, major accidents and scandals. Whether this response will be successful in the long term can be questioned. Two main insecurities emerge from our analysis. The first is whether or not the implied industrialisation of primary dairy production will founder on the relatively high prices for land and labour in the Netherlands. The second concerns the viability of new, alternative arrangements that claim to offer a different and higher quality than can be obtained through industrial production. If the latter trend materialises, then consumers might well shift from the bulk-circuit towards the quality circuit.

NOTES

1. The quantitative data come from the Central Office of Statistics and the Agricultural Economic Institute, unless mentioned otherwise.
2. Farming styles differ considerably. Milk yields, input/output efficiency, cattle varieties, fertilizer levels, the ratio of purchased to self-produced inputs, and the amount of care given to the animals, vary from style to style. The farming style itself, therefore, has a direct effect both on the quality of raw milk produced and the dairy products processed from it. Some farming styles are in line with current tendencies towards industrializing primary dairy production, whereas others follow development strategies that clearly run counter to this trend.
3. This co-operative, *Friesland Coberco Dairy Foods,* is the product of a recent merger by 4 dairy co-operatives, resulting in a dairy company with 16,000 member-farmers, 12,000 employees (6,000 of them working abroad) and a turnover of NLG 9 billion of which two thirds is realised outside the Netherlands (*Koninklijke Nederlandse Zuivelbond FNZ* 1998).
4. The same applies to the module of animal health, where diseases, such as para-tuberculosis or salmonella, are not included in the certification system, although they can affect human health.
5. Unlike independence, which refers to isolation vis-à-vis others, autonomy primarily involves freedom of choice and room for decision in relation to other social actors. It also implies the choice to accept mutual dependence and the accommodation of conflicting interests in dealing with farmer autonomy in agro-food chains (Benvenuti & Frouws: 1998).

REFERENCES

Benvenuti, B., & Frouws, J. (1998). De dialectiek van autonomie en systeemintegratie in de landbouw. Naar een synthese van structuralisme en actor-oriëntatie in de rurale sociologie. [The dialectics of autonomy and system integration in agriculture. Towards a synthesis of structuralism and actor-orientedness in rural sociology]. *Tijdschrift voor Sociaalwetenschappelijk onderzoek van de Landbouw (TSL)*, *13*(4), 212–220.
Bokma, S., Koskamp, G. J., & Biewinga, E. E. (1997). Diergezondheid in het spanningsveld met dierenwelzijn en milieu. [Animal health in between animal welfare and the environment]. In: J. G. de Wilt (Ed.), *Naar een gezonde veehouderij in 2015* (pp. 22–57). The Hague: NRLO.
Broekhuizen, R. van, Klep, L., Oostindie, H., & Van der Ploeg, J. D. (1997). *Renewing the countryside: an atlas with two hundred examples from Dutch rural society.* Doetinchem: Misset Publishers.

Dam, Y. K. van, & Scholten, L. M. (1997). Consument en duurzaamheid: een literatuurstudie [Consumer and sustainability: a study of literature]. In: Y. K. van Dam, C. de Hoog & J. A. C. van Ophem (Eds), *Voeding, Consument en Duurzaamheid* (pp. 47–82). Leuven: Garant Uitgevers.

Eck, W. van, van der Ploeg, B., de Poel, K. R., & Zaalmink, B. W. (1996). *Koeien en koersen; ruimtelijke kwaliteit van melkveehouderijsystemen*. In: 2025 [Cows and courses; spatial quality of dairy farming systems in 2025]. Wageningen/Den Haag: SC-DLO, LEI-DLO.

Elégoët, F., & Frouws, J. (1991). *Stratégies Agricoles. Les quotas laitiers en Bretagne, France, Hollande* [Agricultural strategies. Milk quotas in Brittany, France, the Netherlands] Plabennec: Tud Ha Bro.

Frouws, J. (1998). The Contested Redefinition of the Countryside. An Analysis of Rural Dis courses in The Netherlands. *Sociologia Ruralis, 38*(1), 54–68.

Frouws, J., Oerlemans, N. Ettema, M., Hees, E., van Broekhuizen, R., & Van der Ploeg, J. D. (1996). *Naar de geest of naar de letter. Een onderzoek naar knellende regelgeving in de agrarische sector* [In spirit or letter. An investigation of constraining regulations in agriculture] Wageningen: Circle for Rural European Studies.

Karpik, L. (1992). L'advocatus economicus. *Gérer et comprendre, 26*, 7–16.

Koninklijke Nederlandse Zuivelbond FNZ (1997). *Zuivelzicht*. Voortz. nan: officieel orgaan van de Koninklijke Nederlandse Zuivelbond FNZ, *89*(5), 27.

Koninklijke Nederlandse Zuivelbond FNZ (1998). *Zuivelzicht*. Voortz. nan: officieel orgaan van de Koninklijke Nederlandse Zuivelbond FNZ, *90*(1), 3.

LTO. (1997a). *Uitzicht op een veelzijdige toekomst. De visie van LTO Nederland op de toekomst van de melkveehouderij in Nederland* [View on a many-sided future. LTO's view on the future of dairy farming in the Netherlands] The Hague: LTO.

LTO. (1997b). *Discussienotitie quotumkosten* [Discussion Paper on the Costs of Milk Quota] The Hague: LTO.

McKinsey. (1997). *Benchmark Study of Dutch Economic Performance: the Food Processing Case*. Amsterdam: McKinsey Global Institute Studies.

Menard, C. (1996). On Clusters, Hybrids, and Other Strange Forms: The Case of the French Poultry Industry. *Journal of Institutional and Theoretical Economics (JITE), 152*, 154 183.

Meulenberg, M. T. G. (1996). *De levensmiddelenconsument van de toekomst* [The food consumer of the future] The Hague: NRLO-report 96/4.

Nicolas, F., & Valceschini, E. (1993). Agro-Alimentaire et Qualité. Questions aux sciences sociales [Agro-food and quality. Questions to the social sciences] *Economie Rurale, 217*, 5–11.

Perrier-Cornet, P. (1990). Les Filières Régionales de Qualité dans L'Agro-Alimentaire. Etude Comparative dans le secteur laitier en Franche-Comté, Emilie Romagne, Auvergne. [Regional quality chains in agro-food. Comparative study in the dairy sectors of Franche-Comté, Emilia Romagna, Auvergne] *Economie Rurale, 195*, 27–33.

Ploeg, J. D. Van der (1995). From Structural Development to Structural Involution: The Impact of New Development in Dutch Agriculture. In: J. D. Van der Ploeg & G. van Dijk (Eds), *Beyond Modernization. The Impact of Endogenous Rural Development* (pp. 109–146). Assen: Van Gorcum.

Ploeg, J. D. Van der (1997). On rurality, rural development and rural sociology. In: H. de Haan & N. Long. *Images and realities of rural life. Wageningen perspectives on rural transformations* (pp. 39–73). Assen: Van Gorcum.

Ploeg, J. D. Van der, & Ettema, M. (Eds). (1990). *Tussen bulk en kwaliteit. Landbouw, voedselproduktieketens en gezondheid* [Between bulk and quality. Agriculture, food production chains and health] Assen: Van Gorcum.

Ploeg, J. D. Van der, & Roep, D. (1990). *Bedrijfsstijlen in de Zuidhollandse veenweidegebieden* [Farming styles in South Dutch Peat Areas] Wageningen: WAU.

Ploeg, J. D. Van der, Miedema, S., Roep, D., van Broekhuizen, R., & de Bruin, R. (1992). *Boer Bliuwe, Blinder . . .! Bedrijfsstijlen, ondernemerschap en toekomstperspectieven* [Farming styles, entrepreneurship and perspectives on the future] Wageningen: WAU [in Dutch]

Porter, M. E. (1985). *Competitive Advantage: creating and sustaining superior perform-ance*. New York: The Free Press.

RLG [Council for the Rural Areas]. (1998). *Vertrouwen en zorg: voedselproductie in de 21ste eeuw* [Trust and care: food production in the 21st century] Amersfoort: RLG.

Roep, D., Van der Ploeg, J.D., & Leeuwis, C. (1991). *Zicht op Duurzaamheid en Kontinuteit. Bedrijfsstijlen in de Achterhoek* [Sight on sustainability and continuity. Farming styles in the 'Achterhoek'] Wageningen: WAU.

Roest, K. de. (1990). Een voorbeeld van kwaliteit: de produktie van Parmezaanse kaas. In: J. D.Van der Ploeg & M. Ettema (Eds) *An Example of quality: the production of Parmesan cheese* (pp. 77–87), op. cit.

COMPETING EXPLANATIONS OF SUCCESSFUL DAIRY FARMING IN TEXAS

Wm. Alex McIntosh and Alvin Luedke

INTRODUCTION

Changes in the Texas dairy industry have paralleled those elsewhere in the U.S. During the 1982–92 decade, the number of dairy farms in the U.S. declined by 44%, while average herd size increased by 51%. In Texas, dairy numbers declined by 45% with an increase in average herd size of 98% during the same time period. Furthermore, in 1996–97 alone, the number of dairies decreased by 17% in Texas (Ernestes et al., 1996).

Milk prices were very low in the 1980s. In the 1990s, though the price of milk has increased slightly, so have the prices of inputs including equipment, labor, and land. In Texas, increases in the cost of feed have risen faster than the price of milk (Ernestes et al., 1996). While the pressure on dairy farmers to increase herd size and total milk production continues to be strong, many dairy farmers have either been unwilling to make the needed changes or have been unable to obtain the credit necessary to make such changes (Knutson, 1991). Others have confronted new land and water use restrictions in their local communities (Ernestes et al., 1996). Planning is made more difficult because of the uncertainties created by continued debates in Congress over the agricultural price support system (Siebert et al., 1997). Despite the fact that many of these

Research in Rural Sociology, Volume 8, pages 229–263.
ISBN: 0-7623-0474-X

constraints lie outside the realm of farmer control, some have blamed problems in the dairy industry on the reluctance of some dairy farmers to change (Ernestes et al., 1996; Schwart, 1998). For the most part, the trend in the dairy industry is towards fewer farms with more cows. Many have argued that smaller farms, including dairy, are at the greatest risk of leaving the industry (Schwart, 1998; see also Jackson-Smith, 1999). Some have even argued that dairy farms must grow in size if they are to survive. We assume that some dairies are more successful than others in terms of productivity and/or resource efficiency and that the more successful dairies are more likely to survive (Ernestes et al., 1996). We also argue that dairy operators' satisfaction with their farms represents an important component of success.

Our aim in this chapter is to explore three competing explanations that are commonly offered for dairy success: dairy structure (herd size), regional location of the dairy, and the dairy farmer's orientation. We will take the position, however, that these perspectives actually complement one another in explaining such success.

Dairies as Organizations

Existing research has not dealt with these three hypotheses together within one context and analytical framework. Furthermore, taken as a whole, research on farming has not settled the 'structure' vs. 'agency' nature of such a debate. In other words, extant research provides no clear picture of whether decisions made by farmers vs. factors beyond their control (e.g. input prices) best explain success in agriculture. To contribute towards resolving this issue, at least with regard to the dairy industry, we draw on the complex organization research tradition. There are several reasons for doing so. First, this literature suggests that organizational characteristics such as size or scale of an organization have an impact on the probability of its survival. Second, the environments in which organizations operate clearly affect their success. Third, some have argued that strategic choices made by organizations reflect managerial orientations about how to achieve goals and how to react in the face of changing environments (Hall, 1996; Knoke & Wood, 1981). Strategic choices made by management affect the structure of the organization (including its size), and both choice and structure have a bearing on organizational success (Donaldson, 1996; Shortell et al., 1990).

We argue that there is great utility to be gained from studying farms as organizations. It is commonly perceived, however, that the study of complex organizations requires large organizations and, after all, many farms are small family businesses. Hall (1996) and Dolch & Heffernan (1978) respond to such objections by observing that the majority of organizations in all sectors of the U.S. economy are small, employing less than 10 persons each. Some of these small organizations are family businesses. Yet studies of complex organizations, even those small in size, have benefitted from perspectives drawn from organizational sociology. For example, organizational theory has been used to study the survival of restaurants, many of which are small, family-run businesses. Others have treated voluntary organizations as complex organizations; again many of these tend to have small memberships (Knoke & Wood, 1981; Knoke, 1990). In addition, farms possess many of the same characteristics that organization researchers have found to be important predictors of survival and success, including size, division of labor, and specialization. Finally, a precedent exists for treating farms as complex organizations. Some of the earliest work is that of Dolch & Heffernan (1978), which utilized structural variables such as formalization, hierarchy of authority, and participation in decision making, in order to predict organizational outcomes such as job satisfaction and adaptiveness. Adbu-Ella et al. (1981) employed an organizational perspective in their study of the adoption of agricultural technology. Bennett's (1982) study of Canadian farms drew upon variables from the 'organizational goals approach'. More recently, McIntosh et al. (1990) employed a Weberian approach to organizations and found that farms of greater size, diversity, and division of labor as well as rational management are more likely to employ both economic and non-economic forms of soil conservation practices.

Research Aims

A number of studies have used some of the variables associated with organizational perspectives to explain changes that have occurred in the dairy industry. The researchers involved have not considered all such approaches in a single study nor examined the possible interrelationships among structural, environmental, and managerial characteristics. Our aim in this chapter is to examine the relative importance of organizational structure in terms of size, environmental context in terms of dairy industry growth or decline, and organizational management in terms of orientations toward farming in explaining dairy farm efficiency and success in terms of financial performance and dairy farmer satisfaction.

RESEARCH PERSPECTIVES

Organizational Success

Successful organizations may be viewed as those that survive despite challenges from their environments (Baum, 1996). Thus, organizational researchers have sought explanations for such survival as have rural sociologists interested in predicting the survival of farms in general and dairy farms in particular (see Flora & Stitz, 1985; Albrecht, 1997; Lyson & Gillespie, 1995). Others have focused on performance in terms of efficiency and or effectiveness in producing output or in achieving organizational goals (Yutchman & Seashore, 1967; Etzioni, 1964). Bennett (1982) developed a scale to assess a farm's effectiveness which included measures of consistency of farm output over time, sustainability of the farm practices utilized, rate of return on investment capital, and gross returns from agricultural sales. Cruise & Lyson (1991) have generally studied dairy farm performance in terms of herd average (milk production per milk cow).

Efficiency is often discussed in the complex organization literature (see Hage, 1965, for example), yet it is rarely operationalized. Rural sociologists have eschewed efficiency as well, leaving this to agricultural economists (see Stanton, 1993; Penson et al., 1996) who frequently link increases in efficiency to the adoption of new technology. Johnson & Rutan (1997), for example, have described efficiencies created in the dairy industry by the adoption of artificial insemination. The assumption is usually made that organizations that adopt new technology will enjoy an initial competitive advantage over those organizations that do not (Penson et al., 1996; Rogers, 1995). Some have linked efficiency to the issue of survival in the dairy industry. Lyson & Gillespie (1995) attempted to link aggregate (state) levels of efficiency (i.e. land, labor, or capital per cow) with agreggate changes in the numbers of larger than family-size and family-size dairy farms.

Finally, some organizational researchers have claimed that an important dimension of an organization's success is the degree to which its members are satisfied with either their work or the performance of the organization itself (Georgiou, 1973; Hage & Aiken, 1967). From this perspective an organization cannot be either efficient or effective unless its members have sufficient incentives to work hard. Rural sociologists' interest in satisfaction with farming, however, has had less to do with concerns over whether farmers work as hard as they are capable, but more with the potential connection between satisfaction and leaving farming for other pursuits.

We argue here that in organizations such as farms, the work satisfaction of the operator of the farm is crucial. Farm operators must work long hours and deal with high levels of risk associated with weather, prices, and farm policy. Changes in the industry are likely to affect farmers' perceptions of their work. Others have recognized the importance of farmer job satisfaction and have argued that farming is a more satisfactory way of making a living from the point of view of the participants because it "combines work, residence, and family life" (Wilkening & Ahrens, 1979: 143; cited in Cougenhour & Swanson, 1988). Furthermore, farmers tend to rate their work more favorably than those who work in non-farm occupations (Coughenour & Swanson, 1988).

Some have found that satisfaction with farming depends upon the size and profitability of the farm operation (Coughenour, 1995; McIntosh et al., 1997). Others have linked satisfaction to farmer orientations and perceptions. Those who place higher value on the intrinsic rewards of farming (e.g. working with family members) over the extrinsic rewards of farming (e.g. profits) tend to be more satisfied with farming (Coughenour & Swanson, 1988; Coughenour, 1995). Molnar (1985) found that satisfaction is associated with goals (e.g. desire to expand) and self perceptions (e.g. view self as an innovator). We thus turn our attention to a discussion of organizational size, location, and managerial orientation as predictors of organizational success.

Organizational Size

Contingency theory from organizational sociology argues that resources are scarce and that organizations adapt to resource deficits through the way in which they are structured. No single means of organizing necessarily insures effectiveness (Donaldson 1996), but contingency researchers have consistently found that larger organizations generate resources that help them deal with stable, predictable environments but make them less inclined to adopt new technology. Larger-sized organizations tend also to exhibit greater division of labor and greater diversity of products. Greater size makes economies of scale more likely because larger organizations produce more, usually with lower unit costs (Blau, 1970). For example, artificial insemination is cheaper per cow in larger-sized herds (Johnson & Ruttan, 1997).

Contingency theorists sometimes claim that small organizations survive more readily in rapidly changing environments because such organizations are said to be more flexible. More recently, however, organizational ecologists proposed the 'liability of smallness' hypothesis, which asserts that larger organizations are less likely to fail because: (1) larger organizations tend to provide reliable responses to environmental changes; (2) smaller organizations are less likely to maintain sufficient resource levels to meet ongoing demands; and (3) larger organizations are frequently perceived to be "more legitimate by stakeholders" (Baum, 1996: 79).

There is a well-established relationship between farm size and its efficiency and survival from one generation to the next (Stanton, 1993). Generally, farms relatively larger in size have been more likely to stay in business. Agricultural economists argue that the size-survival effect is due to the interrelationships among size, level of technology, and labor efficiency (see Snodgrass & Wallace, 1964). More recent analyses discuss the relationship between increased farm size and returns to investment. Increases in input lead to increases in return on investment; however, the marginal advantage of continued size increases is eventually lost (Penson et al., 1996). Larger farms are more likely to purchase new technology, which in turn, leads to greater input efficiencies, particularly those having to do with land and labor (see Babb, 1979; McIntosh et al., 1990; Adbu-Ella et al., 1981). Cordtz (1978) has argued, however, that small farms have some advantages over large ones in that operators of small farms can more easily manage a small operation than operators of large farms can.

In contrast to such findings, one aggregate-level study observed that milk production per cow increases with increases in land and labor efficiencies but decreases with efficiencies in capital; furthermore, the same study showed that changes in efficiencies are not related to survival rates of either large or small dairy farms (Lyson & Gillespie, 1995). And Albrecht (1997) has found that small- to medium-sized farms increase their chance of survival by adopting yield-increasing rather than efficiency-increasing technologies. This latter finding may result from small farms having less land available per worker, rendering labor less efficient in such settings.

Organizational research has generally not sought explanations of job satisfaction in the size of the organization employing workers. Instead, workers employed by more highly bureaucratized organizations face an increased probability of alienation and dissatisfaction. As larger organizations tend towards greater bureaucratization, they are more likely to produce such problems. However, there is some evidence that farmers who maintain larger operations are more satisfied with farming than those who operate smaller farms (Schroeder et al., 1985; Coughenour, 1995; McIntosh et al., 1997). The difference between the size-dissatisfaction relationship reported in the formal organization literature and the size-satisfaction relationship found among farmers results from position in the organization. The formal organization studies focus on labor; rural sociological studies concentrate on owners/ managers. We examine the relationship between dairy herd size, measured in several ways, and dairy farm success in Texas. We expect to find generally higher levels of performance, including satisfaction with farming, among larger-sized farms.

Location

The location of an organization also affects its chances for success. Some have found, for example, that the intensity and nature of the competition an organization faces affects the probability of its survival (Baum, 1996). The availability and cost of resources also affects an organization's ability to compete successfully (Donaldson, 1996; Drabenstott & Smith, 1995).

Researchers have examined location factors in the study of dairy success. They have found that the availability of processors and markets for dairy products (Lyson & Gillespie, 1995; Schwarzweller & Davidson, 1997), low cost inputs or transportation systems for lower cost shipment of inputs and outputs in and out of the local community (Gilbert & Akor, 1988), or natural resources such as water (Enestes et al., 1996) are associated with dairy success. Competition over water, particularly by communities for human consumption, has become a major factor in limiting the number of new dairies allowed in some counties and the growth of dairy size in others (Schwart 1999; Ernestes et al., 1996). We hypothesize that factors associated with location such as input prices, transportation, or number of milk processors have an effect on dairy success. These factors are reflected in the history of dairy farm success (growth/decline in the number of dairy farms; growth/decline in amount of the milk produced) at the county level. We will thus create an indirect test of the location effects on current dairy success by classifying counties in terms of dairy success in the past.

Farmer Orientation Typologies

Organizational success, according to some, depends largely on the orientation of management (Hall, 1996; Donaldson, 1996; Shortell et al., 1990). Shortell et al. (1990), for example, believe that the most suitable management strategy for hospital administrators in the changing medical environment is that of 'prospector' or the search for new managerial ideas as opposed to 'defender' or riding out environmental change without altering the organization. Many agricultural economists share this view when it comes to survival and success in the dairy business (Schwart, 1998; Ernestes et al., 1996). Others have found that 'rational orientation' of owner/operators is a good predictor of the adoption of agricultural technologies of various sorts (McIntosh et al., 1990). Cruise &

Lyson (1991) found that rational strategy (measured here by adoption of dairy technologies) is positively related to herd average. Strange (1989), however, suggests that family-oriented farms are frequently as efficient producers of farm products as are agri business farms. In others words, managers of family-oriented farms are capable of making rational decisions. In addition, those who manage large agri business farms are more willing to go into debt than are those who manage smaller farms (Strange, 1989). Entrepreneurs are also likely to operate larger size farms (Salamon, 1992). Walter's (1997) study focuses on the orientations of those farmers perceived to be successful. And Barlett (1991) found that farmers who pursue either high status living or ambitious farm management styles are very likely to face a poor financial situation.

As the above discussion implies, researchers have taken a number of approaches to the study of orientation towards farming. These approaches vary broadly in their views of farming orientation. Most have developed typologies based on ethnicity or some other categorical basis of classification such as family-sized versus larger than family-sized. All such studies seem to have identified the similar kinds of factors that produce one or another of the farm types, yet each offers dimensions the others have ignored. We begin with Salamon (1992), who makes a distinction between yeomen and entrepreneurs. Her typology, while based on two distinct cultural groups, Germans and Yankees, reflects in part the same sort of typological distinctions made by those who characterize differences between modern versus more traditional farmers. Yeomen tend to place a high value on their family's long term continuity in farming. Farming as an activity and land ownership are perceived as ends in themselves. By contrast, the entrepreneur views land and farming more instrumentally; these are perceived as opportunities for profit making. While yeomen strive toward long-run goals of "reproducing a viable farm for the next generation," the entrepreneur pursues shorter-term business goals (Salamon 1992). Thus, the entrepreneur may perceive of the sale of land as a sound business move. Furthermore, entrepreneurs expand in order to make profits and perceive debt as an acceptable means for expansion. Yeomen expand only if the family can manage the extra effort and capital outlay required; debt is an anathema (Salamon, 1992).

Gerry Walter (1997) discovered that the differential weighting farmers give to various values and goals leads to four, rather than two, images of the successful farmer. Managers, for example, are those who wait to see whether new technology will pay off, and seek high levels of production, using a number of rational strategies such as careful record-keeping. Conservatives seek to avoid debt while retaining the farm in the family. Agrarians enjoy farming as a way of life, particularly regarding the work environment. The values and goals used by Walter (1997) to develop his typology overlap considerably with those employed by Salamon (1992) (see also Bennett, 1982).

Strange (1989), like Salamon (1992), draws a contrast between two types of farming, but focuses on the kinds of labor they are likely to employ, arguing that family farms obtain labor and managerial skills from their family members, while industrial-agribusinesses tend to utilize non-family members in these positions. Family-oriented farms attempt to involve family members in the operation in order to prepare them for the eventual take-over of the operation (Strange, 1989; Garkovitch et al., 1995).

Barlett (1991) contributes additional dimensions to farming orientation by contrasting consumption styles with management styles. Furthermore, she finds farm families that opt for a "higher than average household consumption" life style or that practice an "ambitious farm management style" (i.e. expand the operation and accept greater debt) tend to be at much greater risk of failure.

Taken together, these authors have described a number of differences in orientation to farming, which suggests that differences in values and goals with respect to land ownership and land usage, family involvement in the operation, and orientations towards debt and growth, among others, may affect the dairy operation. Each of the authors has captured certain aspects of such orientations and so we have opted for a combined perspective. Furthermore, we believe that the components of farming orientation are better represented as continua rather than simple dichotomies. In our operationalization of farmer orientation, we thus utilize many of the dimensions described by Salamon (1992), Strange (1989), Walter (1997), Garkovitch et al. (1995), Schroeder et al. (1985), and Barlett (1991), but will treat these dimensions as continua. We will then attempt to demonstrate as have Cruise & Lyson (1991) and Barlett (1991), for example, that the goals, values, and behaviors of dairy operators help explain differences in dairy farm success. We hypothesize that those farmers whose orientations towards farming stress economic rewards, the use of debt as a financial tool, or that desire expansion are more likely to perform well in terms of efficiency and financial performance. Those farmers whose orientations place a high value on family involvement and whose goals include increased family involvement are more satisfied with dairy farming than those whose values and goals stress finances and expansion.

In summary, there is thus some evidence that organizational characteristics of dairy farms as well as the orientations of their operators affect dairy farm success. Most studies, however, have considered these factors separately and have often used a limited number of success indicators. The goal of the present research is to examine the effects of location and size of the dairy operation as well as operator farming orientation on the performance of the dairy operation in terms of its financial performance, efficiency, and the satisfaction with farming it provides its operator. Farming orientation will consist of operator farming values, goals, and reliancc on family labor.

METHODOLOGY

Sampling Procedures

Dairies are currently located in 81 of Texas's 254 counties. Over time, a few counties have experienced growth in both the numbers of dairy farms and total milk production, others have retained approximately the same number of farms while expanding milk production, and others have declined in both numbers of farms and milk production. The majority of counties, however, have enjoyed stability. The present study focuses on only those counties that had undergone dairy industry change during the period 1980–89. These trends have continued, for the most part, into the 1990s as well. A stratified sample of counties that fit one of three categories was developed: (1) decline (both in total milk production and numbers of farms), (2) mixed growth (growth in production or numbers of farms, but not both), and (3) growth (increase in both numbers of farms and in total milk production). Counties were then randomly selected for each category, proportionate to the number of counties in the populations of decline, mixed growth, and growth counties. This design resulted in the selection of four counties in the decline category, three counties in the mixed growth category, and one county in the growth category (see Table 1). Hopkins County was classified as a mixed growth county because its decline in number of milk producers accelerated and its growth in total milk production substantially declined in the early 1990s (see Fig. 1 for the location of the sample counties).

A second stage of sampling was the random selection of dairy farms from each county. The number selected was based on the proportion of that county's farms in its location category. The Texas Water Commission provided a list from which the counties' dairies were drawn. This list was cross-checked with a list provided by the Texas Department of Health as well as with listings in local phone books. Sampled dairies were mailed the questionnaire and the Dilman method was followed through all of its stages except the follow-up telephone call. After eliminating those recently out-of-business operations, a response rate of nearly 52% was obtained.

Table 1. Percent Change in Number of Milk Producers and Total Milk Production, 1980–90, Sampled Counties[a]

County Type	% Change in no. of Milk Producers	% Change in Total Milk Production
Decline		
Bexar	−69.2	−62.5
Dallam	−20.0	−3.3
Parker	−52.8	−25.8
Tarrant	−58.1	−28.8
Panola	−10.0	−33.6
Shackelford	0.0	−48.4
Average	−58.7	−33.7
Mixed		
El Paso	−43.8	46.8
Nacogdoches	−30.5	51.8
Hopkins	−2.8	143.0
Average	−25.7	80.5
Growth		
Erath	7.0	172.5
State Total[b]	−16.9	55.7

[a] Data from the Texas Milk Market Administrator (1991); milk producers are those dairy farms that market milk; milk production is measured in pounds.
[b] In the period 1980–1990, 79 of the 254 counties in Texas had 3 or more dairies.

County Descriptions

Table 2 provides a comparison of sample results by county with county characteristics from the Agricultural Census (1992). Note that some of the census data are based on all farms rather than dairy farms. With only two exceptions, the sample dairy farms tend to be larger in terms of number of acres operated. Similarly, the sample of herd sizes tend to be substantially larger than the population herd size for that county, save in the case of Nacogdoches in which the Census indicates that dairy herds average 356.7 cows while the dairy farms in the sample from this county average only 125.2 cows. Average numbers of full time workers are higher in sample data than in the Census for half of the counties (Panola, El Paso, Hopkins, Nacogdoches, and Erath), but are lower in the remaining five counties. Census figures for average dairy product sales tend to be lower than the sample figures for average milk sales in every case save Hopkins County.

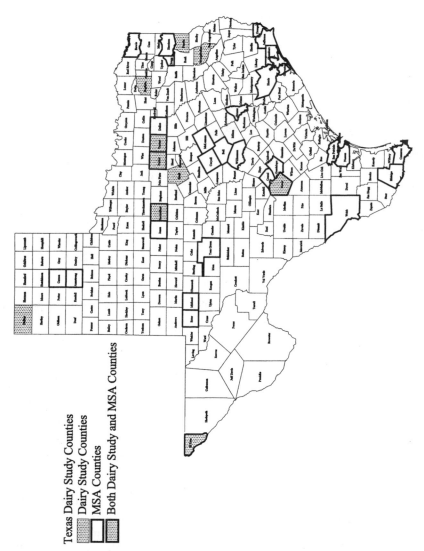

Fig. 1. Texas Dairy Study.

Table 2. Population and Sample Comparisons Across Relevant Indicators

County Type	No. of Dairy Farms		Average Size in Acres		Size Dairy Herd		Average No. of Full Time Workers		Average Dairy Product Sales ($1,000)	
	Pop.	Sample	Pop.[a]	Sample	Pop.	Sample	Pop.[a]	Sample	Pop.	Sample
Decline										
Bexar	43	3	218	300	25	125	4	2	160	248
Dallam	6	2	2,116	1,167	88	200	3	1	150	358
Panola	23	9	247	940	87	395	3	4	332	1,445
Parker	51	4	212	405	110	80	2	2	512	787
Shackelford	8	2	2,391	481	15	135	2	1	–	663
Tarrant	34	5	172	385	39	204	4	2	1,910	2,023
Mixed										
El Paso	18	5	–	358	531	1,026	8	15	1,846	7,860
Hopkins	508	26	220	293	126	200	2	3	2,114	1,802
Nacogdoches	38	7	195	747	357	125	2	4	258	900
Growth										
Erath	224	25	355	848	290	876	4	12	6,421	17,826

Pop. = Population (1992)

[a] All farms in the county (1993–94)

In addition, the sample counties have features that help explain the changing fortunes of the dairy industry within those counties (see Table 3). To begin with, four of the counties are part of the Metropolitan Statistical Areas (MSAs) of San Antonio (Bexar County), El Paso (El Paso County), and Fort Worth-Arlington (Parker County, Tarrant County). Shackleford County is adjacent to the Abilene MSA. Each of these MSAs has continued to grow and urbanize since 1980. Population growth and urbanization represent competition with agriculture for land and water resources. Most of the counties in the study, especially those that were part of MSAs, experienced population growth, sometimes exceeding the state average (see Table 2). Increasing land prices and environmentalist pressures for limits on dairy growth have accompanied this increase in population (Schwart, 1999). Erath, the dairy growth county, also grew at a faster rate than either the state or several of the metro counties did, but in Erath's case, population pressures were low and until very recently, environmental concerns were absent (Schwart, 1999). The most isolated of these counties (Dallam and Shackleford) have not only experienced dairy decline but also lost more than 15% of their populations during the 1980s.

The number of farms and amount of land in production tended to decrease, again with the greater-sized declines in the MSA counties. However, Parker, which is part of the Fort Worth-Arlington MSA, increased in both number of farms and amount of land in production. With the exception of Dallam and Shackleford, whose farm sizes are more than double the state average, the average farm size in the remaining counties fell below the state average.

Despite the decline of agriculture in Bexar, a growing metro county, dairy and beef cattle continue their dominance as income producers from agriculture (Texas Almanac, 1994–95). Tarrant, also a metro county experiencing growth, remains a major agricultural county, producing beef cattle, dairy products, hogs, poultry, and horses. In addition, the county is the home of one of the state's dairy producer organizations. Parker, adjacent to Tarrant, is considered a significant producer of dairy products. Dallam County remains a major producer of beef cattle and cotton. Feedlots produce a significant amount of the county's agricultural revenues. During the 1980s and early 1990s, it experienced a significant decline in dairy farming; however, during the past several years, the dairy industry has staged a comeback in Dallam (Texas Milk Market Administrator 1999). This resurgence is partly the result of a lack of environmentalist pressures there, compared to other counties, where such pressures have increased (Schwart, 1999). Panola is the state's leading poultry producer and has fewer milk buyers than other counties (Texas Almanac, 1994–95).

Table 3. Demographic, Agricultural, and Other Economic Characteristics of Sampled Counties

County Type	Population Change (1980–90) (%)	Population Urban (%)	Labor Force in Agriculture (%)	Average Farm Size (Acres)	Change in no. of Farms (%)	Net Change in land in Farming (%)
Decline						
Bexar	19.9	94.3	1.1	245	-2.9	-4.8
Dallam	-16.4	73.3	22.9	1,981	4.9	-7.0
Panola	6.3	29.5	6.1	221	-2.4	-3.0
Parker	45.2	25.6	3.5	208	9.9	7.1
Shackelford	-15.3	0.0	12.2	2,193	-2.8	-4.2
Tarrant	35.9	98.9	1.0	177	-9.8	-1.9
Mixed						
El Paso	23.3	97.5	1.3	561	-7.4	-13.9
Hopkins	14.2	48.8	12.3	212	5.3	4.9
Nacogdoches	17.0	51.6	5.7	193	0.5	2.2
Growth						
Erath	24.1	59.6	13.1	351	2.2	1.4
State	19.4	80.3	2.3	691	2.0	-0.61

Source: U.S. Bureau of the Census. County and City Data Book. 1994. Washington, D.C.: U. S. Government Printing Office. Texas Almanac 1994-95.

In the counties that make up the region of mixed growth, the MSA county of El Paso had a low percentage of its labor force employed in agriculture (1%). In El Paso, farms declined by 7% and land in farming by 14%. At the same time, the average value of production per farm surpassed $150 thousand, much higher than the state average of $55 thousand per farm. Farm sizes tended to fall below the state average. El Paso's agriculture is dominated by beef cattle, despite its high production of milk relative to many other counties. Hopkins is the second highest producing dairy county in Texas and contains a number of large milk processing plants. Beef cattle, however, have begun to overtake dairy in importance. Dairy farmers in Hopkins not only face urban pressure, but many have also reached a point at which they would have to grow significantly in order to remain in business (Schwart, 1999). Finally, Nacogdoches is considered a leading producer of poultry and timber in the state. Lumber mills are also an important industry. These activities have proven sufficiently lucrative to have begun to displace dairy (Texas Almanac, 1994–95).

The growth county has a greater percent of employment in agriculture than the state as a whole and there was a slight increase in the number of farms and amount of land devoted to agriculture. The average value of agricultural products is somewhat higher in Erath County than for the state as a whole. Erath's dairy production has continued to be the highest in the state, but beef cattle and peanuts are also important. Dairy production is aided by the presence of four milk buyers, including a cheese processing plant. Dairy growth was made possible in the 1980s by the availability of dairy farms and additional land for dairy farm expansion in size at a time in which a number of out-of-state dairy farmers were looking for a location at which to set up new, large-scale dairy operations (Schwart, 1999). A decline in land availability and a moratorium on growth have contributed to a halt in dairy expansion in Erath, although it continues to claim the title of the most productive dairy county in the state (Hale, 1999).

Measurement of Variables

A. *Dairy Farm Success*. As discussed above, organizational success involves a number of factors such as effectiveness, efficiency, and job satisfaction. Some have even suggested that the adoption of new technology is also a good measure of performance. *Success* was measured in four ways. First, the owner/operators were asked to rate the *financial performance* of their dairy farm over the past five years, using a three-point scale that ranged from poor to excellent. Second, *personal satisfaction* with dairy farming was measured by a 4-item scale, which included assessments of their choice of becoming dairy farmers and the income provided by farming. Responses for each of these items ranged from very satisfied to not at all satisfied on a 10-point scale. Principal components analysis of responses to these 4 items resulted in a single factor which explained 59% of the variance in the four items; coefficient alpha was 0.796 for the scale (see Appendix Table A1).

Third, we formed indicators of efficiency. Efficiency measures were based on several considerations. First, efficiency is usually sought with regard to factor inputs associated with the dairy herd itself. Thus, amount of land per cow, assets per cow, and laborers per cow are frequently used measures (see for example, Lyson & Gillespie, 1995). Second, ratios of factor inputs, including number of dairy cows to output (amount of milk produced) are also useful. We used assets per cow, milkers per cow (number of persons employed to milk the cows), and amount of milk produced per cow as our measures of efficiency.

Adoption of dairy technology is the fourth measure of success, which we formed by summing the number of dairy technologies adopted by the owner/ operator. These included pre- and post-dipping of cow teats, use of a veterinarian for regular herd checkups, artificial insemination, ration testing, and use of computers for dairy records. This scale produced a Cronbach's alpha of 0.834.

B. *Structure (Size)*. Herd size is an important structural variable, closely associated with other structural characteristics of farms. We used the total number of cows milked as an interval-level variable in a number of the analyses. For other analyses, we trichotomized this variable into small (26–99 cows), medium (100–199 cows), and large herds (200 cows or more).

C. *Orientation toward farming*. As discussed above, previous work on farming orientations indicates that farmers differ in terms of perceived rewards and desirable characteristics of farming, goals, and behavior. We oper-ationalized each of these characteristics.

Starting with *family and personal rewards from dairy farming*, a 13-item scale was developed with questions regarding the importance of working conditions associated with dairy farming (e.g. working outdoors, working with animals, being one's own boss), the economic rewards of farming, and the ability to work with family members and pass the operation on to the next generation. Response choices to these items ranged from very important to not at all important along a 10-point scale. These reflect the rewards of farming measured by Schroeder et al. (1985), Salamon (1992), and Garkovitch et al. (1995). Cronbach's alpha was 0.924. Principal components analysis produced a three-factor solution reflecting working conditions, economic rewards, and the involvement of family in the dairy operation. The three factors accounted for over 64% of the 13 items' variance (see Table A2). We next examined *financial and family goals*. Farmers have both family and business goals associated with farming. Salamon (1992) argues that some farmers are more likely to be non-risk takers when it comes to setting financial goals. This means a greater willingness to take on debt. Barlett (1991) found that some farmers are more likely to pursue more "ambitious, status-oriented management styles," which involve greater commitments of financial resources to equipment. Other farmers, given their stage in the life cycle, are preparing for retirement. Five questions regarding financial goals such as reducing debt, avoiding debt, preparing for retirement, increasing cash flow were asked. Respondents were asked to rate the importance of each along a 10-point scale. A single factor resulted in the subsequent principal components analysis, which explained 53% of items' variance; Cronbach's alpha was 0.818 (see Table A3).

Garkovitch et al. (1995) and other have identified some of the family goals of farmers as bringing family members into the operation, passing the family farm on to the next generation, and having more time to spend with family. Salamon (1992) describes some farmers as more family-oriented when it comes to farming in that they desire to involve family in current farm work as well as to be able to pass on the operation to the next generation. In addition, such farmers may be more family-oriented in their desire to spend more money and time with their families. Thus, a second set of items that dealt with family goals included the desire to: (1) spend more time with family members, spend more money for family needs, take vacations with family, (2) bring family members into the operation, and (3) prepare to pass the operation on to the next generation. A 10-point response scale for rating the importance of each goal was used. Taken together, the items produced a Cronbach's alpha of 0.677. These items formed two factors, after principal components analysis. The first represents the goal of spending more time and money on family; the second, getting greater involvement of family in the operation. The two factors explain over 82% of the variation in the items (see Table A4). In addition, an attempt to measure personal goals relative to dairying was made. Here the emphasis was on being perceived by others as progressive. Some research has identified this as a goal (see Schroeder et al., 1985). Items included the degree to which an operator thought it desirable to be perceived as an innovator and an entrepreneur; the two items produced a single factor with loadings greater than 0.9. The factor explained 88% of the item's variance and the items as a scale produced a Cronbach's alpha of 0.863 (see Table A5).

Finally, most farms set goals for their *enterprise*. Some desire to remain the same size, others wish to expand. Furthermore, some may wish to diversify their operations or improve herd performance; others desire to improve herd health or safety conditions on their farms (Anoiske & Coughenhour, 1990). Operation goals were measured by eight items that reflected the desire to increase size or production levels or improve the operation by increasing herd health, farm safety, etc, again using the 10-point response scale. A two-factor solution was produced. The first represents the goal of expansion in terms of milk production; the second, improvements in the operation (improve herd health; farm safety; etc.). Sixty-nine percent of the variance was explained by the two factors and the overall alpha was 0.897 (see Table A6).

Another characteristic used to distinguish farm types is preference for *family labor*. A preference for family labor rather than other sources is characteristic of more traditional farms described by Strange (1989) and the Yeoman farms described by Salamon (1992). We lacked a measure of preference of family over other types of labor. We did, however, have measures of the use of family labor on the dairy farm. Reliance on family labor was measured in two ways. First, the proportion of full-time and *proportion of all labor* (full time, part-time, and seasonal) performed by family members was obtained. A second way to capture family member labor contributions is to measure the range of farm tasks in which they are involved (see Wilson et al., 1994). Thus, respondents were asked to indicate which of a series of typical tasks performed on dairy farms (e.g. milking, manure management, calf raising, feed testing, book keeping) were accomplished by family members. These tasks were then summed such that the higher the score, the more *dairy farm tasks performed by family members.*

FINDINGS

Descriptive Findings

On average, dairy farmers in Texas perceived that their dairy farm's financial performance has stayed about the same during the past five years. However, dairy farms that have more than 200 milk cows tend to report improvements in the financial performance of their operations. Satisfaction is highest when it came to being satisfied with being a dairy farmer, but scores are lower for the remaining components of satisfaction (income, financial performance, career alternatives to dairy farming) (see Appendix Table A1). Of the seven kinds of dairy technology that could have been adopted, the sampled members practice 4.9 on average. Dairy farmers in our sample farm, on average, nearly 600 acres of land and milk, on average, nearly 500 cows. They average 6.7 full time workers, with 1.5 persons assigned to the task of milking the cows. Herd average is 16,622 pounds of milk per cow; sample farms utilize 2.08 acres per cow and employ 7.7 milkers for every 1,000 milk cows.

Forty-two percent of full-time labor is contributed by family members; 45% of all labor comes from family. Forty-five percent of the various dairy farm tasks are performed by family members. Texas dairy farmers tend to rate the work conditions of dairy farming (being my own boss, working with animals, etc.) as among the most important aspects of farming (see Appendix Table A2). Economic rewards associated with dairying are next most important followed by family involvement characteristics such as working with other family members, keeping the farm in the family, and bringing their children into dairy farming.

In terms of family goals, spending time with family and taking family on vacations tend to be more important than setting up the farm for the next generation or bringing a family member into the operation (see Appendix Table A3). However, the personal goals of being first in the area to make a change and being seen as a progressive are even less important than the goals of involving family in the operation (see Appendix Table A4).

In terms of financial goals, increasing profitability and increasing cash flow tend to be more important than paying off existing debt or avoiding new debt (see Appendix Table A5). Finally, improving herd health and safety conditions on the dairy farm are more likely to be goals than increasing the total amount of milk sold or production per cow (see Appendix Table A6). The latter two goals however were considered more important than reducing labor costs, minimizing environmental damage created by the farm, or the amount of physical labor involved in dairying.

Average age of the sample members is 48.2. On average, they have been involved with the dairy business for nearly 27 years and have operated their present dairy farm for nearly 18 years, and they derive over 91% of the farm income from the dairy.

Correlations among Structure and Farming Orientation Variables

The farming orientation literature suggests that farm size and farmer orientations are related and implies that those who operate larger farms are less family and more business oriented. Our findings indicate that farmers who operate larger farms place greater importance on both the working conditions and economic rewards associated with dairy farming; larger sized dairy farms tend to use fewer family members to perform farm tasks than smaller dairy farms (see Table 4). Size is not related to family, financial, or operation goals.

Table 4. Inter-relations Among Farm Structure and Farming Orientation Variables

	Rewards/Valued Characteristics					Goals				Family Involvement		
	Working Conditions	Economic Returns	Working with Family	More Time with Family	Greater Family Involvement	Reduce/Avoid Debt	Expand Operation	Improve Operation	Be Seen as an Innovator	% Full-Time Labor by Family	% All Labor by Family	Family Task Involvement
I. Structure												
1. Size	-0.303***	0.376	-0.045	0.161	0.164	0.009	0.106	-0.070	0.050	-0.180	-0.189	-0.348***
II. Farming Orientation												
A. Rewards												
2. Working Conditions	—	0.000	0.000	0.269***	0.288	-0.059	-0.043	0.030	0.204	0.050	0.140	-0.001
3. Economic Returns		—	0.000	-0.011	-0.311	0.204*	0.271**	0.156	-0.092	-0.028	-0.098	-0.170
4. Working with Family			—	0.705****	-0.058	-0.056	0.032	0.172	0.337***	0.257	0.222*	-0.051
B. Goals												
5. More Time with Family				—	0.000	-0.186	0.024	0.099	0.393***	-0.010	-0.067	-0.038
6. Greater Family Involvement					—	0.529****	0.474****	-0.023	0.205*	-0.136	-0.053	-0.089
7. Reduce/Avoid Debt						—	0.635****	0.182	0.002	-0.064	-0.116	-0.339***
8. Expand Operation							—	0.000	0.064	-0.147	-0.203	-0.202*
9. Improve Operation								—	0.046	0.150	0.141	-0.134
10. Be Seen as an Innovator									—	0.098	0.100	0.057
C. Family Involvement												
11. % Full-Time Labor by Family										—	0.952****	0.041
12. % All Labor by Family											—	0.096
13. Family Task Involvement												—

* Significant at the 0.10 level; ** Significant at the 0.01 level; *** Significant at the 0.001 level

Dairy farmers who rate the working conditions associated with dairy farming as important to them are more likely to identify spending more time with their families and being viewed as an innovator as goals than those who value other aspects of farming. Dairy farmers who rate the economic returns of dairy farming as important are more likely to hold debt reduction and expansion as goals.

Dairy farmers who perceive working with family as an important aspect of dairy farming are more likely to desire spending more time with family and being seen as an innovator. Those who value working with family operate farms that employ a greater percentage of family members as either full time or as all types of labor. Those who pursue the goal of spending more time with their families are also more likely to desire being seen as an innovator. Those who wish for greater family involvement either now or in the future also wish to reduce their debt, expand their operations, and be perceived as innovators. Those who wish to reduce debt would also like to expand the size of their operations; such farmers tend to use or involve family in fewer farm tasks. Farmers who wish to expand are also less likely to involve family in farm tasks.

Location Effects on Performance

Based on our reading of the organizational ecology literature, we expected that farms located in areas in which the dairy industry has expanded would be more successful than dairies located in areas of dairy decline. We found some evidence to support that hypothesis. Farmers with operations located in dairy growth counties, when compared with those in mixed growth or decline counties, report greater satisfaction with dairying, higher milk sales, better financial performance, and greater adoption of dairy technology (see Table 5). Farms in dairy growth counties also utilize more acres per cow than those farms in mixed growth counties, but dairy farms in growth and mixed growth counties required fewer milkers per cow. In addition, assets per cow are lower and milk sales per cow are higher in growth counties.

In addition, the type of county in which the dairy is located is also related to the use of family labor on the dairy farm. Farms in areas of decline employ a greater proportion of family members as labor and assign over half of various farm tasks to family members. Farms in areas of growth, by contrast, involve families in fewer tasks and as a lower percentage of the dairy farm's labor force. Dairy farmers located in growth counties are also more likely than those in other county-types to wish to spend more leisure time with family members.

Table 5. County Types Compared by Effectiveness, Efficiency, Size, and Diversity

County Type	Satisfaction With Dairy Farming	Financial Performance	Adopted Dairy Technology	Assets Per Cow	Milkers Per Cow	Acres Per Cow	No. of of Full Time Workers	% of Forage Produced	% of Full Time Labor By Family	% of Total Labor by Family
Decline	0.258[a]	2.353[a]	9.105[a,b]	0.019	0.012[a]	2.933[a,b]	3 188a	69.181[a]	82.480[a]	78.782[a]
Mixed Growth	0.223[a]	2.297[a]	10.000[a]	0.014[a]	0.008[b]	1.711[a]	5.481a	31.395[b]	31.990[b]	35.810[b]
Growth	-.054[b]	1.870[b]	8.720[b]	0.013[a]	0.008[b]	3.617[b]	11.818a	49.808[c]	29.010[b]	27.950[b]

Means with the same letter superscripts are not significantly different from one another.

Size Effects

The complex organization literature predicts that larger-sized organizations perform better than smaller-sized ones. Our findings tend to confirm this hypothesis. Farmers with larger operations are more satisfied with dairy farming, report better financial performance for the past 5 years, and adopt more dairy technology than those with smaller operations (see Table 6). In terms of efficiency, larger sized operations utilize more land per cow, but less full time labor and fewer milkers per cow as well as fewer assets per cow. The efficiency of milk production per cow, however, does not vary by size.

Size and Location

Organizational ecologists have suggested that size and location may interact to affect performance (Baum 1996). Size and location combinations produce a number of differences in performance and farm culture. For example, operators of small- and medium-sized dairies in counties of decline are the least satisfied with dairy farming compared with operators of large-sized farms in growth counties who are the most satisfied. Operators of large farms located in growth counties are more likely to report financial success, adopt more dairy technology, and utilize fewer assets per cow and fewer milkers per cow.

Orientation toward Farming

According to observers such as Salamon (1992), family-oriented farms employ greater proportions of family members, value working with family members, value the working conditions associated with farming in which to spend more time with family, get their families more involved in the operation, pass the farm on to the next generation, and avoid debt. A lower interest in adopting dairy technologies is likely.

We found that those who report good financial performance over the past 5 years are more likely to desire greater family involvement in the dairy operation, but those who wish to spend more time with family members report poorer financial performance (see Table 6). Those operators more satisfied with dairy farming tend to value family involvement on the farm, desire to spend more time with family members, and are less likely to have debt avoidance/ reduction as a goal.

Farmers desiring greater family involvement in the operation of the farm tend to produce less milk per cow. Dairy farmers for whom the goal of debt reduction/avoidance is important employ more assets and more milkers per

Table 6. Dairy Farm Performance, Dairy Farm Size, and Farming Orientation of Farmer

Farm Size/ Family Orientation	Satisfaction With Dairy Farming	Financial Performance	Adopted Dairy Technology	Milk Sold Per Cow	Assets Per Cow	Milkers Per Cow
Farm Size	0.306***	0.285***	0.277***	0.065	0.175	-0.268***
Farming Orientation						
Values						
Good Working Conditions	-0.026	0.050	0.050	0.213	0.243*	0.248**
Economic Rewards	-0.117	-0.108	-0.050	0.209	-0.062	-0.071
Work With Family	0.337***	0.200	-0.033	0.226	-0.228*	-0.185
Goals						
Spend More Time With Family	0.273**	0.223**	0.005	-0.036	-0.038	-0.018
Involve Family in Operation	-0.232**	-0.184	0.041	0.025	-0.206*	-0.090
Be Seen as Innovator	0.089	0.049	0.168	-0.216	-0.049	-0.069
Debt Reduction	-0.269**	-0.202*	-0.006	0.009	-0.384***	-0.227*
Expand Operation	-0.209	-0.070	-0.006	-0.072	-0.260**	-0.150
Improve Operation	0.026	0.015	0.254**	0.116	-0.041	-0.010
Family Labor						
% Full Time Workers by Family	0.104	0.158	0.192	0.051	0.290**	0.424***
% All Workers by Family	0.149	-0.222*	0.208*	0.082	0.410****	0.473****
Family Task Involvement	0.135	0.193*	0.144	-0.026	0.383***	0.195*

* Significant at the 0.10 level; ** Significant at the 0.05 level; *** Significant at the 0.01 level; **** Significant at the 0.001 level

cow and sell less milk per cow. Those less concerned with debt and cash flow, in other words, are more efficient.

Multi-Variate Findings

To develop an overall picture of the factors that affect dairy farm success, we conducted regression analyses, using as independent variables all variables significantly correlated with the success indicators. We included interactions between size and location in these analyses. Size-location interactions and family orientation variables are significant in five of the six success regression models; size alone is significant in only two of these equations.

Two kinds of size-location interactions are important. Small-sized farms located in counties of decline are less efficient in terms of labor and assets. Large-sized farms located in growth counties use less family labor, adopt more technology, produce more milk sales per cow, have better financial performance, and generate greater satisfaction with dairying. This is generally consistent with the size hypothesis posited by both the contingency theorists and organizational ecologists. The findings with regard to county location, which may reflect differences in input prices, transportation costs, markets for dairy products, or land use policies, also tend to support the organizational ecology perspective. This perspective suggests that not only larger size, but favorable environments help organizations to survive and prosper. It would appear, based on our findings, that large organizations are able to take advantage of the resources available in resource rich organizations. In the case of large dairies, for example, this may mean available land for expansion. Alternatively, a large organization may be able to overcome disadvantages associated with their particular location. Because of the amounts of feed they require they may be able to obtain a more favorable price for such inputs.

Family goals and values play an important role as well but the pattern of effects is less clear. We certainly cannot conclude that goals and values associated with family-oriented versus business-oriented farming make a difference in success. Instead the picture is more complex. The findings that those operators who wish to be perceived as innovators employ fewer milkers per cow or that those who hold dairy farm improvement as a goal are more likely to adopt dairy farm technology appear to support this distinction. However, the finding that links financial goals with asset inefficiency (assets per cow) and the finding that family involvement in the operation (as a percentage of the labor force) produces greater satisfaction with farming but less efficiency (in terms of labor and assets per cow) do not support the hypotheses suggested by the farming orientation literature.

SUMMARY AND CONCLUSIONS

These findings, taken together, indicate that dairy farm performance is the product of multiple factors. Size, location, and farming orientations all play a role in determining success. Location and size reflect constraints that, regardless of orientation toward farming, cannot be easily overcome. However, while small farms in counties of decline are less efficient and less successful financially, many have been able to remain in business. They tend to be operated by individuals relatively new to the business of dairy farming. By contrast, larger farms located in growth counties tend to fare better in terms of financial performance and satisfaction. Part of the explanation lies in opportunities that growth counties may offer dairy farmers, but part may lie in the fact that farmers with greater experience in dairy farming who have recently established their present operations are more likely found in growth counties. This suggests that for some, establishment of a new, most likely larger operation in a dairy growth county may represent the means toward greater financial success and greater satisfaction with dairy farming.

While farms that experience better financial performance are associated with operator satisfaction, neither satisfaction nor performance is consistently related to efficiency. It is thus not surprising that those factors associated with satisfaction or financial performance may not be the same factors that associate with efficiency. Family involvement in the operation tends to facilitate rather than hinder satisfaction. The opposite, however, is true of efficiency. The greater the actual family involvement or the value placed on family involvement, the lower the efficiency, particularly that involving labor inputs. Instead, values and goals that stress financial risk-taking and an interest in expansion are associated with the efficient use of land and other assets and the efficient production of milk.

However, there are some cross-cutting features to the size-location influences on financial success and satisfaction with dairy farming. Larger-sized dairies located in counties of dairy growth tend to produce higher satisfaction and better performance. However, such farms also use less family labor, an important predictor of satisfaction. Dairy farms that use more family labor tend to have more satisfied operators. These findings, taken together, suggest that experienced dairy farmers who start a new dairy in a county of dairy growth are likely to be more successful in terms of satisfaction and financial performance. However, in order to increase their chance of success, they will need to establish a large-sized dairy (200 or more cows) and thus will probably have to employ a greater proportion of non-family in their labor forces. This latter consequence will tend to lessen operator satisfaction. At the same time, family involvement tends to be associated with lower efficiencies of various sorts. Thus, as some dairy farmers make changes in their operations, they may find themselves exchanging their satisfaction for not only higher financial performance, but also greater efficiency.

Furthermore, large-scale dairy farms located in growth counties tend to have operators with a greater desire for spending more time with family members. This may be in response to lower family member participation in the operation. It may also reflect a consequence of success. Larger farms located in growth counties tend to be more financially successful, and with that success the operators may develop the ability to devote more time to family activities.

Our findings thus do not give clear evidence that organizational structure (size), location, or management orientations alone provide the answer to what make dairy farms successful. Size and location, largely in combination, explain success in ways we predicted. Farmer orientation, including the use of family labor, also aids in predicting dairy farm success. Farmer orientation includes a number of factors such as financial goals, enterprise goals, family goals, and rewarding aspects of farming along with the use of family labor. None of these factors by themselves predict success; rather various components of success are associated with various aspects of farmer orientation. As suggested by the literature on complex organizations, the size of an organization may affect managerial orientation. The contingency theory literature has argued, by way of contrast, that the managerial orientations lead to decisions to expand or contract. Work on farmer orientations by Strange (1989) suggests that the decisions of those who manage larger farms tend to favor the more business and less family side of a farm firm. We found little evidence that the components of farmer orientation affect size or vice versa. Furthermore, in analyses we have performed elsewhere, we find that farmer orientation has little relationship to the changes made by dairy farms over the past five years in terms of expansion, diversification, or contraction. Size-location is more likely to be associated with these changes.

Because of the importance of the size-location effect on dairy success, future studies need to look more closely at locational variables such as input prices, the availability of transportation and markets, and other resources associated with location. In particular, such studies need to account for the observation that larger sized organizations perform best in locations that foster growth, while small organizations do far less well in environments that hinder growth. Organizational ecologists have not addressed such questions directly, and thus such studies of dairy could contribute to this increasingly important organizational perspective.

The somewhat muddled findings with regard to farming orientations should lead us to re-think the typologies in this area. This is not to claim that the existing typologies are incorrect, but merely to suggest that farmers (and business operators and managers in general) may have orientations towards farming (business, management) that are more complex in nature. It is clear that some of the dairy farmers in our study had orientations that made them both traditional/modern or Yeomen/entrepreneurs at the same time.

Our findings suggest that a multi-theoretical approach will likely provide the best answers to questions regarding performance and efficiency in farming. Size and location, hypothesized by organizational ecologists and agricultural economists, and family orientations, hypothesized by rural sociologists, are both important sets of predictors of farm performance. Both agency and structure count.

ACKNOWLEDGMENTS

We acknowledge the support of the USDA Regional Project NE 177 and the Texas Agricultural Experiment Station. We also wish to thank Harry K. Schwarzweller and Andrew P. Davidson for their helpful comments on this chapter.

REFERENCES

Adbu-Ella, M. M., Hoiberg, E. O., & Warren, R. O. (1981). Adoption Behavior in Family Farm Systems: An Iowa Study. *Rural Sociology, 46*, 42–61.

Albrecht, D. (1997). The Changing Structure of U.S. Agriculture: Dualism Out, Industrialism In. *Rural Sociology, 62*, 474–489.

Anoiske, N., & Cougenhour, C. M. (1990). The Socioeconomic Basis of Farm Enterprise Diversification Decisions. *Rural Sociology, 55*, 1–24.

Babb, E. M. (1979). Some Causes of Structural Change in U.S. Agriculture. In: *Structural Issues of American Agriculture, USDA Economics, Statistics, and Cooperative Research Service* (pp. 51–60). Report 438. Washington, DC: U.S. Government Printing Office.

Barlett, P. F. (1991). Status Aspirations and Lifestyle Influences on Farm Survival. In: D. C. Clay & H. K. Schwarzweller (Eds), *Research in Rural Sociology and Development 5: Household Strategies* (pp. 171–190). Greenwich: JAI Press.

Baum, J. (1996). Organizational Ecology. In: S. R. Clegg, C. Hardy & W. R. Nord (Eds), *Handbook of Organizational Theory* (pp. 77–114). Sage: Thousand Oaks.

Bennett, J. W. (1982). *Of Time and Enterprise: North American Family Farm Management in a Context of Resource Marginality*. Minneapolis: University of Minnesota Press.

Blau, P. (1970). A Formal Theory of Differentiation. *American Sociological Review, 35*, 201–218.

Codtz, D. (1978). Corporate Farming: A Tough Row to Hoe. In: R. Rodefeld, J. Flora, D. Voth, I. Fujimoto & J. Converse (Eds), *Change in Rural America: Causes, Consequences, and Alternative* (pp. 144–151). St. Louis: Mosbey.

Coughenour, C. M. (1995). The Social Construction of Commitment and Satisfaction with Farm and Non-farm Work. *Social Science Research, 24,* 367–389.

Coughenour, C. M., & Swanson, L. E. (1988). Rewards, Values, and Satisfaction with Farm Work. *Rural Sociology, 53,* 442–459.

Cruise, J., & Lyson, T. A. (1991). Beyond the Farmgate: Factors Related to Agricultural Performance in Two Dairy Communities. *Rural Sociology, 56,* 41–55.

Dolch, N. A., & Heffernan, W. D. (1978). Applicability of Complex Organization Theory to Small Organizations. *Social Science Quarterly, 59,* 202–209.

Donaldson, L. (1996). The Normal Science of Contingency Theory. In: S. R. Clegg, C. Hardy & W. R. Nord (Eds), *Handbook of Organization Studies* (pp. 57–76). Sage: Thousand Oaks.

Drabenstott, M., & Smith, T. R. (1995). Finding Rural Success: The New Economic Rural Landscape and Its Implications. In: E. R. Castle (Ed.), *The Changing American Countryside: Rural People and Places* (pp. 180–196). Lawrence: University Press of Kansas.

Ernstes, D., Schwart, R. B. Jr., Outlaw, J., Knutson, R., & Perera, R. (1996). The Texas Dairy Industry: Past, Present, and Future. *Balanced Dairying Economics, 16*(1), 1–7.

Etzioni, A. (1964). *Modern Organizations.* Englewood Cliffs: Prentice Hall.

Flora, J., & Stitz, J. M. (1985). Ethnicity, Persistence, and Capitalization of Agriculture in the Great Plains during the Settlement Period: Wheat Production and Risk Avoidance. *Rural Sociology, 50,* 341–360.

Garkovitch, L., Bokemeier, J. L., & Foote, B. (1995). *Harvest of Hope: Family Farming/Farming Families.* Lexington: University of Kentucky Press.

Georgiou, P. (1973). The Goal Paradigm and Notes Toward a Counter Paradigm. *Administrative Science Quarterly, 18,* 291–310.

Gilbert, J., & Akor, R. (1988). Increasing Structural Divergence in U.S. Dairying: California and Wisconsin Since 1950. *Rural Sociology, 53,* 56–72.

Hage, G. (1965). An Axiomatic Theory of Organization. *Administrative Science Quarterly, 10,* 289–320.

Hage, G., & Aiken, M. (1967). Relationship of Centralization to Other Properties. *Administrative Science Quarterly, 12,* 72–91.

Hale, M. W. (1999). Is Erath Losing Its Grip on the Top Spot? *The Stephenville Tribune,* Sunday, June 13, p. 2.

Hall, R. (1996). *Organizations: Structures, Processes, and Outcomes* (6th ed.). Englewood Cliffs, NJ: Prentice Hall.

Jackson-Smith, D. (1999). Understanding the Microdynamics of Farm Structural Change: Entry, Exit, and Restructuring among Wisconsin Family Farmers in the 1980s'. *Rural Sociology, 64,* 66–91.

Johnson, N. L., & Ruttan, V. W. (1997). The Diffusion of Livestock Breeding Technology in the U.S.: Observations on the Relationship between Technical Change and Industry Structure. *Journal of Agribusiness, 15,* 19–35.

Knoke, D. (1990). *Organizing for Collective Action: The Political Economies of Associations.* New York: Aldine de Gruyter.

Knoke, D., & Wood, J. R. (1981). *Organized for Action: Commitment in Voluntary Associations.* New Brunswick: Rutgers University Press.

Knutson, R. D. (1991). *Dairy Industry Challenges in the Year 2000: A Choice Between Extremes*. Agriculture and Food Policy Center Policy Issues Paper 91-4. College Station: Department of Agricultural Economics, Texas A & M University.

Lyson, T., & Gillespie, G. W. (1995). Producing More Milk with Fewer Cows: Neoclassical and Neostructural Explanations of Changes in Dairy Farming. *Rural Sociology, 60*, 493–504.

McIntosh, Wm. A., Bateman, R., & Cready, C. (1997). *Predictors of Farmers Satisfaction with Dairying: A Five State Study*. Revised and expanded version of a paper presented at the annual meeting of the Rural Sociological Society, Toronto.

McIntosh, Wm. A., Thomas, J. K., & Albrecht, D. E. (1990). A Weberian of the Adoption of Value Rational Technology. *Social Science Quarterly, 71*, 848–860.

Molnar, J. J. (1985). Determinants of Subjective Well-being among Farm Operators. *Rural Sociology, 50*, 141–162.

Penson, J. B., Capps, O. Jr., & Parr Rosson, C. III (1996). *Introduction to Agricultural Economics*. Upper Saddle River, NJ: Prentice Hall.

Rogers, E. (1995). *Diffusion of Innovations* (4th ed.). New York: Free Press.

Salamon, S. (1992). *Prairie Patrimony: Family, Farming, and Community in the Midwest*. Chapel Hill: University of North Carolina Press.

Schroeder, E. H., Fliegel, F. C., & van Es, J. C. (1985). Measurement of the Lifestyle Dimensions of Farming for Small-Scale Farmers. *Rural Sociology, 50*, 305–322.

Schwarzweller, H. K., & Davidson, A. R. (1997). Perspectives on Regional and Enterprise Marginality: Dairying in Michigan's North Country. *Rural Sociology, 62*, 157–179.

Schwart, R. B. Jr. (1998). 20 State Milk Production, December 1997. *Balanced Dairying Quick Letter*, January 16, 1–2.

Schwart, R. B. Jr. (1999). Personal communication.

Siebert, J. W., Anderson, D. P., Knutson, R. D., & Schwart, R. B. (1997). Envisioning a U.S. Dairy Industry without FMMO's. *Balanced Dairying Economics, 17*, 1–8.

Shortell, S. M., Morrison, E. M., Friedman, B., & Associates (1990). *America's Leading Hospital Systems: Lessons in Managing Strategic Adaptation*. San Francisco: Jossey Boss.

Snodgrass, M. M., & Wallace, L. T. (1964). *Agriculture, Economics, and Growth*. New York: Appleton-Century-Croft.

Stanton, B. F. (1993). Recent Changes in Size and Structure in American Agriculture. In: A. Hallam (Ed.), *Size, Structure and the Changing Face of American Agriculture* (pp. 42–70). Boulder: Westview Press.

Strange, M. (1989). *Family Farming: A New Economic Vision*. Lincoln: University of Nebraska Press.

Texas Agricultural Extension Service (1998). 20 State Milk Production, January 1998. *Balanced Dairying Quick Letter*, February 20. College Station. TX.

Texas Almanac and State and Industrial Guide (1994–95). Dallas: Dallas Morning News.

Texas Milk Market Administrator (1991). *Texas Milk Market Report*, February. Carrollton, TX.

Texas Milk Market Administrator (1999). *Milk Marketed from Each County of Texas by All Texas Producers for the Years of 1990–1998*. Carrollton, TX.

U.S. Bureau of the Census (1992). *Census of Agriculture*. Washington, DC: U.S. Government Printing Office.

U.S. Bureau of the Census (1994). *County and City Data Book: 1994*. Washington, DC: U.S. Government Printing Office.

Walter, G. (1997). Images of Success: How Illinois Farmers Define the Successful Farmer. *Rural Sociology, 62*, 48–68.

Wilson, J., Harper Simpson, I., & Laderman, R. (1994). Status Variation on Family Farms: Effects of Crop, Machinery, and Off-Farm Work. *Rural Sociology, 59*, 136–153.

Wilkening, E. A., & Ahrens, N. W. (1979). *Social Determinants of Subjective Well-being in Northern Wisconsin.* College of Agriculture and Life Sciences Research Bulletin R 2968. Madison.

Yutchman, E., & Seashore, S. (1967). A System Resource Approach to Organizational Effectiveness. *American Sociological Review, 32*, 891–903.

APPENDIX

Table A1. Principal Components Analysis of Satisfaction with Dairy Farming Variables

Satisfaction with Various Aspects of Dairy Farming	Mean	Standard Deviation	Satisfaction with Dairy Farming Loading
Being a Dairy Farmer	3.24	2.78	0.688
Income from Dairying	6.29	3.29	0.869
Financial Performance from Dairying	5.92	3.01	0.870
Employment Alternatives to Dairying	5.80	2.99	0.613

Variance Explained (%) = 59.1
Cronbach's Alpha = 0.769

Table A2. Principal Components Analysis of Important Aspects of Farming Variables

Important Characteristics of Farming	Mean	Standard Deviation	Working Conditions Loading	Family Aspects of Farming Loading	Economic Rewards Loading
Economic Rewards	1.44	0.54	0.036	0.069	0.886
Do Things Own Way	1.24	0.53	0.352	−0.038	0.674
Good Place to Raise Family	1.25	0.61	0.536	0.248	0.035
Work Outdoors	1.29	0.64	0.795	0.287	0.042
Work with Animals	1.34	0.62	0.882	0.104	0.049
Physical Labor	1.86	0.91	0.625	0.161	0.014
Challenge to Management Skills	1.65	0.82	0.803	0.132	0.188
Diversity of Work	1.61	0.83	0.626	0.273	0.191
Work with Other Family	1.80	1.06	0.261	0.728	0.289
Maintain Family Tradition	1.90	1.11	0.138	0.757	0.167
Independence of Work	1.59	0.98	0.499	0.513	−0.023
Keeping Farm in Family	1.92	1.23	0.333	0.792	0.245
Bring Children into Farming	2.16	1.24	0.160	0.884	−0.056

Variance Explained (%) = 64.1
Cronbach's Alpha = 0.924

Table A3.   Principal Components Analysis of Economic Goal Variables

			Economic Goals
Economic Goals	Mean	Standard Deviation	Loading
Pay Off Debt	1.99	2.32	0.740
No More Debt	2.56	2.33	0.657
Increase Cash	1.59	1.32	0.810
Increase Profits	1.31	0.85	0.817
Prepare for Retirement	2.05	1.89	0.600

Variance Explained (%) = 52.7
Cronbach's Alpha = 0.818

Table A4.   Principal Components Analysis of Family Goal Variables

			Prepare for Next Generation	More Time With Family
Family Goals	Mean	Standard Deviation	Loading	Loading
Spend Time With Your Family	1.78	1.43	0.027	0.900
Take Family Vacations	2.78	1.55	0.185	0.866
Set Up Farm For Next Generation	4.07	3.45	0.909	0.138
Bring a Family Member Into the Operation	4.89	3.67	0.922	0.074

Variance Explained (%) = 82.4
Cronbach's Alpha = 0.677

Table A5.   Principal Components Analysis of Personal Goal Variables

			Innovator
Personal Goals	Mean	Standard Deviation	Loading
Be First in Area to Make a Change on Farm	7.12	3.39	0.940
Be Seen as Progressive Business Person	6.89	3.44	0.940

Variance Explained (%) = 88.4
Cronbach's Alpha = 0.863

Table A6. Principal Components Analysis of Enterprise Goal Variables

Enterprise Goals	Mean	Standard Deviation	Improve Operation Loading	Expand Operation Loading
Increase Total Milk Sold	1.81	1.61	0.118	0.948
Increase Production Per Cow	1.74	1.64	0.132	0.929
Improve Safety of Farm Operation	1.36	0.91	0.693	−0.032
Reduce Amount of Physical Work	2.61	2.11	0.672	0.085
Reduce Labor Costs	2.30	2.14	0.643	0.160
Improve Herd Health	1.36	0.91	0.576	0.528
Reduce Feed Costs	1.57	1.15	0.613	0.370
Minimize Environmental Damage From Dairy	2.24	1.04	0.612	0.371

Variance Explained (%) = 69.5
Cronbach's Alpha = 0.897

LABOR INPUTS AND OPERATIONAL EFFICIENCIES ON MID-MICHIGAN DAIRY FARMS

Harry K. Schwarzweller

INTRODUCTION

A dairy enterprise's profitability – its ability to provide a decent income for the operator and a reasonably good return on capital invested – depends to a large extent on the efficient use of available labor. This is so for most businesses – agricultural and non-agricultural – and regardless of whether the business employs a large crew of hired workers or relies mainly upon family labor. But, because powerful socio-economic forces are pressing to reshape America's dairy industry and causing very profound changes in many rural communities within which dairy farms are located, the efficient use of labor is becoming an increasingly critical factor in the management of dairy farms.

To survive and prosper nowadays, dairy farms must get bigger. Much research relative to dairying as well as to other industries supports this assertion, namely, that an increase in size of operation, at least to some optimal point, translates into increased profits (Hall & Leveen, 1978; Kumbhakar et al., 1989; Lyson & Gillespie, 1995). Small and mid-sized dairies are advised to expand – to add more cows – and of course to do so while keeping per unit production costs at a minimal level. Any significant degree of herd expansion, however, even when greater efficiencies are subsequently achieved in the use of labor and invested capital (basically in the form of purchased improvements in facilities, technology, and genetic stock), invariably requires some additional

Research in Rural Sociology, Volume 8, pages 265–289.
Copyright © 2000 by Elsevier Science Inc.
ISBN: 0-7623-0474-X

labor inputs. And, in most cases, this means that the farm operator must hire non-family labor, which is often more expensive, probably less experienced, and certainly less flexible than family labor.

Further, in many rural communities it has become extremely difficult for dairy farmers to find potential employees who are reliable, willing to work with livestock (in surroundings that may sometimes be uncomfortable for those not reared on farms), and able to learn the technical skills associated with a modern dairy operation. Throughout rural America, manufacturing and service industries have moved into the countryside and are competing with farms and other businesses for local labor, thereby driving up wages and raising employee expectations about fringe benefits and working conditions.

Thus, dairy farmers – particularly those with mid-size dairies that use mainly family labor – are caught between a need to expand in order to capitalize on advantages that accrue from economies of size and, on the other hand, the high costs and associated frustrations of increasing their labor inputs by hiring non-family workers. Those who choose to get bigger – a decision that is invariably difficult and often stressful – must devise ways to enhance the productive effectiveness of their operation and the efficiency of their labor force, particularly if they are borrowing heavily to build new facilities and to update equipment.

The research reported here – concerned especially, though indirectly, with the expansionist strategies of contemporary dairy farmers – explores differentials in work force characteristics, labor inputs, and operational efficiencies relative to some basic structural features that distinguish dairy farms in a mid-Michigan context. Consistent with the economies of size principle, one would expect larger dairies to be more efficient than smaller dairies (Bruun & Adelaja, 1990; Hallam, 1988; Matulich, 1978; Perez, 1994; Richards, 1996). But other structural features too are often very closely associated with herd size – enterprise specialization, technological modernization, the use of non-family labor – and may affect a dairy enterprise's operational efficiency and, ultimately, its profitability.

ASSESSING OPERATIONAL EFFICIENCIES

An efficient operation is one that minimizes the per unit cost of production, thereby maximizing profits. The term 'dairy labor (or work) efficiency' refers to the ratio between labor inputs (a cost of production) and the subsequent production outputs (a basis for profits) that can be attributed to that work activity. Gains in production obtained by a decreasing expenditure of labor per unit, all other things being equal, are regarded as the more efficient, yielding the greatest profit. Conversely, gains in production obtained by an increasing expenditure of labor per unit are inefficient, and may eventually result in a net loss for the enterprise. Economists, for comparative purposes, prefer to standardize the expression of costs, outputs, and gains in dollar terms. But this is often difficult and generally not necessary, provided that the measures of costs and outputs are clearly associated with enterprise profitability, as they are in the case of dairy farms for labor inputs, a major cost, and milk, the dairy enterprise's main source of revenue.

Dairy labor efficiency is commonly expressed in two ways: (1) number of milk cows managed per worker, and (2) pounds of milk produced per worker (Smith, 1996; Kadlec, 1985; Carley, 1979). The validity of each of these measures is influenced to a large extent by how one determines the magnitude of labor inputs, and ultimately, their cost.

Work time, measured in hours, days, weeks, etc., is generally the basis for an employee's wages, and a convenient standard for assessing labor inputs. Indeed, employees on some large, industrial-style dairy farms are required to punch a time clock. And, paralleling research in manufacturing industries relative to improving the efficiency of an assembly line, some agricultural researchers, concerned about enhancing the labor efficiency of farm workers, have made precise observations on how much time a worker devotes to various farm chores and activities (Sauer, 1981). But time inputs alone are not the equivalent of productive inputs, for workers vary considerably in skills, physical strengths, intelligence and other attributes. Basically, a hired worker's wage level is determined by what the dairy farm manager believes his or her abilities and attributes are worth, taking into account the prevailing labor market situation, i.e. the hired worker's employment alternatives elsewhere. Most dairy farms in Michigan and throughout rural America are family enterprises, with family labor constituting a major portion of the workforce. The dairy farm operator's financial compensation for his/her contributions to the enterprise, both managerial and hands-on, are extremely difficult to ascertain, given that he/she is often both owner and worker/manager and that a cost/benefits accounting is a tedious, technically complicated undertaking. Further, it is well established that family members working on their family's dairy farm are grossly underpaid, if at all, relative to the productive value of their work inputs. Hence, most researchers who are concerned about dairy labor efficiency for assessing the advantages or disadvantages of one system of dairying over another, rely upon one or the other of the two measures of dairy efficiency noted above. Both measures – work efficiency (cows per worker) and production efficiency (milk produced per worker) – are used here. A third variable, herd average (milk produced per cow per year on average), is inextricably linked with production efficiency and must also be taken into account

CHARACTERISTICS OF MID-MICHIGAN DAIRIES[1]

Located in the lower mid-section of Michigan's lower peninsula, Gratiot County, the study site, is one of Michigan's premier agricultural counties. It ranks especially high in the production of corn, soybeans, dry beans, and milk (15th of 83 counties in number of milk cows.) The quality of dairy herds is exceptionally good, with milk per cow averaging more than 20,000 pounds per year; highest in the state (Michigan Department of Agriculture, 1996: 134.) Less than an hour drive from the Lansing metropolitan area, the county has been aggressively committed to a policy of industrial growth (Aronoff, 1993) and, along with a neighboring county, has been designated one of the state's two 'rural renaissance' zones, which enables specified localities to offer tax breaks and other inducements to attract new businesses. Given an increasing range of alternative non-agricultural employment opportunities for local people, the study site provides an excellent chance to research the rapidly changing labor problems that many dairy farmers in many other rural industrializing regions of America and elsewhere will have to deal with in the years ahead.

Information was obtained for 65 of the county's 66 dairy farms in the spring of 1997 by personal interviews with the lead operators or their partners.[2]

Herd Size

These dairies range in size from 930 lactating cows to as few as 26 (late 1997). The average herd is 121 cows, considerably greater than the Michigan average of 75; about 50% of the dairies milk fewer than 90 cows. Most have other stock as well: calves, bred heifers, steers, a bull. But, some dairies contract out for the raising of replacements, a specialization that is becoming increasingly common throughout mid-Michigan.

Herd size is closely associated with many other structural characteristics of dairy enterprises, though, as Vieira (1996) has shown, it does not fully reflect how dairy farm families use the resources available to them and the complex strategies they employ to achieve their goals. For present purposes the observations are noted in terms of four herd size groupings. These are: small, fewer than 70 cows; medium (or mid-sized), from 70 to fewer than 100 cows; large, from 100 to 200 cows; and very large dairies, more than 200 cows. The 'very large' category is skewed upwards to nearly 1,000 cows, and includes only 7 herds.

Acres Managed

Total acreage managed (owned plus rented) is generally consistent with size of herd, though the correlation is not strong ($r = 0.47$). There are many exceptions. Some differences in acreage per cow are noted: small dairies average 5.8 acres per cow; mid-size dairies 5.5; large dairies 4.7; and very large dairies 5.0 acres. On the face (Table 1), it appears that the availability of land may not be an especially critical factor in limiting the expansion of small dairies; the operator's age, the possibility for generational transition, and the availability of investment capital, may be more important. A strong negative correlation between acres of farm land managed and degree of dairy specialization ($r = -0.56$) is observed; farms with more land have a greater proportion of income from cash crops and other non-dairy enterprises, whereas farms with less land are more specialized in dairying. But size of herd and enterprise diversification are not associated. The fact that small and mid-sized dairies have higher land-per-cow ratios than larger dairies probably indicates less intensive land use management practices and/or land that is of lesser quality.

Most dairies here, even those that are diversified, rent some additional land from neighbors. Significantly, the larger dairies, with more than 100 cows, rent in 31.5% of their total acreage, while the smaller dairies rent in only 16.5%. Indeed, dairies with fewer than 70 cows, as a class, actually rent out more land than they rent in (and thus, they manage less land than they own!) To expand their operations, smaller dairies would have to gain access to more land, and that they do not or can not suggests that the pattern of land rentals and rental prices in this area favors the larger dairies. Basic differences in household survival strategies may affect differences in pattern of land utilization by the smaller dairies, but there is no doubt that the larger dairies are more aggressive in contracting for land to enhance their production of forage and grains.

Dairy Specialization/Enterprise Diversification

There is no difference in the degree of dairy specialization (i.e. farm diversification) among smaller and larger dairies, as measured by the percentage of gross farm income deriving from milk sales. Most mid-Michigan dairies rely heavily upon milk sales for their income, with about 82% of gross sales, on average, from milk. In terms of alternative uses of agricultural land, the production of forage and grain as feed for milk cows is a better source of income than most cash crops, such as corn grain, soybeans, and dry beans. Nevertheless, cash crops are a significant enterprise for about a third (33.8%) of the dairies. Livestock other than dairy are of minor importance. In general,

Table 1.   Characteristics of Mid-Michigan Dairy Farms by Herd Size

	small dairies n = 22	mid-size n = 15	large n = 21	very large n = 7	all dairies n = 65
Herd size					
average no. of cows	40	82	134	419	121
range no. of cows	26–69	70–99	100–176	220–930	26–930
Acres managed					
average acres	231	441	629	2106	610
Milk % gross sales					
average %	83.5	80.6	81.7	77.6	81.6
Multi households					
% multi	9.1	20.0	28.6	85.7	26.2
Age, lead operator					
average years	50.8	45.7	45.1	42.9	46.5
range	34–76	30–59	26–68	29–52	26–76
number 60+ years	2	0	2	0	4
Farm workers total					
average equivalents	1.87	2.78	4.19	10.24	3.73
Hired farm workers					
average equivalents	0.25	0.62	1.85	7.25	1.61
Dairy workers total					
average equivalents	1.83	2.59	3.86	9.16	3.27
Family dairy labor					
average %	91.3	85.5	69.7	47.8	79.3
Non-family dairy					
labor average %	8.7	14.5	30.3	52.2	20.7
Facilities age					
% old	77.3	53.3	52.4	0	55.4
score (hi = newer)	2.68	3.67	3.52	4.71	3.40
Equity strong, 80% +					
% farms	45.5	26.7	38.1	28.6	36.9
Debt risky, 39% +					
% farms	31.8	53.3	28.6	57.2	38.5

degree of enterprise diversity is a function of total land managed (r = 0.56) not herd size (r = 0.03)

Almost all of the larger dairies are self sufficient in forage production, whereas about one-fourth of the smaller dairies (with less than 100 cows) must buy additional forage, probably because they have chosen to expand despite limited land resources.

Contracting with neighboring farmers for the raising of replacement heifers is a strategy that some dairies, particularly the smaller ones, use to facilitate herd expansion. Although not yet widespread, this practice is gaining in favor. About 14% of the smaller dairies, but only about 4% of the larger dairies, have their replacements raised by another farmer.

Facilities/Modernization

Cows are housed in various ways in mid-Michigan, from modern free stall or open systems with adjoining milking parlors equipped with the latest technology, to traditional stanchion type systems with milk piped to a nearby milk room and cooling/holding vat. Some barns and milking parlors are very new, designed to take advantage of the latest ideas about how to maximize worker efficiency and to assure cow health and safety. But some are very old, with hand hewn barn timbers that date back 75 years or more. Remodeling of older milking facilities and barns occurred over the years, as the government toughened milk handling standards and made it nearly impossible for any dairies to avoid extensive and expensive remodeling.

By taking into account age of barn, age of adjoining milk house or parlor, and if and when any major renovations were made to them, a five-point scale was devised to reflect the relative modernity of a dairy farm's facilities. It assumes that the more recent the construction/renovation, the more modern the dairy plant and the greater the investment in newer technologies. It also assumes that constructing a new barn and/or milking parlor is a far greater investment and a more radical overhaul than is a 'remodeling'.[3]

Table 1 notes, by size of herd, the average 'facility's age score' and the percent of dairies with older facilities. Very small dairies are likely to have older facilities. All of the very large dairies have facilities that are more modern, undoubtedly because the formation of large dairies, whether by expansion or as new developments, is a relatively recent phenomenon that, in either case, required major investments in new buildings and equipment. The overall correlation between the age of facilities and herd size is moderately strong (r = 0.385).

Equity/Debt

One of the more important factors affecting, or affected by the decision to expand is the farm operator's equity situation: the debt load. Financial analysts generally recognize that a debt-to-asset ratio greater than 70% indicates severe financial stress (i.e. the owner/operator's equity is less than 30%.) Only a few (10.8%) of the mid-Michigan dairies are in serious debt trouble; all but one are smaller dairies, with fewer than 100 cows.

Table 1 notes the percentage of dairies, by herd size, that have an exceptionally strong equity margin of more than 80%, and those that are burdened with a rather heavy (and risky) debt load of 40% or more. Slightly more than one-third of the dairies are in a very secure financial position and, at the other end of the spectrum, another set of more than one-third are in risky financial straits. The medium-sized and the very large dairies appear to be more solidly set financially; the smaller dairies, with fewer than 70 cows, and the large dairies, with 100–200 cows seem to be less secure. But of course, debt situations must be interpreted in light of many other farm business considerations, particularly the long and short term strategies of expansion and modernization.

It can be generalized though, that dairy farms in this mid-Michigan context are in rather good financial health. Many are in an excellent position to expand their operations or to float safely over the current swirl of milk pricing uncertainties.

Dairy Operator Households

All of these dairies are managed as family enterprises, and generally as 'owner/ operator' situations, except in a few cases where a transition from one generation to the next is in process. Most are one-household operations, usually with a spouse and often one or more children participate directly in the day-to-day managerial decisions. It is rare for small dairies to have more than one household involved in management, or for very large dairies to have only a single household involved. But, in this and similar dairy localities elsewhere, there are many different kinds of household arrangements. Social circumstances vary, and the inter-relationships between family and business are adjustable, aimed at optimizing the pursuit of both family and business goals.

Dairies involving two or three households in the management decisions usually represent two generations. The older couple is more likely to live alone or with an unmarried adult son or daughter. The younger couple (or couples) may or may not have children. In either case, most of these households also tend to be heavily dependent upon income from farming (70–80%) and, where they are not, it is often the wife who works off-farm.[4]

Senior operators average about 47-years-old, but the range is wide, from 26 to 76. The operators' level of education is quite high and especially so for the junior partners on larger dairies. About one-half of the younger dairy farmers (and their wives) had completed at least some college.

Dairy Work Force

A rather large work force is involved, directly and indirectly, with the production of milk in this mid-Michigan county. At the core are those households where one or more members play some role in managing the dairy and where one or more members contribute some (and often considerable) work time to the family's farming activities.

Additionally, there are a large number of more-or-less permanent year-round hired workers and most dairies employ some temporary help during the busy season. Smaller dairies, with fewer than 100 cows, are not likely to have a full-time hired worker (only 8.7% do), whereas most larger dairies (78.9%) have at least one full-time hired worker. The very large dairies prefer to hire full-time employees than part-timers.

Clearly, the necessity of recruiting and managing hired workers is what distinguishes large dairies, most of which rely upon a workforce that derives from their immediate family group. But, there are many differences in how a dairy farm work force is organized and to make comparisons it is necessary to standardize some of this variability.

An indicator of 'adult work-year equivalents' was devised to determine the labor inputs of both family and hired labor (Schwarzweller, 1988,1992, 1999). The base, an index number of 1.0, implies the amount of labor equivalent to that contributed by an adult who works 50 hours a week throughout the year. Labor inputs by those under 16 years are also included, but discounted by a factor of 20% for every year of age under 16. In effect, this is a rather conservative index of the farm workforce.

Total worker equivalents on the surveyed dairies ranges from 1.0 to 16.0, and averages 3.73. Hired help accounts for 43.2% of the total, and family/household labor for 56.8%. But, the very large farms hire more than 70% of their labor whereas the smaller dairies, with less than 100 cows, rely mainly on family/household labor (more than 80%).

Not all workers on dairy farms are engaged in activities directly related to dairying, for there is some enterprise diversity. Further, some dairies purchase a significant proportion of their forage and feed requirements, and others contract out the raising of replacement heifers. Such variations are treated as out-sourced labor inputs (acquired indirectly) and equivalent to hired labor managed directly by the farm operator. This adjusted measure of 'dairy labor equivalents', which is used as a basis for estimating dairy labor efficiency, roughly reflects the number of workers specifically involved with the dairy enterprise portion of a farm operation.[5]   Not surprisingly, the number of dairy worker equivalents tends to parallel size of herd (r = 0.93). About 80% of the labor used for the care and feeding of milk cows is family labor. Only about 20% is hired non-family labor. 'Family labor' includes the dairy farm operator(s), his or her spouse, members of their households, and close relatives who work on the farm (unpaid or for wages.) Small and medium-sized dairies, with fewer than 100 cows, rely almost exclusively on family labor (more than 85%). Very large dairies, on the other hand, depend heavily on non-family labor.

OPERATIONAL EFFICIENCIES OF MID-MICHIGAN DAIRIES

Three critically important criteria are used to assess how various structural characteristics – herd size, in particular – affect the operational efficiencies of these dairies: (1) work efficiency (cows managed per worker); (2) herd average (pounds of milk produced annually per cow); and, (3) production efficiency (pounds of milk produced annually per worker). Table 2 reports averages and ranges for each of the four herd size groupings.

Work Efficiency

The number of cows managed per worker is calculated by dividing herd size by the adjusted 'dairy labor equivalents' (i.e. the number of workers involved with the dairy enterprise portion of the farm operation.)[6]

Table 2 notes that work efficiency on these mid-Michigan dairy farms averages 32.7 cows per worker.[7] But, the range in work efficiency is extremely wide, from 10.5 to 85.4 cows per worker. And, as expected, the larger the herd, the greater the work efficiency (r = 0.42). It is at the extremes in herd size that the greatest differences are observed. Very small dairies manifest exceptionally low efficiency on average (44% less than mid-sized dairies) and very large dairies exceptionally high (37% greater than large dairies). But, there is not a great difference in averages between the mid and large dairies (about 5%).

Table 2. Dairy Efficiencies, by Herd Size

	Herd Size (range)				
Efficiency Variable	very small (26–69)	small (70–99)	large (100–199)	very large (200–930)	all dairies (26–930)
Work efficiency					
cows per worker	24.1	34.7	36.3	49.7	32.7
range	10.5–45.9	19.6–64.5	24.9–60.0	35.6–85.4	10.5–85.4
	(n = 22)	(n = 15)	(n = 21)	(n = 5)	(n = 63)
Herd average					
lbs. milk per cow	17,058	21,307	22,271	24,220	20,650
range (hwt)	100–230	150–270	189–255	204–290	100–290
	(n = 19)	(n = 14)	(n = 21)	(n = 7)	(n = 61)
Production efficiency					
milk (hwt.) per worker	4,064	6,996	8,082	12,351	6,892
range (1,000 lbs)	150–872	332–1,299	480–1,338	762–1,964	150–1,964
	(n = 19)	(n = 14)	(n = 21)	(n = 5)	(n = 59)

Herd Average

Cows that are consistently strong milk producers during the course of their lifetimes and dairies that record high herd averages year after year, reflect not only good breeding (genetic stock), but also the operator's managerial skills and his/her ability to provide quality feed and quality care. High producing herds are generally more profitable, because the costs of labor, housing, and equipment do not increase proportional to increases in per cow production. One might argue that raising show cattle (cows classified as 'excellent' by the breed association) is a way of adding value over and above milk sales. To some extent it is, but nowadays, even beautiful cows and heifers need strong production records (and a notable ancestry) to command a significant premium in the sales ring.

Our information on herd averages derives from what the dairy farm operators told us, and/or from what was reported by the Dairy Herd Improvement Association (DHIA). Where available, the recorded DHIA average was used (for 36 dairies).[8] But most dairy farm operators, even if not on DHIA or some other testing program, have a pretty good idea of their herd's average. Monthly milk checks, for instance, are accompanied by a statement of total pounds sold and, taking account of the number of cows in milk that month, it is fairly simple to calculate average production. It is more difficult to keep track of average production over the course of a year. Occasionally, a farmer will report herd average in terms of gallons of milk produced per cow on a given day (at time of interview). This is not a good basis for yearly estimates; daily milk production is variable by season, and so is composition of the herd.

Dairies in this area are doing exceptionally well in terms of milk production, averaging 20,650 pounds per cow per year (Table 2). But there is a wide range, from 29,000 lbs. to fewer than 15,000 lbs. The very smallest dairies have the weakest averages and, as a class, fall considerably below (25% below) that of mid-sized dairies; many are handicapped by inadequate resources. Differences in herd average between mid-size and very large dairies (14% difference) and between large and very large dairies (8% difference) are not nearly as distinctive or as daunting as the wide gulf in herd average that separates small dairies, with fewer than 70 cows, from the rather impressive records being achieved by their neighbors, dairies with larger herds.

Production Efficiency

Combining the above two measures – taking account of efficiencies in the use of labor and in the quality and care of the dairy herd – a broader, overarching indicator of operational efficiency is devised. Other important efficiencies, of course, affect the success (i.e. profitability) of a dairy enterprise – efficiencies in the management of land, crops, equipment, available capital, and even of family/household relationships and obligations. Managerial efficiency is an enormously complex, multi-dimensional variable, but we are confident that the measure of production efficiency used here represents the essence of this configuration.

Specifically, herd size is multiplied by herd average. This total annual production is then divided by dairy labor equivalents yielding pounds of milk per year per worker. Obviously, by its very nature production efficiency parallels the other two indicators and will have similar structural antecedents and correlates. Nevertheless, there will be shadings of difference (in the magnitude of correlations, for example) that will help to better interpret and explain the determinants of success in managing a dairy enterprise.

These dairies averaged 689,200 pounds of milk per year per worker unit, ranging from about 150,000 to nearly 2 million pounds. Differences between the medium and large dairies are not especially great (15.5%). But differences in production efficiency at either end of the herd size continuum are exaggerated – extremely high for the very large dairies and extremely low for the very small dairies. Observations on herd size effect parallel those for cows per worker and herd average; their independent effects are compounded, since both basic variables are drawn into the measure of production efficiency (the greater the herd average and the greater the number of cows managed per worker, the greater the production efficiency).

STRUCTURAL CORRELATES OF OPERATIONAL EFFICIENCIES

Four factors are considered that distinguish important structural differences among dairy farm operations in the mid-Michigan context: size (number of milk cows, total acres managed, total dairy work force); labor (percent family labor); diversity (milk sold as percent of gross agricultural sales); and technology (age of facilities). Table 3 reports correlations between these structural variables and each of the three operational efficiency indicators. To assess the conditioning or contingency effects of herd size, Table 4 compares smaller dairies (fewer than 100 cows) with larger dairies (100 cows or more.)

Operational Size and Efficiencies

Herd size, as expected, is a major determinant of dairy labor efficiency and a major factor associated with herd average. Larger dairies appear to be more

Table 3. Structural Correlates of Dairy Efficiencies

	work efficiency (cows per worker) n = 63	herd average (lbs milk per cow) n = 61	production efficiency (milk per worker) n = 59
Size			
cows #	0.42*	0.51*	0.59*
acres managed	0.39*	0.18ns	0.48*
dairy labor total	0.14ns	0.51*	0.37*
Labor			
% family labor	–0.22ns	-0.49*	–0.46*
Specialization			
milk % of gross	–0.16ns	-0.06ns	–0.09ns
Technology			
facility age	0.33*	0.30*	0.42*

* = significant at alpha 0.05 (ns = not significant)

Table 4. Structural Correlates of Dairy Efficiencies, by Herd Size

	small dairies (fewer than 100 cows)			large dairies (100 cows or more)		
	work efficiency	herd average	production efficiency	work efficiency	herd average	production efficiency
Size						
cows #	0.58*	0.55*	0.68*	0.31*	0.57*	0.50*
acres managed	0.38*	0.13ns	0.44*	0.09ns	–0.06ns	0.15ns
dairy labor equiv	–0.40*	0.31*	–0.12ns	–0.01ns	0.62*	0.21ns
Labor						
% family labor	–0.016ns	–0.24ns	–0.14ns	–0.22ns	–0.54*	–0.36*
Specialization						
milk % of gross	–0.27ns	–0.02ns	–0.32*	–0.02ns	0.31ns	0.07ns
Technology						
facility age	0.00ns	0.18ns	0.06ns	0.59*	0.23ns0	0.62*

* = significant at alpha 0.05 (ns = not significant)

efficient, presumably because of economies of size. There is a strong positive correlation (0.59) between herd size and production efficiency (Table 3) and similar positive correlations, though somewhat more modest in magnitude, between herd size and the two components of production efficiency – work efficiency (0.42) and herd average (0.51).

But one should not speak in absolute terms about a herd size effect, for there are many dairy farms whose operational characteristics deviate from this basic line of generalization. The competitive advantages and disadvantages of smaller vs. larger herds can be and are moderated, at least to some extent, by various structural features, organizational strategies, and management practices that are more or less independent of herd size. Nevertheless, as Table 4 shows, production efficiency is enhanced by additional increments in number of milking cows and this effect is manifested for both small dairies (fewer than 100 cows) and large (100 cows or more); the positive influence of herd size on operational efficiencies is especially strong (and consequently especially important) for smaller dairies.

Total number of acres managed (owned plus rented) is not associated with herd average, but is modestly correlated with work efficiency and, consequently, with production efficiency. But the effect of land availability on work efficiency is conditioned by herd size. It is the smaller, not the larger dairies whose work efficiency is affected by how much land is available; perhaps because smaller dairies have more difficulty in balancing available labor with available land. For instance, it takes a much greater percentage increase in net equity and land holdings for a small dairy, as compared with a large dairy, to expand its cow herd to a size that is sufficient to effectively utilize the addition of an adult son to the dairy work force. Large dairies generally are already at a size level to sustain two or more co-principals. (Land availability, of course, is not the only factor that constrains generational transfers, but, for smaller and mid-size dairies, it is exceedingly important.)

Total labor devoted to the dairy operation, another way to measure size, has a strong association with herd average, and in the case of larger dairies. This is probably a reflection of the herd size effect, for total dairy labor equivalents is highly correlated with herd size.

What is most surprising and especially noteworthy is that, although the relationship between dairy labor total (the availability of labor for the dairy operation) and work efficiency is not significant for larger dairies, it is substantial and negative for smaller dairies. For smaller dairies, the more labor invested in the dairy operation, the lower the work efficiency! This suggests that, for whatever reasons, some surplus labor is 'stacked up' on many of the smaller dairy farms and we are probably witnessing a manifestation of the tension that occurs (and conflicting values that have to be dealt with) in managing a dairy farm as both a tightly run business and as a family enterprise that, in setting priorities, assigns considerable weight to the well-being of all family members.

Clearly, the efficiency of a dairy operation – in terms of herd quality and work effectiveness – is conditioned by an increase in herd size and regardless of whether, at the point of expansion, the dairy is relatively small or relatively large. The problems of surplus labor (underemployment of the available work force) and shortage of land are serious constraints to improving the productive capabilities of smaller dairies (those with fewer than 100 cows.)

Labor Characteristics and Efficiencies

All of the dairies in this particular mid-Michigan context are family-managed enterprises, and most rely heavily upon family labor. On smaller dairies, only a minor proportion of the labor is non-family (11.0%). On larger dairies, however – particularly the very large dairies – a substantial proportion of the labor is non-family (averaging 34.5%). Does it matter in terms of work productivity? Is hired, non-family labor any less efficient than family labor? This question bears heavily on arguments about economies of size, and is especially interesting because it is such a fundamentally important structural issue relative to American agriculture.

Basically, a strong negative association is observed between herd average and percentage of the dairy farm work force that is family; this relationship, subsequently, is manifested as a negative association between production efficiency and percentage of family labor. Work efficiency is not affected by percentage of labor that is family. Thus, it appears that dairies that do not hire much non-family labor, but rely in large measure upon family labor, tend to have weaker herd averages. This negative effect, however, obtains only for larger dairies, not the smaller dairies with fewer than 100 cows; few smaller dairies utilize any non-family labor.

In the case of larger dairies, the lower the percentage of dairy labor that is family, the greater the herd average (−0.54) and, consequently, the greater the overall production efficiency (−0.36). Or, said another way, among large dairies, those that rely more upon non-family labor also tend to have higher production records per worker. The negative associations between percentage family labor and herd average/production efficiency are perplexing. As noted, it applies only to large dairies, with 100 cows or more and mainly to very large dairies, with more than 220 cows.

Certainly these observations cannot be interpreted to mean that family labor is less effective or less reliable than hired, non-family labor. Rather, it is likely that when there are many workers, such as on very large dairy farms, the role of family members should become basically managerial; giving directions, assigning tasks, arranging schedules, overseeing the work, trouble-shooting, etc. As managers (bosses, planners, strategists), their knowledge and skills are multiplied, increasing the efficiency of the operation over and above what they themselves could do directly, without additional non-family hired help. Such increased managerial efficiency is probably expressed most directly through the better care, feeding, and management of the dairy stock and, in turn, the resulting production increase per cow helps to maximize the overall production efficiency of the hired work force.

Enterprise Diversity and Efficiencies

It has been said that dairy farmers who also raise cash crops, beef cattle, or even dairy steers in addition to producing milk, "can't make up their minds about being dairy farmers." An argument often accompanying this comment is that it is more efficient (and profitable, in the long run) for a dairy farmer to focus all of his time, energies, and managerial skills, and all of the farm's land, investment capital, and labor resources, on the production of milk. Enterprise diversification diffuses commitment; a concentration of effort enhances work efficiency. In mid-Michigan, however, and throughout the Midwest generally, dairy farms are not very diversified – and haven't been for a long time. Only a small proportion of dairies get a substantial percentage of their gross agricultural income from sources other than the monthly milk check. Nevertheless, enterprise diversity is an important structural feature of some farms, and so, an exploratory inquiry was undertaken.

Enterprise diversity – or the converse, dairy specialization – does not appear to affect directly any of the three indicators of dairy efficiency. But, when size of operation is taken into account a tendency is observed, in the case of small dairies, for enterprise diversity to be associated, though weakly, with greater work efficiency, which in turn is reflected in higher milk production efficiency on small dairies that are more diversified. (This effect is especially strong among mid-sized dairies, ranging from 70 to 100 cows.) A comparable work efficiency effect deriving from enterprise diversification does not obtain among larger dairies. Among larger dairies, however, increased specialization in milk production is associated with increased herd average. (This effect is especially strong among very large dairies, with more than 220 cows.)

Thus, there is some evidence that enterprise diversity may be a useful strategy for mid-sized dairies to more effectively employ their available labor force. Very large dairies, on the other hand, gain in terms of milk production efficiency by focusing managerial attention on their dairy operation, i.e. specializing, as a way of maximizing their investments.

Modern Technology and Efficiencies

The technological modernization of a dairy farm's facilities for milking and handling its cattle represents, in large measure, the owner/operator's commitment, expressed through capital investments, to enhance the productivity of both cows and workers. Remodeling or rebuilding, and the associated new equipment and improved ways that routine chores are performed, enables a worker to get more done during a given period of time, i.e. to be more efficient. At least, that is the theoretical rationale generally given for such major investments. Further, it is also argued that better facilities for milking and housing the stock mean healthier cows that give more milk for more years. These propositions are explored, insofar as possible, with information provided by the surveyed dairy farmers.

In this mid-Michigan context, the facilities (barns, milk houses/milking parlors) of the very small dairies tend to be older, relatively speaking, than those of the mid-sized and larger dairies, and most very small dairies are one-person operations that will probably not survive as dairies beyond the present generation. On the other hand, all of the very large dairies – probably because very large dairies are a rather recent phenomenon in this area – have relatively new facilities.

Facility age, it appears (Table 3), is moderately associated with all three dairy efficiency indicators; the newer the facility, the greater the work efficiency, herd average, and overall production efficiency. But the observed effect of facility age on herd average disappears when herd size is taken into account (Table 4); facility age does not affect herd average independent from herd size.

Further, the effect of facility age on work efficiency and on milk production efficiency is conditional, applying only to larger dairies, not to smaller dairies. Additional analysis, using four size categories, confirms these observations, and reveals, surprisingly, a strong negative effect of facility age on work efficiency and production efficiency among mid-sized dairies of 70–100 cows. The latter finding is quite puzzling, for it implies that newer facilities might hinder work efficiency. Perhaps it is a transitional phenomenon, as mid-sized dairies initially (and rather abruptly) upgrade their milking facilities prior to expanding (gradually) their cow herd. If so, the operators of mid-sized dairies would be well advised to reconsider their investment priorities, and to focus more deliberately on management procedures and labor saving technologies that will contribute more immediately to an improvement in the worker/cow ratio.

SUMMARY

Herd size is a dominant organizational variable that affects, directly or indirectly, the successful management of a modern dairy farm. This is demonstrably so in mid-Michigan (Gratiot county), where dairy farms are family enterprises and where the largest, with about 1000 cows, does not approach the huge scale of mega-dairies in California, New Mexico, and southwest Texas.[9] Herd size here is strongly associated with work efficiency and, as well, with herd average; thus, it is a major determinant of production efficiency and, ultimately, of the profitability of a dairy operation.

Furthermore, even smaller dairies stand to gain from expanding their operations. Indeed, enhanced efficiencies associated with incremental increases in herd size seem to be especially evident for very small dairies, with less than 70 cows. At the lower end of the herd size range, the underemployment of available labor may significantly undercut dairy profitability.

Total size of land holdings is also an important factor that affects the work and production efficiencies of smaller dairies. Land constraints make it difficult for small dairies to employ their workers more fully and more productively. And, when land for the production of forage and feed grains is limited, smaller dairies can and generally do direct their available labor to cow care and cow management. Herd average is thereby increased to some extent, though the overall work efficiency is decreased – for the number of cows that smaller dairies can accommodate is determined more by the lack of land and the lack of investment capital, than by a lack of available labor, which, because the workforce is mainly family, cannot be easily reduced or more fully employed.

Dairies with a larger workforce than is typical for their herd size class are more likely to have stronger herd averages. But, regardless of herd size, such increased production per cow (presumably stimulated by better management and care) does not necessarily result in greater overall production efficiency nor in greater profitability.

Smaller dairies rely almost exclusively on family labor, whereas a significant proportion of the labor force on larger dairies – and particularly on very large dairies – is non-family. This increased dependence on hired, non-family labor is, arguably, the most important structural feature that distinguishes larger from smaller dairies.

However, the degree to which the dairy work force is family or non-family does not seem to matter very much in terms of work efficiency. This is not surprising in the case of smaller dairies, where there are few non-family workers and where relationships between supervisor and hired worker (milkers, summer temporaries, and the occasional hired full-time worker) are more personal and less like a boss/employee situation. But the absence of a significant association between work efficiency and percent family labor in the case of larger dairies is noteworthy, for it suggests that how the available dairy labor is managed is more important in determining the work efficiency of large dairy operations than whether the dairy labor force is mainly family or non-family.

Why is it that among larger dairies, the greater the percentage of family labor, the lower the herd average and, consequently, the lower the production efficiency? No doubt, the operators of large dairies that employ much non-family labor must be more business-like (less personal, less familistic) in dealing with workers, in assigning specific tasks and duties, and in making farm and herd management decisions. Because their position in the work context is formally contracted, non-family hired workers expect to be supervised directly and authoritatively (which often is not an acceptable manner of communication for family members.). Dairy farm managers who hire a lot of non-family labor cannot assume nor afford a hands-on leadership style, where they work side-by-side with other family members, and where kinship expectations may (and sometimes must) take precedence over the demands of getting a specific task accomplished in a timely fashion.

Most dairy farms in mid-Michigan, regardless of herd size, are specialized, focused primarily on milk production. For dairies that have significant sources of income other than milk sales, their enterprise diversity does not appear to detract from the dairy segment's operational efficiencies (an observation that derives from comparison with dairy farms that are more specialized.). Indeed, among smaller dairies, with less than 100 cows, enterprise diversity enhances production efficiency (total milk produced per work unit). This is probably because any available labor that might otherwise be under-utilized for dairy work is directed toward supplemental enterprises. Alternatively, of course, improvements in work/production efficiencies could also be achieved (perhaps) via herd expansion, but that would require larger capital investments than by adding a secondary enterprise, such as cash cropping.

Larger dairies, typically, have newer facilities than smaller dairies. The barns and milking parlors (or milk houses) of very small dairies are generally quite a bit older, less modern. But, in trying to account for variations in the operational efficiencies of dairies, we find that these two important character-istics, herd size and facilities age, are inextricably linked. Indeed, facilities age alone, independent of herd size, does not explain herd average. Rather, it is because larger dairies tend to have newer facilities, that dairies with newer facilities manifest higher herd averages.

Whether the modernization of a dairy's physical plant and equipment – for the milking, housing, handling, feeding, and caring of cows – affects herd average over and above what can be attributed to herd size (and the associated operational economies) is not ascertainable here: virtually all very large dairies in this mid-Michigan context have invested heavily in recent years to upgrade their buildings and equipment.

Work efficiency, though, is affected by the age of facilities, but only in the case of large dairies. Among large dairies, newer facilities are associated with greater work efficiency and, consequently, higher production efficiency. By making it easier and faster to do routine chores, such as milking, feeding, and handling the stock, the effectiveness of labor is enhanced and, for a given amount of work time inputted, more can be accomplished (and more cows managed per year per worker.) This may also be so for small dairies, but because they must be fiscally conservative and are therefore not as likely to have made significant and costly improvements in their facilities in recent years, we are not able to discern the impacts of such changes (34% of the dairies in this mid-Michigan context have less than 70 cows and 77 % of these very small dairies have relatively 'old' facilities.)

Whether a dairy farmer gains, in a cost/benefit sense, from investing heavily in new facilities and equipment depends on a multitude of factors, not the least of which are his long-term plans for the dairy (generational transition), the availability of investment capital (equity), and the alternative uses for and current pressures on the farm workforce. There is no question that most improvements in dairy facilities and equipment will result in specific tasks being accomplished more efficiently. But, unless there is a concomitant expansion of the dairy herd or a reduction in the total labor inputs that are assigned to the dairy operation (by downsizing the dairy workforce or by adding or expanding supplementary non-dairy farm enterprises), the overall work efficiency of the dairy operation, i.e. the number of cows managed per year per worker, will not be increased and, more seriously, the dairy's profitability will be decreased.

SOCIOECONOMIC REALITIES AND HERD EXPANSION

Size of operation is an important structural characteristic that affects a dairy operation's production efficiency and, ultimately, its profitability as an economic and family enterprise. The findings here strongly support this generalization. Larger dairies have a distinct advantage over smaller dairies through economics that derive from a decreasing expenditure of labor per unit of production, i.e. per cow. Such decreases in labor inputs mean that the available workforce is being more fully (productively) employed; and this happens when the ratio between work units and number of cows cared for and/ or total pounds of milk produced is increased.

But it is not feasible for every dairy to add more cows to the herd so as to achieve a more favorable utilization of available labor (or, similarly, though it is not likely to be problematic – so as to achieve a more rational use of available investment capital.) There are many constraints to expansion, particularly for smaller dairies. Consider, for instance, some of the *circumstances and problems that smaller dairies must deal with* in order to become more efficient:

* *scaling down an underemployed farm family work force*
  Production efficiency can be increased, of course, by reducing total labor inputs while holding the size of operation constant. But it is exceedingly awkward to downsize family members who rely on the farm for their livelihood or who are in line to take over the farm some day, and it is very

stressful for a dairy farmer to hold an off-farm job in addition to managing the dairy and doing the necessary chores and seasonal work.

• *inadequate or marginal land base*
Without the necessary acreage to grow additional forage and grain, and thereby to more fully employ its available labor, a small dairy, to expand, would have to purchase or rent additional land plus the equipment to till it effectively, or would have to buy-in the necessary forage and grain. Either alternative, in most cases, is financially risky, necessitating the commitment of scarce capital, weak equity, and the family's modest cash-flow. A third alternative, to till the available land more intensively, generally requires a change in farming practices and work routines.

• *scarcity of investment capital*
A lack of investment capital to expand and to modernize is the bottom-line economic reality that most small dairy farmers must live with, and it limits their opportunity to adjust aggressively to industry demands. Invariably, the short-term financial margins of small dairies are too narrow to sustain an upgrading of basic essentials, and their equity – in land, buildings, stock, equipment – is too weak to secure long-range loans from lending agencies for the major improvements that must accompany herd expansion.

• *lack of special skills to manage a larger work crew*
To substantially expand a small dairy, say from 80 to 180 cows, means that the senior operator must adjust from a basically hands-on, familial style of management to a more supervisory, non-familial style, and this requires special personality attributes plus appropriate training and/or experience.

• *uncertainties of generational transition*
In making long-range economic decisions, small dairies, like most businesses, must reckon with the problem of generational transition. But a small dairy's relatively tenuous economic viability, particularly in our contemporary societal context where rural children, like their urban counterparts, are urged to go to college, to build a challenging career for themselves in the larger society, and to enjoy the material rewards of individual achievement, tends to transform the uncertainties of generational transition into the inevitability of having to close out the family dairy upon the current manager's retirement. A powerful incentive for expanding a dairy operation, modernizing its facilities, and taking some serious economic risks is the anticipation that a son of daughter will one day assume managerial control of the family farm. If herd expansion means jeopardizing the family's quality of life and basic security and then, after many years of hard work when the operator retires, selling the farm and dispersing the herd, it is not necessarily a rational decision relative to the family's well-being.

For most dairy farms then, herd expansion and its requisite structural modifications bring into play economies of size that enable a dairy operation to produce milk more efficiently. Larger dairies (generally) are more efficient than smaller dairies; smaller dairies (generally) stand to gain in efficiency by adding more cows. But, many and sundry problems constrain small dairies from expanding and, indeed, expansion may not be a wise decision for some dairy farm families. Further, and very important, the observed correlation (0.42) between herd size and work efficiency is modest, as is the observed correlation between herd size and herd average (0.51). There are many exceptions to the general rule; there are many outliers to one side or the other of the regression line. The pattern for achieving efficiency – for increasing the number of cows managed per worker and/or for increasing the overall herd average – is open to innovation, smallness does not condemn a dairy to irreconcilable inefficiency; neither does largeness provide an automatic ticket to the goal of enterprise profitability.

ACKNOWLEDGMENTS

Work on this research was sponsored by the Michigan State University Agricultural Experiment Station as a contribution to U.S. Department of Agriculture regional research project NE177. Tina Turnbull and Beth Dunford merit special thanks for their exceptionally competent help with all phases of the project. The facilitating cooperation of the Gratiot County Extension Director, Van Varner, and his office, is appreciated. Most importantly, we wish to acknowledge the kindness and patience of dairy farm families in Gratiot County.

NOTES

1. To overview the structural and operational characteristics of dairy farms in Michigan, see Bokemeier et al. (1995) and Harsh et al. (1996).

2. For more details about the surveyed dairies, see Schwarzweller (1999). Especially relevant is information about management practices (performance testing and use of bovine somatotropin hormone to stimulate milk production) and the operators' plans to expand or down-size.

3. The specific scoring procedure for this five-point 'facility's age scale' is reported in Schwarzweller (1999). Total scores average 3.4 points, and range from 6 to a low of 2. Most of the dairies (55.4%) are on the 'older' side, scoring 2 or 3 points. Only a relatively small proportion (15.4%) score 'very new', with 5 or 6 points.

4. A total of 349 persons were enumerated in the 85 households. Many are infants and schoolchildren (41.5%), and some of the adults (e.g. a spouse or an older son) hold off-farm jobs and are only peripherally involved with the dairy. But shoolchildren are

often assigned regular chores on the farm, and those who work full-time elsewhere but live at home often assist with farm work on weekends, holidays, and particularly during the busy summer months.

5. For detailed information on these adjustments, see Schwarzweller (1999: 21–23). Labor requirements for the various crop and livestock enterprises are based on Michigan Telfarm statistics compiled by researchers at the MSU Department of Agricultural Economics (Nott, et al., 1995). Labor inputs estimated for the production of cash crops and livestock raised for sale are subtracted from a farm's total labor equivalents. Labor inputs estimated for the production of purchased forage and feed, and for the raising of replacement heifers on contract by other farmers are added to a farm's total labor equivalents. The resulting adjustments provide a reasonable estimate of dairy labor inputs.

6. This measure of work efficiency, admittedly a rough estimate, indicates a dairy's current situation. Two cases were dropped from the analysis. Both were in the process of shifting from cash cropping to more intensive dairying and, consequently, their farm workforce was in an extremely transitional state.

7. This statistic derives from information obtained directly from the surveyed dairy farmers. Labor inputs were inventoried; adjustments were made to take account of labor devoted to other enterprises and of labor supplemented by the outsourcing of feed, forage, and the raising of replacements; and any unusual circumstances that might affect measurement reliability were considered. The observed average of 32.7 cows per worker is remarkably equivalent to what can be calculated from Michigan Telfarm statistics (Nott et al., 1995). Using Telfarm estimates and assuming a 50-hour week per worker for 52 weeks per year, and labor inputs of 54 hours per cow with replacements (producing 19,000 lbs of milk per year) plus 28.4 hours per cow for the production of feed (corn grain, silage, and dry hay), it is estimated that one worker can care for 31.6 cows. Or, assuming a more strenuous 55-hour week per worker (with very little, if any, vacation time), it is estimated that one worker can care for 34.7 cows.

8. The match between farmer statements of herd average and published DHIA records was explored. Some discrepancies were observed, but they are minor (no significant deviations) and, in most cases, statements that varied from the published record were merely an updating from more recent tests. We also assessed, case by case, whether the stated averages (if not on DHIA test) are reasonable estimates. Four cases were dropped for lack of information or because the stated estimates were grossly erroneous. For the remaining 61 cases we are fairly confident of the reported information on herd averages.

9. Elsewhere in mid-Michigan, however, there are some extremely large, mega-size dairies. Not far from Gratiot county a huge, family owned and managed dairy farm with over 2000 cows has been in operation for many years and has become an integral and vital part of the local community, socially as well as economically.

REFERENCES

Aronoff, M. (1993). Collective celebration as a vehicle for local economic development: a Michigan case study. *Human Organization, 52*(4).

Bokemeier, J., Allensworth, E., & Skidmore, A. (1995). *Decisions for the Future: Dairy Farming in Michigan.* MSU Agricultural Experiment Station Research Report 540, East Lansing, MI.

Bruun, M. C., & Adelaja, A. O. (1990). *Economies of scale and output flexibility in Northeastern U.S. dairy.* Paper presented at the AAEA meetings, Vancouver, B. C., Canada.

Carley, D. H. (1979). *Labor Utilization and Costs on Georgia Dairy Farms.* The University of Georgia College of Agriculture Experiment Station Research Bulletin 241.

Hall, B., & Leveen, E.P. (1978). Farm size and economic efficiency: the case of California. *American Journal of Agricultural Economics,* 60(4): 589–600.

Hallam, A. (1988). Economies of size: theory, measurement, and related issues. In: *Determinants of Farm Size and Structure.* Proceedings of a program sponsored by NC–181, San Antonio, Texas. (Michigan Agricultural Experiment Station Journal Article No. 12899, 65–93).

Kadlec, J. E. (1985). *Farm Management: Decisions, Operation, Control.* Englewood Cliffs: Prentice-Hall.

Kumbhakar, S. C., Biswas, B., & Von Bailey, D. (1989). *Review of Economics and Statistics,* 71(4).

Lyson, T. A., & Gillespie, G.W. (1995). Producing more milk on fewer farms: neoclassical and neo-structural explanations of changes in dairy farming. *Rural Sociology,* 60(3).

Matulich, S. (1978). Efficiencies in large-scale dairying: incentives for future structural change. *American Journal of Agricultural Economics,* 60(4): 642–47.

Michigan Department of Agriculture. (1996). *Michigan Agricultural Statistics.* Department of Agriculture, Lansing, MI. 1996.

Nott, S. B., Schwab, G. D., Jones, J. D., Hilker, J. H., & Copeland, L. O. (1995). *1995 Crops and Livestock Budgets Estimates for Michigan.* East Lansing. MI: Michigan State University Agricultural Economics Report No. 581.

Perez, A. M. (1994). *Changing Structure of U.S. Dairy Farms.* Agricultural Economics Report No. 690. Washington, D.C.: U.S. Department of Agriculture.

Richards, T. J. (1996). Positioning your dairy farm business for a profitable future: a western Canada perspective. http: //www.afns.ualberta.ca/wcdairy/wcdairy/wcd96/wcd96175.htm

Sauer, H. (1981). *Arbeitswirtschaftschafliche Untersuchungen und Methoden Ueberpruefung Durch Modell Kalkulationen in der Milchviehhaltung.* [Labor Economics Studies of Dairy Cow Management and an Overview of Methodology and Model Calculations.] Freising-Weihenstephan: Deutschen Forschungsgemeinschaft.

Schwarzweller, H. K. (1999). *Dairy Farms in Mid-Michigan: Structural Characteristics, Labor Inputs, and Operational Efficiencies.* MSU Agricultural Experiment Station Research Report 564, East Lansing, MI.

Schwarzweller, H. K. (1992). *Dairying in Michigan's Thumb: Restructuring for the Future.* MSU Agricultural Experiment Station Research Report 490, East Lansing, MI.

Schwarzweller, H. K. (1988). *Agricultural Structure and Change in the Lower Hunter Valley of New South Wales.* MSU Agricultural Experiment Station Research Report 490, East Lansing, MI.

Smith, T. R. (1996). Positioning your dairy farm business for a profitable future: a U.S. perspective. http: //www.afns.ualberta.ca/wcdairy/wcd96/wcd96135.htm.

Vieira, A. (1996). Dairy Farm Household Survival Strategies in Michigan's Thumb Region. MA thesis. Michigan State University.

KENTUCKY DAIRY FARMS AND TOBACCO PRODUCTION

Lorraine Garkovich, William Crist and Patricia Dyk

Tobacco and dairying have not been a real compatible combination, even though a lot of dairymen and a lot of tobacco farmers are one and the same, because the dairy is a seven-day-a-week, twenty-four-hour-a-day job nearly, so a lot of them do not want to have to take away from management of the herd to produce tobacco.

Comment of an agricultural extension specialist at the University of Kentucky

There is an intuitive truth to this assessment of the potential conflicts in merging dairying and tobacco production, given the labor and management demands of each. What is surprising is that so few of the dairy farmers in Kentucky share this assessment. Tobacco has been the mainstay cash crop of Kentucky farmers since the late 1700s, and long before there was a commercial dairy industry in Kentucky there was commercial tobacco production. It would be hard to find farmland in Kentucky that has not raised tobacco at some time or another, and most dairies began operating on farms where tobacco was already being raised. Today, tobacco remains an important second commodity on a significant proportion of Kentucky's dairy farms and the question to be addressed here is: What are the implications of raising tobacco for Kentucky's dairy enterprises?

At a time when the population and the demand for milk in the South continues to grow, Kentucky's dairy industry is in decline. The decline is, in fact, speeding up despite the fact that Kentucky has many advantages that should contribute to growth in its dairy sector. Kentucky is within a six hour drive of nearly two-thirds of the U.S. population; there is a well-developed interstate highway system; the climate is relatively mild; there is ample pasture

Research in Rural Sociology, Volume 8, pages 291–307.
Copyright © 2000 by Elsevier Science Inc.
ISBN: 0-7623-0474-X

land; and, there is a significant base of grain production. Moreover, in 1997 the state's milk deficit was 467 million pounds, projected to rise to 703 million pounds by 2000 (Hallady, 1998). Yet between 1992 and 1997, total milk production in Kentucky declined 15.6%; the number of commercial dairy farms declined by 29.0%; and, the number of dairy cows declined by 21.1%. Although milk production per cow increased 7.3% between 1992 and 1997, income from the sales of milk products declined 15.6%. Nationally, Kentucky ranked 19th in total milk production in 1997, but 48th in average milk production (12,517 lbs/cow), nearly 4400 pounds below the national average (16,916 lbs/cow).

In the face of many opportunities to build an expanding dairy sector, what accounts for Kentucky's lagging dairy industry? Nearly three quarters of all of Kentucky's commercial dairy enterprises also raise tobacco and derive 12.5 cents of every farm income dollar from the sale of tobacco (U.S. Census of Agriculture, 1992). Is there a relationship between the structure of Kentucky's dairy industry and the prevalence of tobacco production on these farms? What factors influence the decision to raise tobacco and, are there differences among dairy operations given the amount of tobacco they raise? To begin answering these questions we first examine the extent to which tobacco production is integrated into Kentucky's dairy farm operations.

OVERVIEW OF KENTUCKY'S DAIRY FARMS

The 1997 Census of Agriculture reports 3,393 dairy farms in Kentucky, down 51.5% since 1987. 1,985 of these dairies earn over half of their total farm income from the sale of dairy products, and so are classified as commercial dairies.[1] These commercial dairy farms own 82.3% of all milk cows in Kentucky, yet are less than six in ten of all farms in Kentucky with milk cows. Half of these commercial dairy farms have 10 to 49 cows, and another third (35.2%) have between 50 and 99 (Table 1). These commercial dairies represent 72.7% of total milk sales in Kentucky.

Kentucky's dairy farms are significantly smaller than the national average (Table 1). In 1994, less than 20% of all milk cows were on operations with herds of 49 or less, while, nearly one third were on operations with herds of 200 +. Indeed, during the 1990s, national trends were toward ever larger dairies, so that by 1998, fully one quarter of all milk cows in the U.S. were on operations with herds of 500 or more (National Agricultural Statistics Service, 1999).

Sixty five percent (1,285) of Kentucky's commercial dairy farms also grow tobacco and, on average, derive 12% of their farm income from the sale of

Table 1. Dairy Farms in Kentucky, by Herd Size, 1997 and 1992[a]

| Herd Size | 1997 | | 1992 | | 1994[b] |
	number	%	number	%	U.S. %
1–49	993	50.0	1,568	54.8	18.6
50–99	699	35.2	960	33.5	28.7
100–199	248	12.5	299	10.4	19.3
200+	45	2.3	36	1.3	33.4
Total	1,985	100.0	2,863	100.0	100.0

[a] A commercial dairy farm derives 50% or more of the value of total farm sales from the production of milk and other dairy products and the raising of dairy heifer replacements.
[b] National data for 1994 from the Statistical Highlight 1998–1999: Livestock report of the National Agriclltural Statistics Service.

tobacco. One hundred and forty of these dairies (10.8%) have tobacco sales of $50,000 or more, representing more than one-third (37.1%) of the total tobacco sales from Kentucky's commercial dairy farms. This suggests that while dairy sales are spread somewhat evenly across all commercial dairy farms, among those that raise tobacco, more than a third of all sales is accounted for by just one in ten of these dairy/tobacco operations.

Nearly six in ten (57.5%) of Kentucky's commercial dairy farms grow more than 5 acres of tobacco compared to less than a third (34.9%) of all commercial tobacco farms. Overall, nearly half of all Kentucky farms (including commercial tobacco farms) grow less than 3 acres of tobacco. Thus, a higher proportion of Kentucky's commercial dairy farm operators produce larger quantities of tobacco than do all Kentucky farmers raising tobacco, even the commercial tobacco farms.

'FITTING' TOGETHER DAIRYING AND TOBACCO PRODUCTION

What accounts for the high proportion of Kentucky dairies also producing tobacco? To begin to answer this question, it is necessary to understand three characteristics of the burley tobacco commodity system that might influence the decision of dairy operators to also raise tobacco. First, there is the structure of the marketing system. In the 1930s, in order to stabilize tobacco prices, all farm land owners who had raised burley tobacco in the previous years were allotted a quota for the tobacco poundage they could market. 'Barn-door' sales of tobacco were prohibited; anyone found selling tobacco anywhere other than through an authorized warehouse would lose their right to a marketing quota. In exchange for limiting their production, farmers were guaranteed a market price. If the actual price at the warehouses dropped below this, the government would buy and store the crop until market prices rose and the government could sell the surplus. This program, funded by the producers through a charge on all tobacco sold, restricted the amount of tobacco to be legally sold in order to stabilize prices and thereby guaranteed farmers' income based on the marketing quota a producer either owned or could lease. Since most farms in Kentucky were producing some tobacco at the time the program was implemented, most having a marketing quota.

Second, while burley tobacco does not require a considerable investment in equipment or facilities – a tractor, a setter, a flat-bed wagon and a barn with tiers – it does require a significant investment of labor during four to five months of the year. In May, plants, whether from field or floating beds, are hand-bundled and set in the fields. 'Setting' is done by at least three people – one to drive the tractor and two on the 'setter' who place the plants – one-by-one – into the setter for planting and watering. Some farmers have double-row setters which require four 'setters'. During the next two months, one person with a tractor, cultivator, and sprayer can handle forty acres of tobacco, cultivating and spraying for weed, insect, and disease control. But in mid- to late July, it takes several workers to move through the fields, removing by hand the emerging flowers to force growth into the leaves.

In late August and early September, twenty-one days after topping, the tobacco is ready to harvest and house. This is a time of peak labor demand for two reasons. The quality of the crop depends both on moving it from the fields quickly to limit damage due to dust or pitting of the leaves as well as uniformity in time in the barn to cure. Harvesting is still done by hand with a knife, because mechanical harvesters cannot perform all the activities required and there is a strong belief that mechanically harvested burley tobacco leaves are damaged too easily. In a typical harvesting and housing operation, there may be as many as nine people working – one or two on the wagon, five to seven in the tiers, and one or two on the ground picking up dropped sticks or plants. By November, the tobacco is ready to be 'stripped' and taken to market. This stage – stripping and marketing – may last through early January depending on the size of the crop and when the tobacco was hung in the barn to begin curing. Once again, a fairly large crew of labor is required to bring the tobacco down from the barn, take the plants off the sticks, strip the leaves from the stalks, and hand tie them in bundles (van Willigen & Eastland, 1998).

Finally, the economic value of tobacco production for Kentucky farmers must be acknowledged. Tobacco accounts for one quarter of total agricultural cash receipts from just 1% of farmland in production. There are few, if any, other crops which can match the financial return of tobacco on a per acre basis. The state average in 1997 was 2,400 pounds per acre, and at the 1997 market price of $1.84 per pound, an average acre yielded just over $4,400. Tobacco prices have been relatively stable throughout the 1990s, and given the high return per acre, it is easy to understand the financial attraction of raising tobacco. Moreover, while top quality attracts the best price, the marketing arrangement for tobacco assures that even poor quality crops can be sold for a quota price (Snell & Goetz, 1997).

This discussion suggests three key points. First, there is a strong economic imperative underlying tobacco production. Second, most farmers have the essentials for tobacco production; a marketing quota, a barn, a tractor and available labor. Third, tobacco production requires considerable labor inputs during three key times; May, August/September, and October through early January. In two of these periods, transplanting in May and harvest in August/September, there are real time constraints that influence the quality and quantity of production.

Dairying is also a labor intensive enterprise, with key labor – milking and feeding – performed two or three times daily year-round. Since most dairy operations also raise their own hay and silage, these also require a commitment of labor, much of it during the same time of peak demand for tobacco. However, while tobacco has been described as a crop that doesn't require much more than hard work and time to generate a profit, the management demands of dairying are significantly greater. Herd management and record-keeping, feed analysis, facilities maintenance and sanitation are all essential to maximize returns on investments. Moreover, the future for dairy products is far more secure than the future for tobacco. The current debate over tobacco use and the tobacco program create considerable uncertainty as to the size and stability of future markets, and indeed, there is speculation as to whether tobacco will remain a legal commodity in the U.S.

Thus, it could be argued that the economic value of tobacco combined with the historic stability of the tobacco market represent strong incentives for all Kentucky farmers to produce it, even dairy farmers. Yet, the future stability of the tobacco market is highly uncertain, while the demand for milk and dairy products in the South is certain to grow. Still, a majority of Kentucky's dairy farmers continue to grow tobacco. Does tobacco production have labor or management implications for dairy farmers? Do dairy farmers who choose to limit their tobacco production have different life and enterprise goals from those who invest more heavily in the production of tobacco?

Two sources of information will yield some answers to these questions. A 1994 state-wide mail survey of a sample of commercial dairies provides detailed information on farm characteristics, management practices and operators' perspectives on aspects of farming. In-depth personal interviews in 1988 and 1989 with farm couples in four Kentucky counties (two of which had a substantial number of dairies) provide additional insights on the character- istics and attitudes of dairy farmers who do or do not raise tobacco.

The 1994 state-wide mail survey had a response rate of 44.6% from a pool of 417 potential respondents. A total of 186 useable surveys were returned and of these, 134 were still actively involved in a commercial dairy, and another 52 had retired from dairying in the last five years. Participants in the 1988–89 in- depth interviews were selected from a list of active farmers provided by county extension agents in the sample counties. Counties were selected to represent the types of farming in Kentucky. Following an initial telephone contact, both husbands and wives participated in two to three hour personal interviews. The interviews were taped and transcribed.

In the sample of Kentucky dairies (N = 134), nearly one third (34.4%) milk less than 40 cows, slightly less (29.6%) milk 40 to 65, and one third (36.0%) milk 66 cows or more. The largest dairies, those milking 66 cows or more are most likely to be at the extreme, either raising no tobacco or raising four acres or more. Overall, one in five of all the reporting dairies raise no tobacco at all and just under one in five raise ten or more acres (Table 2).

For present purposes, a composite variable was constructed, based on the number of cows milked and the number of acres of tobacco raised. The distribution of the composite variable is as follows: all dairies with *no* tobacco acreage (N = 24, 22.2%); small dairies (milking 1–54 cows) with small tobacco acreage (less than 5 acres of tobacco) (N = 22, 20.4%); small dairies (milking

Table 2.   Tobacco Acreage, by Herd Size (Percentage of Sampled Dairies)

Number of head milked	Percentage of Dairies Raising Given Acres of Tobacco				
	None	1–3.9	4–9.9	10+	Total
1–39	12.1	48.5	33.3	6.1	100.0
40–65	20.0	25.7	37.1	17.1	100.0
66+	31.0	11.9	26.2	31.0	100.0
% Total Sample	21.8	27.3	31.8	19.1	100.0
(Number)	(29)	(36)	(43)	(26)	(134)

1–54 cows) with large tobacco acreage (more than 5 acres of tobacco) (N = 21; 19.4%); and large dairies (milking 55 + cows) with some tobacco acreage (more than 2.5 acres of tobacco) (N = 41, 38.0%). Twenty six dairies were dropped from the analysis due to missing data, leaving 108 dairies for the remainder of this analysis. Analysis of variance was then performed to assess differences in management and attitudes among different sized dairies.

ENTERPRISE AND OPERATOR CHARACTERISTICS

Whether a dairy farm also raises tobacco and the amount of tobacco a dairy farm raises influence farm characteristics over and above differences generally associated with herd size (Table 3). For example, dairies that raise no tobacco, milk an average of 63 cows, maintain 48 replacements, and sold 749,927 pounds of milk in 1993 for an income of $119,762. Finally, income from milk sales represents 76% of total farm sales. For each of these variables, dairies that raise no tobacco are above the sample mean, yet below the mean for the larger dairies that also raise tobacco. On the other hand, the dairies that raise no tobacco are smaller than those that raise tobacco with one exception (dairies milking less than 55 cows) and own the smallest percentage of acres that they operate. Finally, the dairies that raise no tobacco are most likely to keep herd production records.

Among the dairies that do raise tobacco, the smaller dairies, those that raise five acres or more, compared with those that raise less tobacco, have fewer dairy replacements, sell less milk, and have less income from milk sales, even though they milk more cows. The larger dairies that raise tobacco, milk more cows, have more replacements, and sell more milk than all other dairies, yet milk sales represent only 73% of their total farm sales. Moreover, less than half of these large dairies maintain herd production records.

There is a significant difference in farm size among all these types of dairies. Dairies that raise no tobacco are neither the largest nor the smallest in total acreage, but do own the smallest percentage of acreage that they operate. Furthermore, they raise less than the sample mean of silage and alfalfa. Among dairies that do raise tobacco, the smaller dairies that raise less tobacco operate the smallest acreage, raise the smallest acreage of silage and alfalfa. Yet, they own the highest percentage of acreage that they operate. Finally, Those operating smaller dairies without much tobacco are the oldest and have the lowest level of educational attainment. How the investment in large scale tobacco production might influence the time and effort invested in other aspects of the operation is explained by one dairy farmer.

Tobacco comes in spurts. You have to do this or that at a certain time. When the tobacco's ready, you can't wait. One of our major problems was tobacco was ready to house when silage was ready to chop. We'd let the silage go. We'd always let it go and then we'd complain all winter long because our silage wasn't good enough quality so we couldn't get the milk out of the cows.

– Milking 60 cows, raising 30,000 pounds of tobacco, alfalfa, corn on 200 acres

Table 3.   Characteristics of Kentucky Dairies Raising Tobacco

	Herd Size and Acres of Tobacco			
	Any no. of cows No tobacco	< 55 cows < 5 ac	< 55cows > 5 ac	55 + cows > 2.5 ac	Total Mean %
Farm Characteristics					
Cows milked***	63.3	31.2	34.4	92.2	60.6
No. of Replacements***	47.8	16.9	16.5	56.1	36.4
No. of Bulls*	1.4	1.2	1.3	2.6	1.7
Pounds of Milk sold***	749,927	372,217	358,009	856,426	609,090
Income of Milk sales***	119,762	44,740	40,583	186,082	112,442
Farm Sales***	157,061	51,191	59,209	255,028	154,202
Assets Level[a]***	2.0	1.59	1.8	2.4	2.0
Total Acres**	271.2	166.6	313.4	547.3	352.9
Acres owned**	133.2	123.0	171.9	319.7	214.0
Silage acres***	41.5	19.0	18.5	64.8	43.3
Alfalfa acres**	39.8	14.5	21.2	52.3	40.2
Tobacco acres*	0.0	2.4	7.0	15.6	9.3
Operator Characteristics					
Age	48.1	48.6	46.0	47.8	48.5
Education[b]	4.2	3.4	3.9	4.1	3.8
Keep production records[c]*	62.5%	20.0%	33.3%	47.5%	39.1%
(No. farms =)	(24)	(22)	(21)	(41)	(108)

Differences in means significant at the following levels: * = 0.05, ** = 0.01, *** = 0.001

[a] Assets level is a categorical variable. "What is the total value of your farm assets?" 1 = More than $100,000, 2 = Between $100,00 and $500,000, 3 = Between $500,000 and $1 million, 4 = $1 million or more.

[b] Education is a categorical variable. 1 = less than 8th grade, 2 = completed 8th grade, 3 = some high school, 4 = complete high school or equivalent, 5 = completed a 2 year college degree, 6 = completed a 4 year college degree, 7 = completed a graduate or professional degree.

[c] Percent responding they do maintain production records.

USE OF BEST MANAGEMENT PRACTICES

Kentucky's dairy industry, as we've noted, has yet to reach the production levels of dairies found in most other states. The persistent failure of Kentucky dairies to improve herd productivity to anything near national or regional levels is a serious threat to the economic viability of the industry. The failure to improve productivity is not the result of a lack of information or technical assistance, for there are well developed public (i.e. Cooperative Extension Service) and private (e.g. herd improvement associations and feed companies) technical assistance programs within the state. Kentucky dairy operators are well aware of best management practices. Yet, a significant number choose not to use these practices, and the proportion of Kentucky dairymen who do use best management practices is substantially below the level of adoption in several other states. For example, while 39% of Kentucky dairy operators test their forage, comparable figures are 54% in Texas, 62% in Michigan, and 77% in Maryland. A similar gap among dairy operators in these four states also appears with respect to balancing rations (Bokemeier, Allensworth and Skidmore,1995; McIntosh, Bateman & Cready, 1998).

Our analysis suggests that the choice of whether to use best management practices may be related to the competitive need for management invested in tobacco production (Table 4). The dairies that raise no tobacco are most likely to participate in DHIA, maintain regular visits by a veterinarian, use AI on at least 75% of heifers, postdip teats and, predip teats at the same rate as the largest dairies. Among those dairies that also raise tobacco, the larger dairies are more likely than smaller dairies, regardless of the amount of tobacco they raise, to use management practices that are closely associated with higher levels of production. Interestingly, however, the larger dairies are no more likely than the smaller dairies to use artificial insemination on at least 75% of their heifers. Indeed, the largest dairies also report the highest average number of bulls on their farms. Among the smaller dairies, the relationship is not as clear. Those raising much tobacco are less likely to test their forage rations at least three times a year, less likely to have regular visits by a veterinarian, and slightly less likely to use AI on at least 75% of their heifers. A very small proportion of all dairies, regardless of size of the dairy or the amount of tobacco raised, test manure, a practice that many dairy specialists argue is a key component to assuring effective nutrient management.

For many of the dairy farmers we talked with, a key issue influencing the adoption of some management practices is how the practice influences their use of time, given the commodity-mix in their operation and the production cycle of tobacco. While some recognize the ways that tobacco production diminishes the efficiency of their dairy operation, they have not considered dropping tobacco from their commodity mix.

> *I guess the reason we haven't got into AI is we just don't have time to stay with the cows and watch them as we should. We turn a bull in with them and we can let him worry about that. We've got eighteen and a half acres of tobacco. All this hay to put up. We'll do about a thousand rolls of hay each year. We've got a hundred and fifty acres of alfalfa to take care of too. That is a big job.*

— Milking 70 cows, raising $18\frac{1}{2}$ acres of tobacco, 350 beef cattle on 350 acres

> *Q: Why do so few dairy farmers in Kentucky use artificial insemination?*
> *A: I tell you it's tobacco. It's tobacco. Because when tobacco has to be set, it has to be set. A farmer can't be following these cows around to see if they're in heat and getting them bred. They have not really gone with heat detectors like we have . . . . When men are doing the milking and running the dairy, they have the hay they have to get in. They have to get*

Table 4. Management Practices on Kentucky Dairy Farms, by Herd Size and Tobacco Acreage

Management Practice	Herd Size and Acres of Tobacco (Percent Using Practice)				
	Any no. of cows No tobacco	<55 cows <5 ac	<55 cows >5 ac	55+ cow >2.5 ac	Total Mean %
Predip teats***	79.0	24.0	44.0	79.0	61.0
Postdip teats**	1.00	73.0	90.0	95.0	89.0
Test forage 3 times/yr**	54.0	20.0	16.0	58.0	39.0
Test manure for nutrient and moisture content*	0.0	5.0	0.0	15.0	7.0
Balance rations 4 times/yr**	46.0	20.0	42.0	58.0	42.0
Regular visits by veterinarian*	71.0	38.0	26.0	56.0	48.0
Participate in DHIA program*	50.0	14.0	21.0	33.0	29.0
AI on at least 75% of heifers	58.0	43.0	42.0	43.0	45.0
(No. farms =)	(24)	(22)	(21)	(41)	(108)

Responses were coded 0 = No and 1 = Yes. Differences in means significant at the following levels: * = 0.05, ** = 0.01, *** = 0.001

the corn planted, the tobacco to set. They have to do all these other things. So, they want to get the milking done and get out. They don't spend the time that it takes . . . because there are other things that they need to do. It's easier to let the bull do it.

— Milking 86 cows, no tobacco raised on 178 acres

Another farmer noted he had begun leasing out his tobacco because his wife, who used to manage the tobacco enterprise is no longer able to physically run that phase of the farm operation. As a result, they have increased their herd size, increased their alfalfa to 120 acres, and increased their beef herd in the hopes of making up for the income lost from raising tobacco themselves. These comments suggest that Kentucky dairy farmers mix their production activities to provide a diversity of sources of income for the farm business. While some may argue that it would be more efficient and productive to invest all of their management energies into the dairy, many believe that less risk comes from diversification rather than from intensification of dairy production.

PERSPECTIVES ON FARMING AND FARM LIFE

We also considered whether there is a relationship between a dairy operator's perspectives on farming and farm life and the dairy operation's commodity mix. Many Kentucky tobacco farmers refer to their crop as 'the tax/mortgage payment' or, 'the Christmas money', and indeed, given the scale of much of the tobacco production and when the crop is sold, the income from tobacco comes just at the time when property taxes and the annual mortgage are due, or when the Christmas bills arrive. Is there a difference in the career goals and farming perspectives of operators of large and small dairy operations given their commitment to tobacco production?

First, it is interesting to note the similarities among operators of small and large dairies in the importance they attach to enhancing aspects of their dairy operations (data not shown). Nearly all dairy farm operators, regardless of the number of cows milked or the amount of tobacco raised, place a great importance on increasing production per cow, total milk sold, and the health of their cows. Interestingly, nearly all give little importance to increasing the size of their herds. Moreover, nearly everyone asserts that they place high importance on avoiding more debt and paying down their debts, increasing their cash on hand, and increasing their income and profits. So, in terms of general goals for their dairy operations, Kentucky dairy farmers, regardless of the amount of tobacco raised, do not differ significantly. But, there is a degree of inconsistency among these goals and in the ways that many of these dairy farmers have structured their operations. Increasing their herd average and volume of milk sold may not be possible without reducing tobacco production.

And, while improving the dairy's productivity and increasing its milk sales would be reflected in a larger monthly milk check, it would be at the cost of decreased tobacco production. For many Kentucky dairy farmers, giving up the certainty of high returns from tobacco for the potential returns from increased milk sales is not necessarily viewed as an equal exchange.

The only significant differences among large and small dairy operations are those related to their family goals (Table 5). Regardless of the size of the dairy, those who raise tobacco are more likely than those who raise *no* tobacco to attribute greater importance to bring a family member into the operation, to set up the farm for the next generation, to maintain a family tradition, to keep the farm in the family, to have an opportunity to bring their children into the operation and, to save for their children's future. In other words, those dairy operations that also raise tobacco, regardless of the size of their herds, place

Table 5.   Kentucky Dairy Farmers' Goals (Importance Scores)

How important is it to you to:	Herd Size and Acres of Tobacco				
	Any no. of cows No tobacco	< 55 cows <5 ac	<55 cows >5 ac	55+ cows >2.5 ac	Total Mean
Bring a family member into the operation?***	2.00	2.95	3.42	3.61	3.02
Set up the farm for next generation?**	2.42	3.55	3.60	3.76	3.36
Maintain a family tradition?*	2.96	4.10	3.55	3.41	3.47
Keep the farm in the family?*	3.08	4.41	3.67	3.78	3.68
Have an opportunity to bring your children into the operation?*	2.58	3.29	3.55	3.68	3.29
Save for your childrens' future?**	3.09	3.90	4.45	4.15	3.82
Reduce labor costs?*	3.42	4.41	3.86	3.93	3.92
(No. farms =)	(24)	(22)	(21)	(41)	(108)

Questions are coded as follows: 1 = Not at all important through 5 = Very important. Analysis of variance for differences in means among groups. * = significant at 0.05, and ** = significant at 0.01, and *** = significant at 0.001.

greater emphasis on family-related goals than those dairies that do not raise tobacco.

One explanation for this may be that given the income that is possible with raising large quantities of tobacco, it might be that tobacco production is a strategy for generating the cash flow essential to maintaining and/or expanding the operation so that it can be transferred intergenerationally or at least maintained long enough for another family member to assume ownership of the enterprise. Another explanation for these differences may lie in the nature of tobacco work. Raising tobacco has been the quintessential family enterprise on Kentucky's farms for generations. Because of the labor demands, tobacco brings the family, often two generations of family, together in a common enterprise. Even after children leave for college, the cycle of tobacco production brings them back to the farm to help with planting, harvesting, housing, and stripping. From this perspective, the persistence of tobacco production might be viewed in terms of how it contributes to the maintenance of a family tradition as much as its economic contributions to the farm business.

This is not to say that there are not differences in the importance attributed to family-related goals among large or small dairies that raise different amounts of tobacco. The larger dairies attribute greater importance to all the family-related goals but two (i.e. "maintain a family tradition" and "save for your children's future"), than do the smaller dairies. Among the smaller dairies, those raising less tobacco give greater importance to "maintaining a family tradition" and "keeping the farm in the family" than do the smaller dairies raising more tobacco. Finally, it is interesting to note that the smaller dairies with small acreages of tobacco attribute the greatest importance to reducing labor costs.

When asked to assess their financial situation, past and future, the pattern of responses by dairy operators reveals some interesting differences (Table 6). The smaller dairies with small tobacco acreages are most likely to say that their financial situation has gotten worse in the last five years and to predict that it will continue to get worse in the next five years. On the other hand, the smaller dairies raising the most tobacco are most likely to say that their financial situation has gotten better over the last five years and to predict that it will get better in the next five years. The dairies with *no* tobacco and the largest dairies raising tobacco share similar perspectives on their past financial situation, and those raising no tobacco are less optimistic about their future financial situation. It would seem that having a substantial tobacco acreage leads to a greater sense of financial optimism for dairy operators than does the size of their dairy herds.

Table 6. Kentucky Dairy Farmers' Perceptions of Their Financial Situation (Improvement Score)

	Herd Size and Acres of Tobacco				
Perspective on financial situation:	Any no. of cows No tobacco	<55 cows <5 ac	<55 cows >5 ac	55+ cows >2.5 ac	Total Mean
In the last 5 years Financial situation has changed[a]	1.96	2.09	1.57	1.93	1.93
In the next 5 years Financial situation will change?[b]*	1.91	2.19	1.48	1.67	1.82
(No. farms =)	(24)	(22)	(21)	(41)	(108)

[a] Question: "In the last 5 years how has your financial situation changed?" Response codes are: 1 = has gotten better, 2 = stayed the same, 3 = has gotten worse.
[b] "In the next 5 years, will your financial situation change?" Response codes are: 1 = will get better, 2 = will stay the same, 3 = will get worse.

Additionally, we asked dairy farmers to assess their overall life satisfaction (Table 7). There is no statistically significant difference in the level of

Table 7. Kentucky Dairy Farmers' Life Satisfaction

	Herd Size and Acres of Tobacco				
How satisfied are you with:	Any no. of cows No tobacco	<55 cows <5 ac	<55 cows >5 ac	55+ cows >2.5 ac	Total Mean
Income for family living?*	2.83	2.14	3.29	2.63	2.60
Financial performance of dairy?*	3.38	2.62	3.57	3.00	2.98
Your decision to be a dairy farmer?	4.08	3.77	4.24	3.83	3.84
(No. farms =)	(24)	(22)	(21)	(41)	(108)

Questions are coded as follows: 1 = Not at all satisfied, through 5 = Very satisfied. Analysis of variance for differences in means among groups: * = significant at 0.05.

satisfaction reported with the decision to operate a dairy. It is striking that those milking less than 55 cows and raising more than five acres of tobacco report the highest level of satisfaction with the decision to be a dairy farmer. This may be related to the fact that this group of dairy farmers (milking less than 55 cows and raising 5 acres or more of tobacco) also report the highest level of satisfaction with the financial performance of their dairy and the income they have available for family living. On the other hand, their counterparts who raise less than five acres of tobacco report the lowest level of satisfaction with the financial performance of their dairies and the income they have for family living. Overall, the low level of satisfaction with the financial aspects of their business that all the dairy farmers report does not bode well for the future of Kentucky's dairy industry.

SUMMARY AND CONCLUSIONS

Given the current debate over what will happen to the federal tobacco quota system, we might ask to what extent having a marketing quota encourages farmers to raise tobacco. The reality is that most farmland owners with a marketing quota lease out their entire quotas, and of those that do raise their own quota, the majority do not acquire by lease additional poundage. Having a tobacco marketing quota is not sufficient to 'encourage' dairy farmers to raise tobacco. Rather, there seems to be strong economic and family motivations attached to both the decision to raise tobacco and the decision of how much tobacco to raise. Indeed, an alternative question might be asked: If dairy farmers in other regions had the opportunity to raise a commodity – tobacco – that provided a guaranteed high return per acre raised, would they too make the choice to include tobacco in the mix of commodities on their farms?

Does the decision to raise large quantities of tobacco influence the dairy operation? Our analysis suggests that it does and in some very important ways. Firstly, raising no tobacco is associated with milking more cows and selling more milk. Secondly, raising no tobacco influences the use of best management practices. A higher proportion of dairies that raise no tobacco use a set of management practices (e.g. predip teats, regular visits by a veterinarian, participating in DHIA, and AI on at least 75% of their heifers). Interestingly, although there is a consensus by dairy farmers – large herds or small, much tobacco grown or little – on improving the productivity of their dairies, there is little preference for expanding herd size, regardless of current size. This, despite the fact that nearly all the dairy farmers surveyed attribute great importance to improving the performance of their dairy. Perhaps these results indicate that Kentucky's dairy farmers recognize that larger dairies would require diverting labor and management from tobacco production, which historically has provided the most reliable cash flow for the farm operation.

Dairies raising no tobacco place the least importance on family-related goals for their operations. On the other hand, the smaller dairies that raise less tobacco place the highest importance on keeping the farm in the family and maintaining a family tradition. On the other hand, small dairies growing larger acreages of tobacco are most likely to say that their financial situation has improved and will continue to improve, while their counterparts who raise less tobacco are most likely to say their financial situation has and will continue to stay about the same. Moreover, the smaller dairies raising more tobacco are also most likely to be satisfied with their decision to be a dairy farmer and the financial performance of their dairies. This suggests that for many of Kentucky's dairy farmers, investing in tobacco production provides a greater level of economic certainty than investing in their dairies.

While many have argued over the years that dairying and tobacco production are not compatible, it is clear that a substantial proportion of Kentucky dairy farmers do not agree with this assessment. Indeed, more Kentucky dairy farmers raise tobacco than not, and increasing the size of the dairy does not necessarily imply abandoning tobacco production. The emphasis on family traditions and the sense that economic security comes from a diversified operation may help explain the persistence of tobacco production on Kentucky's dairies.

NOTE

1. SIC dairy farms derive half or more of their total farm sales from the production of milk and other dairy products and the raising of dairy heifer replacements. SIC dairy farms can be considered primarily commercial dairies.

ACKNOWLEDGEMENTS

The research reported here was conducted as part of the regional project, NE–177 'Structural Changes in the Dairy Industry'. Appreciation is extended to the Agricultural Experiment Station, University of Kentucky for support of this research.

REFERENCES

Bokemeier, J., Allensworth, E., & Skidmore, A. (1995). *Decisions for the future: Dairy farming in Michigan*. Research Report 540. East Lansing, MI: Michigan Agricultural Experiment Station, Michigan State University.

Hallady, D. (1998). U.S. Dairy Statistics and Trends: 1997. *The Western Dairyman, 79*(5), Unnumbered special insert.

McIntosh, W. A., Bateman, R., & Cready, C. (1997). *Dairy farmer goals, production practices, and satisfaction with dairy farming: A five state comparison.* Paper presented at the 1997 Rural Sociological Society annual meetings.

National Agricultural Statistics Service (1999). *Statistical Highlights 1998–1999: Livestock.* Washington, D.C.: U.S. Department of Agriculture (http://www.usda.gov/nass/pubs/stathigh/1999/lv-mc-htm)

Snell, W., & Goetz, S. (1997). *Overview of Kentucky's Tobacco Economy.* Publication AEC–83. Lexington KY: College of Agriculture, Cooperative Extension Service, University of Kentucky.

VanWilligen, J., & Eastland, S. (1998). *Tobacco Culture: Farming in Kentucky's Burley Belt.* Lexington KY: University of Kentucky Press.

COMMUNITY ENGAGEMENT AND DAIRY FARM PERFORMANCE: A STUDY OF FARM OPERATORS IN UPSTATE NEW YORK

Thomas A. Lyson, Amy E. Guptill, and
Gilbert W. Gillespie Jr.

INTRODUCTION

Dairy farming throughout the United States, but especially in the traditional dairy states of the Northeast and Midwest, is undergoing a major structural transformation that began at least 50 years ago. In New York the number of dairy farms decreased from 60,715 in 1950 to 8,732 in 1997; most of those lost were family-labor dairies, typically milking fewer than 100 cows and operating with the labor of one family or of two related families. During this same period, average herd size increased from 24.1 cows per farm to 80.2. Over the past 20 years, large-scale dairy farms, those with 200 or more cows, is the only size category that is growing. In 1982, New York had 231 dairies of 200 or more cows, but now it has over 570. In short, small-scale, family-labor dairies are giving way to large-scale, industrial-like operations.

   The long-term decline in small, family-run dairy farms has led researchers to investigate the causes and trajectories of structural change. One line of inquiry shows how the structure of the milk market in a region affects the structure of farming in that area (see DuPuis, 1993; Lyson & Geisler, 1992; Lyson & Gillespie, 1995; Schwarzweller & Davidson, 1997.) DuPuis (1993), for

Research in Rural Sociology, Volume 8, pages 309–323.
2000 by Elsevier Science Inc.
ISBN: 0-7623-0474-X

example, found that dairy farms located in peri-urban fluid milksheds tend to be larger and more technologically sophisticated than are dairies located in milksheds that are smaller, more remote, and where most of the milk is used for producing cheese. In a similar vein, Lyson & Gillespie (1995) note ". . . the size structure of dairy production responds to the structure of milk markets." Simply put, small dairy processors tend to articulate with small dairy farms and, conversely, large processors tend to deal with large dairy farms.

These and most other explanations of changes in dairy farming are fundamentally economic, because they presuppose that the emerging structure of the dairy industry is shaped almost entirely by market forces. While a link between dairy farm structure and dairy product markets is both theoretically justified and empirically supported, a second, newly-emerging line of inquiry gives primacy to non-economic, community-based factors as engines of change in the dairy sector. Researchers pursuing this line of inquiry are identifying how the food system could be structured so that family-size dairies could not only survive, but prosper (Lyson & Gillespie, 1995; Lyson & Geisler, 1992; Schwarzweller & Davidson, 1997). In a study of retired dairy farmers in St. Lawrence County, New York, Harper & Lyson (1995) identified the potential for the dairy industry to redevelop with a new system of family-scale, economically-competitive farms. They provide an historical account of how dairy production has become rationalized along mass production lines with a concomitant decline of community-based labor exchanges. They note that "Earlier forms of production agriculture were embedded within a web of household and community relations. The U.S. may have reached the point where the pendulum of production may once again swing back to be embraced and nurtured by local culture" (Harper & Lyson, 1995: 212). Piore & Sabel (1984: 298) set forth the contours of a modern, community-centered system of production which entail ". . . sharing of skills, technical knowledge, information on opportunities and definitions of standards. Structure here shades into infrastructure, competition into cooperation, and economy into society."

The re-emerging line of sociological inquiry on civic engagement and civic community (Dionne, 1998; Tolbert et al., 1998) is important to inform thinking about community-centered systems of agricultural production because these are among the key structural foundations for a more community-based economy. Therefore, we draw upon scholarship focusing on community-based explanations of production performance to show how this relates to variables that tap engagement in community-related activities and events. Civic engagement exists in localities where there is ". . . widespread participation in civic affairs on the part of those able to benefit a community by voluntary management of civic enterprises" (Mills & Ulmer, 1946: 22). Civic community, then, implies a dense network of local institutions and organizations including schools, churches and voluntary organizations. The social structure of a civic community serves as a glue that anchors people to their locality (Barber, 1995; Irwin, Tolbert & Lyson, 1999). In a society in which 'bigger is better' is a widely-accepted precept of economics, and in which small- and medium-scale enterprises find it difficult to produce price-competitive products for the global marketplace, communities are challenged to mute the effects of unregulated competition and accumulation. New ways of sheltering workers, protecting local economies, and nurturing local development are needed if communities are to be considered good places to live and invest.

Drawing on earlier research (Goldschmidt, 1947; Mills & Ulmer, 1946), Tolbert, Lyson & Irwin (1999) introduce the term 'local capitalism' to refer to networks of small and medium size firms, including farms, that ". . . are often linked together . . . to form adaptive systems which continually reinforce and support local socioeconomic climates geared toward long-term vitality and enhanced welfare." The economic base of a civic community rests on a plethora of locally-controlled commercial enterprises that use local labor and local resources and that provide for local needs in culturally-acceptable ways.

Akin to the industrial districts described by Piore & Sabel (1984), agricultural (or dairy) districts would be a possible manifestation of local capitalism. In an agricultural district, farms and farmers would not be merely atomized economic units operating independently and rationally in a free market with core goals of increasing efficiency, decreasing costs, and increasing profits. Rather, farms and farmers would be part and parcel of (and embedded in) community social structures. Dairy farmers and others participating in the organization and institutional life of a local community would generate social cohesion which, in turn, would foster communication and collaboration across a community's seemingly divergent and competitive sectors.

A scenario of family-scale producers would not only be fundamental to a community's economic foundation, but would also be fundamental to its social fabric as well. Family-scale dairies would be able to compete successfully against large-scale dairies by sharing information, cooperating with one another, and remaining organizationally flexible for responding to market changes. Some might process the milk they produce into cheese, yogurt, or other products and some might market milk and other products directly to local citizens.

In this study we examine the organizational, institutional, and interpersonal linkages of a population of dairy farmers in upstate New York to assess the potential for the emergence of a new economy based on *local capitalism* to emerge. Given the lack of a large body of previous empirical research in this area, our study is exploratory. Our guiding hypothesis is that dairy farm performance and farm viability are directly related to a farm operator's level of involvement in local community affairs, his participation in organized agricultural events and activities, and the breadth and depth of his interpersonal networks. Taken together, dairy farmers' involvement and participation in different facets of community life results in a 'civic community' that could be a foundation for a system of local capitalism. The organizational and associational structure of a community can also be seen as a problem solving mechanism. Farmers who participate in local organizations and associations and regularly interact with members of their communities are likely to be exposed to a variety of viewpoints, perspectives, and strategies directly related to the operation and performance of the dairy sector in general and their dairy farms in particular.

RESEARCH METHODS

This study is part of a larger, multi-state research project that was designed to explore organizational and structural changes in the dairy industry and the effects of these changes on communities. In New York, dairy farm operators in four upstate localities were surveyed in the spring of 1997. The localities were selected, in consultation with animal scientists at Cornell University who are familiar with dairy farming in New York, to represent key characteristics that differentiate dairy farm localities in the state. Each of the four localities was coterminous with a 'service area' of the major artificial insemination (AI) service in New York. These service areas ranged in size from including only two or three towns to as many as seven or eight towns. The AI service representatives distributed the survey questionnaires to their clients and later picked up the completed ones. Each farmer was offered a coupon for two 'free' inseminations for his cows for completing the survey and returning it to the representative.

Overall, 325 questionnaires were distributed and 162 completed questionnaires were returned for a response rate of 49.8%. After eliminating cases with missing data on the outcome variables, we were left with 139 cases or 43% of the total. Using AI service representatives to distribute the questionnaires allowed us to survey a diverse set of localities. Unfortunately, this strategy did not allow us to implement any follow-up procedures to increase response rates, such as sending reminder postcards or delivering a second questionnaire.

The characteristics of each of the four areas are summarized in Table 1. Southwestern New York, specifically Chautauqua and Cattaraugus counties, is a marginal farming area. Dairy farming is the primary agricultural enterprise in this region and dairy farms tend to be relatively small-scale, family-labor operations. With growing numbers of farmers leaving dairying, the future economic viability of dairying in this area is unclear. Similar to Southwestern New York in many characteristics, the Mohawk Valley Region is located between Albany and Syracuse. Dairy farms here are smaller than the state average. Although this area is located closer to major urban markets than is Southwestern New York, poor soils and rough terrain inhibit farm consolidation and, therefore, have contributed to declines in dairying there in recent decades. The 'North Country' is located along the St. Lawrence river valley that borders

Table 1. New York Dairy Study Locations

Regions and counties (no. of respondents in parentheses)	1997 Average Herd Size*	1996 Herd Average**	Description
Southwestern NY			Marginal dairy area, many
Cattaraugus(2)	62.9	16,600	communities in these counties
Chautauqua(27)	72.0	16,400	are isolated, weak dairy infrastructure
Mohawk Valley			Marginal dairying area, poorer
Oneida(9)	69.0	16,200	soils, major downsizing in the
Herkimer(12)	70.2	16,200	dairy sector has been occuring
Montgomery(22)	72.7	16,100	since the early 1980's
North Country			Dairy is the only viable
St. Lawrence(26)	69.5	15,400	agricultural enterprise in the region, several large-scale, industrial-type dairies located here in the 1990's
Lake Ontario			Best dairy area in NY, good
Wyoming(28)	156.7	17,800	soils, highest herd averages and
Genessee(3)	176.9	17,700	largest herd sizes, many
Erie(10)	98.2	17,000	industrial-type dairies are being established

* 1997 U.S. Census of Agriculture (NASS, 1999). Averages are for counties, not respondent farms.
** New York Agricultural Statistics, 1996. Averages are for counties, not respondent farms.

Canada. Because of harsh winters and a relatively short growing season, dairy farming has been one of the few economically viable agricultural enterprises in the region. Over the last 30 years, however, the number of dairy farms in this area has dropped precipitously. The main counter trend during the 1990s has been the emergence of several very large operations of 500 or more cows.

In contrast to the other three dairy areas, the Lake Ontario region has good soils and a solid dairy infrastructure, along with the conditions that enable expanding dairy enterprises to absorb small dairy farms to create larger units. These conditions, not found elsewhere in the state, are reflected in the larger and generally more prosperous dairy operations that characterize this region.

In the multivariate analyses that follow, we tested for locality-specific differences. In general, we found that locality was not related to performance or future plans net of a set of control variables. Consequently, we have chosen to only report findings for the pooled data.

Measuring Community Engagement

Dairy farmers and dairy farm households participate in the civic life of their communities in many different ways. We operationalized community engagement as several measures, including the farm operator's: (1) *organizational involvement* in the local community; (2) *attendance at local agricultural events*; and (3) *breadth of participation* in the network of local dairy farmers and service providers. Descriptive information about these scales is provided in Table 2. Our guiding hypothesis is that a dairy farmer's level of civic engagement is associated with the viability of the dairy farm business.

Organizational involvement was scored '1' if the farm operator regularly attended meetings or participated in any *one* of the following kinds of organizations or groups: (1) civic organizations (e.g. Rotary, Kiwanis, VFW); (2) farm organizations (e.g. Farm Bureau, Grange); (3) athletic/recreational groups (e.g. bowling leagues, softball); (4) educational school groups (e.g. PTA, band boosters); (5) community government (e.g. village, town, county boards); (6) church groups (e.g. choir, church board); and 7) any other type of community group or association not listed above. If the operator reported attending or participating in *two or more* categories, this variable was scored '2'. A score of '0' was assigned to farmers who indicated *no* participation in the any of the organizations.

Farm operator's attendance at agricultural events is a scale constructed from responses to the following question: "During 1996 how many times did you attend a meeting, field day or demonstration which was sponsored by each of the following groups?" The groups were: (1) Cooperative Extension; (2) farm supply companies or cooperatives; and (3) other government agencies (e.g. FmHA). For each of the three groups, farmer's were scored '1' if they attended at least one event sponsored by the groups during the year and '0' if they did not attend an event. The scores for the three categories were summed to form a scale with scores ranging from 0 to 3. Cronbach's alpha, which is the average interitem correlation of the items in the scale for the scale, is 0.586.

Third, the farm operator's breadth of participation in agricultural networks was measured by summated responses to the following question: "In an average week, how many times do you talk either by telephone or on a face-to-face basis about farming with each of the following types of people?" The people listed included: (1) other farmers living in the community; (2) other farmers living outside the community; (3) extension personnel in your

Table 2. Three Measures of Community Engagement: (1) OrganizaTional Involvement; (2) Attendance at Local Agricultural Events; (3) Breadth of Agricultural Networks and their Contributions to a Composite Community Engagement Scale (Factor Loadings).

Organizational Involvement	% of farmers who regularly attend
Civic organizations	7.7
Farm organizations	33.4
Athletic/recreation groups	16.9
School groups	11.5
Community government	19.2
Church groups	22.3
Other groups	15.4
Community engagement scale factor loading	(0.739)
Attendance at local agricultural events	% of farmers attending at least one event
Cooperative extension	61.5
Farm supply companies/cooperatives	84.6
Other government agencies	25.4
Community engagement scale factor loading	(0.790)
Breadth of participation in agricultural networks	% of farmers who speak at least once a week to:
Other farmers in community	84.6
Other farmers outside community	49.2
Extension personnel in community	20.8
Farm service/supply personnel	94.6
Agricultural professionals	84.6
Community engagement scale factor loading	(0.843)

community; (4) farm service or supply dealers, salesmen, buyers; and (5) professionals such as veterinarians, management consultants, bankers. Responses ranged from 'almost never' (scored '1') to '15 or more times' (scored '5') for each category. Because a simple additive scale of these items was highly skewed, the items were recoded to be dichotomous with a '0' assigned to farmers who almost never had contact during contact with the type of people and '1' assigned to farmers who spoke with these types of individuals at least once in an average week. These items were summed yielding scores ranging from 0 to 5. The Cronbach's alpha for the scale was 0.578.

Finally, although the concept of community engagement has many different dimensions comprising the numerous and diverse ways in which farmers could be integrated into their local communities, we used principal component analysis to construct a composite of the three measures noted above so as to approximate a comprehensive scale of orientation to community life. The community engagement scale then is a factor index (loadings are reported in Table 2) of organizational involvement, attendance at local agricultural events, and breadth of participation (eigenvalue = 1.882; percentage of variance = 62.7).

Table 3 reports descriptive statistics for, and correlations among, the variables in the analysis. On average in 1996, each farm operator in the study participated in one community organization and one or more events sponsored by either Cooperative Extension, a farm supply company or cooperative, or a government agency. And, in an average week, farmers spoke about farming issues to three other persons, including farmers, county agents, educators, or agribusiness representatives.

The intercorrelations among the four measures of community engagement range from $r = 0.348$ for organizational involvement and attendance at agricultural events to $r = 0.522$ for farm operators' attendance at agricultural events and his/her breadth of participation in agricultural networks. The three measures of community engagement overlap to a degree, but they are not isomorphic and this suggests that we are tapping different ways in which farmers and their households connect to their local communities. Some farm operators are involved in numerous and varied aspects of their communities, representing both agricultural and non-agricultural activities, while others are tied narrowly to particular aspects.

Dairy Farm Performance

The future performance and viability of smaller scale, family-size dairy farming in a particular area depends on many factors. All other things being

Table 3. Correlations and Descriptive Statistics.

Variables	1	2	3	4	5	6	7	8	9	10	Mean (SD)
1. Organizational involvement	—										1.00 (0.842)
2. Attendance at agricultural events	0.348**	—									1.72 (0.933)
3. Breadth of participation	0.447**	0.522**	—								3.36 (1.15)
4. Herd average	0.316**	0.347**	0.222*	—							16,594 (3673)
5. Gross farm sales	0.417**	0.368**	0.427**	0.561**	—						5.22 (2.23)
6. Plan to expand	0.261**	0.323**	0.366**	0.245**	0.341**	—					7.20 (2.44)
7. Plan to contract	-0.255**	-0.219**	-0.304**	-0.196*	-0.312**	-0.538**	—				4.79 (1.99)
8. Herd size	0.353**	0.234**	0.344**	0.354**	0.791**	0.364**	-0.249**	—			92.53 (91.55)
9. Operator's educational level	0.165^{ns}	0.027^{ns}	0.088^{ns}	0.155^{ns}	0.225**	0.113ns	0.012^{ns}	0.279**	—		3.76 (1.30)
10. Operator's years of management	-0.089^{ns}	-0.061^{ns}	-0.140^{ns}	0.167*	0.094^{ns}	-0.162^{ns}	0.120^{ns}	0.021^{ns}	-0.204*	—	20.72 (11.54)
11. Level of technology	0.346**	0.425**	0.394**	0.505**	0.689**	0.520**	-0.319**	0.574**	0.275**	-0.050^{ns}	5.62 (2.26)

* $p < 0.05$, ** $p < 0.01$, ns = not significant

equal, localities with highly productive, efficient, and forward-looking farms have a better chance of withstanding the threat posed by large-scale, industrial operations. We measure performance two ways. First, we use the rolling *herd average* of pounds of milk produced on the farm. This is the average amount of milk per cow produced over a period of one year and is a typical measure of farm productivity (see Cruise and Lyson, 1991). Second, we use *gross farm sales* as a measure of the financial strength of the dairy. All other things being equal, including herd size, farms with higher sales have the potential to generate more net income than farms with lower gross receipts.

The viability of dairy farming is also related to the ability of farm businesses to adapt to increasingly competitive operating conditions. In a competitive environment, farmers that seek out practical opportunities to expand and modernize will have the best opportunities for success. To tap the orientations of dairy farmers in this study, we constructed two additive scales related to the goals and plans of the farm operator. Farmers were asked: "As you look ahead to the next three to five years, what changes do you see in your dairy farm? (1) add more cows; (2) add or expand into other enterprises; (3) make major improvements; (4) reduce the number of cows; (5) disperse the herd; (6) close down completely." Response categories for each of these items ranged from 'very unlikely' (scored '1') to 'very likely' (scored '4'). When summed, items 1, 2 and 3 differentiated farmers who planned to expand from those who did not (Cronbach's alpha = 0.744). Inversely, items 4, 5 and 6 separated farmers who planned to contract from the others (surprisingly with a nearly identical Cronbach's alpha = 0.743).

Control Variables

For dairy farmers' community engagement to be considered an important correlate of dairy farm performance and viability, it must manifest an independent statistical effect over and above those farm structure character-istics and farm operator characteristics that previous research has shown to be related to gross farm sales, herd average, and operator's future plans. In this research we draw on the findings presented in Cruise & Lyson (1991), DuPuis (1994), Schwarzweller & Davidson(1997), and elsewhere and control on *herd size* (number of cows currently milking), *operator's education* (measured on a metric ranging from 1 – 'less than a high school diploma' to 7 – 'post graduate degree'), *operator's years of management* experience (number of years managing current dairy farm) and *level of technology* (summated scale, Cronbach's alpha = .728).[1]

Operator's educational level and operator's years of management are indicators of farmers' human capital that we expect should relate directly with dairy farm performance indicators. Similarly, herd size and level of technology are farm-level factors that should also correlate directly with performance. Both of these farm-level factors are, of course, results of the management decisions of individual operators. However, they also represent characteristics of a farm operation and, as such, should manifest effects over and above the farmers' human capital.

The zero-order correlations between the four dependent variables (herd average, gross farm sales, plan to expand, and plan to contract) and the three measures of community engagement range from $r = -0.255$ to $r = 0.427$. All relationships are in the expected direction and all statistically significant at the $p < 0.01$ level. Among the control variables, both level of technology and herd size are positively related to each of the community engagement variables at the $p < 0.01$ level. However, operator's educational level and operator's years of management are either weakly related or not associated with the community engagement variables.

RESULTS

Table 4 presents the partial correlation coefficients for relationships of each of the three measures of community engagement with the two indicants of dairy farm performance and with the two measures of future plans. These coefficients indicate the net effect of the community engagement variables on the outcome measures, after accounting for the effects of the control variables. In this

Table 4. Partial Correlation Coefficients: Community Engagement Variables Associated with Dairy Farm Performance and Future Plans (Controlling on Herd Size, Operators' Education, Operator's Years of Management, and Level of Technology).

Community engagement variables	(1) Herd Average	(2) Gross Farm Sales	(3) Plan to Expand	(4) Plan to contract
Organizational involvement	0.184^{**}	0.198^{**}	0.073^{ns}	-0.147^{*}
Attendance at agricultural events	0.198^{**}	0.175^{**}	0.114^{ns}	-0.069^{ns}
Breadth of participation	0.053^{ns}	0.205^{**}	0.168^{*}	-0.170^{**}

* $p < 0.10$, ** $p < 0.05$, ns = not significant

analysis, operator's education, operator's years of management, herd size, and level of technology are held constant. With the exception of breadth of participation in agricultural networks, all of the community engagement variables are positively and significantly related to both herd average and gross farm sales. On the other hand, only breadth of participation is significantly and positively related to plans to expand the dairy operation, while organizational involvement and breadth of participation are negatively associated with plans to reduce or abandon the dairy operation, net of the control variables. Overall, these results show clearly that community engagement is important in understanding the performance and operational strategies of dairy farmers in New York.

To explore more fully how the level of community engagement is related to dairy farming in New York, we regressed a composite measure of community engagement and four other variables on two measures of dairy farm performance and two indicants of future plans (Table 5). In the herd average equation (column 1) and in the two future plans equations (columns 3 and 4), level of technology is the most important predictor. The coefficient in the plan to expand equation is positive and that in the plan to contract equation is

Table 5. Regression Analysis: Effect of Community Engagement on Dairy Farm Performance and Dairy Farm Plans (Unstandardized Coefficients in Parentheses).

	(1) Herd average	(2) Gross farm sales	(3) Plan to expand	(4) Plan to contract
Community engagement (composite scale)	0.187**	0.161**	0.158*	−0.189*
	(688.2)	(0.359)	(0.386)	(−0.375)
Herd size	0.038^{ns}	0.555***	0.094^{ns}	−0.101^{ns}
	(1.51)	(0.001)	(0.000)	(−0.000)
Operator's educational level	0.067^{ns}	−0.003^{ns}	−0.066^{ns}	0.136^{ns}
	(188.6)	(−0.000)	(−0.124)	(0.208)
Operator's years of management	0.222**	0.117**	−0.138*	0.117^{ns}
	(70.52)	(0.002)	(−0.003)	(0.002)
Level of technology (scale)	0.384***	0.298***	0.400**	−0.200*
	(623.0)	(0.293)	(0.419)	(−0.175)
Constant	(10778.3)***	(1.87)***	(5.62)***	(4.78)***
Adjusted R^2	0.298	0.726	0.295	0.167
F	12.71***	74.26***	12.56***	5.31***

* $p < 0.10$, ** $p < 0.05$, *** $p < 0.01$, ns = not siginificant

negative, suggesting that farmers who are more up-to-date on technology tend to see a more favorable future for themselves in dairying. In the gross farm sales equation (column 2) level of technology is also an important predictor, but as might be expected, herd size is a stronger predictor of gross farm sales. More importantly for our purposes, in equations 1 through 3, *community engagement* is positively associated and statistically significant, whereas in equation 4 it is negatively associated and statistically significant. This finding supports our guiding hypothesis that involvement in community affairs is one key element in a viable system of dairy farming.

CONCLUSIONS

This research was designed to advance a small, but growing body of theory and research on the effects of community engagement on different social and economic outcomes across a broad range of socio-economic settings. Building on the theoretical insights of Piore & Sabel (1984) and Mills & Ulmer (1946) and earlier empirical work by DuPuis (1993), Lyson & Geisler (1992), Schwarzweller & Davidson (1997) and others, we examined the relationships among different indicators of farm operators' community engagement (including involvement in non-agriculturally-related organizations, involvement in local agricultural activities, and interpersonal networks), and two measures of dairy farm performance and two measures of future plans. Our results provide consistent empirical support for relationships between farmers' and farm households' integration into the social and economic fabric of their community and their dairy farm performance and forward-looking plans.

While we believe that the social cohesion and trust that are developed through participation in community level activities affect both dairy performance and future plans, we also realize that more successful farmers have both a vested interest in maintaining community viability and have a certain validation of their worth as community participants in their farming success. Thus, as we noted in the introduction, farmers are 'part and parcel' of a community. Successful farmers are key parts of the economic bulwark of the community and through their interactions with others in the agribusiness sector, form an adaptive system which reinforces and supports the drive to maintain the long-term viability of agriculture and, in so doing, enhance socio-economic welfare.

Can a system of family-scale dairy producers sustain itself against the onslaught of large-scale, industrial-type producers? In the short-run, at least, technological advances that favor larger dairies and changes in the market for fluid milk that favor the lowest-cost producers will likely further erode the already waning system of family-scale operations. However, we believe that in many localities throughout the Northeast and Lake States, the interpersonal and organizational networks of community engagement and civic community are strong enough to provide a viable alternative to the complete industrialization of dairy production that seems to have occurred throughout the West and Southwest (Lyson & Geisler, 1992). An agenda to support and strengthen a family-scale system of dairying must be based on an understanding of the community dynamics that undergird the models of production identified by Mills & Ulmer (1946), Piore & Sabel (1984), Lyson & Geisler (1992), and Schwarzweller & Davidson (1997). A community-focused system of production provides an alternative to the dominant, market-driven, industrial model that is being offered as the future of agriculture by most land-grant scientists and agribusiness spokespersons.

ACKNOWLEDGMENTS

We are particularly grateful to Charles C. Elrod of the Dairy Initiative at Cornell University for collaborating with us on the project, to Christy A. Gagliano and Lori L. Tyler for data entry and other assistance, to the dairy farmers for completing the questionnaires, and to the AI technicians for distributing and collecting the questionnaires. We acknowledge the comments of Harry Schwarzweller and Andrew Davidson. Funding and support for the project were provided by the Cornell University Agricultural Experiment Station and by the Cornell College of Agriculture and Life Sciences and its partners in the New York Dairy Industry Initiative, especially Genex Corporation. This paper contributes to USDA/SCREES Regional Research Projects NE–177 and NC–208.

NOTE

1. *Level of technology* is a summated scale of responses to the following multiple-response question: "Which of the following practices or technologies do you currently use on your dairy farm?" (1) predip all teats before milking; (2) postdip all teats after milking; (3) use regularly scheduled veterinary services; (4) balance feed rations at least four times a year; (5) use a total mix ration; (6) use artificial insemination on at least 75% of heifers; (7) use freestall housing for milking herd; (8) keep farm records on a computer that you own; (9) use the Internet to get information for the farm; and (10) keep farm production records. For a discussion of a similar scale see Cruise & Lyson (1991).

REFERENCES

Barber, B. (1995). *Jihad vs. McWorld*. New York: Times Books.

Cruise, J., & Lyson, T. A. (1991). Beyond the Farmgate: Factors Related to Agricultural Performance in Two Dairy Communities. *Rural Sociology, 56*, 41–55.

Dionne, E. J. (1998). *Community Works: The Revival of Civil Society in America*. Washington, D.C.: Brookings Institution Press.

DuPuis, E. M. (1993). Subnational State Institutions and the Organization of Agricultural Resource Use: the Case of the Dairy Industry. *Rural Sociology, 58*, 440–60.

Goldschmidt, W. (1947). *As You Sow*. Glencoe, IL: The Free Press.

Harper, D., & Lyson, T. A. (1995). Labor Exchange among Dairy Farmers: Lessons from the past for a More Sustainable Future. *Research in Rural Sociology and Development: Sustainable Agriculture and Rural Communities, 6*, 193–214.

Irwin, M., Tolbert, C., & Lyson, T. (1999). Non-migration and Civic Engagement: How Churches, Associations, and Small Scale Economic Organizations Anchor People to Metropolitan and Nonmetropolitan Places. *Environment and Planning-A, 31*, 2223–2238.

Lyson, T. A., & Gillespie, G. W. Jr. (1995). Producing More Milk on Fewer Farms: Neoclassical and Neostructural Explanations for Changes in the Dairy Industry. *Rural Sociology, 60*, 493–504.

Lyson, T. A., & Geisler, C. C. (1992). Toward a Second Agricultural Divide: the Restructuring of American Agriculture. *Sociologia Ruralis, 32*, 248–263.

Mills, C. W., & Ulmer, M. J. (1946). *Small Business and Civic Welfare*. Report of the Smaller War Plants Corporation to the Special Committee to Study Problems of American Small Business. U.S. Senate, 79th Congress, 2nd Session, Document No. 135. Washington, DC: U.S. Government Printing Office.

National Agricultural Statistics Service (1999). *1997 Census of Agriculture, Vol 1, Geographic Area Series*. Washington, DC: U.S. Government Printing Office.

New York Agricultural Statistics (1996). Albany, NY: New York Crop Reporting Service.

Piore, M. J., & Sabel, C. F. (1984). *The Second Industrial Divide*. New York: Basic Books.

Schwarzweller, H. K., & Davidson, A. P. (1997). Perspectives on Regional and Enterprise Marginality: Dairying in Michigan's North Country *Rural Sociology, 62*, 137–179.

Tolbert, C. M., Lyson, T. A., & Irwin, M. (1998). Local Capitalism, Civic Engagement, and Socioeconomic Well-being. *Social Forces, 77*, 401–28.

REMODELING A DAIRY PRODUCER COOPERATIVE

Jerker Nilsson and Martina Bärnheim

INTRODUCTION

The Swedish dairy industry is struggling to adjust to disruptive changes in the political economy of agriculture. In 1990 the government abolished its long-standing protective support of agriculture, but this process of liberalization was interrupted after a couple of years as Sweden applied for membership in the European Community. In 1995, with very little educational and organizational preparation that might have eased the transition, the nation and its agricultural sector were joined into the Community, then labeled the European Union.

Completely dominated by a few cooperatives, the Swedish dairy industry experienced problems of unsatisfactory competitiveness in relation to producers in other EU member states. Consequently, the cooperatives are now seeking more effective ways to serve their members. In this chapter we focus on one small dairy cooperative that is trying to invent a new organizational form that would better fit with the demands of the new market conditions.

To set the stage for presenting the rationale of a new organizational model for this dairy cooperative we begin by considering some of the challenges that must be dealt with and some of the choices available to the largest dairy producer cooperatives. After a brief over-view of the Swedish dairy industry, we explore the situation facing the small dairy producer cooperative, and what its alternatives are for gaining market strength. This cooperative's current economic problems follow from the fact that it is presently organized in accord with an organizational model that is more suitable for conditions prevailing

Research in Rural Sociology, Volume 8, pages 325–353.
2000 by Elsevier Science Inc.
ISBN: 0-7623-0474-X

under the former national agricultural policy. Hence, we will scrutinize this model as well as others considered by the cooperative.

The particular cooperative in question has settled on a new model, the core of which is the introduction of a type of shares that cooperative members are invited to buy voluntarily and which thereby gives them the right to profit from the cooperative's value-added operations. These shares are intended to be freely tradable within the membership at a market price whereby the members get an incentive for long-term participation. At the same time all members are permitted to sell as much milk as they want to the cooperative, but for these volumes the price paid is only the true market price, i.e. the intervention price paid by the European Commission.

It is an innovative model. Nothing like this has been tried by any other cooperative. Thus, we are especially interested because this model could be adapted advantageously by other cooperatives in similar situations, particularly in the dairy industry.

MARKET CHALLENGES

Strategies of Large Dairy Cooperatives in Europe

Due to the ongoing internationalization of the dairy industry, competitive pressure is increasing. Multinational corporations are moving into the lucrative markets for value-added products. Many European dairy producer cooperatives, notably the largest ones, are challenging the multinational conglomerates on the most profitable market segments. For this to succeed, the cooperatives are forced to seek radically new routes. Hence, the cooperatives are striving for extended capital, low cost operations and stronger market positions. (Van Bekkum & van Dijk, 1997; Zwanenberg, 1997).

Meeting the competition requires large investments in research and development as well as in branding, advertising and other marketing efforts. The subsequent growing need for capital has caused some of the large dairy cooperatives to seek new financial solutions. All Dutch dairy cooperatives have recently introduced a variety of financial instruments which mean increased individual ownership through more allocated capital, and hence, also stronger member involvement. At the end of the 1980s, four Irish dairy cooperatives became Public Limited Companies listed on the Dublin stock exchange, though with the dairy farmers as majority owners (on two occasions the farmer ownership later fell below 50%). MD Foods put all its foreign operations in a subsidiary, owned jointly with a number of Danish banks, insurance companies and pension funds (in 1998, however, it again turned into a fully-owned subsidiary).

In their attempts to reap economies of scale, some dairy cooperatives have expanded internationally by purchasing dairies. By acquiring several local dairies, Danish MD Foods is now the second largest milk supplier in the U.K. with a 19% market share. In 1991, Campina-Melkunie of the Netherlands became the largest player in the Belgian dairy market after buying Comelco, and then continued to buy Südmilch (1993) and half of Tuffi (1997), both in Germany. The Irish dairy cooperatives Golden Vale and Glanbia run operations in the U.K., whereby they purchase milk from British farmers. (The British, Belgian and German dairy farmers are solely suppliers to the dairy cooperatives, not members.) Several dairy cooperatives (Danish, Swedish, Finnish, Dutch, etc.) have subsidiaries with production plants in the former communist countries.

The recent years have witnessed some remarkable amalgamations between already large cooperatives. In 1995, most of the Austrian dairy cooperatives merged into two large cooperatives – Bergland Milch and NÖM. Avonmore and Waterford, both Irish PLC cooperatives, merged in 1997, adopting the name Glanbia. In the same year, Coberco merged with another large Dutch dairy cooperative, Friesland Frico Domo, as well as with two smaller ones. In 1999 there were rumours about ongoing merger negotiations between Friesland Coberco and Campina-Melkunie – the result would be that nine-tenth of the Dutch milk production is processed within one cooperative.

A similar dominating position is attained in Denmark, after MD Foods and KløverMælk in 1999 agreed upon a merger. The two German cooperatives Westmilch Milchunion and Milchwerke Westfalen merged in 1998, to form the then largest dairy group in Germany, called Humana Milchunion with a total of 7,200 members. In late 1998, four other German dairy cooperatives, viz. MZO Oldenburger Botterbloo, Nordmilch, Bremerland Nordheide Molkerei and Hansano Milchhof decided to merge, thereby creating the fourth largest dairy processing firm in Europe.

This chase for a larger financial basis, lower cost operations and stronger positions on the international markets directly effects the farmer-members. Being a member of and supplier to a strong cooperative, the farmer's position is strengthened, thus enhancing his economic survival chances. He is still exposed to troublesome price squeezes and market fluctuations, but not to the same extent as the members of weaker dairy cooperatives or those that are serving investor-owned dairies. This is a general trend, though there are many exceptions may.

A Small Cooperative Searches for a New Strategy

What can the members, board, and management of small dairy cooperatives do, with insufficient resources for expansion, and being less attractive as merger partners? A small Swedish dairy cooperative, Skånemejerier, has been struggling to solve its problems of low and decreasing profitability and weak market power. A new organizational model is being proposed with the aim of adapting to market conditions insofar as possible, in order to avoid the market distorting price signals normally found in traditionally organized cooperatives.

The aim is to explore the Skånemejerier situation and the organizational changes that are being planned. The Skånemejerier re-modeling would introduce a type of shares that will be tradable among the membership, i.e. a market for shares is established. To the extent that a farmer-member owns such shares, he be entitled to profits from the value-added activities of the cooperative. Without shares, a farmer will receive only the EU intervention price for his milk (which is the correct market price). This organizational model is expected to change the incentives of members so that they are more in line with the demands put of competitive markets.

In May 1997, the board of directors of Skånemejerier established a working group to determine how the profitability of the cooperative could be enhanced. Perhaps its pricing policy needed to be revised or its organizational structure modified, or some other things had to be done. It was clear that the existing structure and practices of Skånemejerier would not help them gain strength in the competitive markets. The working group consisted of two board members, one rank-and-file member and two executives. Two models to solve the cooperative's problems were developed. As far as is known, neither of them have ever been applied previously by any other dairy cooperative, nor by any other agricultural cooperative.

The first model involves the introduction of multiple-pricing within the existing organizational framework. This was rejected, however, as being too rigid. The second, more radical model implies that members must buy shares to acquire the right to the cooperative's profits; it was presented in the working group's report to the board in April 1998, and gained the board's unanimous acceptance.

Since then, the restructuring plan has been discussed by members at numerous local meetings. Having a tradition for genuine member democratic governance, everyone involved is eager that an eventual solution should be thoroughly understood and debated by the members. At a meeting in March 1999, the board decided upon a cardinal plan; the model shall be implemented and in operation by January 1st, 2001. In the meantime further details will be investigated as well as uncertain effects will be further analysed.

As far as can be judged at this point (July 1999), the proposed model promises to be instrumental in helping the cooperative and its members to design a profile and marketing strategy that is different from its main competitors. Specialty products for selected niche markets will be emphasized.

The next section presents the structure of the dairy industry in Sweden and how some remarkable political decisions have radically changed the conditions for this industry. An understanding of this is necessary to grasp the subsequent analysis of Skånemejerier's current competitive position, its deliberations as to market strategies and its willingness to find ways for adapting to the new business environment.

THE SWEDISH DAIRY INDUSTRY

Context of Dramatic Change

Sweden joined the European Union on January 1st, 1995. Though it had a long history of protective agricultural policies, no transition rules and no temporary economic supports were granted to agriculture, nor even applied for. Finland and Austria, on the other hand, upon joining the European Union were permitted to provide some transitional adjustments for their agricultural sector. The rationale for treating Sweden differently was that the government considered its agriculture already to be competitive in the European markets because the national protective support to agriculture had been abandoned in 1990.

The dissolution of the old agricultural policy was to have taken place over a five-year period, but when the government submitted its application for membership in the European Union, the process of deregulation was brought to a halt. Hence, only a minor part of the agricultural policy had actually been abolished and farmers and the processing industries had only taken few and small adaptive measures to adjust to a non-regulated business environment. Agricultural production costs were still higher than in competing countries because Sweden still had too many and too small farms, many in remote locations, and machinery was very expensive. Swedish farmers had never been exposed to tough competition in any markets, and hence, most of them were slow to adapt and not open to new ideas (Nilsson, 1997b).

Today, imported food products have a strong foothold on the markets. Prices have fallen drastically for all agricultural products, and the price cuts came quickly and mercilessly. Because the Swedish farmers' production costs were basically adapted to a generous national agricultural policy, the sudden and large price reductions caused grave financial problems. Most seriously hit were the dairy, pork, beef and egg industries, while grain producers have managed better.

Since 1995, great changes have taken place in Swedish agriculture. The number of farmers is nearly half of what it used to be, and those who have survived are more prone to try new ideas, such as new crops, new technologies and new animal breeds. In the processing industry a number of mergers have occurred. Cooperatives have strengthened their efforts to develop new products, and their pricing policies have undergone considerable changes, with the purpose of attaining better coordination in the processing chain.

In spite of these changes, Swedish agriculture has a long way to go until it is internationally competitive. Production costs are still much higher than in competing countries. The former agricultural policy was so generous that farmers could count upon a stable income, and many of the structural conditions of those days are still present:

- Still today, large farmer groups have greater hope for protection-seeking politics than for efficiency-raising and market-orienting measures.
- In the old days, farming in marginal areas and remote regions was economically feasible while today, this agriculture is inefficient.
- Extreme legislation in relation to animal welfare, ecology and other production conditions was introduced (i.e. extreme in comparison with other nations). This constitutes a competitive disadvantage as Swedish agriculture has very high production costs.

Restructuring of the Dairy industry

The food, drink and tobacco manufacturing industries account for 10% of the gross national product, as compared to 26% in the Netherlands. The formerly protected parts of the food industry, such as slaughter-houses, pork-butchers, and dairying, account for 5% of the industrial turnover. These industries have traditionally been socio-economically important as supplying the domestic market for food. Only a few percent of the products were exported.

Although the agricultural sector plays a minor role in the Swedish gross national product (2.2%) milk production is of vital importance for rural development. Milk production accounts for one-third of Swedish agriculture. Especially for full-time farmers, dairy farming is essential; more than half of these farmers are milk producers. A large part of the countryside is dependent

Table 1. Swedish dairy Farms, 1990–1998 (Source: Svensk Mjölk)

	1990	1998	Percentage change
Total cows (number)	576,000	450,000	−22
Milk production (metric tons)	4,130,000	3,278,000	−20
Dairy farms (number)	25,000	13,800	−45
Cows per farm (average)	23.0	29.6	+29
Herd average (kilograms/cow)	7,174	8,103	+13

on milk production; for example, in the north, 84% of the full-time farmers are milk producers.

In 1998 there were 450,000 milk cows. Since 1990 the number of cows has decreased by 22% while the number of dairy farms decreased by 45% (Table 1). The average herd is 29 cows, compared to 51 and 41, respectively, in Denmark and the Netherlands. The average yield per cow is 8,000 kilograms per year, which brings Sweden to the top in Europe together with the Netherlands and Denmark.

Milk production, i.e. the quota which is the maximum volume of milk that EU permits the country to produce, is 3,300 million kilograms, compared to 4,500 in Denmark, 11,000 in the Netherlands and 23,700 in France. In 1996 the average milk price was SEK 292 per 100 kg which is higher than in any competing country (SEK 100 = EUR 11 or USD 13). Still, it is not enough to cover the production costs of Swedish farmers.

When the European milk quota system was introduced in 1984, the member states were free to implement the policy at their own discretion. So, regulations differ a lot. The Netherlands, for example, has a liberal policy concerning the quota scheme, which has resulted in the development of quota markets for both purchasing and leasing. When Sweden became a member of the Union, a scheme to avoid capitalization of the milk quota was designed. Hence, Sweden applies strict regulations regarding the transfer of production quotas with some regional constraints, even though this hampers structural improvements. A Swedish farmer who wants to extend (or shrink) his milk production may buy more quota only from (or sell quota to) the Swedish Board of Agriculture (a governmental agency), and the price is not a market price but administratively set.

Almost all milk is processed by dairy cooperatives. Investor-owned dairies are few and insignificant. The total number of dairy processors is 16, eight of whom process 99.7% of the total milk production (Table 2). These eight

Table 2.   Swedish Dairy Cooperatives in 1997

Cooperative	Milk volume, metric tons	Milk volume, SEK million[1]
Arla	2,112	13,298
Skånemejerier	419	2,591
Nedre Norrlands Producentförening	179	1,961
Norrmejerier	190	1,342
Milko mejerier	240	1,378
Falköpings mejeri	67	280
Gefleortens mejeriförening	43	245
Gäsene mejeriförening	16	53
Total	3,2662	21,148

(Source: Svensk Mjölk)
[1] SEK 100 = EUR 11 or USD 13

cooperatives have 50 plants. In 1985 and 1990 the number of processing firms were 28 and 20 with 99 and 71 plants, respectively.

More than 43% of the milk is processed into fresh products: liquid milk, fermented milk in the form of yoghurt and other sour milk products, butter and spread, and cream (Table 3). The consumption of liquid and fermented milk per capita is 154 kg, which is the third largest in the European Union next to Finland and Ireland.

Sweden's entry into the European Union in 1995 dramatically changed the operational conditions for the dairy industry. Previous agricultural policy had

Table 3.   Milk Products as Percentage of Total Milk Processed in 1992 and 1997

Products	1992	1997
Fluid milk, sour milk, butter, spread, and cream	45	43
Skimmed milk	1	1
Cheese (semi-hard)	34	34
Milk powder and condensed milk	14	14
Other products	6	8
Total percent	100	100

(Source: Svensk Mjölk)

the primary aim of supplying the domestic market with domestically produced food. Exports were mainly a way of handling seasonal variations, and the principal exports were generic products such as butter and skimmed milk powder. Now the European dairy exporters have full access to the Swedish market. To defend their market position, Swedish dairy processors have embarked on new strategies, among them:

- Prices have been reduced to a level where retail chains and other buyers are less attracted by foreign products. Today, the prices of dairy products are comparable to those of foreign products.
- A larger share of the milk intake is processed into products that are less vulnerable to the fierce price competition.
- Product development is more and more focused on highly processed or value-added products, (e.g. specialty milk powder products, fruit yogurts, and some cheeses).
- Marketing accounts have been boosted, as the importance of investing in market development such as brand names has increased.
- The Swedish dairy industry has developed new distribution channels not only abroad by also domestically.
- Considerable efforts have been made to increase the know-how and skills required to compete internationally (dairy cooperatives used to sell only on national, or regional markets).
- There are limited exports of some products to selected foreign markets. All exports, however, are not profitable as the revenues are often lower than the farmers' production costs. This remarkable strategy is justified by the argument that a price fall on the domestic market can be avoided by sending some production abroad.

SKÅNEMEJERIER – A SMALL DAIRY COOPERATIVE WITH MIGHTY NEIGHBORS

Structural Characteristics

One Swedish dairy cooperative, Skånemejerier, has taken significant steps to solve the problems of low (even negative) profitability both at the dairy level and at the member-farmer level. It has businesses in the southernmost part of the country, the province of Scania. Even though Skånemejerier is Sweden's second largest dairy processor, its share of the total volume is only 13%. The largest processor, Arla, has 62% of the milk production. Hence, Skånemejerier is squeezed in between two giant dairy cooperatives, Arla in the north and

Denmark's MD Foods in the south, both of which have a considerably broader product mix, and a size that may foster low unit costs in processing operations. The 1,600 members of Skånemejerier deliver annually 419 thousand metric tons of milk, compared to 2.118 thousand tons from Arla's 9.000 members and 3.220 thousand tons from 8.000 MD Foods members in Denmark.

Skånemejerier wants to remain an independent dairy cooperative. The option would be a merger but the two neighboring cooperatives are for different reasons excluded. The Swedish Competition Board would not permit a merger with Arla as that would mean even more concentrated market power than at present, and a merger with a Danish cooperative would be cumbersome due to differing legal systems. A merger with another cooperative is hardly realistic as the distance to the partner would be so large that the advantages would be smaller than the problems.

Skånemejerier is a cooperative of the traditional type, just like almost all other farmer cooperatives in Sweden. This is basically an effect of the old agricultural policy; in the years when the agricultural policy could safeguard the economy of the farmers, they (i.e. their organizations) had no reason to lobby for a liberal regulation of the cooperative business form. The legislation on cooperative societies is more ideologically and less economically under-pinned in Sweden than in the major competing countries.

The traditional cooperative business form of Skånemejerier is seen in, among others, the following traits:

• Organized as a cooperative society with open membership policy.
• Governance according the principle of one member, one vote.
• All member supplies must be accepted by the cooperative.
• Mainly unallocated equity capital.
• The members' share capital is not remunerated.

Skånemejerier's production consists of roughly equal portions of fresh products (fresh milk, yogurt, cream, butter, etc.), cheese, and processed bulk products (industrial butter, condensed milk, milk powder). The latter category is composed of those products that are subject to the milk policy of the European Union, though Skånemejerier generally succeeds to find other buyers of these products, thereby not having to sell to the European Commission's intervention inventories. Until 1990 the national agricultural policy included a policy of profit balancing. Profits from the product categories mentioned were equalized between the dairy processors, so firms with a large share of the profitable fresh milk products subsidized processors with a large share of cheese and industrial products, both with low profitability.

The effects of this policy are still to be seen. Skånemejerier still has a larger share of cheese and industrial products (34% and 28%, respectively) today and with even poorer profitability. Fluid milk accounts for the rest, 38%. According to information from the cooperative, only about 50% of the milk processed contributes positively to the milk price paid to the farmers. All other products reduce the members' milk price.

Current Strategies

To avoid dependence of generic products, such as non-branded cheese and industrial products, Skånemejerier tries to transform as much of the deliveries as possible into branded, highly processed, products and to find new markets. Product development and flexibility are the best ways to improve earnings for semi-processed products. Further, Skånemejerier is trying to reorient itself from a regional dairy to an international food company. Hence, new non-milk products are introduced and new markets developed outside the region.

In recent years, Skånemejerier has established several strategic alliances within the European food industry, as, for example an alliance with two dairy cooperatives in Denmark and Germany: MD Foods and HansaMilch. Likewise, alliances have been formed within the research world. As a small food processor Skånemejerier can allocate only one per cent of its turnover to R&D. Instead of a costly development department, one employee sweeps the market for innovative ideas, networking with universities and colleges. This strategy has been successful with new products in the range of smart foods and functional foods. These strategic alliances form the basis of Skånemejerier's export operations (Göransson & Kuiper, 1997). The essence of the exporting strategy is to reach profitable markets with unique value-added products. It is admittedly a time-consuming and costly endeavor but there is no option, and until now considerable success has been harvested.

All in all, Skånemejerier is in the process of being transformed from a product-oriented to a market-oriented firm. In relation to its members, however, only a few changes have been made. Market-signals are not transferred correctly to the members. Farmers are paid an average price for their milk, whereby the marginal revenues which the cooperative gains when selling the processed products are hidden from the farmers.

In addition, members have few incentives to individually contribute to the cooperative's equity capital. This is especially problematic as the new strategies of product development and market development require costly investments. In order to retain a cooperative feature in the future, more risk-bearing capital has to be provided by the members.

Competitive Weaknesses

One may conclude, therefore, that Skånemejerier has many problems that could develop into a crisis if radical measures are not taken quickly. The economic difficulties are serious:

- Because of its small production volume, the unit costs of processing are high, and so the product mix must be very limited.
- Its small size also means that the firm has limited capital for investing in new products and new markets.
- Skånemejerier's 'domestic market' (the province of Scania) is small in relation to the volume of milk produced in the cooperative, i.e. the supply exceeds the demand. It is difficult to convince retailers and consumers further north to buy Skånemejerier's products rather than Arla's. Also, the oligopolistic structure should be taken into account – challenging Arla would be unwise by Skånemejerier, as Arla has the capability to retaliate in a hard way. Hence, in order to sell all the volume produced, Skånemejerier has to reduce its sales prices. Thereby, the price for raw milk also becomes comparatively low, which means dissatisfaction among the members: the milk prices do not cover their production costs.
- Production costs at the farm level may be equal to those in other regions of Sweden, but they are higher than in other countries, as an aftermath of the national agricultural policy that did not stimulate efficient operations. Generally, Swedish agriculture is not able to compete with a cost-leadership strategy, to use the vocabulary of Porter (1980). High production costs pose a great danger especially to Skånemejerier and its members, because foreign competitors have easy access to the southernmost tip of Sweden.

Consequently, the prospects for success in competition with other dairy processors, all much larger than Skånemejerier, are meager. The only option seems to be going for specialty products, aimed at selected niche markets, i.e. a differentiation strategy according to Porter (1980). Skånemejerier has already had some success with this type of operation. The existing organizational structure, however, has turned out to be an obstacle for a differentiation strategy with an emphasis on value-added products.

So, Skånemejerier's board established a working group to explore how the organization could be changed. In 1998, a proposal for reorganization was presented to the membership. The organizational remodeling dilemma could be expressed as a shift from: (1) a *traditional cooperative model (with average price policy)* towards either (2) a *similar cooperative model but with multiple-pricing,* or (3) a *composite model where the members own tradable shares* – the working group settled for the latter. These three organizational models are discussed below.

TRADITIONAL MODEL WITH AVERAGE PRICING

Micro-economic Perspectives

Ever since agricultural cooperatives were established they have utilized the principle of average prices when paying their members for the milk. Total revenues are divided by volume supplied, arriving at a unit price. Because this price policy implies that all profits made by the cooperative are distributed to the farmers in the form of product prices, signals to the farmers about prevailing market conditions are more or less distorted, compared to the marginal price philosophy of investor-owned firms (Bateman et al., 1979; Cotterill, 1987). Higher prices induce the membership to produce and supply a volume that is larger than the market's demand for products. Nevertheless, average pricing has functioned reasonably well over the decades, resulting in the dominance of cooperatives in the marketing of most agricultural commodities in most countries (Van Bekkum & van Dijk, 1997).

Two conditions, however, must be fulfilled for this pricing policy to be successful: (1) the cooperative's production function must be characterized by substantial economics of scale, and (2) the prices that the cooperative meets when selling the products should not be influenced by the volumes (Nilsson, 1998). The last requirement could be met due to either agricultural policy regulations or the cooperative's volumes being too small to affect the market price (the market being large).

Given these two conditions, a cooperative that is organized according to traditional cooperative principles will make the best possible profits for its farmer members. These cooperative principles are: open membership; low or no interest on member investments; sizable unallocated funds; democratic governance; ideological demands for fairness; equity; equality; and solidarity; etc. The economic benefit from implementing these principles is increased production volume, both by stimulating existing members to supply larger volumes (capital remuneration paid in the form of prices; certain cross-subsidizing between member categories), and by attracting more members (socially attractive arguments; better prices).

For traditionally organized cooperatives to be efficient, the inflow of raw products should be fairly homogeneous, and consequently the membership must be relatively homogeneous. Likewise these cooperatives should be dealing with unprocessed or slightly processed products. Thereby, the cooperative gets low costs, and it can compete successfully in the large markets where price is the only effective sales parameter. The price paid to the farmers is better than it would be with any other marketing arrangement, and there are market forces within the farming population, assuring that each farmer is as cost-efficient at his farm as possible.

If these two conditions are not met, problems arise. First, when a traditionally organized cooperative extends it operations into processed or highly processed (value-added) products, the profits made in these operations are due to raise the prices paid to the farmer-members even further beyond the market value of the raw product, resulting in the members increasing their production level even more. Traditionally organized cooperatives are obliged to accept all deliveries from all members, thus the total volume handled by the cooperative will substantially exceed the demand. The only way for a cooperative to clear the market is to reduce its salesprice, especially for product lines that face the least price elasticity. If a cooperative is working with highly processed products, it is operating in a more defined market. Therefore, the cooperative's price is hardly independent of its sales volumes, and so, the cooperative's sales may result in a lowered market price to the detriment of the farmers. In the end, perhaps not very much is gained from the value-added operations of the cooperative.

Second, if a cooperative extends it operations into processed products, it will come to work on a larger number of markets and more diverse markets. So, there is a greater richness and complexity in the market signals. When calculating an average price to be paid to the farmers, however, this richness of information is lost, and the message to the farmers is extensively distorted. Higher profits give the signal that the production should be increased which is in the interests of nobody.

The situation described above is a classical problem, posed and discussed in the literature on agricultural cooperatives. "Producers have the incentive to increase output because they can make a profit by expanding output. . . . it is profitable for the individual to overproduce" (Schmiesing, 1989, p. 162). There appears, however, to be no effective way of dealing with the situation:

• A cooperative may supplement faulty price signals with additional information provided through newsnotes, personal communication, etc., with the purpose of guiding the members about production decisions. It is, though, not likely that the farmers would adhere the advice as they have economic incentives to take advantage of high prices through increased production.

- Sexton (1986) says that profits should be paid to the farmers as 'wind-fall money', which would not have the effect of raising the farmers' production volume. This method would be very difficult to implement in real life.
- Vercammen and colleagues (1996) advocate price differentiation according to the volume delivered; another option is price differentiation based on quality, whereby quality is given a wide interpretation – also hard to do in practice.

Property Rights Perspectives

According to property rights theory, inefficiency will result when traditionally organized cooperatives engage in processing raw commodities into value-added products. The core issue is that there are no markets for the residual rights, i.e. the expectations as to future profits are not given a value (Condon & Vitaliano, 1983; Vitaliano, 1983; Cook & Tong, 1997). A member may join the cooperative without paying the market value of the membership rights, or future flow of net benefits. Hence, "the multiple interpretations of . . . vaguely defined property rights lead to conflicts over residual claims and decision control, especially as cooperatives become increasingly complex in organizational structures" (Hackman & Cook, 1997, p. 105). A number of problems follow:

- *The joint property or free-rider problem:* Free-riding behavior is encouraged, i.e. self-interest seeking members reap benefits without contributing accordingly.
- *The horizon problem:* No member wants the cooperative to make investments with a longer pay-back period than his own remaining member period, and hence, cooperatives are normally under-invested.
- *The portfolio problem:* Given heterogeneity within the membership as regards risk preferences, a cooperative's investments will be inoptimal for practically all the members.
- *The control or follow-up problem:* An individual member has very limited incentive to control the management, and also very limited capability.
- *The influence cost or decision-making problem:* Because memberships are heterogeneous, the management has difficulties in judging which actions to take and how these affect different member categories.

The root of these problems is that the members are individualistic actors and will behave in ways that do not fit with the collectivist traits of traditional cooperatives. This argument is easy to understand, and the cooperative business sector is abundant with examples of these problems that cause economic hardships of many cooperative organizations.

Nevertheless, cooperative organizations have existed for ages, so this critique cannot be generally applicable. Considering the traditional cooperative organization model and the task for which it was designed, these problems must be re-evaluated:

- *The joint property or free-rider problem:* If cooperatives are very limited in the processing of members' products, not much equity capital is needed. Hence, the members' latitude for free-riding is small.
- *The horizon problem:* A traditional cooperative's business activities are so simple that only quite small investments are needed, mainly as recurring reinvestments, and so, they are not much in conflict with the members' planning horizons.
- *The portfolio problem:* The traditional cooperative performs the same task for each and everyone, and members are fairly homogeneous, and so, the portfolio problem is negligible.
- *The control or follow-up problem:* Monitoring a traditional cooperative is fairly uncomplicated, as it performs only few and simple tasks for the members.
- *The influence cost or decision-making problem:* If the membership is homogeneous and the business operations are simple, the management has an easy task.

One may conclude that when traditionally organized cooperatives are working within their proper domain, the problems are so small that the benefits from the cooperative organization, both in terms of exploiting economies of scale and in terms of transaction cost reduction for the members, surpass the property right problems. These problems arise when the cooperative leaves this domain, i.e. when it acquires a large amount of capital, produces advanced products, develops complex business operations, gets heterogeneous interests within the membership, etc. The five problems stated above could be regarded as having validity in these instances.

Skånenemejerier as a Traditional Cooperative

The mechanisms described above concern agricultural cooperatives generally, and so, they apply also to dairy cooperatives such as Skånemejerier. As Skånemejerier is a traditionally organized cooperative with a varied product mix, ranging from bulk products to value-added products, an average of the final markets' prices gives poor information to its members. The incorrectness of the price signals is especially alarming as it hides the fact that part of the volume is sold at a loss for Skånemejerier. The cooperative has to market almost half of the volume at a price that is lower than the price it pays for the farmers' raw milk, and this loss is not signaled to the farmers. It should, however, be recognized that a loss on part of the cooperative's volume does not necessarily mean that the farmers make a loss. This is so only if the price attained by the cooperative is lower than the farmers' production costs.

The difference in relation to theoretical reasoning is that the EU quota system prevents Skånemejerier members from expanding their production as they otherwise would do in response to the prices being higher than the market value of the products. Instead, the distorted price has the effect of impeding the farmers' incentives to conduct cost-reducing changes on their farms. The problem of negative profitability would be insignificant if the farmers at large were able to produce at a cost that is lower than the cooperative's price for the lowest paid share of the volume, but this seems not to be the case. With the present payment practice, the farmers have little reason to cut their production costs to a level that would turn also the existing loss business into a profitable one.

Skånemejerier's management has tried to ameliorate the situation by considerable cost-cuttings in the cooperative's operations and by introducing more and more cost-price signals to the farmers (price differentiation based on different quality dimensions). All this has proven insufficient, however.

Further, Skånemejerier's competitors are considerably larger, and consequently their unit costs are lower and their product mix is broader. Hence, Skånemejerier has a marketing disadvantage which makes reconsidering the price policy even more compelling. The anticipation of still greater competitive pressures also contributes to the worries.

TRADITIONAL MODEL WITH MULTIPLE PRICING

The Problem: Negative Profitability

The problems described above were perceived as acute by Skånemejerier in 1997, because the milk prices fell for the first time below that of its main competitor, Arla. Hence, a working group was asked to investigate how the problem of low and decreasing profitability could be solved. Initially, the focus was on the pricing policy, as the figures revealed that part of the operations gave negative profitability. For some products, the prices paid to the farmers for their milk were higher than the prices that the customers paid for the processed products. So, the group started out by developing a new model for the cooperative's pricing policy, though still keeping to the traditional cooperative organizational model.

Table 4. Skånemejerier's Price and Cost Structure (Approximates)

Product line	Share of total volume	Sales price expressed as raw milk price[1]
Fresh: fluid milk, fermented milk (sour milk and yogurt), butter and spread, cottage cheese, etc.	38%	SEK 4.10/kg
Semi-hard cheeses	34%	SEK 3.00/kg
Processed bulk: industrial butter, condensed milk, milk powder	28%	SEK 2.20/kg
Milk price paid to the farmers		SEK 2.85/kg

[1] SEK 100 = EUR 11 or USD 13

Table 4 illustrates the problem. The product mix is divided into three lines according to profitability per kilogram (= sales revenues minus all processing and marketing costs). Fresh goods are the most profitable, while the industrial products line is a loss business, producing only SEK 2.20 per kilogram as opposed to SEK 2.85 which is the average price paid to the farmers (SEK 100 = EUR 11 or USD 13).

An observer might wonder how prices could differ that much between product lines. Under market conditions, economic theory tells us, prices converge as manufacturers aim for the more profitable markets and try to withdraw from the least profitable markets. There are many market imperfections in the dairy markets. Fresh goods are costly to transport and store; rival firms have difficulties attaining economies of scale because the markets are small; the market structure is an oligopoly meaning that each competitor has the possibility of retaliating against any other competitor's hostile action.

In Table 4, the problematic product line is industrial products. Still, one can not claim that this product line should be cut, i.e. that the farmers should reduce the production, perhaps even up till 28%. The figures are averages, and what counts are the marginal figures. If the farmer's marginal production cost (the cost for producing the last kilogram) is less than SEK 2.20, it pays to produce as much as possible, up till the limit set by the quota.

Multiple Pricing – Pros and Cons

The working group considered a pricing policy that would introduce flexibility by differentiating of the raw milk price paid to farmers according to the profitability of the various lines of processed products. The three product lines noted in Table 4 could serve as a basis, although any other way of categorizing the products would be possible. Indeed, it is not necessary to have a number of steps, for a continuous scale would do.

Using such a formula, a dairy farmer would be paid a higher price for the first 38% of his quota, a lower price for the subsequent 34%, and a much lower price for the remaining 28%. Thus, more realistic market signals would reach the farmer. Since the formula percentages will fluctuate over time, farmers would be informed each month about how the cooperatives' sales are developing.

Based on his own economic situation and according to his own discretion, an individual member could vary his milk production within limits set by his quota. A less efficient, high-cost producer, i.e. one whose marginal costs exceed SEK 2.20, would be encouraged to reduce his production. He would perhaps only produce 38% of his present volume (quota) for which he would get a very high price, plus 34% which would render him a fairly high price, thus eliminating the remaining, low-priced, 28% of his present production. The fact that EU has granted a farmer a certain production quota, does not mean that he is obliged to produce all the volume that this quota permits him to produce. At present, all farmers produce to the limit of their quota because the average pricing policy encourages them to do so.

Provided that a farmer's marginal production costs are below SEK 2.20 he could make a profit by selling all the milk he may produce. Hence, the more efficient, low cost producer would continue to produce the same volume as he does today, or he would even like to extend his operations by buying more quota from the Board of Agriculture.

Such a multiple-pricing model would increase the profits made by the totality of farmers and cooperative. Nevertheless, the total volume of milk, produced by the members of Skånemejerier would undeniably be reduced, as some high-cost producers would cut their volume. Hence, the cooperative's processing costs per unit may rise as a consequence of overcapacity in some processing plants, i.e. lost economies of scale would reduce the gains.

The arguments for this model are:

- Skånemejerier would continue as a traditionally organized cooperative. The multiple-pricing model does not require any cumbersome re-structuring.
- The model is easily understood and communicated to members, and it is considered to be 'fair'. All members will be offered the same conditions by the cooperative, and then they may make their own decision about production volume, based on their individual cost structure.

- Market signals to the farmer would be more clear and powerful, and on the basis of this improved information, the farmer make wiser decisions about his own production volume (based on the profits of each product line) and about actions in the cooperative to improve the profitability (based on the balance between product lines with different profit levels).
- Hence, the profitability of the farmers and the cooperative would rise.

There are also a number of drawbacks:

- A study was done of the cooperative's membership (Andersson, 1998) and it revealed that a multiple-pricing policy would hamper the structural development within the membership. There would be weaker incentives for farmers to search for cost-savings in their operations and especially unfortunate is that high-cost producers would not close out nor become more efficient, but would only reduce their volume.
- Without lower production costs it would be difficult to defend dairying's long-term position in the region. Regardless of how successful a producer cooperative is in developing attractive products, if the farmers can not produce at a lower cost than the raw milk can be bought on the open market, the members may sooner or later find it more profitable to simply close-out their operations and continue more comfortably as share holders in a milk-processing firm, that buys its raw milk from elsewhere.
- There would be large administrative costs associated with the system as the sales prices vary a lot over time and the profitability is difficult to assess accurately. The profitability of some cheeses, e.g. might be very satisfactory, but not of others.
- The model can hardly take into account the fact that many products are technically linked to each other, e.g. wastes from one production process serve as inputs to another one.
- The fact that the cooperative's members do not produce to their maximum quotas might prove to be a mistake in future agricultural policy negotiations.
- If or when the EU quota system is abolished, a multiple-pricing model will not work.
- If Skånemejerier is the only cooperative to introduce this pricing model, some members would find it profitable to extend their production volume by buying more production rights (quota), and these can only be acquired from members of other cooperatives (though indirectly via the Board of Agriculture). If so, the problem is not solved as the volume produced would again become larger than the volume demanded.

• The property rights problems would not be a alleviated significantly. Greater member involvement is probable as the members become better informed about the businesses of the cooperative, but all the five problems would remain unsolved.

The Skånemejerier working group found that the drawbacks outweighed the advantages, and the model was rejected. Instead, a basically different type of cooperative organizational model was proposed.

COMPOSITE MODEL WITH TRADABLE VALUE-ADDED RIGHTS

Objectives

A more radical model evolved that would challenge the traditional cooperative business. Instead of the present average pricing policy or the rejected multiple-pricing policy, a dual pricing model was explored. The duality consists in one low (open market rate) price for all milk delivered and one higher price for part of the deliveries – provided that the member has bought B shares giving right to the profits originating from the cooperatives value-added operations.

The two most profitable product lines could be expanded (Table 4). Hence, more R&D as well as market development efforts would be desirable, but if so, more capital is required. Because of its geographical location, Skånemejerier can not expand in territory served, nor in terms of volume. The expansion route open to it is in terms of product and market development, attaining a larger share of the profitable value-added markets. This might be difficult to accomplish for a traditional cooperative where all members want everybody else to supply money – cf. the common property and the horizon problems.

So, two main goals were advanced: the system should stimulate the development of: (1) more efficient, low-cost dairy farms, and it should facilitate the (2) mobilization of more equity capital. For this to be realized, the property rights problem must be solved. Collective ownership and vaguely defined property rights is at the root of this problem. Thus, a new type of share should be introduced, to be offered the members to buy voluntarily for cash, and then it should be traded freely within the membership. While traditionally the profits of a cooperative are distributed to the members in proportion to the volumes of milk supplied, the new system implies a profit distribution in proportion to the number of shares that the member has bought. With the resultant individualized ownership the presently diffuse property rights will be clarified.

A third goal was to (3) retain the traditional cooperative business form. It is desirable to introduce clearly defined property rights which will result when there is a market for shares which give the holders the right to residuals of the firm. However, abandoning the existing organizational form completely was neither advisable nor legally possible:

- Swedish legislation on cooperative societies requires agricultural cooperatives to adhere to the so-called cooperative principles, i.e. open membership, and acceptance of all supplies from the members.
- The milk volume produced by members is so small, compared with competing dairy processors, that maximum production (the quota) is desirable in order to benefit from economies of scale in the processing operations. Because of unallocated equity, low dividends and several other attributes, the traditional cooperative model has an advantage in achieving low average costs through economies of scale.
- To better serve the retail chains, Skånemejerier has to offer a reasonably broad product mix, and so, the production volume must not fall below the quota.

Composite Model Proposed

By combining clearly defined property rights with the traditional cooperative model, a composite organizational model was created, with tradable value-added rights as its core component. Tradable delivery rights are not new in agricultural cooperative contexts whereby the members have rights to deliver specified volumes to the cooperative (Bärnheim, 1996). Such rights help to streamline the production chain, adapting the raw material production to consumer demand, via the multitude of processing activities. Tradable delivery rights have for many years been used in, for example, starch and sugar beet cooperatives, and during the nineties they became widespread in the so-called New Generation Cooperatives in North America (Harris et al., 1996; Nilsson, 1997a; van Dijk, 1997).

Tradable value-added rights are also comparable to tradable owner shares, which are found in PLC cooperatives (Harte, 1997) and in some subsidiaries owned jointly by cooperatives and individual members. Both give the right to returns on equity, but do not give benefits to the member in his role as a patron (Van Bekkum & van Dijk, 1997). Anyhow, the effects are the same, for they encourage long-term planning by the owners and limit free-riding behavior, i.e. property rights problems are dealt with directly.

Tradable value-added rights as proposed for Skånemejerier, differ in important ways from the existing models of tradable delivery rights and tradable owner shares:

- Value-added rights would be introduced into the structure of an existing cooperative while tradable delivery rights are built into the structure of newly established cooperatives.
- By law, Swedish agricultural cooperatives must have open membership, while tradable delivery rights by necessity imply closed memberships.
- Tradable delivery rights give members the right to deliver commodities to the cooperative, while in Skånemejerier's case it would be a right to receive the profits made in the cooperative's value-added operations.
- Value-added rights can be owned only by active members (producers), while owner shares may in some cases can be held by others, such as former members.

Thus, the cooperative would pay the prevailing open market price for all milk delivered by its members. Presently this is the EU's intervention price. But none of the dairy farms associated with Skånemejerier would be able to survive very long on just that base price, for it would not cover the farmers' average costs of production. (Hopefully, however, it will exceed most farmers' marginal cost of production, i.e. their costs of producing the last kilogram of milk.)

If the cooperative paid only the EU intervention price to the farmers, the cooperative would make tremendous profits. The profits, of course, would be the result of accumulated equity, know-how, market assets, physical plants, good-will, etc., assets which are not a consequence of the milk deliveries from the members. Nevertheless, these profits belong to the members and should be distributed among the members in one way or another.

The value-added profits would be distributed to the members via a new type of shares (B shares) to be sold to the members. Each share entitles a member to receive a high price for a specified volume of raw milk. The total number of shares is calculated on the basis of the total volume of milk that the cooperative expects to be processed and marketed at an acceptable over-all price. It might be 80% of the current volume, corresponding roughly to the products necessary to be an attractive partner to the retailers.

A farmer who has bought a certain number of B shares (= value-added rights), will get a higher price for the volume of milk corresponding to those shares. The more B shares he holds, the higher the revenues he will get for his total production. However, the cooperative can not in advance promise any specific milk price for the holders of B shares because this price depends on the profits made on the cooperative's value added operations and the market for these products. Given that the base price is very low (the EU intervention price), these profits may though become substantial.

All farmers would have a chance to buy such B shares; this decision is solely the farmer's. The price of the B shares, when the cooperative is offering them to the members, would be set at a level that is acceptable both for the members and for the tax authorities, i.e. a market level that does not represent any subsidies to the share buying farmer. Neither must it be a bad business for the farmer, or be perceived by the members as being unfair.

After B shares have been sold to members, they may be freely traded between members. This encourages long-term planning. The price of a share would be anticipated on the basis of the farmers' expectations concerning future prices on the value-added products.

Expectations

Tradable shares will have the effect of stimulating cost-reducing and efficiency raising measures. While the multiple-price system may give high-cost producers disincentives to reduce costs and rather limit production, a system of value-added rights gives different signals, leading to the opposite effect.

When members are trading B shares, value-added rights will represent a higher value for low-cost (efficient) producers than for high-cost (less efficient) producers. The former can make more money when owning value-added rights than the latter can. Hence, low-cost producers will be willing to pay a higher price and will want to increase their ownership of B shares. High-cost producers will find it more profitable to quit the business and sell their value-added rights to low-cost producers, if it is not possible to enhance their production efficiency.

After some years, a large proportion of the value-added rights may be expected to be possessed by low-cost producers, and these farmers will have an interest in reducing their production cost level still more. Hence, tradable B shares will introduce dynamic forces in this dairy community. In the long run, the dairy farmers will be very efficient, and the farmers who close-out will do so without as much transitional strain as often occurs in dairy re-structurings. The survival chance for milk production in the region is increased.

Value-added rights also affect other incentives. Participating farmers will become more interested in the cooperative and will encourage the development of processed products and the addition of more value-added products. They will be more willing to invest money, for a net profit can be expected. Over the years value-added products may account for a major share of Skånemejerier's product mix. The participating farmers, traditionally oriented toward production, have incentives to become market oriented.

Also the incentive systems within the cooperative enterprise become more attuned to the demands of the markets. The managers have stronger reasons to attain results, as the objectives of the business operations become clearer.

The composite model with tradable value-added rights has certain advantages:

- It is independent of the EU quota system.
- New shares can be issued, if the need should arise (for development capital).
- Other types of shares could be issued and offered to members on other terms. To keep property rights clearly defined, such new business ventures must be organized within separated business units (profit centers) with market based prices in the dealings with the cooperative. Thereby the dual price model may become a triple or quadruple price model.
- For greater capital needs it would be possible to invite external investors as co-owners of subsidiaries. This would not threaten the farmer members' position since the external owners would not supply any milk; the remuneration of their capital would be set at a fixed rate.
- The total volume of milk that is linked to the value-added rights (maybe 80%) could be increased or decreased, in light of marketing conditions. The higher the percentage, the lower the market value of the value-added rights.

Thus, with respect to the three objectives set forth by the working group, the expected positive effects of this composite cooperative model are:

(1) More efficient, low-cost dairy farms.
- Lower costs of primary production due to efficiency raising measures at the farms as well as development towards a more efficient structure of agriculture.
- Stronger market orientations among the membership as well as in the cooperative's management, implying higher profitability.

(2) Mobilization of more equity capital.

- The sales of value-added rights (B shares) to members will raise the equity capital of the cooperative whereby more money can be invested in R&D and in market development.

(3) Retain the traditional cooperative business form.
While keeping to a traditional cooperative organizational form, the introduction of trade in B shares means that property rights in the cooperative are individualized and clearly defined:

- *The joint property or free-rider problem:* The propensity to be a free-rider is reduced: in order to get a larger share of the profits, members have to contribute with risk-bearing capital.
- *The horizon problem:* Because the value of B shares is decided by expectations of future prices, members' time horizon is extended.
- *The portfolio problem:* The investment portfolio of the cooperative will correspond to members' interests as these can be expressed as maximizing the long-term milk prices, i.e. the value of the B shares.
- *The control or follow-up problem:* In the traditional cooperative model with average pricing, individual members have little incentive as well as limited capability to control the management. The proposed model implies strengthened ownership by the members, and they can be expected to keep a closer eye on how the cooperative firm is run.
- *The influence cost or decision-making problem:* The long-term maximization of the B share value constitutes unambiguous criteria for management decisions.

There are, however, also certain pitfall that must be avoided (Moore & Noel, 1995). For this model to perform well, the Skånemejerier board and management must take some action to secure a well-functioning market for the B shares (value-added rights):

- The exchange value cannot be easily established for the prospective buyers and sellers.
- Further, financial advisors and brokers can hardly be expected to show much interest, as the volume of trade is too small.

CONCLUSIONS

During the last ten years or so considerable changes have taken place in the European dairy industry. Multinational food corporations, many of them with a stake in the dairy sector, are the driving force. To meet the challenge from these giants, dairy farmer cooperatives have embarked on new and varied strategies, involving mergers, acquisitions, external financiers, increased individual farmer ownership, etc.

Smaller dairy cooperatives which reject being absorbed by the larger ones, have difficulties following that route. Without adapting to the new business environment, however, they may end up as either sub-suppliers to large supermarket chains and processing firms, or as suppliers to a local consumer markets. Both options are less attractive, the first one implying very low prices and the latter considerable uncertainties.

One small dairy cooperative that for legal and geographical reasons can not amalgamate with any larger cooperative, is Skånemejerier, located at the south tip of Sweden. As the members have very low profitability on their dairy farms, and the board and management of the cooperative can project only a bleak economic future, the board appointed, in 1997, an internal working group to come up with a plan that could rescue dairy farming in the region.

The working group suggested a new organizational model that is designed to change the system of incentives for its members in such a way that the members' short-term aspirations are brought more in line with their long term interests. With this new organizational model, the cooperative's price paid to farmers will consist of two parts. First, *the basic price* which is a true market price and thereby very low (in today's Europe it is the EU intervention price). Second, *the value-added price,* which derives from the cooperative's total assets in the form of accumulated capital, market position, product development capabilities, staff competencies, etc. All members get the basic price for all delivered milk, while the value-added price, on top of the basic price, is paid to the farmers who have bought a specific type of B shares from the cooperative or from other members. To each B share is linked a specified volume of milk, which gives the owners of those shares a right to the better price.

Through the flexibility that this organizational model brings to Skånemejerier, the cooperative and its members should be better prepared for the future. The cooperative will get more resources and stronger reasons for product and market development activities, thereby avoiding the most intense price competition. Because there will be a free market for trading the B shares (value-added rights) within the membership, property rights relative to the cooperative's business ventures become more clearly defined, which has several advantages:

- The members will have an interest in providing equity capital to the cooperative.
- Through tradable shares, all good investments in the cooperative will benefit the members, even if the investments may involve non-milk products.
- The members will maintain a long-term interest in the cooperative firm's performance, and thereby be willing to supply more.
- The members can be expected to keep a closer eye on the cooperative's operations.
- The management will be guided by clear goals relative to the cooperative's businesses.

Further, the new model will lead to efficiency-raising measures within the membership. After a few years, value-added rights will probably be possessed by the most efficient (low-cost) dairy farmers as these have the most to gain by owning the B shares. This will strengthen the position of the dairy industry in the region.

There are also some gains for the farmers who are forced to quit their farming operations due to high costs of production and difficulties of cutting their cost level. At present, they leave the cooperative almost empty-handed as they redeem only the par value of their investment in the cooperative, made probably several decades ago. With the new system, they have a chance to profit from selling B shares, bought at a lower price.

The working group presented its report to the board in April 1998. After the proposal has been scrutinized at numerous member meetings, the board decided in the Spring of 1999 that the new organizational model should be introduced as from January 1st, 2001.

REFERENCES

Andersson, F. (1998). *Alternativa prismodeller för mejerikooperationen [Pricing Models for Dairy Co-operatives]*. M.Sc. thesis, Department of Economics, Swedish University of Agricultural Sciences, Uppsala (In Swedish with English summary).

Bärnheim, M. (1996). *Financing Agricultural Co-operatives – The Case of the Dutch Dairy Sector*. M.Sc. thesis, Department of Economics, Swedish University of Agricultural Sciences, Uppsala.

Bateman, D. I., Edwards, J. R., & Levay, C. (1979). Agricultural Co-operatives and the Theory of the Firm. *Oxford Agrarian Studies, 8*, 63–81.

Condon, A., & Vitaliano, P. (1983). *Agency Problems, Residual Claims, and Cooperative Enterprise*. VPI Working paper #4, Virginia Polytechnic Institute and State University, Blacksburg, VA.

Cook, M. L. (1995). The Future of U.S. Agricultural Cooperatives: A Neo-Institutional Approach. *American Journal of Agricultural Economics, 77*(5), 1153–1159.

Cook, M. L., & Tong, L. (1997). Definitional and Classification Issues in Analyzing Cooperative Organization Forms. In: M. Cook, R. Torgerson, T. Sporleder & D. Padberg (Eds), *Cooperatives: Their Importance in the Future Food and Agricultural System* (pp. 113–118). Washington, D.C.: The Food and Agricultural Marketing Consortium.

Cotterill, R. W. (1987). Agricultural Cooperatives: A Unified Theory of Pricing, Finance, and Investment. In: J. S. Royer (Ed.), *Cooperative Theory. New Approaches* (pp. 171–258). Washington, D.C.: USDA/ACS.

Göransson, G., & Kuiper, E. (1997). Skånemejerier: Functional Foods Through Research. In: B. Traill & K. G. Grunert (Eds), *Product and Process Innovation in the Food Industry* (pp. 163–174). London: Blackie Academic & Professional.

Hackman, D. L., & Cook, M. L. (1997). The Transition to New Cooperative Organizational Forms: Public Policy Issues. In: M. Cook, R. Torgerson, T. Sporleder & D. Padberg (Eds), *Cooperatives: Their Importance in the Future Food and Agricultural System* (pp. 105–112). Washington, D.C.: The Food and Agricultural Marketing Consortium.

Harris, A., Stefanson, B., & Fulton, M. (1996). New Generation Cooperatives and Cooperative Theory. *Journal of Cooperatives, 11*, 15–29.

Harte, L. (1997). Creeping Privatisation of Irish Co-operatives. A Transaction Cost Explanation. In: J. Nilsson & G. van Dijk (Eds), *Strategies and Structures in the Agro-Food Industries* (pp. 31–53). Assen: Van Gorcum.

Moore, C. V., & Noel, J. E. (1995). Valuation of Transferable Delivery Rights for Marketing Cooperatives. *Journal of Cooperatives, 10*, 1–17.

Nilsson, J. (1997a). New Generation Farmer Co-ops. *Review of International Co-operation, 90*(1), 32–38.

Nilsson, J. (1997b). Inertia in Cooperative Remodeling. *Journal of Cooperatives, 12*, 62–73.

Nilsson, J. (1998). The Emergence of New Organizational Models for Agricultural Cooperatives. *Swedish Journal of Agricultural Research, 28*(1), 39–47.

Porter, M. (1980). *Competitive Strategy*. New York: Free Press.

Schmiesing, B. (1989). Theory of Marketing Cooperatives and Decision Making. In: D. Cobia (Ed.), *Cooperatives in Agriculture* (pp. 156–173). Englewood Cliffs, NJ: Prentice-Hall.

Sexton, R. J. (1986). The Formation of Cooperatives: A Game-Theoretical Approach with Implications for Cooperative Finance, Decision Making, and Stability. *American Journal of Agricultural Economics, 72*(?), 214–225.

Svensk Mjölk [Federation of Swedish Dairy Co-operatives]. Personal communication.

van Bekkum, O.-F., & van Dijk, G. (Eds) (1997). *Agricultural Co-operatives in the European Union – Trends and Issues on the Eve of the 21st Century*. Assen: Van Gorcum.

van Dijk, G. (1997). Implementing the Sixth Reason for Co-operation: New Generation Co-operatives in Agribusiness. In: J. Nilsson & G. van Dijk (Eds), *Strategies and Structures in the Agro-Food Industries* (pp. 94–110). Assen: Van Gorcum.

Vercammen, J., Fulton, M., & Hyde, C. (1996). Nonlinear Pricing Schemes for Agricultural Cooperatives. *American Journal of Agricultural Economics, 78*(3), 572–584.

Vitaliano, P. (1983). Cooperative Enterprise: An Alternative Conceptual Basis for Analyzing a Complex Institution. *American Journal of Agricultural Economics, 65*(5), 1078–1083.

Zwanenberg, A. (1997). *European Dairy Cooperatives Developing New Strategies*. Utrecht: Rabobank International Marketing.

DISTRIBUTION OF DAIRY PRODUCTION RIGHTS THROUGH QUOTAS: THE NORWEGIAN CASE

Anne Moxnes Jervell and Svein Ole Borgen

INTRODUCTION

Since the early 1980s, the quota system has had significant effects on the situation of Norwegian dairy farmers, conferring certain rights and imposing certain obligations. Through delivery quotas, dairy farmers gain access to the protected domestic consumer market and to a share of the significant financial support provided by the state to Norwegian agriculture. On the other hand, decisions made by farmers relative to capital investments, herd expansions and such must take account of and are constrained by quota limits. During the quota period, the potential yield levels per cow have increased substantially due to technological improvements. The observed over-capacity indicates that total production on existing dairy farms could increase more than 25% if quotas were abolished (Giæver et al., 1995).

Milk production quotas have been widely used during the last quarter of the 20th century as a policy instrument to regulate national or regional markets. In 1989, 30% of the world's milk production was produced under quota regimes (IDF 1989). EU introduced the super-levy system in 1984 (Petit et al., 1987; Hairy & Perraud, 1988) while the first Canadian fluid milk quotas were introduced as early as 1968 in Ontario, followed by market sharing quotas for industrial milk in 1971 (Hamm & Nott, 1986; Gouin & Morriset, 1988). The quota systems curb surplus production but are also instruments to redistribute

Research in Rural Sociology, Volume 8, pages 355–378.
ISBN: 0-7623-0474-X

income to dairy farmers without stimulating production beyond demand. According to Kola (1991), production quotas can be a more efficient way to redistribute income to farmers than other policy instruments. But as noted by Burrell (1990b):

> Dairy programmes vary considerably between OECD countries in terms of their basic design and details of their routine management. These variations reflect differences between countries in the distribution of herds by size, the method and degree of assistance to the dairy sector, the degree of self-supply in milk products and the institutional framework within which the dairy sector is regulated (Burrell, 1991: 1).

Previous studies of dairy quota systems have dealt with aspects of efficiency both at the policy and farm level, and with the consequences for structural development and competitiveness on a national level (Jacobson, 1988; Kirke, 1989; Burrell, 1989a, b, 1990; Murphy, 1989; Dawson & White, 1990; Kola, 1991; Jervell, 1994). Our objective here is to explore the Norwegian dairy quota system – focusing in particular on its design and implementation during the past two decades. In effect, the Norwegian system illustrates how a policy instrument such as this, namely production quotas aimed at regulating the milk market, is affected by broader concerns and the institutional context that condition its implementation. It also demonstrates that when a number of actors with divergent and conflicting interests take part in policy design, the formulation of policy over time may take unexpected and unforeseen directions. Dairy farmers who will be impacted will invariably assume strong positions and try to influence the evolving system in ways that reflect their own individual and collective interests.

We will briefly present some of the main characteristics of the Norwegian dairy quota system, focusing on problems that have been encountered in quota implementation. Some of the implementation problems are still not resolved. Questions of distributive and procedural justice are highlighted, as they have been important in the debate. Information for our observations and discussion derives from reports and documentary materials that were obtained from the organizations involved and previous research (Jervell, 1993, 1997). In addition we interviewed some key actors in late 1998 including: a long-time member of the quota system secretariat; a member of the steering committee of the Norwegian Smallholders Union (NSU); and, a leader of the Norwegian Farmer's Union (NFU). In order to understand the functioning of the quota system in Norway, one must have some comprehension of the institutional context within which the quota system is applied. Consequently, we begin our exploration with an overview of the Norwegian dairy sector and its corporative structure.

THE NORWEGIAN DAIRY SECTOR

Small-scale Farm Structure

Norway has only 3% of total land area as agricultural land, marginal conditions for many crops, and a relatively low level of self-sufficiency in agricultural products. Subsidies and income transfers make up a large part of the average farm revenue. The smaller the farm, the larger the subsidies and income transfers measured per unit produced. Dairy farming is the most important agricultural activity in Norway, measured both in worth of produce and in importance for farmer income and regional rural settlement. Transfers are higher in dairying than in agriculture at large. In Norway the PSE (Producer Subsidy Equivalent) for the dairy sector has been higher than 80% (OECD, 1990). Income transfers have been mediated through a system of quantitative import regulations, import tariffs, price deficiency payments, investment subsidies and direct payments tied to input use such as acreage or animals. In the 1990s and after the WTO Uruguay round, import regulations are less strict while direct payments have become more important.

One third of all Norwegian farms have dairy cows. The average dairy farm has 13 dairy cows and around 15 hectares of land, some of which is rented from nearby holdings. The farms are predominantly small-scale family operations, family owned and family worked. Restrictions on investments in dairying and the exit of smaller farms are factors that have contributed to a more uniform dairy sector. In 1997 more than 50% of the dairy farms had between 10 and 19 cows. On the upper end of the scale, the largest farms (10% of all) had 'only' 20% of the total cows. Table 1 shows some features in the development of the Norwegian dairy industry from 1969 through 1997. Farm size is small and the structural change has been slow compared to what has been happening in most other European countries. For instance, the number of farms with dairy cows in

Table 1. Changes in the Norwegian Dairy Farm Sector, 1969 to 1997.

	1969	1979	1989	1997
Total supply (and deliveries to dairies), mill liters	1679 (1528)	1816 (1742)	1945 (1835)	1827 (1682)
Yield per cow, liters per year	4001	4900	5787	5830
Number of holdings with dairy cows	82177	38906	29100	24100
Average number of cows per holding	5.3	9.6	11.6	13.3

Denmark was halved in the 1979 to 1989 period. Countries that in 1980 had a structure more similar to Norway's, such as Ireland, Finland, Sweden and Germany, have all experienced a more rapid increase in average herd size in the 1980 to 1990 period (Flaten & Giaever, 1998: 2–4).

As a result, the cost of milk production is greater in Norway than in many other countries. But even if the producer price for milk is more than twice the price in New Zealand, producer prices constitute only part of the dairy income. Subsidies and direct payments have grown in importance since the 1970s. Payments are regionally and structurally diversified to compensate small farms in remote parts of the country. In 1997 the average dairy farm received a total of subsidies of more than NOK 4.4 per liter milk, while a farm with 40 cows received approximately NOK 2 per liter (Flaten & Giaever, 1998: 128).

Due to relatively small operations, Norwegian dairy farm families are increasingly involved in pluriactivity and income gaining activity outside the farm. The average labor input outside the farm by operator and spouse on dairy farms has increased by around 350 hours over the last decade, while labor input on the farm decreased by 200 hours (Jervell & Loyland, 1998). It is increasingly more common that the spouse has an off-farm occupation, and more seldom that both partners work full-time on the farm.

Role of Dairy Co-operatives

Until recently, all dairy farmers have been co-operatively organized and all milk produced in Norway has been delivered to and sold through a nationally federated dairy co-operative. Since the 1930s, these cooperatives have played a major role as implementers of national agricultural policy. The legal basis for this role is first and foremost constituted by the 1930 Marketing Act (Omsetningsloven). This act, carried unanimously by the Norwegian Parliament (Furre, 1971; Isaksen, 1984: 43), gave dairy co-operatives the responsibility for regulating market supply to stabilize prices. It presupposed that a *nation-wide apparatus* would implement the overall objectives specified by the law (Holmgren, 1981: 175). The nationally organized producer co-operatives were valued as a proper instrument for the government. One objective of the Marketing Act was to provide co-operatives the means they needed to carry on effective market regulation. A main purpose of market regulation was the stabilization of prices and quantities supplied in all regions of the country.

Subsidies through price support and direct payments have also been channeled through marketing co-operatives. The Norwegian Dairies co-operative (NM) has controlled all milk supplied and is obliged to receive any milk that producers (with quota) want to deliver. To prevent the Norwegian Dairies (the dairy co-operative) from taking advantage of its dominating position in the dairy market, the wholesale prices of milk products have, since 1951, been regulated. A nation-wide system adjusts the price differentials for milk that goes to the fresh milk market and to the cheese/butter market (manufacturing) so that prices paid to farmers are stable throughout the country. This scheme is supervised by a committee which includes representatives of the farmer organizations. (Vale, 1990; Brunstad et al., 1998). The regulatory model in Norwegian agriculture has been built on the idea that farmers are responsible for production, within limits for aggregate supply set by the authorities. Producer co-operatives are delegated the authority to accomplish this regulatory task. This type of regulatory regime represents a nation-wide and centralistic approach to the issue of synchronizing aggregate supplies to fluxes in aggregate demand pattern. It is nation-wide and centralistic in the sense that the main principles and operative arrangements are designed in the annual national agricultural negotiations between the farmer's representatives and the state. In the annual agricultural negotiations on prices and policy measures for the agricultural sector, including the dairy sector, the farmers are represented by two organizations: the Norwegian Farmers Union (NFU) and the Norwegian Smallholders Union (NSU), that generally take different positions on many questions. Representatives from the Ministry of Agriculture and the Ministry of Finance advance the government positions. Agreements are implemented as a standardized arrangement throughout the country.

Internationalization and Policy Changes

The National Agricultural Policy (NAP), developed in the 1950s was at its peak ideologically and in terms of financial transfers to the farm sector in the mid-1970s. Since the mid-1980s, the Norwegian government has been in the process of modifying its regulatory regime, in tune with the international trend to liberalize or deregulate the agricultural sector.

In the early 1990s, Norway entered into membership negotiations with the European Union. A small majority turned down EU membership in the referendum of November 1994, but during the negotiations, much attention was paid to the possible consequences for agriculture. Consumer prices for most foodstuffs are higher in Norway than in the EU and cost reductions and more efficient production structures are being called for.

The most important international agreements to which Norway complies now are the agreements of the World Trade Organisation (WTO) and the EEA agreements (European Economic Area) with EU. Imports of agricultural products are to be increased, whereas tariff barriers and subsidies should be reduced. The possibility for subsidized exports of dairy products to international markets is reduced. This implies that national production must be brought in line with demand and that the 'supply goal' for milk is reduced from 1800 million liters in 1980 to around 1600 million liters in year 2000.

Substantial budget cuts have been undertaken, and more are expected to come. Farmers in general are supposed to draw less on state budgets (subsidies), and to gain a larger proportion of their income directly from the markets. An overall political objective is to reduce consumer prices, through lowering production and transaction costs in value chains from stable to table.

DESIGN OF THE QUOTA SYSTEM

Quotas in a Policy Context

Through the last two decades, various regulatory schemes have been set up to align aggregate milk production to domestic demand. The design of the schemes have been influenced by the market situation, international pressures and by the political ambitions of domestic milk production, farm-based regional settlement, efficient production of consumer goods and an agricultural sector that has positive effects on environmental values. How various dairy quota schemes have been influenced by events affecting the agricultural policy and market situation, is schematically presented in Fig. 1.

As a way to control supply, quotas were first suggested as early as in 1930, and again in 1956 (NML, 1986). Since the exit rate from dairy production was high in the early 1960s, the question was not seriously debated at that time. An increased demand for milk in the years 1975–80 made a rigorous quota system seem unnecessary, and a governmental committee that evaluated dairy policy in the late 1970s (NOU, 1980) concluded that other measures (like the chosen voluntary scheme) might be sufficient.

Norway's first quota-based regulatory scheme was set up in 1983, as a reaction to the increasing problem of surplus production in its dairy sector. From 1978 through 1983, aggregate milk production grew by 10%. Productivity growth and investments in farm development more than made up for the loss of production caused by smaller farms that closed-out. A rapid growth in producer prices and subsidies following the ambitious agricultural policy of the late 1970s stimulated investment and production (Hegrenes & Romarheim, 1989). Moreover, there was a dramatic fall in demand from 1980 through 1982. This development can be connected to a reduction in consumer

AGRICULTURAL POLICY AND MARKET SITUATION	Investments subsidies Income goal for farmers.	Reduced consumer subsidies. Excess supplies.	Reregulating agricultural policy. GATT/WTO.	EU negotiations and referendum. (1994)	New actors compete with national co-op. Next WTO round
	1975-79	1980-84	1985-89	1990-94	1995-99
DAIRY QUOTA SCHEME	Voluntary bonus arrangement. (1979-82)	Two-price quota system. (1983-)	Exemption rules implemented. Yearly modifications.	No entry. Buy-out scheme. Aggregate production goal reduced.	From two-price to levy system. Buy and sell scheme.

Fig. 1. Evolvement of the Dairy Quota Scheme in Norway.

subsidies that started in 1980 (Vatn, 1991: 31). Consequently, there was a production surplus of almost 300 million liters of milk in 1982. The need for stronger production control seemed obvious. Dairy farmers, through the National Association of Norwegian Milk Producers (NML) and other farmer organizations, agreed and were willing to participate in an effort to regulate production more strictly. The two-price quota system was therefore introduced in 1983, and has been redesigned and changed multiple times. We shall now present the design in more detail, and explore some of the perceived advantages and disadvantages.

The Two-price Quota Scheme (Initial Period, 1983–90)

The first quota-based scheme was a two-price quota system. The basic mechanism of this regulatory scheme was that milk delivered without quotas or in excess of quota was paid a low and, over the years, diminishing share of the ordinary milk price. Initial quotas were allocated to producers according to their prior production level in 1980–82. At the outset, the plan was to base a farmer's quota on a moving average of deliveries the last three years. This source of flexibility was left in 1984. However, farmers could apply for exemptions from the main rules for setting quotas. Allowances were automatically made for producers that had participated in the program for voluntary reduction of production.

The so-called 'two-price steering committee', in which parties to the agricultural agreement (the state and the two farmers associations) were represented, was delegated the right to administer the rules and handle exemptions. The Norwegian Milk Producers Organization (NML) was to administer the system and fulfill the secretarial functions. Obviously, the fact that all Norwegian milk producers were organized within the same national co-operative dairy organization facilitated the introduction of farm level production quotas and the control over deliveries.

The two-price quota scheme was to be preliminary. The temporariness of the system made it a yearly topic in agricultural negotiations. Changes in the rules for quota setting were made every year. For example, in 1984 the 'moving average' rule was dropped. Some producers suggested that this rule encouraged farmers to over-produce to increase their future quota. That same year, structurally and regionally diversified factors to modify quotas were introduced. Arguments were advanced that some marginal regions and small farms should not carry the same burden as the larger farms that had caused surplus-production.

In the negotiations on quota rules the two farmer organizations advocated different principles. For instance, to protect small-holders from the possible negative effects of a quota on the income of marginal farms, the small-holders union (NSU) wanted minimum quotas. A minimum quota of 15,000 liters was introduced in 1984. This was later increased to 25,000 liters in 1986 and to 30,000 liters in 1987. For the Farmers Union it was more important to introduce a floor referring to prior production. In 1986 the argument won through that it was necessary to shield also larger producers from too large quota reductions and it was decided that no producer should fall lower than a floor of 84% of initial quota in 1983.

In the meantime, the parties had been evaluating how the farmer's productive resources could be taken into account in setting quota. This stemmed from an earlier debate where imported feedstuff was blamed for the excess supply. By giving more quota to those with ample farm-grown forage crop a perceived imbalance could be corrected. Finding out how to decide the amount of forage crop on the farm proved difficult. An attempt to use local representatives showed itself especially open to an unacceptable degree of individual discretion. How norm yields and acreage could be used without giving unwanted regional or structural effects was arrived upon only after a number of ex ante calculations and hard negotiations.

The multiple exemption rules ('unntaksregler') made many producers eligible receivers of additional quotas. The most important exemption rules were those concerning investments in farm development and entry for new generations or new farms. From 1983 through 1989, almost 50% of the farmers increased their quotas through various types of exemptions (Jervell, 1997). The numerous exemption rules opened up some degree of discretion in administrative decisions for deciding and evaluating a farm's 'productive resources' (building capacity and acreage).

The Quota Buy-out Scheme (1991–94)

After almost a decade of practicing the quota system, the scope for redistributing quotas administratively on the basis of exemption rules dried up in 1990. Market demand for dairy products continued to decline and national production had to be reduced proportionally. Dairy farmers experienced lower production quotas from year to year whereas yield growth and technical development had strengthened their capacity to produce. Discontent with the system grew.

Gouin (1988) argues that some kind of market for quota becomes inevitable over time. Though most Norwegian producers are very skeptical of and principally opposed to any kind of quota market (Jervell, 1993), the next regulatory instrument to be set up in the Norwegiandairy sector was a quota buy-out scheme. This was introduced in 1991, with 1992 as the first year in operation. The buy-out program offered a financial grant to dairy farmers, termed an 'adjustment grant' to stimulate them to reduce or quit production. Farmers who participated in the program were obliged to withdraw from milk production for seven years. They were compensated by an amount which corresponded to average delivered quantity (within quota limits) the last five years. The compensation per liter was relatively low (on average 3.75 NOK per liter), not far above the milk price. Participation in the scheme was limited, only 1.6% of total production was withdrawn in 1992. The withdrawn quota was used to reduce national production, and there was no redistribution of quotas. The following year, the quota buy-out scheme attracted even less interest, and in 1994 it was abolished. Individual quotas were again reduced by a factor to limit production to the reduced 'production goal'.

Other changes also affected the dairy sector during this period. In connection with the Norwegian referendum on EU membership in 1994, Norwegian people focused on the high cost of food. The government and the agricultural ministry advocated increased competition in the dairy sector. Before the referendum, uncertainty as to future agricultural policy was extremely high. Shortly after the referendum, new actors in the dairy sector emerged. A legislative 'hole' in the dairy quota scheme was disclosed when one producer established a private milk processing facility for consumer milk outside the quota system. The quota legislation had till then not been prohibitive towards production or sale without quota, but had depended on the state supported economic superiority of the dairy co-operative as an outlet for dairy farmers. Lately, the Norwegian two-price system has been changed to a levy system and it is no longer permitted to sell milk without a quota.

The Quota Buy and Sell Scheme (since 1996)

The buy-out scheme had been ineffective in restructuring the dairy sector. This triggered the introduction of a revised system: the so-called quota buy and sell-scheme. Other reasons for introducing a quota market was that, in theory, this would reallocate quota to the most efficient farmers (Romstad, 1995; Loyland et al., 1995). Both farmer organizations took positions against this system of quota redistribution that was mainly advocated by the government. The quota buy-sell system was set up in 1996. Its aim was to open up to some degree the reallocation of production quotas, allow farmers some degree of quota increase and farm development and thereby make possible a more efficient industry structure.

Though principally opposed to a quota buy and sell scheme, the Farmers Union did take part in its design. The Farmers Union negotiated a guarantee that the national quota or production goal of 1,700 million liters should not be decreased till after 1999, e.g. that all quota sold should be redistributed. But the Farmers Union had to abandon that position one year later as a result of decreased demand and market pressure.

All parties agreed that the quota buy and sell program should build on administratively set prices, but farmers argued that the prices had been set too high, even though demand for quota proved much higher than supply. Since a market with fixed prices could not be expected to balance quota supply and demand, the reallocation (sale) of quota had to be administered in accordance with certain rules. To maintain the regional structure of production, the country was divided into six trade regions. Quota supplied by farmers selling quota, should, primarily be redistributed within the region. There were disagreements with respect to the principles by which the production quotas were to be reallocated. State representatives argued that the principle of equal proportions should rule the roost ("to everyone according to the absolute size of the existing quota"). The Small-holders Union, however, claimed that the surplus production quantity should be allocated to farmers in equally large quantities. If – on average – 2,000 liters were to be allocated to the farmers, each of them should have precisely 2,000 liters (the principle of absolute equality; to everyone equally much, independent of any other criteria). Finally an in-between solution was selected, which combined three principles:

- All eligible dairy farmers were offered a minimum level of 1000 liters
- Beyond the minimum level, available production quantity was to be allocated to each applicant according to the total amount applied for. The amount bought could not exceed 20% of previous quota.
- An upper limit was specified: The absolute, maximum production quota – after having bought quota for the current year – should not exceed 130,000 liters. There were some exemptions from this rule.

The combinations of these three rules are sketched in Fig. 2.

An amount of 25 million liters was subtracted before redistribution of quota to farmers who wanted to buy quota. These rather complicated rules resulted in quota buyers receiving approximately 2000 liters each in 1997. Thus, the quota buy and sell scheme offered very limited quota increases to existing producers and did not provide opportunities for new entrants to the industry. Entry has only been possible in a limited number of cases as for producers of 'organic

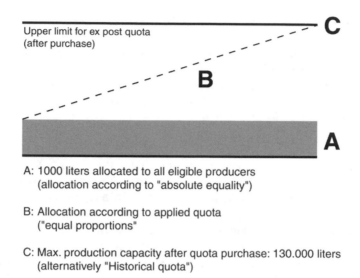

A: 1000 liters allocated to all eligible producers
(allocation according to "absolute equality")

B: Allocation according to applied quota
("equal proportions"

C: Max. production capacity after quota purchase: 130.000 liters
(alternatively "Historical quota")

Fig. 2. Redistribution of Quota Through the 1997 Quota Buy and Sell Program.

milk' near dairies that process organic raw milk, or for farmers that switch from sheep to dairy production in areas with predator problems.

Impediments to newcomers to dairying are seen as a problem by farmer organizations. The Small-holders Union want to recruit new producers and keep up the number of farms, while the Farmers Union gives greater weight to the importance of avoiding privileges and to the relative situation of dairy farmers vis-à-vis farmers in other sectors (such as pigs, beef etc.).

Further, while the government has advocated increased competition in the dairy sector, new processing actors have had to either buy milk from Norwegian Dairies or attract producers who have been delivering to the national co-operative. The entry of private entrepreneurs (processors) in the dairy sector in the 1990s initiated a process by which the quota secretariat was moved to a more neutral body outside the dairy co-operative (Omsetningsrådet).

In 1998, the introduction of quota redistribution on a very local level (municipalities), has brought the quota buy-sell system a little bit closer to a system where quotas are traded between neighbors. Local variations in quota supply and demand caused the average amount of quota bought in different regions in 1998 to vary between zero and 20,000 liters. While all the consequences, and the administrative difficulties involved, do not seem to have been foreseen or intended, the chosen arrangement did give rise to a degree of development on individual farms that has not been possible for many years. But this possibility did not apply to farmers in active dairy regions, where by definition very few farmers have sold quota.

JUSTICE AND IMPLEMENTATION PROBLEMS

The design of the Norwegian quota system has been a complex process and there have been many problems in its implementation. We have touched on some of these, but we have not addressed them in detail. We shall do so now. Policy design and policy implementation are closely associated, but one finds that the study of policy decision-making processes is much more researched than the strategies and consequences of policy implementation (Flyvbjerg, 1998; Sætren, 1998). One reason may be that implementation research must attend to a broader range of social, economic and political variables. Policy implementation depends on the patterns of interaction among many organizations and interest groups that act within multiple decision-areas covering different process stages. In the case of Norwegian dairy policy, at least three levels must be taken into account: (1) At the *policy* level the quota system is legitimated as an arrangement within the existing dairy policy. (2) At the *organizational* level rules and regulations are decided in the agricultural negotiations and the administrative quota committee (steering committee) under direct influence of the state and the two farmers associations. (3) At the *operational* level, there is substantial interaction between farmers and the quota administration at local processors, regional government offices and the apex of the national dairy cooperative.

The outcomes of the quota policy are assessed by and may influence both the policy level and the organizational level. Moreover, the policy process spans an extended timeframe, and it is often difficult to draw a clear line between the process and the context within which it takes place. Having these complexities in mind, we shall now briefly discuss some selected implementation issues that relate to the concern for distributive and procedural justice, as well as the evolvement of investments and the structural pattern of the industry.

Distributive Justice

Through the last two decades, there has been a multifaceted stream of critique from farmers about the functioning and consequences of the various quota schemes. A significant part of this critique relates to perceived injustices. From very different standpoints, many farmers have voiced the same overall concerns, claiming that the schemes do not pass a fairness test. This observation is in accordance with Elster's proposition that justice-related issues are often put to the forefront in non-market organizations (Elster, 1992). At the organizational and operational levels, the distributing of quota within the farmer community can be seen as a 'local justice' problem. Therefore, distributive justice is a natural component of any review of implementation. The right to produce and sell milk within a protected and regulated market may be seen as a limited good. The allocation and redistribution of quotas between producers emerges as a question of distributing a scarce good.

Elster (1992) explains the principles of local justice through three different levels of decision making. First-order decisions are made by political authorities and influence the supply of a scarce good. Third-order decisions are decisions made by potential recipients that affect their likelihood of receiving a scarce good. Second-order decisions are those that specify how a good should be allocated. Normally, different actors will have different motivations. Political authorities will be motivated mainly by efficiency, second-order actors by equity, procedural justice and local efficiency and third-order actors mainly by self-interest. Public opinion may intervene and is most typically concerned with equity.

Albeit quotas are not goods in a strict sense, they are crucial with respect to a farmers' opportunity of generating income from his farm. Quotas are limited and the demand for quotas has proven large. What allocation principles are applied and what concepts of fairness prevail with respect to the allocation of quotas? Based on thorough empirical studies of institutions in multiple western institutions, Elster (1992) classifies the principles of local distribution as follows:

(1) Equality (absolute equality, equal deviation from a base-line)
(2) Time-related principles (queuing)
(3) Principles defined by status (regional residency, age etc.)
(4) Principles defined by welfare effects (need, social efficiency, incentive effects)
(5) Mechanisms based on power (purchasing power)
(6) Mixed principles (in practice almost all actual allocative systems are based on mixed principles, one example of which is post allocation trade).

Judged by our analysis of quota allocation, most principles (except perhaps for the queuing principle) seem to be used to some degree. The initial principle for quota allocation was that of equal percentage deviation from the baseline (former production). Both the principles of absolute equality (to everybody equally, independent of any other variable) and equal proportions have been influential in distributing quota reductions and in the redistribution of quota through the buy-sell scheme. However, there seem also to be shifts away from the initial principle (equal percentage deviation from a baseline of former production) towards a situation where other principles have gained larger weight. Therefore, the current implementation practice seems to rest on a blend of allocation principles.

In the policy implementation process, there is a systematic link between interests and arguments. Most systematically, the NSU-representative has been advocating need as the most relevant allocation principle. The essential line of argument put forth by the NSU is that small producers should be positively discriminated, in order to retain the traditional structure of the dairy sector (with respect to regions as well as size of holdings). On the other side, the NFU-representative has systematically advocated the allocation principle of equal proportions, in order to avoid discrimination based on size. Both parties have appealed to those principles of distributive justice which are closest to their own interest. What we observe is strategic use of arguments (Elster, 1995).

With respect to the implementation of the quota schemes, there are of course also conflicting interests within the two farmer organizations. For instance, there is an underlying controversy that the more quota is distributed to new entrants or by exemption rules, the more severe the quota cuts will be for the 'ordinary' producer who falls outside these rules. Generally, the small-holders (NSU) have been more in favour of administrative redistribution than the Farmers Union (NFU).

As quotas have become a more valued asset, and as the possibility of entry into dairying without quota has decreased, the exit rate from the dairy sector has been low. Slow structural development and a decreasing milk market were the reasons for introducing a quota buy-out system in 1991. An argument that attracted some support from the Farmers Union was that it would be better to let some farmers leave the industry than to let all farms suffer from inefficient use of their productive resources as quotas were cut.

The general impression is that the various quota schemes have been subject to substantial conflicts of interests, but nevertheless implemented effectively. The consequences of the distribution of quotas on production in different regions and on farm structure has been subject to annual evaluations. The parties have agreed that rules may be altered next year, depending on what is observed this year. Despite differences in rhetoric and strategies, all parties involved seem to have acted rather pragmatically, and have shared the concern for a relatively even geographical distribution of milk production capacity. Representatives for the parties involved have obviously been able to make compromises that have been widelyaccepted by the majority of the farmers. The fact that farmers are represented in the annual agricultural negotiations also enhances the overall legitimacy of the final results among members.

Procedural Justice

We believe that the end result of any quota allocation system must pass a so-called fairness test. Though this test is of an informal nature, the consequences of failing this test, is that the system loses trustworthiness in the eyes of the farmers. Another aspect of the fairness test is that all *decision procedures* must be perceived of as fair. Unless the farmers and other involved persons trust the procedures by which quotas are allocated, they will not trust the end results of the procedures.

With respect to different versions of the quota system, multiple implementation issues seem to question the assumptions of procedural justice. The quota system has changed over time, spurred by fluxes in the market, identification of unintended effects, and by unforeseen strategic adaptations. The system has also been adapted to policy changes. Our interviews indicate that the two-price committee and the negotiating parties to the agricultural agreement have been more preoccupied with the end results of the system, than with making stable rules that dairy farmers can adhere to and rely on for a longer time span. Some of the changes in rules and implementation have also been the result of changing power relations between the interests involved.

Farmers have been charged with the difficult task of adapting strategically to a specific set of rules, under the condition that the rules in question are valid only in a very limited period of time (one year). In principle, too short a time horizon may be the source of many problems for the agents in question as well as for the effectiveness of the entire system. Commitments may be perceived difficult, since what the authorities decide does not bind them more than one year ahead. The farmer's strategies may be tailor-made to the current rules, but not necessarily relevant within the next quota scheme.

One example can illustrate the instability of the system and how and why rules are changed: The national steering committee has been concerned that the quota buy-sell scheme should not significantly influence the geographical distribution of milk production. The political concern for regional supply and farm-based settlement has already been mentioned. One argument from the farm side was to protect the system of local, professional milk producers against the disintegration of professional knowledge and support. To remain effective and motivated, all milk producers need some professional and social stimulation from local colleagues; they also need a local support structure. An exit rate that is too high could harm the local processing industry and infrastructure. Therefore, it was argued that the quota buy-sell scheme should be implemented, as long as the geographical distribution of production was not seriously altered. In 1997, trade was mediated within six large regions. Still some localities lost production, especially within the large Northern Norway region where there was a significant geographical redistribution. It was therefore suggested to divide the trade regions further.

During the agricultural policy negotiations in 1998, the Minister of Agriculture interfered, by suggesting the rule that all exchange of quotas should be organized within each municipality. The farmer's organizations agreed to this without much hesitation. For the minister, the symbolic value of imposing this rule seemed high; he was facing expectations within the government parties to maintain regional industry. However, a decision was made without careful consideration of the possible consequences of implementing this rule. The national steering committee and the quota administration were left with the very complex task of linking a general idea with smooth working routines. And dairy farmers who the year before could buy only a small part of the quota they had wanted to purchase, suddenly faced quite different possibilities, some 'obliged' to buy 20,000 liters (and pay 100,000 NOK), while others were offered nothing. This result created a lot of noise, and provoked suggestions of altering the rules within the quota year, ensuring that all eligible farmers received at least some quota.

The short time horizon of the rules in the quota scheme creates substantial inconsistency over time. There are, however, path dependencies that restrict the future scope for changes of the current quota buy-sell scheme. Quotas have gradually gained a financial value and through the quota buy-out and buy-and-sell scheme a price has been attributed to the quota. It is now difficult to abolish the buy-and-sell scheme without compensating the holders in accordance with the financial value of their quotas. The situation for some farmers may be that they stay in dairying because of the financial value of the quota rather than because of the value to the operation of the farm.

All in all, however, our impression is that the procedural justice issues that stem from the apparent risk of inconsistent governance over time, have never unfolded completely in the Norwegian dairy sector. What seems to stabilize the system, is the extent to which the quota system has been embedded in the nation's agricultural policy, and the use of a central quota committee with farmer representation. Farmers' trust in the rule makers seems to compensate the lack of stability.

Investments and Structural Development

One important aspect of production quotas is their impact on productive efficiency. Quotas at the farm level may impede structural development, and thereby damage the competitive ability of a national industry. Those who institutionalize an enduring quota system can not disregard the problem of investment needs and structural development. Thus, questions of structural development and investment possibilities have constituted a major part of the debate on policy design and implementation. In many countries the introduction of a quota market has been the main instrument for allowing structural development within a quota system. In his study of the Canadian quota system, Jacobson (1988) concludes that due to the quota market, the quota system has not hampered structural development.

Norwegian farmers and farmer organizations have been strongly opposed to the introduction of quota markets (Jervell, 1993). They seem to prefer an administrative redistribution of quotas with an upper limit on farm size, even after a quota buy and sell system is introduced. In Norway, farmers have influenced both their own quota and the quota regulations through individual and concerted action. By keeping informed they have been able to act strategically to achieve extra quota and/or voice their opinions on the regulatory policy.

In a rigid system the influence of the design and implementation of the quota system on milk production structure increases over time. During the 1980s a large part of the need for investments related to farm succession was taken care of through exemption rules. During this period, more than 50% of the farms had their quota level increased to an administratively set level based on farm resources. Since quota size was always limited upwards, a number of investment decisions were influenced. Jervell (1997) shows that farmers who were making capital improvements in the 1983–90 quota period were investing in smaller capacity buildings than farmers in 1960–1970. For individual farmers however, the motivation was to increase farm quota. Decisions to pass over the farm to the younger generation, or to till new land were, at least in some cases, strategic (third-order) decisions to make the farm eligible for additional quota. All decisions on quota redistribution were eventually made by the central steering committee, to ensure a high degree of fair treatment. Local authorities could still influence the decisions to some degree through the planning of and differential granting of loans and subsidies to new farm buildings.

A decreasing market for dairy products left dairy farmers in the 1990s with little scope for production growth. The possibilities for exemption and administratively evaluated quota increases disappeared. The quota buy out and buy-sell schemes have to a large extent been used to withdraw milk from the market, and the possibilities to develop farms through buying quota have been very limited. This implies that the pressure from and the perceived uncertainties by farmers who need to make investment decisions for the future, has increased. Some farmers in situations where important long-term decisions must be made, opt to sell their quota and leave dairying altogether.

Joint operation is an alternative solution particularly for farmers in more active and expansive regions. An interest in this type of dairy farm organization is increasing and the number of joint operations has doubled during the last three years. There are now (2000) almost 500 joint operations and more than 1000 farmers are involved. Establishing a joint operation enable farmers to invest in new technology and exploit size economies, while keeping their individual quotas and most of the dairy production subsidies. The full time dairy operation may in practice be handled by one of three active farmers, the other two having their main employment elsewhere but providing replacement and labor in peak seasons. There are rules as to the participants input in the joint operation, but on the part of the quota administrators there is a concern that what is called joint operations is in some cases more of a concealed quota leasing. Another concern is the serious question of what will happen when the next generation is to take over the operation and what should be done with the quota if one partner withdraws.

DISCUSSION

The Norwegian quota system demonstrates how a policy instrument introduced for one main purpose – to regulate milk production – can be redesigned, implemented and modified in accordance with overall policy concerns and the institutional situation. Since its introduction in the early 1980s, the dairy quota system has been intimately tied to the wider agricultural policy system. The most profiled policy objectives have been to secure domestic milk production and a regional and structural leveling of production and income. The quota schemes have demonstrated their effectiveness with respect to influencing the structure of the industry in line with the overall policy objectives. For the state and the corporatist parties, the quota systems have served as crucial and flexible instruments.

Obvious conflicts of interests between farmers have been negotiated in a structured manner, and softened by the state. Conflicting goals and interests have unfolded both in the design phase and in the implementation phase. Nevertheless, all parties seem to have been pragmatically focusing the resulting distributive and structural outcome of the various quota schemes. They have been far less oriented towards problems caused by inconsistency over time. There have been unforeseeable changes in rules, regulations and administrative practices. Some types of unintended effects have constantly accompanied the intended effects, and triggered a redesign of the regulatory system. The Norwegian quota system demonstrates that when a number of actors with divergent and conflicting interests take part in policy design, the development of policy over time tends to take unexpected and unforeseen directions. Modifications of a scheme is in itself one way to handle conflicts:

> because any scheme will create objections in some quarters, and because the faults of the system in place tend to be more vivid than the flaws of the alternatives, we often observe unstable oscillations and perpetual modifications (Elster, 1992: 137).

Distributive conflicts, which are normal and typical in most federate organizations, have also been systematically softened in the case of the Norwegian dairy sector, due to financial support from the state. The state subsidies can also explain why the principles of equal distribution of quotas (absolute equality or equal proportions) have gained so much emphasis. Both the frequent changes, the risk of time-inconsistencies and potential injustices seem to have been widely accepted by the parties and the farmers they represent. We believe the corporatist governance structure is the major cause for the calmness of the implementation. Through their professional organizations and the dairy co-operative, dairy farmers have had a profound involvement in the design and implementation of the national agricultural policy. The farmers organizations are deeply involved and responsible in both the design and implementation phases. A further reason why frequent changes are accepted is the way the quota system is embedded in the agricultural policy process. An indicator is how special concerns have been included in the system, like the introduction of quotas for new organic dairy farmers in certain areas, or the introduction of quotas for sheep farmers who could solve a predator problem by shifting to dairying. In short, the quota system has served as a flexible tool for implementing a wide set of political objectives and enterprises, within the framework of an advanced corporatist governance regime.

FUTURE PERSPECTIVES

So far, the story of the quota governance model in Norwegian dairy sector in the late 1990s is one of soft re-regulation rather than tough deregulation, as most clearly demonstrated in the case of the quota buy and sell scheme. This scheme was argued for by the state as a means to reintroduce market forces in a very regulated sector, but the final design of the system was thoroughly embedded in a policy of administrative redistribution. The market for dairy quotas in Norway is not similar to the quota markets at work in Canada or the United Kingdom. From other countries we know of quota systems that are designed more for market or industry requirements for raw milk (approaching production contracts). The policy change within the European Union dairy sector is to lower milk prices and compensate some of the income loss through direct payments connected to production or the number of cows. This is believed to reduce the pressure on quotas, as well as their financial values, and over time make it feasible to abolish quotas. Up to now, the situation in the Norwegian dairy industry has been different and the principles for the redistribution of quota sold are close to the principles that have traditionally governed agricultural policy and the two-price system.

What is the future of quota regulatory models in the Norwegian dairy industry? The following factors will undoubtedly impact heavily upon the Norwegian dairy industry and its current regulatory system:

First, the development of the demand for dairy products, and the extent to which foreign competitors will enter and penetrate the Norwegian market are important sources of uncertainty. New nationally based processing industry actors within Norway have started competing with the national co-operative Norwegian Dairies for milk deliveries. Measured by their production capacity and market share, they currently represent a negligible threat to the national dairy co-operative. The new entrants, however, represent a signal of the future structure in the Norwegian dairy industry. The entrants are not to the same degree member organizations and part of the national corporatist system and may in the future cooperate with international actors and look outside Norway for new sources of raw milk.

Second, the four dominating retailer chains in Norway are in the process of increasing their market power relative to industry and agriculture. Together the four chains control the end consumer market, and there is no way for the dairy industry to bypass them. Recently, one of the retailer chains has voiced that it will actively support competitors to the dairy co-operatives. To verify their statement, one retail chain is financially supporting one of the private dairy processors. If the retailer chains are given the option to import milk and other dairy products at lower prices, they will probably do so.

Third, the political situation in Norway is characterized by substantial ambiguity when it comes to the future of market regulation, and the role of the agricultural co-operatives. So far the politicians give no clear-cut message. It is not clear whether they expect the dairy co-operative to be a market-oriented competitor, or an administrative body. The twin roles imply very different notions of efficiency. For decades, the dairy co-operative has learned to compromise between very different expectations from the market arena, the political/administrative arena and the membership arena. Signals from the political arena are inconsistent. For instance, dairy co-operatives are expected to reduce production costs and prices substantially, but not to shut down plants in remote districts. The dairy co-operative is expected to behave like any other market competitor, but also obliged to deliver milk to competitors. The co-operative is expected to rationalize the production structure, but also to accept deliveries from all producers, independent of volume and location. Today, the mission and identity of TINE Norwegian Dairies is unclear, and future role of the co-operative in market regulation is under increased public scrutiny.

Fourth, an expensive farm structure may become an impediment for the industry in the light of World Trade Organization agreements to reduce agricultural support and decrease the barriers to trade. A diminishing domestic market will have immediate impacts on the total national quota. Farmer organizations can not in the future expect to negotiate agricultural agreements that sets national quota well beyond domestic demand. Decreasing markets, whether due to increased competition from imported dairy products or from dairy substitutes, could make it necessary to withdraw all the quotas farmers sell and return the quota buy and sell system to a buy-out system. If the market decreases rapidly it will be impossible to achieve a balanced market without either a significant reduction of milk prices and dairy farm subsidies, or a significant increase in the price paid for withdrawn quota, or both.

With respect to the immediate future, none of the important actors seem willing to abolish the quota system and to let go of the significant control this gives them over the dairy sector. However, the divergent structural development of the dairy sector in Norway and other countries, the emerging conflicts of interest between the dairy industry and other parts of the food system, and the limits international agreements put to national subsidies, represent substantial pressure towards more radical changes in the future.

REFERENCES

Banks J., & Marsden, T. (1997). Reregulating the UK Dairy Industry: The Changing Nature of Competitive Space. *Sociologia Ruralis*, 37(3), 382–404.

Brunstad, R. J., Gaasland, I., & Vårdal, E. (1998). *Deregulation of the Norwegian market for milk products*. Discussion Paper 14/98. Department of Economics, University of Bergen, Bergen.

Burrell, A. (Ed.) (1989a). *Milk Quotas in the European Community*. Wallingford: CAB International.

Burrell, A. (1989b). Dairy Herd Size and Efficiency under EC Milk Quotas. *Farm Management*, 7(3), 145–151.

Burrell, A. (1990a). Producer response to the EC milk superlevy. *European Review of Agricultural Economics*, *17*(3), 43–55.

Burrell, A. (1990b). *The management of dairy quotas in OECD countries*. Consultants report. OECD. Paris.

Dawson, P. J., & White, B. (1990). The post-quota performance of dairy farms in England and Wales. *Applied Economics*, *22*, 1399–1406.

Elster, J. (1992). *Local Justice. How Institutions Allocate Scarce Goods and necessary Burdens*. New York: Russell Sage.

Elster, J. (1995). Strategic Uses of Arguments. In: K. J. Arrow et.al. (Eds), *Barriers to Conflict Resolution*. New York: W.W.Norton & Company.

Flaten, O., & Giæver, H. (1998). *Strukturendringer i norsk mjølkeproduksjon*. (Structural changes in Norwegian milk production.) Melding nr. 18. Institutt for økonomi og samfunnsfag, Norges landbrukshøgskole, Ås-NLH.

Flyvbjerg, B. (1998). *Rationality and power: Democracy in practice*. Chicago: University of Chicago Press.

Furre, B. (1971). *Mjølk, bønder og tingmenn. Studiar i organisasjon og politikk kring omsetningen av visse landbruksvarer 1929–30*. (Milk, farmers and politicians. Studies in the political organisation of the distribution of some agricultural products 1929–30). Oslo: Det norske samlaget.

Giæver, H., Jervell, A. M., Flaten, O., & Hegrenes, A. (1995). *Kostnader og omstillingsmuligheter på norske mjølkeproduksjonsbruk*. (Production costs and adjustment possibilities on Norwegian dairy farms.) NILF-rapport 1995:3. NILF Oslo/ NLH Ås.

Gouin, D. M. (1988). Peut-on se passer d'un marche des quotas? *Cahiers d'Economie et Sociologie Rurales*, *7*(2), 179–192.

Gouin, D. M., & Morriset, M. (1988). Vingt ans de contigent laitiers: l'experience canadienne. *Cahiers d'Economie et Sociologie Rurales*, *7*(2), 37–56.

Hairy, D., & Perraud, D. (1988). Crise laitiere et quotas: l'evolution de la politique laitiere en France et dans la Communaute. *Cahiers d'Economie et Sociologie Rurales*, *7*(2), 9–36.

Hanninl, L. G., & Nott, S. B. (1986). *The Canadian Milk Quota System: An Analysis and Comparison to the Michigan and U.S. Dairy Industry*. Agricultural Economics Report No 489 September 1986. Department of Agricultural Economics, Michigan State University, East Lansing.

Hegrenes, A., & Romarheim, H. (1989). *Investering og kapital i landbruket 1970–1988*. (Investment and capital in agriculture 1970–1988). Landbrukspolitisk forskningsprogram. Arbeidsrapport 24. NILF. Oslo.

Holmgren, K. (1981). *Norges Kjøtt og Fleskesentral. Jubileumsskrift 1931–1981*. (The Norwegian Meat Co-operative. Jubilee Edition 1931–1981). Oslo: Norbok.

IDF (1989). Quota Controls. On Milk Supplies and Supply Management. *Bulletin of the International Dairy Federation No. 245* (2nd ed.). Brussels.

Isaksen, G. (1984). *Politiske mål, offentlig styring og samhandling innen jordbruket. En studie av de muligheter og begrensninger markedsorganisasjonene i kjøttsektoren gir for offentlig styring*. (Political objectives, public governance and cooperation in agriculture. A study of the potential and pitfalls of the sales cooperatives in the meat sector with respect to governance). Aas, Norway: Agricultural University of Norway.

Jacobson, R. E. (1988). Supply Management Options: National Impact and Policy. *Journal of Dairy Science*, *71*(8), 2297–2303.

Jervell, A. M. (1993). Farmers' attitudes to milk quota policy in Norway. *Sociologia Ruralis*, *XXXIII*(3/4), 365–382.

Jervell, A. M. (1994). *Mulighetene for norsk melkeproduksjon. Konkurranseevne og kostnadssam-menligninger.* (Opportunities for Norwegian milk production. Competitiveness and relative costs.) Det landbrukspolitiske forskningsprogrammet, arbeidsrapport nr. 31. Institutt for økonomi og samfunnsfag, NLH, Ås.

Jervell, A. M. (1997). *Farm quota management. A farm level study of the Norwegian two-price milk quota system 1983–1990.* Doctor scientarium theses 1997: 9. Department of economics and social sciences. Agricultural University of Norway.

Jervell, A. M., & Løyland, J. (1998). Endringer i jordbrukshusholdenes inntekt utenfor bruket 1986–96. (Changes in agricultural household's off-farm income 1986–1996.) *Landbruksøkonomisk forum,* 4/98, 63–75.

Kirke, A. W. (1989). The Influence of Milk Supply Quotas on Dairy Farm Performance in Northern Ireland. In: Burrell (Ed.), *Milk Quotas in the European Community.* Wallingford: CAB International.

Kola, J. (1991). *Production control in Finnish agriculture. Determinants of control policy and quantitative and economic efficiency of dairy restrictions.* Agricultural Economics Research Inst.. Helsinki: Research Publications 64.

Løyland, J., Haglerød, A., Jervell, A. M., Mittenzwei, K., Nævdal, E., & Prestegard, S. S. (1995). Kostnadskonsekvenser av omfordeling av melkekvoter. (Cost consequences of the redistribution of milk quotas). NILF-notat 1995:7, 120p.

NML (1986). *Håndbok for toprisordningen på melk. (Handbook for the two-price milk quota system).* Sekretariatet for styringsgruppen for toprisordningen for melk. Oslo.

NOU (1980). *Mjølkeproduksjonen. Produksjonstilpassende tiltak. (Dairy production. Measures for regulation.)* Universitetsforlaget. Oslo: Norges offentlige utredninger 1980:2.

OECD (1990). *National policies and agricultural trade. Country study Norway.* Organisation for Economic Co-operation and development: National policies and agricultural trade. Country Studies. Paris.

Petit, M., de Benedictis, M., Britton, D., De Groot, M., Henrichsmeyer, W., & Lechi, F. (1987). *Agricultural policy Formation in the European Community: The birth of Milk Quotas and CAP reform.* Elsevier. Amsterdam.

Romstad, E. (1995). Omsettelige kvoter,(Tradeable quotas.) *Landbruksøkonomisk forum 1/95,* 69–78.

Sætren, H. (1998). *Whatever happened to implementation research – And does it matter?* Paper presented at the conference Samples of the future at Stanford University, Stanford, 20–22 September 1998.

Vatn, A. (1991). *Landbrukspolitikk og bondeatferd. Ein studie av tilpassinga til 650 landbrukshushald frå 1975–1990.* (Agricultural policy and the behaviour of farmers. A study of 650 agricultural households from 1975–90). Norges landbrukshøgskole. Institutt for økonomi og samfunnsfag. Melding nr. 4. ÅS-NLH.

REORGANIZATION OF MILK MARKETING ARRANGEMENTS IN THE UNITED KINGDOM, 1994–2000

Jo Banks

INTRODUCTION

The organisation of the United Kingdom dairy sector has undergone a fundamental transformation following the passage of the 1993 Agriculture Act. A shift has taken place away from a 'supply based' regulatory framework, designed and originally implemented primarily to give milk producers (farmers) stable markets and incomes, to a more 'demand-led' regulatory context within which milk marketing arrangements are now able to more rapidly and recognisably reflect evolving market conditions and supply chain dynamics. The 1993 Agriculture Act terminated the existence of five statutory monopoly Milk Marketing Boards (MMBs) across the United Kingdom which had dominated the structure and regulation of the industry for over sixty years. The MMBs were farmer based organisations which acted as the sole broker of milk between dairy farmers and dairy processors in different regions of the U.K. All farmers were legally obliged, unless specifically exempt, to sell their milk through the Milk Marketing Boards.

This chapter concentrates primarily upon milk marketing and the dairy sector in England and Wales. The regulatory change which removed the statutory MMB of England and Wales has initiated a process whereby supply chain relationships have been renegotiated, new balances of power tested, and new conventions established across the dairy supply chain. The impacts are

Research in Rural Sociology, Volume 8, pages 379–405.
Copyright © 2000 by Elsevier Science Inc.
All rights of reproduction in any form reserved.
ISBN: 0-7623-0474-X

evidenced in the changing organisation and structure of the industry. I wish here to tell something of the story of milk marketing in the U.K., beginning with an overview of the industry prior to 1994, and then going on to examine how the industry has evolved since that time. Within this, particular consideration is given to the emergence and relative effectiveness of new forms of producer co-operation, the changing structure of the industry, and the process and discourses of reregulation which here are revealed as both contested, hierarchical and social in nature. However, before going on to do this, consideration is given to the use of the term reregulation to describe the removal of the statutory milk marketing framework.

REREGULATION NOT DEREGULATION

Polanyi (1944) originally introduced ideas of market embeddedness in social and political structures in an examination of how regulatory institutions develop. His approach highlighted the fact that, as markets exist within social and political frameworks, markets are always regulated. In the U.K. the term deregulation has become synonymous with the privatisation by the state of services formerly held in public ownership, for example, the privatisation of the railways, water services, gas and electricity supplies in the U.K. However, in using the term deregulation we risk implying that regulation is only something carried out by the state, and that once the state has withdrawn from direct intervention, regulation has effectively been removed, leaving industries to operate in a regulation free environment. Such a view denies other potentially significant forms of non-statutory regulation. Therefore, the term used to describe the withdrawal of direct state intervention in the sector throughout this chapter is not *de*regulation but *re*regulation. The concept of *re*regulation, allows us to move away from a polarised notion which sees regulation as something only undertaken by the state. Christopherson (1993) comments that 'on-off' concepts of regulation are not broad enough to encompass forms of regulation which blur the distinction between public and private sectors, and that a second, broader conception of regulation is required, where continuous regulation, by private as well as public sectors is assumed. Adopting such an approach therefore invites contemporary analysis of the U.K. dairy sector to observe how new forms of public and private regulation emerge and are reproduced.

Having moved away from a solely state focused interpretation of regulation to a definition which encompasses the role played by other actors in establishing alternative forms of social and economic regulation across supply chains, or between groups of individuals, the process of reregulation itself becomes a key focus. Taking this perspective and applying it to the dairy sector of the 1990s raises a series of questions: (1) Whose interests are being best served by reregulation? Farmers, processors, retailers? (2) Which actors (in the agro-food complex) are being empowered, and which weakened by the process of reregulation? (3) What are the discourses of empowerment, advantage and differentiation, and who is defining them? (4) What implications do these changes have for the processes of uneven development at different spatial and structural scales? Before going on to examine some of these questions, our attention must first turn to the dairy sector under the statutory Milk Marketing Scheme as this provides the context for change.

THE U.K. DAIRY SECTOR 1933–1994

In examining the reorganisation of the dairy sector in the 1990s it is necessary to understand something of the industry prior to that time. The structure of the U.K. dairy industry is unique within Europe. This uniqueness has resulted from the historical development of a regulatory framework between 1933 and 1994 (the Milk Marketing Scheme or MMS) which encouraged the separation of processing and production activities in the sector and had at its core the operation of the MMBs. Throughout the industrial world by far the most common response to the mutual reliance between dairy processing companies and milk producers has been the formation of vertically integrated producer-processor co-operatives, these never emerged in the U.K. Back in the 1920s and 1930s the British dairy processing sector was consolidating and expanding rapidly. Lacking effective mechanisms for co-operation in the market, dairy farmers faced very low incomes, insecure markets and a weak negotiating position within the supply chain. Consequently, farmers would undercut one another in the drive to sell their highly perishable commodity before it became worthless (Baker, 1973).

The problem of poor co-ordination among producers was tackled through the passage in 1931 and 1933 of Agricultural Marketing Acts. These Acts established the monopoly Milk Marketing Board in England and Wales. The key objectives of the MMB were to provide stable markets and to increase farm incomes, goals reflected in the organisations motto 'Together in Enterprise'. Later the MMB would also played a key role in improving standards and levels of efficiency through encouraging the adoption of artificial insemination technology, improved stock genetics, and through milk recording. Although established by state statute, the MMB was not a government organisation. However, a very close relationship developed between the MMB and the Ministry of Agriculture Fisheries and Food, a relationship which become widely regarded as an exemplar of agrarian corporatism (Grant, 1985; Cox et al., 1990). As Winter (1984) observed, "By approaching the M.M.B. from the standpoint of corporatist theory it is possible to avoid the twin pitfalls of considering the Board either solely as a producers' association (or lobby) or as a government body. As a corporatist arrangement it shares aspects of both."

Operation of the MMB

The MMB acted as a monopoly raw milk buyer and broker, selling all farmers milk on their behalf and returning to farmers a 'pool' price based on the returns from all the milk when sold. The 'end-use' pricing system employed by the MMB meant that milk destined for manufacture into lower value processed commodities (e.g. butter, skimmed milk powder) cost dairy processing companies less to purchase than identical milk destined for processing and sale in the (premium) liquid milk market. Within the 'end-use' pricing system, priority of supply was also given to servicing the liquid milk market. This system was not universally endorsed by the industry, particularly once competition among retailers (notably the large supermarkets) reduced the profit margins on liquid milk. Objections also came from quality cheese manufacturers and others producing high value-added processed diary products since they could not guarantee receiving specific volumes of milk on a daily basis all year round. The ability to operate a pool pricing system was only made possible because the MMB was responsible for transportation of milk from farm to the first destination of processing. If transportation had been in the hands of processors then they would have wanted to minimise their costs rather than giving equality of market access to all producers.[1]

Prior to 1973 the MMB set the price of milk for various end uses in consultation with the processing industry. The presence of Government officials on the MMB Board and rules governing its operation were intended to prevent the abuse of monopoly against the consumer interest. From 1973 to 1994 milk prices were negotiated annually within the Joint Committee which contained equal representation of both dairy processors and milk producers (the Dairy Trade Federation and MMB respectively). Furthermore, from 1973 onward prices for certain bulk commodities were set under the CATFI (Common Approach to Financial Information) system raw milk pricing formula. This formula of milk pricing was based upon a target return on capital of 12.5% to the dairy processor and did much to stifle innovation.

Spatial and Structural Development Under the MMB

The MMB had an impact on the spatial development of the dairy industry. A number of policies and features were central in this regard and would generate opportunities for differentiation and respatialisation after 1994. Firstly, under the MMB farmers had equal market access irrespective of how much milk they produced or where they were located relative to the market (processing facility) within an MMB region. Secondly, assuming quality criteria were met, farmers were paid a fixed price per litre. Thus, a farmer producing one million litres of milk a year on a farm located very close to processing facilities would receive the same price for each litre as a farmer producing just one hundred thousand litres located at considerable distance from processing facilities. Geographical cost factors of production were therefore removed from the production side of the industry. The pool pricing system meant that farmers located close to markets were effectively subsidising more geographically remote producers. The MMB had full control over transport and distribution, and milk prices to processors were calculated to include such charges.

The MMB also shaped the structure of the industry Despite being operated on behalf of dairy farmers, the MMB did not result in a fossilisation of the production base. The trend toward fewer, larger farms, and increasing capital intensity continued in line with productivist agricultural policies (see Table 1), and in many cases were encouraged by the MMB. The introduction of EU milk quotas in 1984 placed a ceiling onproduction increases. Subsequently dairy farmers focused increasingly upon improving yield per cow relative to inputs, especially through improved stock genetics.

Furthermore, despite maintaining a broad level of support among farmers, by the 1990s the Milk Marketing System was widely regarded as being responsible for stifling innovation and new product development in the processing sector. The Milk Marketing Scheme continued to give priority of supply to liquid milk up to 1994 and the CATFI system, did little to encourage the industry to rationalise and innovate away from the manufacture of low

Table 1. Dairy Structure, England and Wales, 1934–1994

	Cows ('000)	Producers	Milk/Cow (litres) April to March
1934	2,206	141,000	n.a
1950	2,491	161,937	2,830
1960	2,595	123,137	3,320
1970	2,714	80,265	3,755
1980	2,672	43,815	4,715
1994	2,218	28,033	5,265

Source: The Residuary Milk Marketing Board. Cited in J.Empson (1997).

value bulk commodities into new higher value-added growth sectors. There was little incentive to risk capital on new ventures when margins (albeit low) were effectively guaranteed for the manufacture of bulk commodities due to the low milk price related to such products and the European Union's intervention buying mechanisms (which placed a floor on market prices). Playing the system rather than addressing emerging markets became widespread.

A second impact of the Milk Marketing Scheme on the processing sector was the development by the MMB of its own processing operation. This occurred very early in the MMB history and was caused by the refusal of Nestle (a processor) to enter into a contract with the MMB.[2] As a response to this early challenge the MMB established a creamery which could be used as a buyer of 'last resort' when no other buyers could be found, and also as a sink for surplus milk. These processing facilities eventually developed into a company called Dairy Crest which would go on to become the largest dairy processing company in Britain. In establishing a processing division, the MMB was playing an active role in strengthening the position of milk producers within the market place, and developing strategies to minimise the risk posed by dissident dairies who might attempt to by-pass the monopoly MMB and throw the whole system into crisis. Having processing capacity also provided greater security to those producers located far from major markets. As we shall see, the attempt by the MMBs successor to develop processing capacity would become a critical issue in reshaping the sector and an ongoing cause of uncertainty.

It was estimated by the Dairy Industry Newsletter[3] that by 1997 there were around 400 milk processors in the U.K., nearly 300 in England and Wales, 25 in Northern Ireland and 100 in Scotland. Together, these companies processed more than 13,600 million litres of milk a year. Nearly three-quarters of these companies were small liquid processors (including farm based milk bottlers). There were also more than 200 small cheese makers. In 1997/8 four processors together accounted for 51.7% of raw milk purchases, each purchasing more than 1.5 billion litres of milk. Three processors, who each purchased more than 500 million litres, accounted for a further 17%, so that the seven largest companies out of around 400 in the U.K., purchased two-thirds of the raw milk in Great Britain (see Table 2). In terms of whole milk utilisation by dairies in 1997 51% of milk in England and Wales went to the liquid market, 26% into the production of Cheddar cheese, 10% other cheeses, 6% condensed milk, 3% other products and 5% other disposals (NDC, 1998).

While the MMB existed for over 60 years, the markets for dairy products and their means of reaching consumer did not remain unchanged. This is particularly true with liquid milk sales which have shifted from doorstep

Table 2. Major UK Milk Processors, 1997, with UK Market Share

Company	Volume	Share of raw milk purchases in U.K.
Express Dairies	< 1.5 billion litres each	13.6%
AWG		13.1%
Unigate		12.5%
Dairy Crest		12.5%
Total		51.7%
MD Foods	< 500 million litres each	6.1%
ACC		5.8%
Wiseman		5.1%
Total		17.0%
Other processors (10 companies)	100–500 million litres	14.1%
Small processors	> 100 million litres each	17.2%

Source: Adapted from MMC 1999 p.159.

deliveries to supermarket sales. According to figures from the National Dairy Council (1999), doorstep delivery accounted for just 35% of the liquid volume sold, down from over 70% in the 1980s. Apart from the 17% used in schools or catering, the rest of the U.K.'s liquid milk – approximately half – is sold in supermarkets or other retail outlets. This shift in liquid volume from doorstep to supermarket shelf sales has significantly reduced the margins available to dairy processors supplying the liquid market and placed processors in direct competition with one another to secure the highly important retail supply contracts (see Table 3).

Table 3. UK Milk Prices, Pence Per Pint, 1993, 1995, 1996

	1993	1995	1996
Retail Price (A)	104	84	95
Manufacturers Price (B)	90	80	84
Raw Milk Costs (C)	56	60	62
Retail cash margin (A-B)	14	4	11
Manufacturers cash margin (B-C)	34	20	22

(Price based on a 4 pint, standard large retail container.)
Source: BZW estimates 1996.

The globalisation of the dairy industry and the advent of a more diverse marketplace exposed the inefficiencies of the U.K. dairy sector and the weakness of the end-use pricing structure and milk allocation system. By the late 1980s and 1990s processors were increasingly arguing that the MMS was preventing them effectively meeting the challenges of emerging markets and new retailing structures.

Challenges to the MMB

Throughout the post-war period the duel model of agrarian corporatism and agrarain productivism[4] was reflected in the supply-led regulation of the dairy sector. End-use pricing; liquid milk premiums; annually set prices; the removal of geographical cost factors in production; all of these factors reflect how the sector was regulated in a way which promoted the interests of milk producers.

However, the development of more complex markets and new retailing structures, alongside a gradual but inevitable evolution of Common Agricultural Policy system away from price support and market intervention, meant that statutory measures developed under very different conditions were bound to come under considerable pressure for change. Indeed, by the late 1980s even some farmers were beginning to question whether the MMB, which had served former generations so well, was really the most appropriate structure through which to meet the challenges of a new century. Farmers complained that U.K. prices were among the lowest in Europe, despite having a monopoly co-operative and some of the highest quality of milk available in Europe. Farmers could also see that milk prices were likely to come under increased pressure as trade liberalisation advanced, and questioned whether the bureaucratic MMB, with transaction costs as high as 2 pence per litre by the 1990s, really had the capacity to act in their long-term interests.

Throughout the 1980s and early 1990s the impetus for change built from many sources. The following factors were particularly important in instigating change: (a) European Union objections to the monopoly position of the MMB following the introduction of EU wide competition policy and the Single European Act; (b) wide spread dissatisfaction among U.K. farmers with the low price they received for milk relative to their European counterparts; (c) dairy industry objections to the operation of a state sanctioned monopoly, and to the end-use pricing system which it (and the Milk Marketing Board) recognised as discouraging innovation and investment in new products; (d) the increasingly high costs of running the bureaucratic MMB; and, (e) strong ideological objections by the Conservative government to the continued existence of a producer monopoly distorting the operation of 'the free market'. On this last point, it was clear by the early 1990s that continuation of the status quo in the dairy sector was an increasingly untenable option. The ideological objections to the continued existence of the MMB structure were reflected by Marsden & Wrigley (1995) when, in the broader context, they observed that,

> While the retailers were viewed by government as the embodiment of Thatcherite free-market growth, the farmers were, more embarrassingly, seen to be the recipients of large amounts of public funds and of old-style corporatist regulatory support (p. 39).

The desire on the part of the government to reregulate the dairy sector was clearly expressed during the passage of the 1993 Agriculture Act through Parliament. The following statement was made which most appropriately summarised U.K. government policy regarding state intervention in the British dairy sector at that time.

> When the Milk Marketing Scheme was introduced 60 years ago, its very characteristics as a monopoly were hailed as the salvation of producers. Times have changed, however, and the scheme is now the farmer's gaoler not his saviour . . . The ending of the milk marketing schemes will amount to a major deregulation measure *replacing bureaucratic control with freedom of action.* It will liberate much creative potential which is suppressed at the moment and help our processors and producers challenge their foreign competitors in *providing what the consumer wants* . . . In the context of the Single Market, we need to enable our producers to compete on level terms with their continental counterparts . . . We must beware of falling into the situation of the dairy industry, where the high added value products come increasingly from abroad and we are left with the commodity end of the business . . . I am not prepared to be seen as a Minister who was so unable to confront short-term fears that he allowed an industry to destroy itself . . . we have shown our concern to improve our ability to compete and to give our producers and manufacturers better opportunity to win a larger share of the market for added value products . . . *the opportunities presented by our supermarkets can be fullyseized only by businesses big enough to negotiate satisfactory terms and to deliver the required quantity and quality consistently* . . . Our aim is to help the industry do its job better, to liberate it from the shackles of the past and to realise its potential. At a time when there is so much talk of restrictions and quotas this Bill is a move to set the industry free. (MAFF, 1993) [my emphasis].

NEW TIMES: REREGULATION AND REORGANISATION

On what became known as Vesting Day, November 1st 1994, all dairy farmers across the U.K. were able, for the first time since 1933, to freely negotiate the sale of their milk directly with milk processing companies who, in turn, could now write their own contracts and invite producers to sign-up to them. Althernatively, producers could form new producer operated groups or co-operatives. What emerged reflects Jessop's (1990) observed that while capitalism may have inviolable laws, it also has a plurality of logics.

New Mechanisms for Marketing Milk

The 1993 Agriculture Act placed a requirement on the MMBs to prepare a reorganisation schemes for the marketing of milk in their areas. In England and Wales the MMB reorganisation scheme involved the establishment of a large voluntary farmer owned co-operative company called Milk Marque Limited. This company was promoted as the successor to the MMB and was obliged to act as buyer of last resort if farmers were not offered, or did not choose to accept, alternative contracts. Of couse, if farmers did not wish to join Milk Marque then there was nothing stopping them establishing other producer-controlled co-operatives or in developing supply relationships directly with private dairy companies.

Under the MMB milk collection, transportation, quality and compositional testing, and price negotiations were all centrally organised. Since Vesting Day two main types of organisation have emerged through which these activities are variously undertaken or managed. These are referred to as 'quota-holding' and 'non-quota holding' groups, or more simply as independent brokering groups (IBGs) and direct contract groups (DCGs) respectively. These are now examined in turn. Fig. 1 overviews the new milk marketing framework.

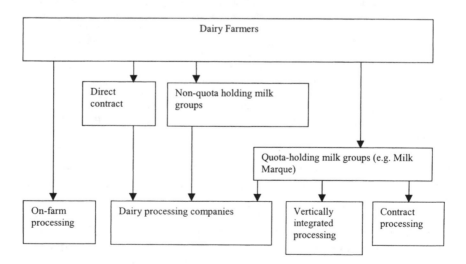

Fig. 1. From Producers to Processor through the U.K.s Reregulated Dairy Sector.

Quota-Holding Milk Groups

Milk Marque, the successor the MMB, was the major quota-holding group to be established in England and Wales in 1994, although a handful of much smaller groups have also been formed since then. The term 'quota holding' is used to describe such groups because, under the milk regime operated through the CAP in the U.K., farmers have to register their wholesale milk quota with the first buyer of that milk, with the first buyer subsequently becoming liable for the payment of any wholesale levy (overproduction fine) which is then recovered from individual producers. Under the former Milk Marketing Scheme, only the MMB was approved as a first buyer by the Intervention Board. Today quota-holding groups are responsible for the collection, testing, and transportation of their milk. They run their own systems for invoicing customers (processors), making payments to their members for their milk, and managing their members milk quota. Quota-holding groups often supply more than one processing company, and some have chosen to vertically integrate through investment in their own processing capacity.

Since Vesting Day Milk Marque has been obliged under the rules of its formation as a successor body to the MMB, to offer all dairy farmers formerly selling through the MMB a new supply contract. As a co-operative whose membership was voluntary, Milk Marque wished to sign contracts with as many farmers as possible in order to control a large proportion of available raw milk supplies, and thereby place itself in a strong negotiating position with processing companies. The argument that strength would come through numbers was bolstered by the general acceptance that, with the growing dominance of the multiple retailers and the continuing and expected rationalisation in the processing sector, to have anystrength in the market, producers needed to be part of a large farmer controlled business. Unsurprisingly there was a degree of animosity between dairy farmers supporting and promoting Milk Marque and those who wished to experiment with other trading arrangements. With imaginations fuelled by memories of the 1920s and 1930s, many farmers, uninvolved in milk marketing for many years, feared that large dairy processing companies would seek once again to exploit farmers if they did not stick 'together in enterprise' once more. The potential to build strength through numbers was further aided by the belief that in a market constrained by milk quotas, and where total quota only accounted for around 90–95% of U.K. domestic consumption in the early 1990s, dairy companies would be forced to compete for available supplies, and that this would help maintain or increase farm-gate prices. At Vesting Day, Milk Marque has signed contracts with over 20,000 farmers and controlled 66% of available milk supply in England and Wales, 58% nationally.

Non Quota-holding Groups

A significant minority of farmers (approximately one third in England and Wales) did not wish to join Milk Marque or other smaller quota-holding groups, but rather to establish relationships directly with dairy processing companies. Dairy companies themselves, foreseeing the new marketing situation post-MMB encouraged dairy farmers in the run up to Vesting Day to sign contracts directly with their companies (making the dairy processor the body registered with the Intervention Board and hence the 'holder' of the quota). Some farmers, especially those supplying smaller processors, were happy to simply have one-to-one direct contracts and dealings with the processing company involved. This was particularly the case where personal networks existed and the dairies in question were manufacturing high value-added products forwhich farmers could see growth markets. However, in most cases, dairy farmers came together within groups affiliated to a particular processor. Nearly all the large processing companies sought to develop supplies from non-quota holding groups. Many of these groups were formed by farmers themselves as a result of informal discussions on how to respond to the abolition of the MMB leading up to Vesting Day. Many dairy processors were very keen to reduce their reliance upon Milk Marque as the dominant raw milk supplier. Hence, even through, as members of non-quota holding groups, farmers contracts were directly with dairy companies, as members of an affiliated group they had the opportunity to use their combined strength (milk volume) as a means of negotiating prices higher than those being offered to Milk Marque members, and other bonuses. If members of non-quota holding groups felt their terms of trade were unsatisfactory and could be bettered elsewhere, members could vote to terminate their contracts *en masse*, and move as a whole group to supplying another dairy processor. In the period immediately following Vesting Day, such groups became highly effective in obtaining prices 5–10% over those being paid to members of Milk Marque. On average the volume of milk produced by members of non-quota holding groups has been much greater than those supplying Milk Marque. This feature, in conjunction with often tight geographical coherence, enabled processors to off-set premium prices against overall cost-savings in transportation. If farmers were located relatively close to a large processing company it was likely that if they signed a contract with Milk Marque their production would still be going to the same plant. For some, loyalty to the ideals of co-operative marketing through Milk Marque had to be weighed carefully against the potential opportunity costs such a decision could entail.

Aside from higher prices, another reason some farmer were willing to move away from the continuity and security offered by Milk Marque was the fact that they had developed close ties with their local creameries under the MMB. Through the ex-farm allocation system operated by the MMB many farmers knew which dairy was processing their milk, and came to take pride in the products of those companies. Therefore, when the MMB was abolished, the opportunity was seized by many to move into a closer relationship with the businesses processing their milk, rather than join Milk Marque which was, due to disagreements over new milk selling systems, developing antagonistic relationships with processing companies even before it was formally launched.

In 1994 farmers hopes were high that the new milk marketing arrangements would result in higher milk prices at the farm gate for members of quota-holding and non-quota holding groups alike. In line with these expectations the immediate impact of the new milk marketing arrangements was to raise the farm-gate price of milk from an average of 22.1 pence per litre (ppl) to 24.5 ppl., and the cost of milk to processors from an average of 23.9 ppl to 26 ppl. (DIN 1998). Producers of commodities such as cheese or butter, no longer cushioned from the market by end-use pricing and CATFI, were particularly hard hit, seeing raw milk prices increase by nearly 20% in one year All milk processors now had to compete on an equal basis for supplies, irrespective of whether they were producing high value-added products or low value commodities.

With control over the majority of milk being produced in England and Wales, and in the context of a market constrained by milk quota, Milk Marque's milk price effectively became the base price for milk nationally, and the price upon which other milk groups based their premiums or bonuses. The Monopolies and Mergers Commission report into the supply of raw cow's milk in the U.K. neatly summarised the Milk Marque selling system as follows (MMC, 1999: 3)

> Milk Marque sells most of its milk on six-month or longer contracts in selling processes held twice a year. Under its 'volume-bid' auction system, buyers bid for the volume of milk they require under one or more 'service contracts', which are offered at specified prices that include delivery. The service contracts differ chiefly in the extent to which they permit Milk Marque or its buyers, respectively, to vary the volumes of milk that Milk Marque supplies daily, each month or over the entire contract period. Its 'market-led' contacts give buyers relatively even volumes of milk over these periods and are therefore more highly priced than the 'supply-led' contracts, under which the volumes of milk supplied may be far less stable and predictable. Milk Marque uses its supply-led contracts to manage daily and

seasonal fluctuations in production and demand. Typically, fresh liquid milk processors, whose products cannot be stored, require even supplies of milk to meet a fairly predictable retail demand for their product. Processors of storable products such as cheese and milk powder can more readily handle fluctuating supplies.

DISCOURSES OF REREGULATION

As already noted, the majority of the major dairy companies attempted (with variable degrees of success) to purchase at least part of their basic milk requirements from sources other than Milk Marque. The justification of such strategies varied considerably between companies. However, a set of common priorities and discourses emerged which have been redefining differentiation (competition and forces driving uneven development) in the sector in the periodleading up to, and in the years immediately following, vesting day. What follows is an examination of these dimensions of differentiation. From these responses we can begin to understand how new supply-chain relations, and the parameters which define them, variously empowered different groups of actors and agencies as well as restructuring and re-spatialising dairying.

Security of Supply and the Formation of New Producer Groups

In the context of a national market constrained by milk quota, and with great uncertainty over new milk marketing arrangements, ensuring a secure supply of milk became a key objective of dairy processors in 1993, 1994 and 1995. Initially it was a common view among dairy companies that the security of supplies (required daily) could not be assured satisfactorily by a 100% reliance upon Milk Marque since the price bidding and allocation systems operated by the co-operative could potentially lead to bids (made by processors for set amounts of milk at set prices) being scaled back if total demand exceeded total supply. As it has emerged, security of supply has become less of an issue over time, particularly as milk prices have fallen and processors have contracted a greater proportion of the milk requirements directly or from other quota-holding groups. From late 1996 onward dairy companies were less concerned with attracting new sources of supply as with improving the quality of existing supplies. Indeed, as milk prices have fallen so raw milk sourced from Milk Marque has becoming a cheaper alternative to directly contracted supplies (see Table 4).

In the heady days following reregulation, when milk prices were rising and producers were desperately trying to develop independent sources of supply, it was widely considered that both quota holding and non-quotaholding groups

Table 4. Price Paid for Milk by Processors and Amount Received by Farmers (England and Wales 1994–1998), Pence Per Litre.

	94–95	94–95	95–96	96–97	97–98
Paid by dairy companies	24.1	26.1	26.1	25.8	22.5
Paid to dairy farmers	22.4	24.5	24.5	24.2	20.5

alike would be able to maintain prices for producers. Although this has not materialised in the longer-term, the groups do still have an important role to play in negotiating milk prices and represent an important new form of producer-based activity and co-operation. Several dairy companies initially had misgivings about milk groups, particularly non-quota holding groups. However they quickly warmed to the idea once it became clear that producers favoured these groups, and that they provided an effective and efficient means of communicating with large numbers of producers. Direct contract groups also allowed dairy companies to develop close working relationships with farmers in specific areas and/or for specific projects or product developments. However, only one milk group, which controls the majority of organically produced milk in the U.K., has been effective in maintaining high producer prices and true price independence from Milk Marque. As relations between dairy processors and dairy farmers have evolved since 1994, the negotiating power of milk groups has not been able to over ride external factors (most notably the strength of Sterling) exerting downward pressure on prices.

Price, Volume and Geography

The fact that farmers who were willing to sign contracts directly with dairy companies in the immediate period following reregulation (1994–96) wanted a price premium for doing so led analysts to question whether dairy companies could afford the luxury of sourcing milk directly. Working from prices offered for a standard litre during the period November 1994 to June 1995, Fearne & Ray (1995) noted how the average price paid to members of non-quota holding groups was over 1 ppl more than the average price offered by Milk Marque during this period. The extra money paid to members of non-quota holding groups being variously made up from direct incentives, loyalty bonuses, and group bonuses. Despite the price premium for direct supply, Fearne and Ray showed that, in general, milk sourced directly by dairy companies was cheaper than that supplied by Milk Marque. Efficient transport networks based on geographically rational 'milk fields' and (potentially) reduced brokering/ negotiating fees were both important factors enabling this saving to be made whilst still offering price premiums to dairy farmers. In most cases, direct sourcing takes place from farmers located within a 20–30 mile radius (or equivalent cost-rational zone) surrounding processing facilities. Some large companies with more than one production site, and thus able to balance milk supplies between sites if necessary, have worked to build milk fields which, if not contiguous to a processing facility, retain a high concentration of volume in a restricted geographical area. Since 1994 there has been a continued entrenchment of contract geographies based in large part around non-quota holding groups.

In addition to the efficiencies offered by tightly organised milk groups, by sourcing a proportion of milk supply directly via non-quota holding groups, dairy companies could also purchase milk from Milk Marque on cheaper supply-led contracts (which allow daily deliveries to fluctuate) rather than the more expensive demand-led contracts. Through direct contracts dairies could guarantee minimum volumes necessary to maintain processing efficiencies. Costs could be further reduced since purchases from Milk Marque included a transportation fee in the price. Hence, many processing companies used Milk Marque to supply processing facilities furthest from their own milk fields and in doing so externalised transportation costs.

Two years after reregulation it was clear that Milk Marque had lost much of its former ability to maintain high milk prices, and its selling system was coming under increasing pressure. Initially the system whereby dairy companies bid for available milk supplies encouraged processors to collectively oversubscribe the volumes available. This enabled Milk Marque to re-start the bidding process at a higher milk price until demand met with supply. Once dairy companies had overcome their initial uncertainty and became more confident and accustomed to the new milk buying system this situation reversed. From 1996 Milk Marque frequently received bids for volumes of milk from processors which failed to accommodate the supplies available. In this situation the co-operative's selling system required that a new round of bidding was initiated at lower milk price. Evidence of the growing ability of the major dairy companies to operate the Milk Marque selling system their advantage is the shift in volumes of milk bid for under the different types of contracts offered by Milk Marque. According to the National Farmers Union,[5] in the first milk auction after deregulation, 4.5% of the milk offered was bought on the most expensive premier contracts, while 26.1% was bought on the cheaper fluctuation/residual supply contracts. By the time of the last full scale sellinground before Milk Marque abandoned their selling system in the summer of 1998, premier contracts accounted for only 1.1% of the milk bid for while fluctuating/residual covered 74.9%. By standing back from the Milk Marque bidding rounds, large processors forced Milk Marque to reject all bids and restart the selling round at lower prices. This action eventually led in 1998 to Milk Marque abandoning its selling system in favour of individual price negotiations with its customers.

Since 1996 the milk price received by dairy farmers in the U.K. has declined rapidly, tumbling from over 25 ppl in 1996 down to 17 ppl and below by 1999. Members of direct contract groups have seen their prices fall roughly in line with those of Milk Marque members, although premiums of 1–2 ppl still remain. Currency revaluations and changing markets in Europe and around the world have, of course, played their role (notably the strengthening of £ sterling relative to the Euro) in this decline. In their submission to the House of Commons Agricultural Select Committee report on the Marketing of Milk in 2000, the National Farmers Union made the following statement with regard to falling milk prices.

> In the two years after deregulation dairy farmers benefited from strong milk prices as the private processing companies adapted to the milk selling system operated by Milk Marque Ltd and sought to increase the volumes of their direct supplies. In the years following, this immediate gain has been reversed as sterling re-valued and as the private dairy companies learned how to operate the Milk Marque selling system to their advantage. However the fall in farm gate milk prices has been greater than is justified by the stronger pound ... We believe that the key factor contributing to the decline in producers' milk prices in excess of that justified by the foreign exchange rate is the weakness in the Milk Marque selling arrangements for milk.

It would appear therefore that the initial motivations of dairy farmers who fought to maintain one strong farmer-controlled co-operative operating 'together in enterprise' in the hope that controlling volume alone would guarantee market strength, were somewhat misplaced.[6]

Since 1994 the relative share of the U.K. milk supply market controlled by Milk Marque has diminished. In 1995/6 Milk Marque had 20,300 members, with a raw milk market share of around 58% in the U.K., 66% in England and Wales. However, by 1998/99 membership had fallen to 15,500 farmers, and a market share in the U.K. and England and Wales of just 46% and 55% respectively. By comparison, the popularity among dairy farmers of other groups either selling their milk direct to dairy companies or through other independent farmers co-operatives had grown. By the beginning of the year 2000 it was estimated that 45% of all milk in the U.K. was being sold direct by farmers to dairy companies, with a further 5% being purchased by independent farmer-controlled quota-holding groups (House of Commons, 2000).

Economies of Scale and Scope

The improved efficiency of dairy processors direct milk sourcing arrangements has been a key factor placing pressure on Milk Marque to reduce their milk charges. As a co-operative Milk Marque paid a pool price to producers for the milk it sold on their behalf. The problem of this system in the reregulated milk market was that those members with larger production units capable of highly efficient production became frustrated that they were, in effect, compensatingfor smaller or higher cost producers, and thus incurring opportunity costs. Faced with competition from dairy companies trying to secure supplies direct from farms (and offering higher prices), Milk Marque was forced to introduce a system of payment based upon volume with extra price bonuses for those producers with sufficient milk storage capacity on-farm to necessitate collections only every other day instead of daily. For example, a farmer producing over 2 million litres of milk a year and with every other day collection (EODC) received 23.5 ppl between April and September 1997 whereas a farmer producing less than 100,000 litres a year and requiring every day collection received only 18.5 ppl even if the milk was of identical quality. So, farmers in different parts of the country and with herds of different sizes found that these factors had a direct bearing not only on their ability to enter into different contracts (which may or may not be available to them), but also on the price they receive for their milk. As the chairman of the National Farmers Union's national milk committee commented relating this issue to farmers in west Wales,

> From April 1st (1997) they [dairy farmers signed with Milk Marque] will have to cope with a higher collection charge and a 2.6 or 2.7 pence per litre cut in milk price . . . They will be getting around 25% less for their milk even before the next green pound revaluation. Inevitably some will get out of milk (Farmers Weekly, 28.3.97).

Quality Differentiation

In 1994/95 the contacts offered by many dairy processors wishing to engage supplies direct from farmers were, in large part, identical to the contracts offered by Milk Marque. Over time, however, dairy companies have increasingly initiated supply contracts with farmers whichdiffer from those offered by Milk Marque. By financially rewarding particular production characteristics (such as protein content over butterfat or vice-versa) processors have attempted to source milk which more closely meets their production requirements and which helps to maximise the return for producers in the context of a butterfat quota.[7] When buying from Milk Marque, dairies could only be certain that the milk they received would meet minimum levels of butterfat and protein.

Another means of differentiation initially used by direct contract groups was based upon the discourse of traceability. The drive towards greater product traceability, especially in the light of the Bovine Spongiform Encephalopathy (BSE) crisis and other food scares in the U.K., is evident throughout the agro-food sector. Seeking to meet consumer concerns as well as control risk through the supply chain, it has been retailers, and in turn processors, who have pushed the hardest for full traceability of milk back to the farm of origin. In the first year following reregulation there was widespread dissatisfaction among both dairy companies and the major supermarket chains regarding the traceability of milk sourced via Milk Marque - although the legitimacy of these claims has to be balanced against attempts by these companies to discredit Milk Marque. In keeping with the principles of 'due diligence' outlined by the 1990 Food Safety Act[8] processors were encouraged by retailers to provide ever more product traceability and assurances. Direct sourcing gives processors the ability to trace milk back to source (i.e. the individual farm). The composition, hygiene, age, and origin of milk is all known. Having taken onboard the criticisms of processors, Milk Marque began offering full traceability. However, in the event of a problem, specific information on the culpable farm would not be made available to dairy companies.

Some processors foreseeing the end of the MMB and ex-farm allocation system were not prepared to receive milk whose specific origin they could not determine, even if it did meet quality standards. Many producers also place a high value on knowing where the milk they produce is going to be processed (reverse traceability), and hence the ability to identify with specific products in the market. Traceability as a discourse was not therefore purely a consumer-led or economically motivated phenomenon. However, traceability is becoming increasingly important in the marketing of certain dairy products, especially cheese, where marketing and product branding are often based geographical or regional provenance.

Finally, the definition of 'quality' has come to include the welfare of animals involved in the production process. Mounting consumer awareness and concern for the welfare and management of animals within agro-food system has run parallel with drives for greater product traceability associated with product hygiene. The seemingly contradictory position of the government as both guardian of consumer safety and facilitator of economic growth within agri-business has further legitimised the retailers' position as representative of the consumer interest, and in defining or demanding assurances of quality and safety in production from suppliers. In response processors have been pro-active in establishing codes of practice for animal welfare and stockmanship and it is likely that this will lead to various formal forms of farm accreditation. Milk Marque and the National Farmers Union introduced a welfare scheme following consultation with members and retail multiples and several other large dairy companies have introduced their own standards. As the retail multiples intensify their own battles over the provision of 'quality' and 'value' the dairy sector is facing increased pressure to assure welfare and stockmanship standards, especially given the market context in which processors have to continually compete with each other to win supply contracts in anoversupplied market. However, it is also true that the costs of implementing welfare and other such schemes has fallen onto farmers and dairy companies without remuneration through increased prices.

Farmers unable to keep pace with the quality treadmill, whether they are members of Milk Marque or not, are going to find it more difficult to operate viable businesses in coming years as contracts, backed up by EU legislation,[9] and pricing structures impose severe financial penalties on low quality milk (be this defined by hygienic cleanliness, composition, welfare, traceability or volume). Similarly, groups of farmers capable of producing high quality milk may empower themselves through this process. The strategy of using directly sourced milk from specific groups of producers to supply specific products (especially fresh products) is currently being employed by several major processors, and is variously justified by claims of extended shelf-life and greater product yield.

Vertical Integration

Just like the MMB before it, Milk Marque soon began to face problems of excess supply at certain peak times of the year and in certain regions of the country. Despite protestations from the representatives of the processing industry who questioned the legality of Milk Marque investing in processing capacity, an independent subsidiary of the Co-operative called Milk Marque Developments (MMD) did establish a relatively small cheese processing operation in 1996. The Dairy Industry Federation (DIF) was very concerned that in undertaking processing through MMD, Milk Marque was taking milk out of the market and thereby giving the co-op the opportunity to artificially raise prices. In reality, so long as processing activity remained limited, this was never a very serious threat. However, the announcement by MMD in 1999 that it intended developing processing facilities with the capacity to process over one billion litre of milk forced the DIF to mount a more vigorous challenge, and was a key factor in the Monopolies and Mergers Commission's decision in 1999 that Milk Marque should be disbanded and restructured. The MMC concluded that the new facilities would have given Milk Marque opportunity to exploit its scale monopoly in milk supply and thereby the price of milk, which was regarded as against the public interest.

IN SEARCH OF STABILITY

Between 1994 and 2000 the reregulated dairy sector, but most obviously Milk Marque, has selectively struggled and failed to achieve a mutually acceptable and harmonious trading relationship between dairy farmers and milk processors. Ongoing uncertainties and conflicts in the sector, largely based around the legitimacy of the new selling system operated by Milk Marque, eventually led in 1999 to the announcement by the Monopolies and Mergers Commission (now Competition Agency) that Milk Marque was to be disbanded and reformed as three smaller regional quota-holding groups. These smaller groups would not control sufficient milk to represent a scale monopoly, and would be able, if they wished, to invest in processing capacity. Representing the dairy processing industry, the DIF successfully argued that, even though prices to producers had fallen, Milk Marque was using its position as the major supplier of raw milk to maintain prices at an artificially high level, and thereby act as a scale monopolist against the rules of competition. Among the MMC conclusions it was noted that,

> Milk Marque has been able to price discriminate and raise the average price of milk above levels that would otherwise have been reached by engaging in the following practices. It has increased the required tolerances of its supply-led contracts to a degree greater than was necessary if its objective was to balance overall supply, and widened the price differentials between its different contract types more than was justified. It has forces its smaller processor customers to pay a higher price for their milk than its larger customers to an unjustified extent. By imposing restrictions on the use of milk bought in its lowest-priced contracts in the summer 1998 selling process, it has obliged some processors to purchase milk at higher prices than they would otherwise have had to pay. It has entered into individually negotiated contracts with certain large processors on terms that were neither disclosed nor made available to the generality of customers. Finally, it has been able to exploit the particular aversion of some of its customers to the risk of obtaining inadequate supplies of milk or supplies obtained on adverse terms (MMC, 1999: 4).

and went on;

> Milk Marque's behaviour has resulted in greater uncertainty and higher costs for the dairy processing industry in Great Britain, resulting in lower levels of investment by them, than would otherwise have been the case. Consumers pay more for fresh liquid milk than they otherwise would. Milk Marque's exploitation of its monopoly position thus operates and may be expected to operate against the public interest (MMC, 1999: 5).

In reviewing the development of the dairy sector since 1994, and seeking to find a way through the complex battle being fought between Milk Marque and the DIF, the MMC reached the following conclusions which would subsequently be accepted by the government:

> Deregulation has not brought about a competitive market for milk. Milk Marque and the dairy processors have become increasingly confrontational and this has damaged the industry as a whole. The consumer has not been well served . . . We judge that many of the problems are attributable to the ability of Milk Marque to exercise in a number of ways its significant market power, which derives from the considerable discretion it has over the operation of its selling system and its 49.6% share of the supply of milk in Great Britain . . . we therefore recommend that Milk Marque should be divided into a number of independent, quota-holding bodies having an approximately equal share of Milk Marque's supply of milk at the time the division take place . . . the purpose of our recommendation is to eliminate the market power of Milk Marque, to create a more competitive market for the supply of milk, and to provide fresh opportunities for producers and processors to develop commercial relationships that serve their interests, as well as the interests of consumers. The new bodies *should be allowed to engage in their own processing* as, in the absence of market power, this should not prove a threat to competition (MMC, 1999: 5).

The prospect of Milk Marque being split into three smaller regional quota-holding milk groups provides new opportunities but also new threats which will doubtless continue to shape the U.K. dairy industry in the coming years. What follows is a brief summary of some of these issues, tackling first the negative aspects of the Milk Marque split and then the more positive aspects.

The split up of Milk Marque has implications for the ability of producers to exercise market power through effective co-operation. Processing companies already have significant leverage over milk producers, a situation worsened for Milk Marque by the fact that it was not allowed to vertically integrate and enter into processing. Even the Secretary of State for Trade and Industry acknowledged, when asked if farm gate prices would fall as a result, that "this may well be the outcome." (MMC, 1999a). Furthermore, recognising the dependence of the U.K. milk price on the strength of Sterling, indicates that even the most powerful milk group could not bring about salvation for struggling dairy farmers since the guidelines used by either side to determine the price of milk are set in Euros. A second potentially negative implication will be the increased costs resulting from duplicated services and administrative systems across three operations, which will all deduct from farm-gate prices. Third, and perhaps more worrying for many small or remote producers, there is (as yet) no guarantee that the new co-operatives will be buyers of 'last resort'. This could mean that farmers in remote locations are not able to find buyers for their milk, and subsequently be forced out of operation. However it should be remembered that the new groups will be members organisations and as such they will be driven by their members. Finally, while the Government plan to split Milk Marque into three groups based on geographical areas, once up and running there will be nothing stopping members from switching between these groups. It is probably that one group will be left 'high and dry' with high overhead costs, including collection and transport costs, and low incomes to farmers due to lack of power in the market to command premiums for members milk.

More positively, the new milk marketing arrangements give many producers an opportunity to start a fresh relationship with processors and leave behind the acrimony and recriminations which were a feature of Milk Marque's dealings with sector. For example, dairy companies were often accused of wanting to destroy Milk Marque by offering farmers premiums to go direct. There is now an opportunity to leave behind the mutual lack of co-operation and respect which some might argue was established through the MMB and perpetuated through Milk Marque, and to develop an industry based upon a new philosophy of flexibility and one-to-one relationships. It is true that in the current market processing companies are likely to welcome the opportunity to work with the new co-ops as imploding them through a lack of co-operation would not help the industry as a whole.

Another positive outcome of the Milk Marque split will be the ability of the new co-ops to legitimately engage in value-added activities (through vertical integration and investment in processing capacity). Formerly, the strange situation existed where, on the one hand the Government was encouraging farmers to develop new co-operative structures and to add value to primary production across the agricultural sector, and on the other hand was criticising the largest producer co-operative in the country, Milk Marque, for trying to do just that! Unlike Milk Marque, the new co-operatives will not be subject to limitations on their investment in processing. The MMC had ruled that, while Milk Marque remained a single entity it should be prevented from vertical integration and expanding of its existing processing activities – a decision which had been instrumental in the Government's decision to allow Milk Marque to be split. While generally welcomed, some farmers have voiced dissent, claiming that the opportunity to add-value is a false hope. They argue that many farmers cannot afford to invest in processing capacity, and that even if they do, adding more capacity to the U.K. sector will only have a negative impact on prices. Furthermore, even if a venture is successful, such investments take a long time to yield payback, time which is scarce farmers currently struggling to stay in business. The report by the House of Commons Agricultural Select Committee into the Marketing of Milk saw fit to comment on this issue:

> In the current climate, processing is often presented as an instant salvation for hard-pressed farmers. We are sympathetic to their desire to earn a higher percentage of theretail price of their product, but rash investments in processing capacity for its own sake, for example, producing intervention products, will not necessarily bring the rewards farmers seek and in the case of the new successor bodies could seriously weaken their financial stability. Investment in products for the retail market, by the producer co-operatives, alone or in convert with other companies, is a different matter altogether and we believe that there could be many opportunities which will open up for the new co-operatives in this way (House of Commons, 2000).

Finally, the prospect of a new start with three new co-operatives will bring to an end the constant attention brought to bear on the sector by competition authorities examining the validity of claims regarding Milk Marque's trading practices. That constant attention has caused real problems for the industry as a whole since 1994, has cost everybody involved a lot of time and money, and has only acted to fossilise the industry by discouraging processors from investing as a reaction to ongoing uncertainties. Milk Marque's decision to accept the recommendation to split into smaller co-operatives has therefore not only been welcomed with great relief by the industry, but also removes the threat of further references of the industry to the competition authorities which would most likely have occurred if attempts had been made simply to rework the old Milk Marque selling system. The Farmers Union of Wales, taking onboard this view, stated of the new opportunity that "the biggest advantage is if the new co-operatives were allowed to carry on without control or interference from Government."

CONCLUSION

The evolution of the milk marketing in England and Wales over the course of the 1990s reflects a purposeful move by the state away from direct intervention in the day to day management and operation of the sector. The shift away from a close corporatist relationship between state and dairy farmer is now complete. The next ten years will doubtless see ongoing rationalisation within the milk supply sector, both at the farm level and among milk groups and processors. The reintroduction of geographical cost factors in production and the growing legislative burden will only serve to accelerate this process.

Finding themselves in a position where they have to produce goods defined in composition, quality and format by the market, processing companies and producers have responded to the abolition of the MMB by adopting a series of different sourcing strategies designed to provide security and maximise quality and traceability. These strategies are leading to new patterns of uneven spatial development often centred around new milk groups. The break-up of Milk

Marque is now likely to accelerate this process as there will no longer be a buyer of 'last-resort' obliged to offer a market to all farmers capable of producing milk which meets legal standards. Quality discourses related to hygiene, traceability, welfare and environment will increasingly drive the process of differentiation alongside more traditional cost factors. In this sense traditional price and cost factors are becoming encased by a variety of new qualitative value criteria which 'commoditise' milk products in new more complex ways. Reregulation is acting to differentiate producers in new ways, highlighting the competitiveness of some groups of farmers, and exposing the vulnerability of others. Compounded by the BSE crisis, the high value of Sterling relative to the Euro (making imports cheaper and EU price intervention relatively lower), new costs associated with traceability and welfare auditing, and falling milk prices, many farmers have entered the new millennium with a serious headache. It is likely that many small scale dairy farmers will leave the sector in the coming five years, and that milk production will become even more concentrated within specific areas of the country. All milk is no longer to be judged as equal. Special opportunities and markets now exist for organic milk; milk of very high hygienic standards; milk with high protein levels; milk from particular regions of the country that can be linked to product marketing; milk which can be traced back to a specific farm; or milk from farms which have made special efforts to maximise animal welfare. In view of these possibilities, we should not fall into the trap of seeing farmers responses to reregulation as simply reactive. The history of the 1990s shows that farmers have the ability and desire to be highly pro-active in exploring new contractual arrangements, differentiating their production, and working to develop strategic alliances. This said, it is at the level of individual producers that the impact of reregulation appears to be greatest.

As for whether or not quota-holding milk groups will be successful in developing vertically integrated enterprises capable of challenging directly the dominant privately owned dairy companies, only time will tell. We do know however, that the outcome of reregulation is a more complex, contingent and dynamic sector. The process of reregulation has opened new opportunities for groups of farmers to work with processors to meet specific market requirements. It has also enabled issues of concern to consumers and the agenda of near consumer agencies (notably retailers) to be translated into quantifiable and deliverable standards (regulations) and procedures within the supply chain. Yet, despite the growing importance of intra-supply chain regulation and regulators, it should be remembered that the State still has a critical role to play, most notably in representing the interests of the U.K. dairy sector within Common Agricultural Policy renegotiations, as these over shadow every other question about the future of the dairy industry in Europe. Moving beyond direct interventionin the domestic milk marketing framework, the state also now has a new role in monitoring international developments and assessing new regulatory demands against the competitive situation of the industry so as to maintain a level playing field between it and its European counterparts.

NOTES

1. Under the MMS all producers in England and Wales were charged a flat rate per gallon moved with some very small variations based upon the distance of the production region from the London market.

2. Nestle, it can be presumed, was seeking to break the monopoly of the MMB in milk supply by forcing local producers to by-pass the MMB and sell direct to the dairy on different terms.

3. The Dairy Industry Newsletter is a key source of information in the deregulated dairy sector publishing both bi-annual reports on the milk market and monthly newsletters for the trade.

4. A model which encouraged the growth in scale and efficiency of agricultural production through mechanisms such as CAP price support.

5. Quoted in evidence provided by the NFU to the House of Commons Select Committee on Agriculture Second Report – The Marketing of Milk (February 2000).

6. If Milk Marque had received over 70% of milk supplies in England and Wales at vesting day then it is likely that there would have been some intervention on behalf of the Monopolies and Mergers Committee to ensure that the company did not abuse its market power.

7. Milk quotas within the Common Agricultural Policy are not a strict cap on the volume of milk which can be produced, but rather a quota on the volume of butterfat which can be produced.

8. The 1990 Food Safety Act in the U.K. placed a responsibility and obligation on food processors and retailer to show that they had taken all 'due diligence' in ensuring product safety and hygiene. This legislation represented a significant shift in the role of the state relative to the food sector, with the industry now being responsible for its own regulation.

9. EU legislation (EC Directive 92/46) to be implemented in 1997 will mean that milk with a somatic cell out of 400,000 cells/ml or greater will be deemed unfit for human consumption. The somatic cell count, or SCC, refers to the number of cells present in milk that have originated from the cow itself (as distinct from invading bacterial cells).

REFERENCES

Baker, S. (1973). *Milk to Market – Forty Years of Milk Marketing.* London: Heinemann.
Barclays de Zoete Wedd Research (1996). *Dairy Industry: Radical thinking required.* London: BZW Research Limited.

Christopherson, S. (1993). Market Rules and Territorial Outcomes: The Case of the USA. *International Journal of Urban and Regional Research, 17*, 274–288.

Cox, G., Lowe, P., & Winter, M. (1990). Agricultural Regulation and the Politics of Milk Production. In: C. Crouch & R. Dore (Eds), *Corporatism and Accountability* (pp. 169–199). Oxford: Clarendon Press.

Dairy Industry Newsletter (1995). *U.K. Milk Report – 97/98*. Cambridge: Eden Publishing.

Empson, J. (1997). The History of the Milk Marketing Board, 1933–1994: British Farmer's Greatest Commercial Enterprise. *Journal of the Royal Agricultural Society of England*, 21–36.

Farmers Weekly (1997). 'Double whammy' threat to small milk producers. *Farmers Weekly*, 28/3/97, 18.

Fearne, A., & Rey, D. (1996). *Price determination* and discovery in a 'de-regulated' milk market: perspectives on the price of U.K. milk. Wye College: University of London.

Grant, W. (1985). Private organisations as agents of public policy: the case of milk marketing in Britain. In: W. Streek & P. Schmitter (Eds), *Private Interest Government* (pp. 182–196). London: Sage.

House of Commons Select Committee on Agriculture. Second Report (2000). *The Marketing of Milk*.

Jessop, B. (1990). Regulation theories in retrospect and prospect. *Economy and Society, 19*(2), 153–216.

Marsden, T., & Wrigley, N. (1995). Regulation, retailing, and consumption. *Environment and Planning A, 27*, 1899–1912.

NDPC (1998) *UK Dairy Facts and Figures – 1998* National Dairy Publicity Council: London.

Monopolies and Mergers Commission (MMC) (1999). Milk: A report on the supply in Great Britain of raw cows' milk. Competition Commission.

Monopolies and Mergers Commission (1999a). Evidence Question 724.

Pugliese, E. (1991). Agriculture and the new division of labour. In: W. Friedland et al. (Eds), *Towards a New Political Economy of Agriculture*. Boulder: Westview Press.

Winter, M. (1984). Corporatism and Agriculture in the UK: The Case of the Milk Marketing Board. *Sociologia Ruralis, 24*(2), 106–119.

NOTES ON CONTRIBUTORS

Jo Banks is a research associate and Ph.D. candidate in the Department of City and Regional Planning at Cardiff University. His dissertation research examines the changing form and function of regulation across the dairy supply chain in the wake of the abolition of state sanctioned Milk Marketing Boards. He is currently exploring the socio-economic impacts of rural development policies under the EU Fair Programme. He is an established consultant in agrifood supply chain development, with particular reference to the organic, red meat and dairy sectors in Wales.

Bradford L. Barham is associate professor of agricultural and applied economics at the University of Wisconsin-Madison and co-director of the Program on Agricultural Technology Studies. He completed his doctorate in economics at Stanford University in 1988. Currently he is studying agricultural biotechnology issues at both farm and industry levels, examining the determinants of rBST adoption patterns among Wisconsin dairy farmers and the determinants of ag-biotech patents and local economic spillovers at universities. His work has appeared in the *Journal of Development Economics, American Journal of Agricultural Economics, Rural Sociology, World Development, Economic Development and Cultural Change, Canadian Journal of Economics, Land Economics, Latin American Research Review, Journal of Latin American Studies, Hispanic American Historical Review,* and *The Geographical Journal.*

Martina Bärnheim received the degree of Master of Science in agricultural economics at the Swedish University of Agricultural Sciences. Her thesis dealt with financial instruments in Dutch agricultural cooperatives. She is presently researching membership issues, marketing problems and strategic planning relative to Sweden's second largest dairy cooperative (Skanemejerier.)

Erik Berrevoets is currently employed by the Australian National Audit Office. His research interests include agricultural development and the social and political aspects of environmental change.

407

Svein Ole Borgen is researcher at the Norwegian Agricultural Economics Research Institute and associate professor in organization theory at the Agricultural University of Norway. His interests focus on agricultural cooperatives and the food industry. He is currently exploring the strategic options for Norwegian agricultural cooperatives in a more competitive and international setting.

J. J. (Bees) Butler is a dairy extension specialist in the Department of Agricultural and Resource Economics at the University of California – Davis. His areas of research include livestock production and marketing, public policy, intellectual property rights, and the adoption and transfer of technologies. He earned his B.S. at Lincoln University in New Zealand, M.S. at the University of Reading in England, and Ph.D. at Michigan State University. He regularly testifies at national and state hearings on dairy policy, and has published numerous articles on dairy marketing and economic policy.

William L. Crist, Sr. is extension professor and dairy specialist in the Department of Animal Sciences, University of Kentucky. He received his Ph.D. in reproductive physiology from Ohio State University. His extension program focuses on mastitis control, milking management, and dairy facilities layout. Recently, he has been involved in developing a farm management extension education program that emphasizes goal setting, time management and labor relations.

Andrew P. Davidson is a lecturer in the School of Sociology at the University of New South Wales, Australia. His research interests center on economic restructuring, environmental sociology, gender, and tourism. He has published articles dealing with dairy restructuring, farm household responses to soil salinity in Pakistan, women in agriculture, and food and culture in Hong Kong. He is presently writing a book entitled: *Gender, Household Dynamics and Small-Scale Agriculture in Pakistan*.

Patricia Dyk is associate professor in the rural sociology program, College of Agriculture, University of Kentucky. She earned her Ph.D. from Utah State University in family studies. Her research focuses on public policies and programs related to family well-being and family dynamics and stress, especially among rural families. She is currently involved in a multi-year evaluation of Kentucky's family preservation support programs.

Jaap Frouws is assistant professor in the Department of Rural Sociology, Wageningen University, The Netherlands. His research interests include political sociology, the sociology of agriculture and agri-environmental politics. Much of his empirical work is concerned with manure policies and the restructuring of intensive livestock farming in The Netherlands.

Lorraine Garkovich is professor in the rural sociology program, College of Agriculture, University of Kentucky. She earned her Ph.D. from the University of Missouri, Columbia. Her research focuses on rural community and farm family change, while her extension program addresses a wide range of issues related to community development (e.g., strategic planning, socio-demographics, leadership development). She is co-author of *Harvest of Hope: Family Farming and Farming Families* (1995).

Gilbert W. Gillespie, Jr. is a senior research associate in the Department of Rural Sociology at Cornell University. His research interests include the sociology of agriculture and food systems, community development, and the effects of social and technological change.

Amy E. Guptill is a Ph.D. candidate in the field of Development Sociology at Cornell University. Her major research interests include food and agricultural systems, development policy, and political ecology. In addition to participating in research in New York State, she is currently doing her dissertation research in Puerto Rico.

Douglas Harper is professor and chair of the Department of Sociology at Duquesne University. His research interests are in cultural sociology and he has previously published on the sociology of the tramp, the small-shop artisan, the rural informal economy, and visual sociology.

Douglas B. Jackson-Smith is assistant professor of rural sociology and urban and regional planning at the University of Wisconsin-Madison, and co-director of the Program on Agricultural Technology Studies. He is especially concerned with the social and economic dimensions of agricultural change. Currently, he is directing a number of research projects of Wisconsin farmers, including studies of the dynamics of dairy herd expansion, impacts of farm structural change on rural communities and farm families, patterns of agricultural technology adoption, and land use conflicts between farmers and rural residents over farmland preservation and the siting of large livestock facilities. He co-chairs the sociology of agriculture interest group in the Rural Sociological Society.

Anne Moxnes Jervell is researcher and head of the research department at the Norwegian Agricultural Economics Research Institute. Her research interests include agricultural policy, farm households, rural development and pluri-activity, and she has especially focused on the dairy sector. She has published in *Sociologia Ruralis* and has edited a Norwegian journal in agricultural economics and rural sociology.

Thomas A. Lyson is professor of rural sociology and director of the farming alternatives program at Cornell University. Currently, he is researching the processes of local economic development. His interests also focus on the relationships among agricultural and food systems and nutrition and health. He recently served as editor of *Rural Sociology*.

Alvin J. Luedke is a doctoral student in sociology at Texas A&M University. His current research focuses on demographic and economic factors associated with church growth and graduates' evaluations of their university training. He has participated in research on the effects of the 1980 farm crisis and the 1996 Farm Bill on agricultural producers in Texas, and the effects of demographic change on the incidences of diseases/disorders in metropolitan and non-metropolitan areas of Texas.

James H. McDonald is associate professor of anthropology at the University of Texas – San Antonio, and co-editor of the journal *Culture & Agriculture*. Much of his research has focused on the political economy of dairying in Mexico, primarily among small-scale commercial and peasant farmers in the states of Guanajuato and Michoacán. Also, he has been studying Mexican political culture and the area of science and technology. His recent work on agricultural development is published in *Human Organization*, *Research in Economic Anthropology*, and *Culture & Agriculture*.

Wm. Alex McIntosh is professor of rural sociology and sociology at Texas A&M University. His current research focuses on family factors in adolescent nutrition and community hospital adoption of tele-medicine. He is author of *Sociologies of Food and Nutrition* (1996) and a recent paper on rural hospital survival.

Jerker Nilsson is professor of business administration at the Swedish University of Agricultural Sciences. Specialized in marketing and in cooperative business, he has recently edited the book *Strategies and Structures in the Agro-Food Industries,* and has written major parts of *Agricultural Cooperatives in the European Union: Trends and Issues on the Eve of the 21st Century.* His research on the adaptation of farming businesses to current market conditions is published in the *Journal of Cooperatives, Annals of Public and Cooperative Economics, Scandinavian Journal of Management,* and *Swedish Journal of Agricultural Research.*

Harry K. Schwarzweller is professor of sociology at Michigan State University and series editor for *Rural Sociology and Development.* His research deals with issues relating to agricultural change, restructuring of the dairy industry, the survival strategies of farm households, and the development of economically marginal regions, such as Michigan's Upper Peninsula. He has served as president of the Rural Sociological Society and of the International Rural Sociological Association.

Hilary Tovey is a senior lecturer in sociology at Trinity College, Dublin, Ireland. She has research interests and publications in a range of areas, including rural society in late modernity, the sociology of food, the sociology of environment, and minority languages and cultures. She was recently elected President of the European Rural Sociological Association.

Jan Douwe Van der Ploeg is professor of rural sociology at Wageningen University, The Netherlands. His research focuses on rural development processes, technology and policy. He is founder of what has become known as the 'farming styles approach'. He is a member of the Dutch National Council for Rural Areas.

Gerd Vonderach is professor of sociology at the University of Oldenburg in Germany. His research interests are in the sociology of work (*Arbeitssoziolo gie*), rural and agricultural sociology (*Land-und Agrar-soziologie*), labor markets (*Arbeitsmarkt und Soziopolitik*), and in qualitative social research (*qualitativen Sozialforschung*). He has led numerous empirical research projects, and authored many monographs and articles. His various works include studies of the occupational characteristics and concerns of worker/ sailors who navigate the inland waterways, tourism in rural communities, the impacts of unemployment and career change/rehabilitation on the life histories of workers, and the circumstances of dairy farmers in the Wesermarsch region. Since 1998 he has been publishing the biannual *Land-Berichte* (Country Report) relative to the changing situation in rural regions.

Christopher Wolf is assistant professor and extension specialist in the Department of Agricultural Economics at Michigan State University. He earned his B.S. at the University of Wisconsin and Ph.D. at the University of California – Davis. His areas of research include dairy farm size and structural change, risk management, and biotechnology and its market effects.